The Mammoth Book Of

Comic Quotes

The Mammoth Book Of

Comic Quotes

Edited by
Geoff Tibballs

ROBINSON
London

Constable & Robinson Ltd
3 The Lanchesters
162 Fulham Palace Road
London W6 9ER
www.constablerobinson.com

First published by Robinson,
an imprint of Constable & Robinson Ltd 2004

A copy of the British Library Cataloguing in
Publication Data is available from the British Library

ISBN 1-84119-752-1

Printed and bound in the EU

CONTENTS

viii   Contents

x Contents

xvi   Contents

INTRODUCTION

Someone somewhere must once have said that you can learn a lot about a person from his or her favourite comic quote. It's such a question of individual taste. It could be a one-liner from Woody Allen or Steven Wright, a truism from Oscar Wilde or Mark Twain, a witty observation from Dave Barry or Jerry Seinfeld, a profound thought from Homer Simpson, a Dorothy Parker put-down, or even dialogue from a classic TV series such as *Frasier*, *Friends* or *Sex and the City*.

For this collection of over 8,000 wisecracks and one-liners, the world's greatest wits offer their thoughts on every subject imaginable – from banking to bestiality, golf to gluttony, sailing to socks. Hardy perennials sit alongside promising newcomers, seasoned practitioners such as Bob Hope and Joan Rivers being balanced out by younger performers whose names, although possibly unfamiliar now, are surely destined to become mainstays of future collections of humorous quotations.

Some of the most sparkling one-liners are not attributable to any individual, but lack of identification is no reason for omitting quality quotes so these too are included here.

As I have plundered the television archives for some of the material, it is only fair to acknowledge the creators of these much-loved series. So let's hear it for: Jennifer Saunders (*Absolutely Fabulous*), Johnny Speight (*All in the Family*), Richard Curtis, Ben Elton and Rowan Atkinson (*Blackadder*), Glen Charles, Les Charles and James Burrows (*Cheers*), Bill Cosby, Ed Weinberger and Michael Leeson (*The Cosby Show*), Chuck Lorre (*Cybill*), Graham Linehan and Arthur Mathews (*Father Ted*), John Cleese and Connie Booth (*Fawlty Towers*), David Angell, Peter Casey and David Lee (*Frasier*), Marta Kauffman and David Crane (*Friends*), Susan Harris (*The Golden Girls*), Ray Galton and Alan Simpson (*Hancock's Half-Hour*), Roy Clarke (*Keeping Up Appearances*), Garry Shandling and Dennis B. Klein (*The Larry Sanders Show*), Linwood Boomer (*Malcolm in the Middle*), Michael G. Moye and Ron Leavitt (*Married . . . With Children*), Larry Gelbart and Gene Reynolds (*M*A*S*H*), John Cleese, Graham Chapman, Terry Jones, Michael Palin, Eric Idle and Terry Gilliam (*Monty Python's Flying Circus*), Ricky Gervais and Stephen Merchant (*The Office*), John Sullivan (*Only Fools and Horses*), Nat Hiken (*The Phil Silvers Show*), Jim Abrahams, David Zucker and Jerry Zucker (*Police Squad*), Dick Clement and Ian La Frenais (*Porridge*), Matt Williams (*Roseanne*), Larry David and Jerry Seinfeld (*Seinfeld*), Candace Bushnell and Darren Star (*Sex and the City*), Matt Groening (*The Simpsons*), James L. Brooks, Stan Daniels, David Davis and Ed Weinberger (*Taxi*), Bonnie Turner and

Terry Turner (*3rd Rock From the Sun*), David Kohan and Max Mutchnick (*Will and Grace*), and Antony Jay and Jonathan Lynn (*Yes, Minister*). Without the contributions of these talented wordsmiths, this book would have been considerably shorter.

I am also indebted to Nick Robinson, Pete Duncan and Krystyna Green at Constable & Robinson Ltd for their support and suggestions and to the ever-helpful staff at Nottingham Library.

Geoff Tibballs
2004

A

Ability

A man's got to do what a man's got to do. A woman must do what he can't.
RHONDA HANSOME

Competence, like truth, beauty and a contact lens, is in the eye of the beholder.
LAURENCE J. PETER, *The Peter Principle*

Martyrdom is the only way in which a man can become famous without ability.
GEORGE BERNARD SHAW

Ability is the art of getting credit for all the home runs somebody else hits.
CASEY STENGEL

Ability is what will get you to the top if the boss has no daughter.

Abortion

President Bush was *against* abortion, but *for* capital punishment. Spoken like a true fisherman; throw them back, kill them when they're bigger.
ELAYNE BOOSLER

I can't have a baby. I could barely find the time to schedule the abortion.
MIRANDA HOBBES (CYNTHIA NIXON), *Sex and the City*

(*entering hospital for an abortion*) It serves me right for putting all my eggs in one bastard.
DOROTHY PARKER

Accidents

When you're involved in an accident, why does someone always ask, 'Are you alright?' 'Yes, fine thanks. I'll just pick up my limbs and be off.'
BILLY CONNOLLY

I fell off the roof the other day. The insurance man told me the accident policy covered falling off the roof but not hitting the ground.
TOMMY COOPER

I don't know about you, but I intend on writing a strongly worded letter to the White Star Line about all of this.

JACK DAWSON (LEONARDO DICAPRIO), *Titanic*

(*about people bumping their heads*) If it's not a headboard, it's just not worth it.

RACHEL GREEN (JENNIFER ANISTON), *Friends*

Whenever I see an old lady slip and fall on a wet sidewalk, my first instinct is to laugh. But then I think, what if I was an ant and she fell on me? Then it wouldn't seem quite so funny.

JACK HANDEY

The ship is sinking. We must try and save it. Help me get it into the lifeboat.

SPIKE MILLIGAN, *The Goon Show*

That doesn't mean that you should just sit back and just let accidents happen to you. No, you have to go out and cause them yourself. That way you're in control of the situation.

P.J. O'ROURKE

A cement mixer collided with a prison van on the Kingston Bypass. Motorists are asked to be on the lookout for sixteen hardened criminals.

The Two Ronnies

A car hit a Jewish man. The paramedic said, 'Are you comfortable?' The man said, 'I make a good living.'

HENNY YOUNGMAN

Accountants

The company accountant is shy and retiring. He's shy a quarter of a million dollars. That's why he's retiring.

MILTON BERLE

Bloom, do me a favour. Move a few decimal points around. You can do it. You're an accountant. You're in a noble profession. The word 'count' is part of your title.

MAX BIALYSTOCK (ZERO MOSTEL), *The Producers*

This is the accounts department, the number bods. Do not be fooled by their job descriptions, they are absolutely mad, all of 'em. Especially that one, he's mental. Not literally of course, that wouldn't work.

DAVID BRENT (RICKY GERVAIS), *The Office*

People always ask me, 'Were you funny as a child?' Well, no, I was an accountant.

ELLEN DEGENERES

When I asked my accountant if anything could get me out of this mess I am in now, he thought for a long time and said, 'Yes, death would help.'

ROBERT MORLEY

I don't have any use for bodyguards, but I do have a specific use for two highly trained certified public accountants.

ELVIS PRESLEY

With creative accountancy, who needs cheating?

KATHARINE WHITEHORN

An accountant is a man hired to explain that you didn't make the money you did.

An accountant is someone who solves a problem you didn't know you had in a way you don't understand.

An actuary is someone who cannot stand the excitement of chartered accountancy.

Achievement

Herman tried to build a ship inside a bottle. We had to break the bottle to get him out.

LILY MUNSTER (YVONNE DE CARLO), *The Munsters*

Whatever women do, they must do twice as well as men to be thought half as good. Luckily, this is not difficult.

CHARLOTTE WHITTON

Accomplishing the impossible means only that the boss will add it to your regular duties.

The only thing some people can achieve on their own is dandruff.

Acquaintance

Acquaintance: a degree of friendship called slight when its object is poor or obscure, and intimate when he is rich and famous.

AMBROSE BIERCE, *The Devil's Dictionary*

Some of my best friends are acquaintances.

MEL CALMAN

An acquaintance that begins with a compliment is sure to develop into a real friendship.

OSCAR WILDE

Acting

My only regret in the theatre is that I could never sit out front and watch me.
JOHN BARRYMORE

(*on her role as the elf queen in* Lord of the Rings) My husband asked: 'Are you going to wear pointy ears?' I said, 'Yes'. He said, 'Do it.'   CATE BLANCHETT

I love the camera and it loves me. Well, not very much sometimes. But we're good friends.   DIRK BOGARDE

Acting is the expression of a neurotic impulse. It's bum's life. The principal benefit acting has afforded me is the money to pay for my psychoanalysis.
MARLON BRANDO

(*of his movie debut*) I got the job because I could belch on cue.
CHARLES BRONSON

Someday I'd like a part where I can lean my elbow against a mantelpiece and have a cocktail.   CHARLES BRONSON

When I played drunks I had to remain sober because I didn't know how to play them when I was drunk.   RICHARD BURTON

My acting technique is to look up at God just before the camera rolls and say, 'Give me a break.'   JAMES CAAN

You get paid the same for a bad film as you do for a good one.
MICHAEL CAINE

I wanted to win an Oscar so that I'd get more scripts without other actors' coffee-stains on them.   MICHAEL CAINE

I used to get the girl; now I get the part. In *The Quiet American* you may have noticed I got the part and the girl. It's a milestone for me because it's the last time I'm going to get the girl. I'm sure of it, now I'm nearly seventy.
MICHAEL CAINE (*2002 interview*)

My first part was playing the front end of a horse. He was a serious horse, though.   SIMON CALLOW

Filming is like a long air journey: there's so much hanging around and boredom that they keep giving you food.   JOHN CLEESE

(*advice to an actor*) My dear boy, forget about the motivation. Just say the lines and don't trip over the furniture.
NOËL COWARD

The difficulty of doing a sex scene is that sex is the one thing in movies that your entire audience knows about. Nobody in the audience has been killed and most haven't taken a bullet or been in a brutal fight. Lovemaking, everybody's an expert.
MICHAEL DOUGLAS

I don't use any particular method. I'm from the let's pretend school of acting.
HARRISON FORD

Always remember before going on stage, wipe your nose and check your flies.
ALEC GUINNESS

A movie camera is like having someone you have a crush on watching you from afar – you pretend it's not there.
DARRYL HANNAH

Acting is the most minor of gifts and not a very high-class way to earn a living. After all, Shirley Temple could do it at the age of four.
KATHARINE HEPBURN

I got into acting so that I could meet girls. Pretty girls came later. First, I wanted to start off with someone with two legs.
DUSTIN HOFFMAN

It's a Peter Pan profession. If you are still doing it when you're old, there's something badly wrong with you. Particularly actresses – they get madder and madder as they get older.
JANE HORROCKS

The important thing in acting is to be able to laugh and cry. If I have to cry, I think of my sex life. If I have to laugh, I think of my sex life.
GLENDA JACKSON

I didn't even know my bra size until I made a movie.
ANGELINA JOLIE

Acting has been good to me. It has taken me to play golf all over the world.
CHRISTOPHER LEE

I phoned my mum and said I had the lead in *Will and Grace*. When she asked me who Will was, I answered that he was a lawyer and he was gay. And then my mum said, 'Oh, Eric, not a lawyer . . .'
ERIC MCCORMACK

(*on his RAF 'Top Gun' pilot brother, Colin*) He flies at 500mph, 200ft above the ground, whereas I wear make-up for a living.
EWAN MCGREGOR

My acting range? Left eyebrow raised, right eyebrow raised.   ROGER MOORE

The embarrassing thing is that the salad dressing is out-grossing my films.
PAUL NEWMAN

My acting is a bit like basketball. Most females in my films come off very well.
I give great assist. And if I'm lucky, I even score.   BURT REYNOLDS

Acting is merely the art of keeping a large group of people from coughing.
RALPH RICHARDSON, *An Actor's Life*

To act with my clothes on is a performance; to act with my clothes off is a documentary.   JULIA ROBERTS

This isn't exactly a stable business. It's like trying to stand up in a canoe with
your pants down.   CLIFF ROBERTSON

The sitting around on set is awful, but I always figure that's what they pay me
for. The acting I do for free.   EDWARD G. ROBINSON

I like working with people I've seen in just a towel.   ADAM SANDLER

My only problem is finding a way to play my fortieth fallen female in a different
way from my thirty-ninth.   BARBARA STANWYCK

I play John Wayne in every picture regardless of the character.   JOHN WAYNE

(*advice on acting*) Talk low, talk slow, and don't talk too much.   JOHN WAYNE

I stick to simple themes. Love. Hate. No nuances. I stay away from psychoanalysts' couch scenes. Couches are good for one thing.   JOHN WAYNE

Acting is like sex. You should do it, not talk about it.   JOANNE WOODWARD

Action

There's a fine line between participation and mockery.   SCOTT ADAMS

Action is the antidote to despair.   JOAN BAEZ

If we can't alter the tide of events, at least we can be nearby with towels to
mop up.   PETER DAVID, *Q-in-Law*

The world is divided into people who do things and people who get the credit.
DWIGHT D. MORROW

If you see a snake, just kill it – don't appoint a committee on snakes.
H. ROSS PEROT

It is amazing what you can accomplish if you do not care who gets the credit.
HARRY S. TRUMAN

You have to keep busy. After all, no dog's ever pissed on a moving car.
TOM WAITS

Actors

In real life, [Diane] Keaton believes in God. But she also believes that the radio works because there are tiny people inside it.   WOODY ALLEN

(*on Jean-Claude Van Damme*) Acting is not his forte. Neither is being humble.
ROSANNA ARQUETTE

There are five stages in the life of an actor: Who's Mary Astor? Get me Mary Astor. Get me a Mary Astor type. Get me a young Mary Astor. Who's Mary Astor?   MARY ASTOR

(*of Pola Negri*) Couldn't act her way out of a paper bag.   TALLULAH BANKHEAD

Nowadays, Robert Redford's skin looks like a child's sandpit after heavy rain.
LYNN BARBER

I like to be introduced as America's foremost actor. It saves the necessity of further effort.   JOHN BARRYMORE

(*on Mel Gibson*) He seems to think he's Lee Marvin – except he's two feet shorter and about one third the talent.   JOHN BOORMAN

All I can say about Gary Cooper is he's hung like a horse and can go all night.
CLARA BOW

An actor's a guy who, if you ain't talking about him, ain't listening.
MARLON BRANDO

(*on Montgomery Clift*) He acts like he's got a Mixmaster up his ass and doesn't want anyone to know it.   MARLON BRANDO (*on James Dean*) Mr Dean appears to be wearing my last year's wardrobe and using my last year's talent.   MARLON BRANDO

(*on Esther Williams*) Wet she's a star, dry she ain't.   FANNY BRICE

(*on an unnamed actor*) Like acting with 210 pounds of condemned veal.
                                                                    CORAL BROWNE

A character actress is an actress too ugly to be called a leading lady.
                                                                    KATHY BURKE

(*advice to fellow actors*) If you're going to make rubbish, be the best rubbish in it.   RICHARD BURTON

(*on Greta Garbo*) Dry and draughty, like an abandoned temple.
                                                                   TRUMAN CAPOTE

Life is difficult enough without Meryl Streep movies.   TRUMAN CAPOTE

Ricardo Montalban is to improvised acting what Mount Rushmore is to animation.
                                                                  JOHN CASSAVETES

Bogart's a helluva nice guy till 11.30 p.m. After that he thinks he's Bogart.
                                                                    DAVE CHASEN

(*to Peter O'Toole*) If you'd been any prettier it would have been 'Florence of Arabia'.   NOËL COWARD

(*of Judy Garland*) I didn't know her well, but after watching her in action I didn't want to.   JOAN CRAWFORD

I was in Hitchcock's *Lifeboat*. So was Tallulah Bankhead, who didn't wear panties, and each morning when we climbed into a lifeboat — up on a mechanical rocker — she gave the cast and crew a hell of a view, hiking up her skirt! Eventually someone complained to Hitch, who didn't want to get involved. He explained that it was an inter-departmental matter — involving wardrobe, costume, and possibly hairdressing . . .   HUME CRONYN

(*on Jayne Mansfield*) Dramatic art in her opinion is knowing how to fill a sweater.   BETTE DAVIS

(*on Cary Grant*) He needed willowy or boyish girls like Katharine Hepburn to make him look what they now call macho. If I'd co-starred with Grant or if [Joan] Crawford had, we'd have eaten him for breakfast.   BETTE DAVIS

(*on an unnamed starlet*) She's the original good time that was had by all.

BETTE DAVIS

(*on Hugh Grant*) A self-important, boring, flash-in-the-pan Brit.

ROBERT DOWNEY JR

Show me a great actor and I'll show you a lousy husband.   W.C. FIELDS

(*of Mae West*) A plumber's idea of Cleopatra.   W.C. FIELDS

(*on his ex-wife*) Debbie Reynolds was indeed the girl next door. But only if you lived next door to a self-centred, totally driven, insecure, untruthful phoney.

EDDIE FISHER

There are two things I would never do – climb Mount Everest and work with Val Kilmer again.   JOHN FRANKENHEIMER

Actors are the only kind of merchandise allowed to leave the store at night.

AVA GARDNER

(*on Clark Gable*) He's the kind of guy who, if you say, 'Hiya, Clark, how are you?', is stuck for an answer.   AVA GARDNER

(*of Ingrid Bergman*) Dear Ingrid – speaks five languages and can't act in any of them.   JOHN GIELGUD

(*of Michael Caine*) An over-fat, flatulent, 62-year-old windbag. A master of inconsequence masquerading as a guru, passing off his vast limitations as pious virtues.   RICHARD HARRIS

(*on hearing that a New York theatre was being named after her*) An actress's life is so transitory – suddenly you're a building.   HELEN HAYES

(*on Norma Shearer*) A face unclouded by thought.   LILLIAN HELLMAN

The average Hollywood film star's ambition is to be admired by an American, courted by an Italian, married to an Englishman, and have a French boyfriend.

KATHARINE HEPBURN

Actresses will happen in the best-regulated families.   OLIVER HERFORD

Walt Disney has the best casting. If he doesn't like an actor he just tears him up.   ALFRED HITCHCOCK

I did not give Lee Majors his start in acting – you can't pin that one on me. Anyway, technically he hasn't started acting yet.   ROCK HUDSON

(*to Robert Mitchum*) You're like a pay toilet, aren't you? You don't give a shit for nothing.   HOWARD HUGHES

(*on husband Charles Bronson*) I think I'm in so many of his pictures because no other actress would work with him.   JILL IRELAND

Producers treat actors like mushrooms. They keep you in the dark and pour shit on you.   ROSS KEMP

(*on Sarah Bernhardt*) A great actress, from the waist down.
            MARGARET KENDAL

A stripper is suing *The National Enquirer* for saying she had sex with Ben Affleck. You know your movie bombed when a stripper doesn't want her name associated with yours.   CRAIG KILBORN

After *The Wizard of Oz* I was typecast as a lion, and there aren't all that many parts for lions.   BERT LAHR

(*on Maureen O'Hara*) She looked as though butter wouldn't melt in her mouth – or anywhere else for that matter.   ELSA LANCHESTER

(*on Dame Maggie Smith*) She's better on stage, from a distance. On a screen, close up, she makes you want to dive for cover.   ELSA LANCHESTER

Michael Caine can out-act any, well nearly any, telephone kiosk you care to mention.   HUGH LEONARD

(*on his role in the movie* Humoresque) I played an unsympathetic part – myself.
            OSCAR LEVANT

Sophia Loren plays peasants. I play ladies.   GINA LOLLOBRIGIDA

Clara [Bow] was the idol of the illiterate, and from her dainty lips came nothing more seductive than bubble gum.   ANITA LOOS

(*on Jack Nicholson*) A legend in his own lifetime and in his own mind.
            JENNIFER LOPEZ

(*on Johnny Depp*) He's the kind of guy that would be really sweet to a girl and bring her flowers, but still take a pee in the alley. TRACI LORDS

There's a statue of Jimmy Stewart in the Hollywood Wax Museum, and the statue talks better than he does. DEAN MARTIN

Dudley Moore has a club foot. That's not a problem — for him, his career, or anyone. What I object to is his club wit. JAMES MASON

(*on Dustin Hoffman*) Never argue with a man who is shorter than his Oscar. LARRY GELBART

If Arnold [Schwarzenegger] hadn't existed we would have had to build him. JOHN MILIUS

A Steve McQueen performance lends itself to monotony. ROBERT MITCHUM

Burt Lancaster couldn't pick up an ashtray before discussing his motivation for an hour or so. JEANNE MOREAU

(*on his ex-wife*) To the unwashed public, Joan Collins is a star. But to those who know her, she's a commodity who would sell her own bowel movement. ANTHONY NEWLEY

There are three stages in an actor's career. The first is when he shows up on the set and says: 'You should've seen the girl I was with last night. God! I didn't sleep. She was *amazing*!' In the second stage, he's a leading man and says: 'You know, I found the most wonderful restaurant — you wouldn't believe the fish.' By the third stage, he's a character actor. Now he says: 'Oh, I had the most lovely bowel movement last night.' PAUL NEWMAN

You don't hear about Tom Hanks running around nights. You don't hear about Tom Hanks stealing. You don't read about Tom Hanks in *The National Inquirer*. That's what I like about Tom — he never gets caught. JACK NICHOLSON

(*on Jayne Mansfield*) Miss United Dairies herself. DAVID NIVEN

Keanu Reeves is going to play Superman in a new movie. The villains don't use kryptonite to stop him, they just use big words. CONAN O'BRIEN (*asked the secret of an actor's success*) Sincerity. Once you can fake that, you can achieve anything.   LAURENCE OLIVIER

There are three types of actress: the silly, the very silly, and Shirley MacLaine.
                                                                     P.J. O'ROURKE

Scratch an actor and you'll find an actress.   DOROTHY PARKER

(*on Marion Davies*) She has two expressions – joy and indigestion.
                                                                     DOROTHY PARKER

(*on Frances Farmer*) Cinderella goes back to the ashes on a liquor-slicked highway.
                                                                     LOUELLA PARSONS

In *Dragonheart*, instead of a dragon, I acted with a tennis ball on a stick. I've worked with some actors who've given me less.   DENNIS QUAID

(*on co-star Mae West's movie debut*) She stole everything but the cameras.
                                                                     GEORGE RAFT

(*on Paul Newman*) He has the attention span of a lightning bolt.
                                                                     ROBERT REDFORD

(*on Sylvester Stallone*) He is to acting what Liberace was to pumping iron.
                                                                     REX REED

When an actor marries an actress they both fight for the mirror.
                                                                     BURT REYNOLDS

An actress is not a lady; at least, when she is, she is not an actress.
                                                                     GEORGE BERNARD SHAW

(*on Jack Lemmon*) He has a gift for butchering good parts while managing to look intelligent, thus constituting Hollywood's abiding answer to the theatre.
                                                                     WILFRID SHEED

Paramount paid me by the tear.   SYLVIA SIDNEY

People think, 'Wow, you're an actress, so people must be really nice to you and kiss your ass.' *Nobody* kisses my ass!   ALICIA SILVERSTONE

Why don't actors look out of the window in the morning? Because they'd have nothing to do in the afternoon.   MICHAEL SIMKINS, *What's My Motivation?*

Glenn Close is not an actress – she's an address.   Maggie Smith

(*on Gwyneth Paltrow*) She lives in rarified air that's a little thin. It's like she's not getting quite enough oxygen.   Sharon Stone

Some of my best leading men have been horses and dogs.

Elizabeth Taylor

The physical labour actors have to do wouldn't tax an embryo.

Spencer Tracy

(*on Brigitte Bardot*) She used to sulk in the morning when I had not been nice to her in her dreams.   Roger Vadim

(*on Gary Cooper*) He got a reputation as a great actor by just thinking hard about the next line.   King Vidor

(*on appearing in the 1982 film* Jinxed) The only way I could force myself into kissing [Bette] Midler on-camera was to pretend that I was kissing my dog.
            Ken Wahl

(*of Anita Louise*) As cold as a stepmother's kiss.   Hal Wallis

People find out I'm an actress and I see that 'whore' look flicker across their eyes.   Rachel Weisz

(*on Sean Connery*) Guys like him and [Michael] Caine talk about acting as if they knew what it was.   Nicol Williamson

(*of Fredric March*) He was able to do a very emotional scene with tears in his eyes, and pinch my fanny at the same time.   Shelley Winters

Mamie Van Doren often acted like Mr Ed the Talking Horse.   Paula Yates

An actor is the only ham that can't be cured.

Adultery

(*on the death of her philandering husband, King Edward VII*) Now at least I know where he is!   Queen Alexandra

It seems so lazy to have an affair with your secretary, like always going to the nearest restaurant instead of the best.   Lynn Barber

My wife gives me no respect. I took her to a drive-in movie. I spent the whole night trying to find out what car she was in. RODNEY DANGERFIELD

Last night I caught my wife in bed with the kid who delivers the pizza. She begged me not to tell the butcher. RODNEY DANGERFIELD

Thou shalt not commit adultery . . . unless in the mood. W.C. FIELDS

When you marry a mistress you create a job vacancy. JAMES GOLDSMITH

How dare he make love to me and not be a married man!
ANNE KALMAN (INGRID BERGMAN), *Indiscreet*

If you marry a man who cheats on his wife, you'll be married to a man who cheats on his wife. ANN LANDERS

A mistress is what goes between a mister and a mattress. JOE E. LEWIS

Adultery is the application of democracy to love. H.L. MENCKEN

I think a man can have two, maybe three, affairs while he is married. But three is the absolute maximum. After that, you are cheating.
YVES MONTAND

[Being a mistress] is like having a book out from the library. It is like *constantly* having a book out from the library. LORRIE MOORE

Adultery? Why fool about with hamburger when you can have steak at home?
PAUL NEWMAN

I discovered my wife in bed with another man, and I was crushed. So I said, 'Get off me, you two!' EMO PHILIPS

Adulthood

Adults are just obsolete children. DR SEUSS

An adult is someone who has stopped growing at both ends and started growing in the middle.

You know you've reached adulthood when sleeping on the couch makes your back hurt.

You know you've reached adulthood when 90 per cent of the time you spend in front of a computer is for real work.

You know you've reached adulthood when you get into a heated argument about pension plans.

You know you've reached adulthood when you keep more food than beer in the fridge.

You know you've reached adulthood when 6 a.m. is the time you get up, not when you go to bed.

You know you've reached adulthood when you hear your favourite song in an elevator.

Adversity

Adversity has the same effect on a man that severe training has on the pugilist: it reduces him to his fighting weight.

JOSH BILLINGS

The only person who sticks closer to you in adversity than a friend is a creditor.

Advertising

An advertising agency is 85 per cent confusion and 15 per cent commission.

FRED ALLEN

How can something be 'new and improved'? Which is it? If it's new, then there has never been anything before it. If it's improved, then there must have been something before it.

BILLY CONNOLLY

The very first law in advertising is to avoid the concrete promise and cultivate the delightfully vague.

BILL COSBY

Sure I eat what I advertise. Sure I eat Wheaties for breakfast. A good bowl of Wheaties with Bourbon can't be beat.

JAY 'DIZZY' DEAN

Doing business without advertising is like winking at a girl in the dark: you know what you are doing but nobody else does.

EDGAR WATSON HOWE

Research men in advertising are really blind men groping in a dark room for a black cat that isn't there.

LUDOVIC KENNEDY

Advertising may be described as the science of arresting the human intelligence long enough to get money from it.   STEPHEN LEACOCK, *Garden of Folly*

Half the money I spend on advertising is wasted, and the trouble is I don't know which half.   LORD LEVERHULME

You can fool all of the people all of the time if the advertising is right and the budget is big enough.   JOSEPH E. LEVINE

I'm tired of hearing about money, money, money. I just want to play the game, drink Pepsi, wear Reebok.   SHAQUILLE O'NEAL

Advertising is the art of convincing people to spend money they don't have on something they don't need.   WILL ROGERS

Many a small thing has been made large by the right kind of advertising.   MARK TWAIN

I saw a subliminal advertising executive, but only for a second.   STEVEN WRIGHT

Advice

(*on advice given to him by his father*) Take a bottle by the neck and a woman by the waist and you'll be all right.   GEORGE BAKER

I do what it says on the Aspirin bottle: take two and keep away from children.   ROSEANNE BARR

Never ascribe to an opponent motives meaner than your own.   J.M. BARRIE

Advice is like castor oil; easy to give, but dreadful to take..   JOSH BILLINGS

Find out what she loves most in the world and kill it. That way you'll move up a step.   MIMI BOBECK (KATHY KINNEY), *The Drew Carey Show*

Never stray from the path, never eat a windfall apple and never trust a man whose eyebrows meet in the middle.   ANGELA CARTER, *The Company of Wolves*

You better live every day like it's your last day, because one day you're going to be right.   RAY CHARLES

When a man seeks your advice he generally wants your praise.

LORD CHESTERFIELD

I owe my success to having listened respectfully to the very best advice, and then going away and doing the exact opposite. G.K. CHESTERTON

Always be nice to those younger than you, because they are the ones who will be writing about you. CYRIL CONNOLLY

A word to the wise ain't necessary – it's the stupid ones who need the advice.

BILL COSBY

Keep your nose clean and your chin up, even if it requires surgery.

RAY DAVIES

Never go to bed mad. Stay up and fight. PHYLLIS DILLER

Don't do drugs, don't have unprotected sex, don't be violent. Leave that to me.

EMINEM

Never, ever go to bed with a man on the first date. Not ever. Unless you really want to. CYNTHIA HEIMEL

Always tell the truth. You may make a hole in one when you're alone on the golf course. FRANKLIN P. JONES

Advice is what we ask for when we already know the answer but wish we didn't. ERICA JONG

Be careful not to do your good deeds when there's no one watching you.

TOM LEHRER

When you have got an elephant by the hind leg and he is trying to run away, it's best to let him run. ABRAHAM LINCOLN

Never take notice of anonymous letters, unless you get a few thousand on the same subject. ROBERT MENZIES

Treat a whore like a lady and a lady like a whore. WILSON MIZNER

Don't smoke too much, drink too much, eat too much or work too much. We're all on the road to the grave, but there's no need to be in the passing lane.

ROBERT ORBEN

My mother gave me this advice: trust your husband, adore your husband and get as much as you can in your own name.   JOAN RIVERS

Live fast, die young, and leave a good-looking corpse.
NICK ROMANO (JOHN DEREK), *Knock On Any Door*

Speak softly and carry a big stick: you will go far.   THEODORE ROOSEVELT

Never invest your money in anything that eats or needs repairing.
BILLY ROSE

I want to share something with you: the three little sentences that will get you through life. Number 1: Cover for me. Number 2: Oh, good idea, boss. Number 3: It was like that when I got here.   HOMER SIMPSON, *The Simpsons*

Beware of all enterprises that require new clothes.   HENRY DAVID THOREAU

If you can't convince them, confuse them.   HARRY S. TRUMAN

Always be sincere, even if you don't mean it.   HARRY S. TRUMAN

I have found that the best way to give advice to your children is to find out what they want and then advise them to do it.   HARRY S. TRUMAN

Always acknowledge a fault. This will throw those in authority off their guard and give you an opportunity to commit more.   MARK TWAIN

Never have children, only grandchildren.   GORE VIDAL, *Two Sisters*

If you've got them by the balls, their hearts and minds will follow.
JOHN WAYNE

Don't give a woman advice; one should never give a woman anything she can't wear in the evening.   OSCAR WILDE

Remember that nobody will ever get ahead of you as long as he is kicking you in the seat of the pants.   WALTER WINCHELL

My grandfather likes to give me advice, but he's a little forgetful. One day, he took me aside and left me there.   STEVEN WRIGHT

Advice after mischief is like medicine after death.   DANISH PROVERB

The best way to save face is to keep the lower half shut.

Always use tasteful words. You may have to eat them.

Believe nothing until it has been officially denied.

Never put both feet in your mouth at the same time, because then you won't have a leg to stand on.

Never hit a man with glasses. Hit him with something bigger and heavier.

Never offend people with style when you can offend them with substance.

Never give yourself a haircut after three margaritas.

Never underestimate the power of stupid people in large groups.

When all else fails, read the instructions.

Affection

The most affectionate creature in the world is a wet dog.　　AMBROSE BIERCE

My wife and I always hold hands. If I let go, she shops.　　HENNY YOUNGMAN

Afterlife

There is the fear that there is an afterlife but no one will know where it's being held.　　WOODY ALLEN

I do benefits for all religions – I'd hate to blow the hereafter on a technicality.　　BOB HOPE

I wanna live till I die; no more, no less.　　EDDIE IZZARD

There's no such thing as a soul. It's just something they made up to scare kids, like the bogeyman or Michael Jackson.　　BART SIMPSON, *The Simpsons*

Age and ageing

The man who views the world at fifty the same as he did at twenty has wasted thirty years of his life.　　MUHAMMAD ALI

The best thing to do is to behave in a manner befitting one's age. If you are sixteen or under, try not to go bald.　　　　WOODY ALLEN

I refuse to admit that I am more than fifty-two, even if that does make my sons illegitimate.　　　　NANCY ASTOR

The secret of staying young is to live honestly, eat slowly, and lie about your age.　　　　LUCILLE BALL

Most women are not so young as they are painted.　　　　MAX BEERBOHM

As a graduate of the Zsa Zsa Gabor School of Creative Mathematics, I honestly do not know how old I am.　　　　ERMA BOMBECK

The older you get, the stronger you have to get. Getting old is not for cissies.　　　　PIERCE BROSNAN

Age is something that doesn't matter, unless you are a cheese.　　　　BILLIE BURKE

I'm sixty-three now, but that's just 17 Celsius.　　　　GEORGE CARLIN

Nature gives you the face that you have at twenty, but it is up to you to merit the face you have at fifty.　　　　COCO CHANEL

Things hurt me now. My knees hurt, my back hurts. But your head still thinks it's twenty-three.　　　　GEORGE CLOONEY

Age is just a number. It's totally irrelevant unless, of course, you happen to be a bottle of wine.　　　　JOAN COLLINS

Pushing forty? She's clinging on to it for dear life!　　　　IVY COMPTON-BURNETT

Why on earth do people say things like, 'My eyes aren't what they used to be?' So what did they used to be? Ears? Wellington boots?　　　　BILLY CONNOLLY

I have to be careful to get out before I become the grotesque caricature of a hatchet-faced woman with big knockers.　　　　JAMIE LEE CURTIS

Careful grooming may take twenty years off a woman's age, but you can't fool a flight of stairs.　　　　MARLENE DIETRICH

Whatever you may look like, marry a man your own age – as your beauty fades, so will his eyesight.　　　　PHYLLIS DILLER

Youth is a blunder; manhood a struggle; old age a regret.

BENJAMIN DISRAELI, *Coningsby*

(*on late fatherhood, 2003*) I'm very excited at this age of my life to be starting a new family, but I'd like not to be in a wheelchair for high school graduation.

MICHAEL DOUGLAS

The years between fifty and seventy are the hardest. You are always being asked to do things, and you are not yet decrepit enough to turn them down.

T.S. ELIOT

At eighteen our convictions are hills from which we look; at forty-five they are caves in which we hide.   F. SCOTT FITZGERALD

Women are not forgiven for ageing. Robert Redford's lines of distinction are my old-age wrinkles.   JANE FONDA

At twenty years of age, the will reigns; at thirty, the wit; and at forty, the judgement.   BENJAMIN FRANKLIN, *Poor Richard's Almanack*

Time and tide wait for no man, but time always stands still for a woman of thirty.   ROBERT FROST

I was told when you hit forty men stop looking at you. It's true, until you slip on a mini-skirt.   MARIELLA FROSTRUP

A woman is as old as she looks before breakfast.   EDGAR WATSON HOWE

If you want to know how old a woman is, ask her sister-in-law.

EDGAR WATSON HOWE

Allow me to put the record straight. I am forty-six and have been for some years past.   ERICA JONG

Youth is the gift of nature, but age is a work of art.   STANISLAW LEC

A man's only as old as the woman he feels.   GROUCHO MARX

Age is not a particularly interesting subject. Anyone can get old. All you have to do is live long enough.   GROUCHO MARX

When a woman tells you her age, it's all right to look surprised, but don't scowl.

WILSON MIZNER

There's money in wrinkles. A woman I've known for years said, 'You're almost good looking now.'   BILL NIGHY

The older you get, the better you get. Unless you're a banana.
ROSE NYLUND (BETTY WHITE), *The Golden Girls*

There was no respect for youth when I was young, and now that I am old there is no respect for age. I missed it coming and going.   J.B. PRIESTLEY

A woman is as young as her knees.   MARY QUANT

I'm forty-eight, which worries me, because at twenty-four I had a midlife crisis.
DENNIS REGAN

The easiest way to diminish the appearance of wrinkles is to keep your glasses off when you look in the mirror.   JOAN RIVERS

Life begins at forty – but so do fallen arches, rheumatism, faulty eyesight, and the tendency to tell a story to the same person three or four times.
HELEN ROWLAND

It is a mistake to regard age as a downhill grade toward dissolution. The reverse is true. As one grows older, one climbs with surprising strides.
GEORGE SAND

I think age is a very high price to pay for maturity.   TOM STOPPARD

From birth to eighteen, a girl needs good parents. From eighteen to thirty-five, she needs good looks. From thirty-five to fifty-five, she needs a good person-ality. From fifty-five on, she needs good cash.   SOPHIE TUCKER

Phyllis Diller's so ancient she's just a carcass with a mouth.   RUBY WAX

The three ages of man are youth, middle age and 'my word, you do look well.'
JUNE WHITFIELD

The old believe everything; the middle-aged suspect everything; the young know everything.   OSCAR WILDE, *The Chameleon*

Thirty-five is a very attractive age. London society is full of women of the very highest birth who have, of their own free choice, remained thirty-five for years.
OSCAR WILDE, *The Importance of Being Earnest*

Blanche Devereaux (Rue McClanahan): This is strictly off the record, but Dirk is nearly five years younger than I am.
Dorothy Zbornak (Bea Arthur): In what, Blanche, dog years?

The Golden Girls

Both women and melons are best when fairly ripe.   Spanish proverb

A man is as old as he feels, a woman as old as she feels like admitting.

American proverb

A woman of thirty-five thinks about having children. A man of thirty-five thinks about dating them.

Go for younger men. You might as well — they never mature anyway.

The best ten years of a woman's life are between the ages of twenty-nine and thirty.

Thirty-five is when you finally get your head together and your body starts falling apart.

Agents

My agent gets ten per cent of everything I get, except my blinding headaches.

Fred Allen

My agent went swimming in shark-infested waters but escaped without injury. That's what they call professional courtesy.   Herman J. Mankiewicz

I wish to be cremated. One tenth of my ashes shall be given to my agent, as written in our contract.   Groucho Marx

Agreement

When you say that you agree to a thing in principle, you mean that you have not the slightest intention of carrying it out in practice.   Otto von Bismarck

My idea of an agreeable person is a person who agrees with me.

Benjamin Disraeli

Contracts are agreements made up of big words and little type.

Sam Ewing

The fellow that agrees with everything you say is either a fool or he is getting ready to skin you.   KIN HUBBARD

If two men on the same job agree all the time, then one is useless. If they disagree all the time, then both are useless.   DARRYL F. ZANUCK

Simply because nobody disagrees with you doesn't mean you're brilliant — maybe you're the boss.

Airplanes

The U.S. airline industry is still one of the safest on earth; the only nation with a better safety record is the Republic of Kyrgyzstan, which has only one airplane and can't figure out how to start it.   DAVE BARRY

Did you ever notice that the first piece of luggage on the carousel never belongs to anyone?   ERMA BOMBECK

If God wanted us to fly, He would have given us tickets.   MEL BROOKS

They say that if two airplanes almost collide, it's a near miss. Bullshit, it's a near hit! A collision is a near miss.   GEORGE CARLIN

In airplanes, why is there no window in the toilet? Who on earth is going to see in?   BILLY CONNOLLY

There's no reason to become alarmed, and we hope you'll enjoy the rest of your flight. By the way, is there anyone on board who knows how to fly a plane?
ELAINE DICKINSON (JULIE HAGERTY), *Airplane*

One good thing can be said for all airline food: it's served in small portions.
SAM EWING

Lord Flashheart (Rik Mayall): You should treat your aircraft like you treat your woman.
Edmund Blackadder (Rowan Atkinson): So you should take your plane out to dinner and a movie?
Lord Flashheart: No, get in her five times a day and take her to heaven and back!   *Blackadder Goes Forth*

Nothing is so uninteresting to look at as clouds from the inside.
RICHARD GORDON, *Doctor in the Swim*

Airplane travel is nature's way of making you look like your passport photo.

AL GORE

I love flying. I've been to almost as many places as my luggage.   BOB HOPE

There are only two reasons to sit in the back row of an airplane: either you have diarrhoea, or you're anxious to meet people who do.   RICHARD JENI

Why do airlines put an oxygen mask directly over your seat? You don't need it there. You know where they should put it? Inside the tiny little bathroom. That's where you need the oxygen.   JAY LENO

The average airplane is sixteen-years-old. And so is the average airplane meal.

JOAN RIVERS

Airline food is gastronomic murder.   EGON RONAY

You know the oxygen masks on airplanes? I don't think there's really any oxygen. I think they're just to muffle the screams.   RITA RUDNER

Airline hostesses show you how to use a seat belt in case you haven't been in a car since 1965.   JERRY SEINFELD

Do they need keys to start the plane? Maybe that's what those delays on the ground are sometimes, when you're just sitting there at the gate. Maybe the pilot sits up there in the cockpit saying, 'I don't believe this . . . dammit . . . I did it again.' They tell you it's something mechanical because they don't want to come on the P.A. system: 'Ladies and gentlemen, we're going to be delayed here on the ground for a while. I uh . . . oh God, this is so embarrassing . . . I . . . I left the keys to the plane in my apartment. They're in this big blue ashtray by the front door. I'm really sorry. I'll run back and get them.'

JERRY SEINFELD

Soon the only people flying to Europe will be terrorists. It will be, 'Will you be sitting in armed or unarmed?'   ROBIN WILLIAMS

Why don't they make the whole plane out of that black box stuff?

STEVEN WRIGHT

How do you get off a non-stop flight?

Airports

I had arrived at the airport one hour early so that, in accordance with airline procedures, I could stand around.   DAVE BARRY

If the Lord had wanted people to fly, He would have made it simpler for people to get to the airport.   MILTON BERLE

A new machine for passenger screening at airports can see right through clothing. Listen, if it keeps the screeners awake . . .   JAY LENO

They have luggage stores in airports. Who forgets their suitcase? Have you ever seen a guy with an armload of shirts going, 'Hurray, a suitcase!'?
                                    JAY MOHR

I did not fully understand the term 'terminal illness' until I saw Heathrow Airport for myself.   DENNIS POTTER

Alcohol

I'd rather have a full bottle in front of me than a full frontal lobotomy.
                                    FRED ALLEN

Do not allow children to mix drinks. It is unseemly and they use too much vermouth.   STEVE ALLEN

Alcohol is good for you. My grandfather proved it irrevocably. He drank two quarts of booze every mature day of his life and lived to the age of 103. I was at the cremation – that fire would *not* go out!   DAVE ASTOR

One reason I don't drink is that I want to know when I'm having a good time.
                                    NANCY ASTOR

You can't drown yourself in drink. I've tried, you float.   JOHN BARRYMORE

Whisky is too good to be sullied with water.   BRENDAN BEHAN

I am a drinker with writing problems.   BRENDAN BEHAN

I only take a drink on two occasions – when I'm thirsty and when I'm not.
                                    BRENDAN BEHAN

I saw a notice which said 'Drink Canada Dry', and I've just started.
                                    BRENDAN BEHAN

I know I'm drinking myself to a slow death, but then I'm in no hurry.

ROBERT BENCHLEY

A friend of mine belongs to Alcoholics Anonymous. He's not a fanatic about it. He doesn't go to meetings – he just sends in his empties.   MILTON BERLE

My misdeeds are accidental happenings and merely the result of having been in the wrong bar or bed at the wrong time, say most days between midday and midnight.   JEFFREY BERNARD

(*on soccer star husband George*) I can understand that he doesn't want to go to Alcoholics Anonymous where people keep asking him for autographs.

ALEX BEST

In 1969 I gave up drinking and sex. It was the worst twenty minutes of my life.

GEORGE BEST

Most British statesmen have either drunk too much or womanised too much. I never fell into the second category.   GEORGE BROWN

My favourite drink is a cocktail of carrot juice and whiskey. I'm always drunk but I can see for miles.   ROY 'CHUBBY' BROWN

One tequila, two tequila, three tequila, floor.   GEORGE CARLIN

Alcohol is like love: the first kiss is magic, the second is intimate, the third is routine. After that you just take the girl's clothes off.

RAYMOND CHANDLER, *The Long Goodbye*

When I was younger, I made it a rule never to take a strong drink before lunch. It is now my rule never to do so before breakfast.   WINSTON CHURCHILL

Always remember that I have taken more out of alcohol than alcohol has taken out of me.   WINSTON CHURCHILL

Port is the perfect drink: a combination of aphrodisiac and tranquilliser. If you don't get what you want, you aren't bothered.   BARRY CRYER

I drink too much. The last time I gave a urine sample it had an olive in it.

RODNEY DANGERFIELD

(*on absinthe*) It's like marijuana. Drink too much and you suddenly realise why Van Gogh cut off his ear.   JOHNNY DEPP

I don't drink these days. I am allergic to alcohol and narcotics. I break out in handcuffs.
ROBERT DOWNEY JR

Alcohol is necessary for a man so that he can have a good opinion of himself, undisturbed by the facts.
FINLEY PETER DUNNE

A lot of men get very funny about women drinking – they don't really like it at all. I'm sorry lads, but if we didn't get pissed, most of you would never get a shag.
JENNY ECLAIR

How well I remember my first encounter with The Devil's Brew. I happened to stumble across a case of bourbon – and went right on stumbling for several days thereafter.
W.C. FIELDS

I exercise strong self-control. I never drink anything stronger than gin before breakfast.
W.C. FIELDS

I always keep a supply of stimulant handy in case I see a snake . . . which I also keep handy.
W.C. FIELDS

(on alcoholism) First you take a drink, then the drink takes a drink, then the drink takes you.
F. SCOTT FITZGERALD

Drinking removes warts and pimples. Not from me, but from those I look at.
JACKIE GLEASON

I was in love with a beautiful blonde once. She drove me to drink. 'Tis the one thing I'm indebted to her for.
THE GREAT MAN (W.C. FIELDS), *Never Give a Sucker an Even Break*

I can't die until the government finds a safe place to bury my liver.
PHIL HARRIS

I often sit back and think 'I wish I'd done that' and find out later that I already have.
RICHARD HARRIS

I formed a new group called Alcoholics Unanimous. If you don't feel like a drink, you ring another member and he comes over to persuade you.
RICHARD HARRIS

Be wary of strong drink. It can make you shoot at tax collectors and miss.
ROBERT A. HEINLEIN, *Time Enough for Love*

Am I the only person who gets confused about the amount of alcohol you can safely drink before driving and the amount of alcohol you can take through customs?   HARRY HILL

Martinis before lunch are like a woman's breasts. One is too few and three are too many.   JOHN HUMPHRYS

Even though a number of people have tried, no one has ever found a way to drink for a living.   JEAN KERR

A mixture of brandy and water spoils two good things.   CHARLES LAMB

I distrust camels, and anyone else who can go a week without a drink.
                                                    JOE E. LEWIS

I don't drink any more than the man next to me. It just so happens that the man next to me is Dean Martin.   JOE E. LEWIS

I always wake up at the crack of ice.   JOE E. LEWIS

(*on his Scottish accent*) My wife says I'm Scotch by absorption.
                                                    MAGNUS MAGNUSSON

By the time a bartender knows what drink a man will have before he orders, there is little else about him worth knowing.   DON MARQUIS

Don't put ice in my drink: it takes up too much room.   GROUCHO MARX

Candy
Is dandy,
But liquor
Is quicker.   OGDEN NASH, *Reflection on Ice-Breaking*

They're trying to put warning labels on liquor saying, 'Caution, alcohol can be dangerous to pregnant women.' That's ironic. If it weren't for alcohol, most women wouldn't even be that way.   RITA RUDNER

Alcohol is the anaesthesia by which we endure the operation of life.
                                                    GEORGE BERNARD SHAW

If I had all the money I've spent on drink, I'd spend it on drink.
                                    VIVIAN STANSHALL, *Sir Henry at Rawlinson End*

Edina Monsoon (Jennifer Saunders): You've given up drinking before.
Patsy Stone (Joanna Lumley): Worst eight hours of my life!

Absolutely Fabulous

The last mosquito that bit me had to check into the Betty Ford clinic.

PATSY STONE (JOANNA LUMLEY), *Absolutely Fabulous*

There are two things that will be believed of any man whatsoever, and one of them is that he has taken to drink.   BOOTH TARKINGTON, *Penrod*

An alcoholic is someone you don't like who drinks as much as you do.

DYLAN THOMAS

I don't have a drink problem, except when I can't get one.   TOM WAITS

When I read about the evils of drinking, I gave up reading.

HENNY YOUNGMAN

Abstinence is a good thing, but it should always be practised in moderation.

Alcohol doesn't solve any problems . . . but then again, neither does milk.

Alcohol: a liquid for preserving almost everything but secrets.

Alcohol and calculus don't mix. Never drink and derive.

You know you've drunk too much when you lose arguments with inanimate objects.

You know you've drunk too much when the back of your head keeps getting hit by the toilet seat.

You know you've drunk too much when you can focus better with one eye closed.

Algebra

Stand firm in your refusal to remain conscious during algebra. In real life, I assure you, there is no such thing as algebra.   FRAN LEBOWITZ

Alimony

Alimony is like buying oats for a dead horse.   ARTHUR BAER

You never realise how short a month is until you pay alimony.

JOHN BARRYMORE

Marriage is but for a little while. It is alimony that is forever.

QUENTIN CRISP

Divorce is a system whereby two people make a mistake and one of them goes on paying for it.   LEN DEIGHTON

Alimony: the high cost of leaving.

Alimony: bounty afer the mutiny.

Alternatives

If the grass is greener in the other fellow's yard, let him worry about cutting it.

FRED ALLEN

Women now have choices. They can be married, not married, have a job, not have a job, be married with children, unmarried with children. Men have the same choice we've always had: work or prison.   TIM ALLEN

I believe that it's better to be looked over than it is to be overlooked.

BELLE (MAE WEST), *Belle of the Nineties*

I'd rather spend an evening on top of a ladder in No Man's Land smoking endless cigarettes through a luminous balaclava.

EDMUND BLACKADDER (ROWAN ATKINSON), *Blackadder*

The absence of alternatives clears the mind marvellously.   HENRY KISSINGER

When choosing between two evils, I always like to take the one I've never tried before.   MAE WEST

The greener grass on the other side is probably artificial turf.

Ambition

If all the world's a stage, I want to operate the trap door.   PAUL BEATTY

I will stop at nothing to reach my ambition, but only because my brakes are defective.   ASHLEIGH BRILLIANT

Shoot for the moon. Even if you miss you'll land among the stars.
LES BROWN

When you reach for the stars, you may not quite get one, but you won't come up with a handful of mud either.
LEO BURNETT

It's always been my ambition to be killed by some lover in a fit of passionate jealousy.
MARIANNE FAITHFULL

Everybody wants to be Cary Grant. *I* want to be Cary Grant.   CARY GRANT

What's my loftiest ambition? I've always wanted to throw an egg into an electric fan.
OLIVER HERFORD

If I were a fraction, my goal would be world denomination.   CHRIS LIPE

Ambition is a poor excuse for not having enough sense to be lazy.
CHARLIE MCCARTHY (EDGAR BERGEN)

I really wanted to be the new Shirley Temple.   MADONNA

My dad always used to say to me: 'Riaad, you can do anything you want in this world . . . as long as you become an orthopaedic surgeon first.'
RIAAD MOOSA

My ambition is to host a TV chat show with Neil Armstrong as a guest and never once mention the moon.   ARDAL O'HANLON

Adults are always asking kids what they want to be when they grow up because they are looking for ideas.
PAULA POUNDSTONE

When people come and talk to you of their aspirations, before they leave you had better count your spoons.   LOGAN PEARSALL SMITH, *Afterthoughts*

(*on his legacy to the world*) I just want a conveyor belt at the John Lennon Airport: 'The bags from Malaga are coming up on Conveyor Belt Ringo.'
RINGO STARR

You can only sleep your way to the middle.   DAWN STEEL

Ambition is the last refuge of the failure.   OSCAR WILDE

America

The curtain rises on a vast primitive wasteland, not unlike certain parts of New Jersey.
WOODY ALLEN

America is the country where you buy a lifetime supply of aspirins and use it up in two weeks.
JOHN BARRYMORE

America is the land of permanent waves and impermanent wives.
BRENDAN BEHAN

You have to wonder about a country where the bombs are smarter than the high school graduates. At least the bombs can find Iraq on the map.
A. WHITNEY BROWN

I come from a part of the world where the Egg McMuffin would be a heritage object.
BILL BRYSON

I don't get all choked up about yellow ribbons and American flags. I see them as symbols, and I leave them to the symbol-minded.
GEORGE CARLIN

America is the only nation in history which miraculously has gone directly from barbarism to degeneration without the usual interval of civilisation.
GEORGES CLEMENCEAU

America is dumb, like a dumb puppy that has big teeth.
JOHNNY DEPP

Yes, America is gigantic, but a gigantic mistake.
SIGMUND FREUD

America's one of the finest countries anyone ever stole.
BOBCAT GOLDTHWAITE

Why is New Jersey called the Garden State? 'Cause it's too hard to fit 'Oil and Petro-Refinery State' on a licence plate.
GRACIE HART (SANDRA BULLOCK), *Miss Congeniality*

America is the land of wide lawns and narrow minds.
ERNEST HEMINGWAY

The difference between America and England is that Americans think 100 years is a long time, while the English think 100 miles is a long way.
EARLE HITCHNER

You know, America is a great place, but it doesn't have a place where you can get rid of your kids.   CLIFF HUXTABLE (BILL COSBY), *The Cosby Show*

There's this notion that America has no culture, that it's all garbage. But the fact that everyone in the world wears a baseball cap has to be reckoned with.
                                                                    GLENDA JACKSON

America is a melting pot; the people at the bottom get burned while all the scum floats to the top.   CHARLIE KING

When I was a graduate student at Harvard, I learned about showers and central heating. Ten years later, I learned about breakfast meetings. These are America's three contributions to civilisation.   MERVYN A. KING

The big story: Las Vegas got three inches of snow. So it's official, hell is freezing over.   JAY LENO

A new book lists all the countries that hate the United States. It's called *The World Atlas*.   JAY LENO

The trouble with America is that there are far too many wide open spaces surrounded by teeth.   CHARLES LUCKMAN

America is our neighbour, our ally, our trading partner, and our friend. Still, sometimes you'd like to give them such a smack . . .   RICK MERCER

The U.S. is the most loved and hated country in the world. We're Frank Sinatra.
                                                                    DENNIS MILLER

I'm from England, the country that used to own you people.
                                              DAPHNE MOON (JANE LEEVES), *Frasier*

The United States is like the guy at the party who gives cocaine to everyone and still nobody likes him.   JIM SAMUELS

Don't worry, Marge. America's health care system is second only to Japan, Canada, Sweden, Great Britain, well, all of Europe, but you can thank your lucky stars we don't live in Paraguay!   HOMER SIMPSON, *The Simpsons*

I visited an American supermarket. They have so many amazing products here. Like powder milk. You add water and you get milk. And powder orange juice. You add water and you get orange juice. Then I saw baby powder. And I said to myself, 'What a country! I'm making my family tonight!'   YAKOV SMIRNOFF

I found there a country with thirty-two religions and only one sauce.
CHARLES-MAURICE DE TALLEYRAND

America is a large, friendly dog in a very small room. Every time it wags its tail it knocks over a chair.
ARNOLD TOYNBEE

It was wonderful to find America, but it would have been more wonderful to miss it.
MARK TWAIN, *Pudd'nhead Wilson*

In America, through pressure of conformity, there is freedom of choice, but nothing to choose from.
PETER USTINOV

Every time Europe looks across the Atlantic to see the American eagle, it observes only the rear end of an ostrich.
H.G. WELLS, *America*

Of course, America had often been discovered before Columbus, but it had always been hushed up.
OSCAR WILDE

The thing that impresses me most about America is the way parents obey their children.
DUKE of WINDSOR (formerly EDWARD VIII)

In America half an hour is forty minutes.
GERMAN PROVERB

Americans

Americans like fat books and thin women.
RUSSELL BAKER

If you surveyed a hundred typical middle-aged Americans, I bet you'd find that only two of them could tell you their blood types, but every last one of them would know the theme song from *The Beverly Hillbillies*.
DAVE BARRY

The average Southerner has the speech patterns of someone slipping in and out of consciousness. I can change my shoes and socks faster than most people in Mississippi can speak a sentence.
BILL BRYSON, *The Lost Continent: Travels in Small Town America*

Americans have been brought up to believe that everyone loves them for themselves.
ART BUCHWALD, *I Chose Capitol Punishment*

The IQ and the life expectancy of the average American recently passed each other going in opposite directions.
GEORGE CARLIN, *Napalm and Silly Putty*

You can always trust the Americans. In the end they will do the right thing, after they have eliminated all the other possibilities.   WINSTON CHURCHILL

Americans have two brains – one in the usual place and the other where the heart should be.   MARLENE DIETRICH

The reason that the all-American boy prefers beauty to brains is that he can see better than he can think.   FARRAH FAWCETT

Mr Hamilton (Bruce Boa): Couldn't find the freeway. Had to take a little backstreet called the M5.
Basil Fawlty (John Cleese): Well I'm sorry it wasn't wide enough for you. A lot of the English cars have steering wheels.   *Fawlty Towers*

Americans want grungy people, stabbing themselves in the head on stage. They get a bright bunch like us [Oasis], with deodorant on, they don't get it.   LIAM GALLAGHER

No one can be as calculatedly rude as the British, which amazes Americans, who do not understand studied insult and can only offer abuse as a substitute.   PAUL GALLICO

You cannot gauge the intelligence of an American by talking with him.   ERIC HOFFER

Never criticise Americans. They have the best taste that money can buy.   MILES KINGTON

American men, as a group, seem to be interested in only two things: money and breasts.   HEDY LAMARR

The National Science Society has announced that seventy per cent of Americans do not understand science. The other thirty per cent do not understand what seventy per cent means.   JAY LENO

The men the American people admire most extravagantly are the most daring liars; the men they detest most violently are those who try to tell the truth.   H.L. MENCKEN

The average American's day planner has fewer holes in it than Ray Charles's dart board.   DENNIS MILLER

Americans will eat garbage provided you sprinkle it liberally with ketchup.

HENRY MILLER

More than ever before, Americans are suffering from back problems – back taxes, back rent, back auto payments. ROBERT ORBEN

Americans will put up with anything provided it doesn't block traffic.

DAN RATHER

Americans have different ways of saying things. They say 'elevator', we say 'lift'. They say 'President', we say 'stupid psychopathic git'. ALEXEI SAYLE

Americans adore me and will go on adoring me until I say something nice about them. GEORGE BERNARD SHAW

I like American women. They do things sexually that Russian girls never dream of doing – like showering. YAKOV SMIRNOFF

Americans often seem to be so overwhelmed by their children that they'll do anything for them except stay married to the co-producer.

KATHARINE WHITEHORN

For every American art has no marvel, and beauty has no meaning, and the past has no message. OSCAR WILDE

Amish

We were Pentecostal. That's just a lightbulb and a car away from being Amish.

RENEE HICKS

I heard about an Amish guy getting run over by a car. That's like a Catholic choking on a condom. RENEE HICKS

What's an Amish guy with his hand up a horse's ass? A mechanic.

ROBIN WILLIAMS

Anarchy

We started off trying to set up a small anarchist community, but people wouldn't obey the rules. ALAN BENNETT, *Getting On*

Ancestors

Humans are not proud of their ancestors and rarely invite them round to dinner.
DOUGLAS ADAMS

My ancestors wandered lost in the wilderness for forty years because even in biblical times, men would not stop to ask for directions.   ELAYNE BOOSLER

None of us can boast about the morality of our ancestors. The records do not show that Adam and Eve were married.   EDGAR WATSON HOWE

My folks didn't come over on the *Mayflower*, but they were there to meet the boat.   WILL ROGERS

Julie Andrews

Working with her is like being hit over the head by a Valentine's Day card.
CHRISTOPHER PLUMMER

Julie Andrews is like a nun with a switchblade.   LESLIE HALLIWELL

Anger

If they could figure out a way to channel my anger, they could solve the energy crisis.   WOODY ALLEN

I have only two temperamental outbursts a year – each lasts six months.
TALLULAH BANKHEAD

Experts say you should never hit your children in anger. When is a good time? When you're feeling festive?   ROSEANNE BARR

Great fury, like great whisky, requires long fermentation.   TRUMAN CAPOTE

A tart temper never mellows with age, and a sharp tongue is the only edged tool that grows keener with constant use.   WASHINGTON IRVING

Never speak when you are angry. If you do you'll make the best speech you'll ever regret.   ROBERT LYND, *The Blue Lion*

No man can think clearly when his fists are clenched.   GEORGE JEAN NATHAN

Men are like steel. When they lose their temper, they lose their worth.
CHUCK NORRIS

Anger is one letter short of danger.   ELEANOR ROOSEVELT

When you see a married couple walking down the street, the one that's a few steps ahead is the one that's mad.   HELEN ROWLAND

My Uncle Sammy was an angry man. He had printed on his tombstone, 'What are you looking at?'   MARGARET SMITH

No one can drive us crazy unless we give them the keys.

Animals

As pandas spend fourteen hours a day eating and the rest sleeping, it is not surprising the birthrate is low. There is something about the panda which does not give you a lot of hope. Under those entertaining white fur bloomers, or in the general vicinity thereof, there beats the suicidal and depressive heart of the true comedian.   NANCY BANKS-SMITH

Scientists tell us that the fastest animal on earth, with a top speed of 120 ft per second, is a cow that has has been dropped out of a helicopter.
                    DAVE BARRY

The sooner all the animals are extinct, the sooner we'll find their money.
                    ED BLUESTONE

Isn't it amazing that South American three-banded armadillos, with three flexible joints in their shells, can roll up in a ball, while North American nine-banded armadillos, with nine flexible joints, can't?   CHUCK BONNER

A squirrel is just a rat with a cuter outfit.
                    CARRIE BRADSHAW (SARAH JESSICA PARKER), *Sex and the City*

All bears are agile, cunning and immensely strong, and they are always hungry. If they want to kill you and eat you, they can, and pretty much whenever they want. That doesn't happen often, but – and here is the absolutely salient point – once would be enough.   BILL BRYSON, *A Walk in the Woods*

Apparently bears are attracted to women in their menstrual cycles. A 1,000lb grizzly against a 120lb woman with cramps. I say fair fight.   SIMON COTTER

I ask people why they have deer heads on their walls and they say, 'Because it's such a beautiful animal.' I think my mother's attractive but I have photographs of her.   ELLEN DEGENERES

An elephant – a mouse built to government specifications.

ROBERT A. HEINLEIN, *Time Enough for Love:
the Further Adventures of Lazarus Long*

What is it with chimpanzees and that middle parting? Stuck in the Twenties, aren't they?
HARRY HILL

My favourite animal is steak.
FRAN LEBOWITZ

On the Discovery Channel I saw that the male hyena often gets angry during sex. I'd get mad too if the female was laughing at me.
JAY LENO

Also on the Discovery Channel I learned that minks can have sex for eight hours straight. Sure. They're lying on mink. But how does the guy mink talk her into it? She already has the coat.
JAY LENO

Two bats were hanging up in a cave and one said to the other, 'When I'm older, I hope I don't become incontinent.'
MICK MILLER

The chicken is a noble beast,
The cow is much forlorner,
Standing in the pouring rain,
With a leg at every corner.
SPIKE MILLIGAN

The cow is of the bovine ilk;
One end is moo, the other, milk.
OGDEN NASH

No committee could ever come up with anything as revolutionary as a camel – anything as practical and as perfectly designed to perform effectively under such difficult conditions.
LAURENCE J. PETER

I love animals, especially in good gravy.
FREDDIE STARR

I had a linguistics professor who said that it's man's ability to use language that makes him the dominant species on the planet. That may be, but I think there's one other thing that separates us from animals: we aren't afraid of vacuum cleaners.
JEFF STILSON

A walrus is like Tupperware – they both like a tight seal.

Anniversaries

I asked my wife, 'Where do you want to go for our anniversary?' She said, 'Somewhere I have never been.' I told her, 'How about the kitchen?'

HENNY YOUNGMAN

The biggest surprise you can give your wife on your anniversary is to remember it.

Antiques

Want to have some fun? Walk into an antique shop and say, 'What's new?'

HENNY YOUNGMAN

An antique is a thing which has been useless for so long that it is still in good condition.

Apathy

Hey, just because I don't care doesn't mean I'm not listening.

HOMER SIMPSON, *The Simpsons*

Apology

To apologise is to lay the foundation for a future offence.

AMBROSE BIERCE, *The Devil's Dictionary*

Ellen Morgan (Ellen DeGeneres): I think you owe Joey an apology.
Ed Billick (Bruce Campbell): What am I supposed to say, 'I'm sorry you're a lazy, incompetent slob and I had to fire you?'
Ellen: Now, that wasn't so hard, was it?

ELLEN

It is a good rule in life never to apologise. The right sort of people do not want apologies, and the wrong sort take a mean advantage of them.

P.G. WODEHOUSE, *The Man Upstairs*

An apology is saying the right thing after doing the wrong thing.

An apology is the superglue of life: it can repair just about anything.

The two most essential words for a strong, healthy relationship are 'I apologise.'

Appearance

Claudette Colbert . . . had some difficult angles to her face. The right side of her face was called 'the other side of the moon' because nobody ever saw it.
MARY ASTOR

Gillian Anderson always reminds me of a supply teacher. DAVID BADDIEL

(*on Conservative leader William Hague*) They have elected a foetus as party leader. I bet there's a lot of Tory MPs who wish they hadn't voted against abortion now. TONY BANKS

She was a large woman who seemed not so much dressed as upholstered.
J.M. BARRIE

Prince looks like a dwarf who's been dipped in a bucket of pubic hair.
BOY GEORGE

John Prescott looks like a terrifying mixture of Hannibal Lecter and Terry Scott.
GYLES BRANDRETH

(*on Steve McQueen*) His features resembled a fossilised wash rag.
ALAN BRIEN

(*on Walter Matthau*) Once seen, that antique-mapped face is never forgotten – a bloodhound with a head cold, a man who is simultaneously biting on a bad lobster and caught by the neck in lift doors. ALAN BRIEN

(*on Lionel Richie*) He's got a chin like an ironing board. PETE BURNS

(*on novelist Jacqueline Susann*) She looks like a truck driver in drag.
TRUMAN CAPOTE

She looked a million dollars, I must admit, even if in well-used notes.
ANGELA CARTER, *Wise Children*

You know, I'd almost forgotten what your eyes looked like. Still the same. Pissholes in the snow. JACK CARTER (MICHAEL CAINE), *Get Carter*

He looked as inconspicuous as a tarantula on a slice of angel food.
RAYMOND CHANDLER, *Farewell My Lovely*

The edges of the folded handkerchief in her breast pocket looked sharp enough to slice bread.   RAYMOND CHANDLER, *The Lady in the Lake*

(*on Charles de Gaulle*) He looked like a female llama surprised in her bath.
WINSTON CHURCHILL

(*on Vita Sackville-West*) She looked like Lady Chatterley above the waist and the gamekeeper below.   CYRIL CONNOLLY

Frasier Crane (Kelsey Grammer): I do not have a fat face!
Niles Crane (David Hyde Pierce): Oh, please! I keep wondering how long you're going to store those nuts for winter.   *Frasier*

(*responding to reporters' criticism of his appearance*) I go to a better tailor than any of you and pay more for my clothes. The only difference is that you probably don't sleep in yours.   CLARENCE DARROW

Sylvester Stallone has a face that would look well upon a three-toed sloth.
RUSSELL DAVIES

He had but one eye, and the popular prejudice runs in favour of two.
CHARLES DICKENS, *Nicholas Nickleby*

(*on Jeanette Macdonald's face*) It reminds me of an aardvark's ass.
W.C. FIELDS

(*on actor Ralph Richardson*) I don't know his name but he's got a face like half a teapot.   KING GEORGE VI

She may very well pass for forty-three – in the dusk, with a light behind her!
WILLIAM S. GILBERT, *Trial by Jury*

Prince: Bambi with testosterone.   OWEN GLEIBERMAN

(*on the looks of soccer player Peter Beardsley*) He's the only player who, when he appears on TV, Daleks hide behind the sofa.   NICK HANCOCK

(*of Clark Gable*) His ears make him look like a taxi-cab with both doors open.
HOWARD HUGHES

(*on John McEnroe*) Hair like badly turned broccoli.   CLIVE JAMES

Barbara Cartland's eyes were twin miracles of mascara and looked like two small crows that had crashed into a chalk cliff.   CLIVE JAMES

(*of Robert Redford*) He has turned almost alarmingly blond – he's gone past platinum, he must be into plutonium; his hair is coordinated with his teeth.
PAULINE KAEL

Bob Hoskins is just a testicle with legs.   PAULINE KAEL

If I were two-faced, would I be wearing this one?   ABRAHAM LINCOLN

(*on Calvin Coolidge*) I do wish he didn't look as if he had been weaned on a pickle.   ALICE ROOSEVELT LONGWORTH

The act of chewing makes a man look like a sulky cow.
ROBERT LYND, *The Blue Lion*

Bono would love to be 6ft tall and thin and good-looking. But he's not – he reminds me of a soddin' mountain goat.   IAN MCCULLOCH

My wife has lovely coloured eyes. I particularly like the blue one.
BOB MONKHOUSE

George [Sanders], a giant grizzly of a man, had a face, even in his twenties, which looked as though he had rented it on a long lease and had lived in it so long he didn't want to move out.   DAVID NIVEN

(*on Sinead O'Connor*) She looks like she's had a run-in with a lawnmower. She's about as sexy as a Venetian blind.   MADONNA

(*on Alexander Woollcott*) He looked like something that had gotten loose from Macy's Thanksgiving Day Parade.   HARPO MARX

The girl was built in the way they used to build cars – all the weight at the back.   DENIS NORDEN, *Oh, My Word*

Men seldom make passes
At girls who wear glasses.   DOROTHY PARKER

Boxer Brian London possesses the most unbeautiful face – it looks as if it, at one time, fell apart and was reassembled by a drunken mechanic.
MICHAEL PARKINSON

Every time I find a girl who can cook like my mother, she looks like my father.
TONY RANDALL

You look at Ernest Borgnine and you think to yourself: was there anybody else hurt in the accident?
DON RICKLES

(*on Donatella Versace*) That's the kind of face you hang on your door in Africa.
JOAN RIVERS

(*on Spice Girl Mel C*) In her shell suit she used to look like a single mum on a council estate.
JONATHAN ROSS

(*on Isadora Duncan*) A woman whose face looked as if it had been made of sugar and someone had licked it.
GEORGE BERNARD SHAW

(*on Angelica Huston*) She has the face of an exhausted gnu, the voice of an unstrung tennis racket, and a figure of no describable shape.
JOHN SIMON

(*on Glenda Jackson*) She has the look of an asexual harlequin.
JOHN SIMON

(*on Walter Matthau*) He looked like a half-melted rubber bulldog.
JOHN SIMON

(*on Melina Mercouri*) Her blackly mascaraed eye-sockets gape like twin craters, unfortunately extinct.
JOHN SIMON

I always thought Miss [Liza] Minnelli's face deserving of first prize in the beagle category.
JOHN SIMON

Why do you sit there looking like an envelope without any address on it?
MARK TWAIN

She wore far too much rouge last night, and not quite enough clothes. That is always a sign of despair in a woman.
OSCAR WILDE, *An Ideal Husband*

The only thing that prevented a father's love from faltering was the fact that there was in his possession a photograph of himself at the same early age, in which he, too, looked like a homicidal fried egg.
P.G. WODEHOUSE *Eggs, Beans and Crumpets*

He was a tubby little chap who looked as if he had been poured into his clothes and had forgotten to say when.
P.G. WODEHOUSE, *Very Good, Jeeves*

Uma Thurman looks like a giraffe that has wandered off the Nature Reserve and panicked.

Applause

Applause – the echo of a platitude.   AMBROSE BIERCE, *The Devil's Dictionary*

Carol [Channing] never just enters a room. Even when she comes out of the bathroom, her husband applauds.   GEORGE BURNS

Who decides when the applause should die down? It seems like it's a group decision; everyone begins to say to themselves at the same time, 'Well, okay, that's enough of that.'   GEORGE CARLIN

One person clapping by themselves, always embarrassing . . . particularly after sex, I find.   HARRY HILL

Archaeology

An archaeologist is the best husband any woman can have: the older she gets, the more interested he is in her.   AGATHA CHRISTIE

An archaeologist is someone whose life is in ruins.

Jeffrey Archer

Is there no beginning to your talents?   CLIVE ANDERSON

Jeffrey Archer is proof of the proposition that in each of us there lurks a bad novel.   JULIAN CRITCHLEY

(*on Archer's 'novelography'*) He can't write fiction and he can't write non-fiction, so he's invented a bogus category in between.   IAN HISLOP

He does fifteen drafts of one of his books. If you read one and don't think it's very good, remember it's been improved fourteen times. What must the first draft be like?   PAUL MERTON

The last time I was in Spain I got through six Jeffrey Archer novels. I must remember to take enough toilet paper next time.   BOB MONKHOUSE

Architecture

In my experience, if you have to keep the lavatory door shut by extending your left leg, it's modern architecture.   NANCY BANKS-SMITH

Most architects think by the inch, talk by the yard, and should be kicked by the foot.
CHARLES, PRINCE OF WALES

Architects are people who don't like fields.
MIKE HARDING

I think all modern architects should be pulled down and redeveloped as car parks.
SPIKE MILLIGAN

The Sydney Opera House looks as if it is something that has crawled out of the sea and is up to no good.
BEVERLEY NICHOLS

A doctor can bury his mistakes, but an architect can only advise his clients to plant vines.
FRANK LLOYD WRIGHT

We should learn from the snail: it has devised a home that is both exquisite and functional.
FRANK LLOYD WRIGHT

Argument

I can win an argument on any topic, against any opponent. People know this, and steer clear of me at parties. Often, as a sign of their great respect, they don't even invite me.
DAVE BARRY

Most young couples begin married life knowing very little about how to argue with each other, and are forced to learn through trial and error.
DAVE BARRY

My wife was too beautiful for words — but not for arguments.
JOHN BARRYMORE

The only way to get the best of an argument is to avoid it.
DALE CARNEGIE

Once a woman has forgiven her man, she must not reheat his sins for breakfast.
MARLENE DIETRICH

Nothing is as frustrating as arguing with someone who knows what he's talking about.
SAM EWING

I got in an argument with a girlfriend inside of a tent. That's a bad place for an argument, because then I tried to walk out and had to slam the flap. How are you supposed to express your anger in this situation? Zip it up real quick?
MITCH HEDBERG

If you can't answer a man's argument, all is not lost. You can still call him vile names.
ELBERT HUBBARD

It is impossible to defeat an ignorant man in argument.   WILLIAM G. MCADOO

Unlike your thighs, your argument does not retain water.
JACK MCFARLAND (SEAN HAYES), to KAREN WALKER, *Will and Grace*

There's two theories to arguing with a woman. Neither one works.
ROY ROGERS

You can't reason someone out of something they weren't reasoned into.
MARK TWAIN

Always tolerate other people's opinions, but don't be too broadminded to take your own side in an argument.

Do not argue with a spouse who is packing your parachute.

Aristocracy

Aristocrats spend their childhood being beaten by fierce nannies and their later years murdering wildlife, so it is hardly surprising their sex lives are a bit cock-eyed.
JILLY COOPER

The Grand Old Duke of York
He had ten thousand men.
His case comes up next week.
SPIKE MILLIGAN

An aristocracy in a republic is like a chicken whose head had been cut off: it may run about in a lively way, but in fact it is dead.
NANCY MITFORD, *Noblesse Oblige*

Armour

Armour is the kind of clothing worn by a man whose tailor is a blacksmith.
AMBROSE BIERCE, *The Devil's Dictionary*

Arrogance

Nobody can be so amusingly arrogant as a young man who has just discovered an old idea and thinks it is his own.
SYDNEY HARRIS

Be careful of men who are bald and rich; the arrogance of 'rich' usually cancels out the nice of 'bald'.
RITA RUDNER

Art

Buy old masters. They fetch a better price than old mistresses.
LORD BEAVERBROOK

Painting is the art of protecting flat surfaces from the weather and exposing them to the critic.
AMBROSE BIERCE

This is going to be art's greatest moment since Mona Lisa sat down and told Leonardo da Vinci she was in a slightly odd mood.
EDMUND BLACKADDER (ROWAN ATKINSON), Blackadder

Abstract art: a product of the untalented, sold by the unprincipled to the utterly bewildered.
AL CAPP

A woman is fascinated not by art but by the noise made by those in the field.
ANTON CHEKHOV

Art, like morality, consists in drawing the line somewhere.   G.K. CHESTERTON

Modern art is what happens when painters stop looking at girls and persuade themselves they have a better idea.
JOHN CIARDI

An artist cannot speak about his art any more than a plant can discuss horticulture.
JEAN COCTEAU

There is no more sombre enemy of good art than the pram in the hall.
CYRIL CONNOLLY, Enemies of Promise

I inherited a painting and a violin which turned out to be a Rembrandt and a Stradivarius. Unfortunately, Rembrandt made lousy violins and Stradivarius was a terrible painter.
TOMMY COOPER

The reason some portraits don't look true to life is that some people make no effort to resemble their pictures.
SALVADOR DALI

(*on seeing one of his pictures sold at auction*) I feel as a horse must feel when the beautiful cup is given to the jockey.
EDGAR DEGAS

The murals in restaurants are roughly on a par with the food in art galleries.
PETER DE VRIES

Dada's art is just turpentine intoxication.   MARCEL DUCHAMP

I couldn't have a modern painting hanging in my home. It would be like living with a gas leak.   DAME EDITH EVANS

(*on an art exhibition by Rolling Stone Ronnie Wood*) Wood attacks the canvas with all the skill of a painter-decorator looking forward to being paid in cash at the end of the day. Rolf Harris is Matisse next to Ronnie Wood.
                    BONNIE GREER

(*on winning the Turner Prize*) It's amazing what you can do with an E in A-level art, twisted imagination and a chainsaw.   DAMIEN HIRST

Art has to move you and design does not, unless it's a good design for a bus.
                    DAVID HOCKNEY

When having my portrait painted I don't want justice, I want mercy.
                    BILLY HUGHES

Art is anything you can get away with.   MARSHALL MCLUHAN

I hate flowers – I paint them because they're cheaper than models and they don't move.   GEORGIA O'KEEFE

(*asked how he knew which paintings were his*) If I like it, I say it's mine. If I don't, I say it's a fake.   PABLO PICASSO

I would never have taken up painting if women did not have breasts.
                    PIERRE-AUGUSTE RENOIR

A portrait is a painting with something wrong with the mouth.
                    JOHN SINGER SARGENT

Every time I paint a portrait I lose a friend.   JOHN SINGER SARGENT

An amateur is someone who supports himself with outside jobs which enable him to paint. A professional is someone whose wife works to enable him to paint.   BEN SHAHN

(*on J.W.M. Turner's painting* The Slave Ship) It resembles a tortoiseshell cat having a fit in a plate of tomatoes.   MARK TWAIN

If Michelangelo had been straight, the Sistine Chapel would have been wall-papered.   ROBIN TYLER

It's not hard to understand modern art. If it hangs on a wall it's a painting, and if you can walk around it, it's a sculpture.   SIMON UPDIKE

If Botticelli were alive today, he'd be working for *Vogue*.   PETER USTINOV

If you look at a thing long enough, it loses all of its meaning.   ANDY WARHOL

(*on James McNeill Whistler*) The only thoroughly original ideas I have ever heard him express have had reference to his own superiority as a painter over painters greater than himself.   OSCAR WILDE

(*on Whistler*) He opened the eyes of the blind and has given great encourage-ment to the short-sighted.   OSCAR WILDE

I've been doing a lot of abstract painting lately. Extremely abstract. No brush, no paint, no canvas, I just think about it.   STEVEN WRIGHT

Assassination

You cannot run faster than a bullet.   IDI AMIN

An assassin is one who takes life easily.   LAURENCE J. PETER

Assassination is the extreme form of censorship.   GEORGE BERNARD SHAW

(*before being deposed as President of Georgia, 2003*) I'm getting a little bored. No one has tried to kill me for a couple of years.   EDUARD SHEVARDNADZE

Asthma

I was walking through the park when I had a very bad asthmatic attack. These three asthmatics attacked me. I know, I should have heard them hiding.

EMO PHILIPS

Astrology

You can tell a lot about someone's personality if you know his star sign. Take Jesus, born on 25th December. Fed the 5,000, walked on water – typical Capricorn.

HARRY HILL

Sometimes I'm charmed by the fact that there are women with whom you can discuss the molecular theory of light all evening, and at the end they will ask you what is your birth sign.   ROMAN POLANSKI

Those astrology things where they tell you all the people that have the same birthday as you – it's always an odd group of people, like Ed Asner, Elijah Muhammed and Secretariat.   JERRY SEINFELD

Atheism

An atheist is a man who has no invisible means of support.   JOHN BUCHAN

When I told the people of Northern Ireland that I was an atheist, a woman in the audience stood up and asked if it was the Catholic God or the Protestant God I didn't believe in.   QUENTIN CRISP

An atheist is a man who watches a Notre Dame–Southern Methodist University game and doesn't care who wins.   DWIGHT D. EISENHOWER

What do atheists scream when they come?   BILL HICKS

I once wanted to become an atheist, but I gave up – they have no holidays.
                                    HENNY YOUNGMAN

Atmosphere

I've created an atmosphere where I'm a friend first, boss second, probably entertainer third.   DAVID BRENT (RICKY GERVAIS), *The Office*

Attraction

I can't even tell if women like me. I know when they don't like me, because they say things like, 'Yeah, that's him, Officer.'   KEVIN BRENNAN

Do you really believe in your wildest dreams that a girl like that could possibly be interested in an ageing, Brilliantine, stick insect like yourself?
                                    SYBIL FAWLTY (PRUNELLA SCALES), *Fawlty Towers*

It is said that women are often attracted to men who remind them of their fathers. So when on a date, remember to greet her with: 'You're not going out in that!'   JEFF GREEN, *The A-Z of Being Single*

What's the difference between stalking and overzealous admiration? I guess that's what the jury will decide at my trial next week. DAVE HENRY

I'm always attracted to the wrong kind of guy: like the Pope. CAROL LEIFER

I like a woman with a head on her shoulders. I hate necks. STEVE MARTIN

So, Debbie McGee, what first attracted you to millionaire Paul Daniels?
MRS MERTON (CAROLINE AHERNE), *The Mrs Merton Show*

When a man says he wants to meet a girl with a sense of humour, he means one who will laugh at everything he says while her breasts jiggle.
CHERI OTERI

To attract men, I wear a perfume called 'New Car Interior'. RITA RUDNER

People often ask me what I look for in women. I look for *me* in women!
GENE SIMMONS

Audiences

I wish I could think of a positive point to leave you with. Will you take two negative points? WOODY ALLEN

I was at the bar in a northern workingmen's club when a chap came up to me and said, 'Were you the turn?' I said, 'Yes.' He said, 'Do you mind a bit of constructive criticism?' I said, 'No.' He said, 'I think you're crap.'
LES DAWSON

Hell is a half-filled auditorium. ROBERT FROST

If they liked you, they didn't applaud – they just let you live. BOB HOPE

(*to the audience at the 1963 Royal Variety Performance*) Would the people in the cheaper seats clap your hands. And the rest of you, if you'd just rattle your jewellery. JOHN LENNON

Audiences, like salad dressing, are never the same. ROBERT MORLEY

(*observing a queue at the box office before one of his performances*) There's something about a crowd like that that brings a lump to my wallet.
ELI WALLACH

The play was a great success, but the audience was a failure.

OSCAR WILDE

If all the world is a stage, where is the audience sitting?

Australia

The traditional dress of the Australian cricketer is the baggy green cap on the head and the chip on the shoulder. Both are ritualistically assumed.

SIMON BARNES

(*on Melbourne*) I've always wanted to see a ghost town. You couldn't even get a parachute to open here after 10 p.m.   MAX BYGRAVES

Australians go to work in shorts and that's a good enough reason to hate them.

JEREMY CLARKSON

I don't despair about the cultural scene in Australia because there isn't one here to despair about.   ROBERT HELPMAN

To live in Australia permanently is rather like going to a party and dancing all night with your mother.   BARRY HUMPHRIES

Australia is an outdoor country. People go indoors only to use the toilet, and that's a recent development.   BARRY HUMPHRIES

Australian foreplay consists largely of the words 'Are you awake?'

BARRY HUMPHRIES

We may be a small race, but there's divinity in our cricket.

THOMAS KENNEALLY

Australia may be the only country in the world in which the word 'academic' is regularly used as a term of abuse.   LEONIE KRAMER

New Zealanders who leave for Australia raise the IQ of both countries.

ROBERT MULDOON

Racial characteristics: violently loud alcoholic roughnecks whose idea of fun is to throw up on your car. The national sport is breaking furniture and the average daily consumption of beer in Sydney is ten and three quarter Imperial gallons for children under the age of nine.   P.J. O'ROURKE

Authority

I have as much authority as the Pope; I just don't have as many people who believe it.
GEORGE CARLIN

At work, the authority of a person is inversely proportional to the number of pens he or she is carrying.

Autobiography

He spends most of his time writing, and is currently revising his autobiography to include himself.
WOODY ALLEN, *Getting Even*

I have been commissioned to write my autobiography. Can anyone tell me where I was between 1960 and 1974 and what the hell I was doing?
JEFFREY BERNARD

Autobiography is probably the most respectable form of lying.
HUMPHREY CARPENTER

An autobiography is an obituary in serial form with the last instalment missing.
QUENTIN CRISP, *The Naked Civil Servant*

If you believe the past can't be changed, you haven't read a celebrity's autobiography.
SAM EWING

(*on Gertrude Stein's autobiography*) I found nothing really wrong with this autobiography except poor choice of subject.
CLIFTON FADIMAN

Autobiography is an unrivalled vehicle for telling the truth about other people.
PHILIP GUEDALLA

Automobile racing

I think NASCAR would be much more exciting if, like in a skating rink, every fifteen minutes someone announced it was time to reverse direction.
JEFFREY ANBINDER

You always see gaps in racing. The trick is to make sure they are wider than your car.
MARIO ANDRETTI

Auto racing is boring except when a car is going at least 172mph upside down.
DAVE BARRY

I want to be a race car passenger – just a guy who bugs the driver: 'Say man, can I turn on the radio? You should slow down. Can I put my feet out the window?'
MITCH HEDBERG

(*on deciding to retire, 1999*) I first had doubts at Melbourne this year. We all raced to the first corner and I thought, 'What's the hurry?'
DAMON HILL

(*on Irish driver Eddie Irvine*) He's brash and can be abrasive. He goads people. He's the Ian Paisley of Formula 1.
DAMON HILL

Grand Prix racing is like balancing an egg on a spoon while shooting the rapids.
GRAHAM HILL

My first priority is to finish above rather than below the ground.
JAMES HUNT

(*after a horrific accident in 1976*) There is no point in having a complex about losing half an ear.
NIKI LAUDA

In my sport the quick are too often listed among the dead.
JACKIE STEWART

(*of Ayrton Senna*) He was a fantastic driver, but he had an immense number of collisions. And they could not all have been everybody else's fault.
JACKIE STEWART

(*on success in the Indianapolis 500*) There's no secret. You just press the accelerator to the floor and steer left.
BILL VUKOVICH

Michael Schumacher would remain a formidable challenge if he was driving a pram.
FRANK WILLIAMS

Automobiles

Women are like cars: we all want a Ferrari, sometimes we want a pickup truck, and we end up with a station wagon.
TIM ALLEN

Never have more children than you have car windows.
ERMA BOMBECK

Bumper sticker: 'We Are the Proud Parents of a Child Whose Self-Esteem is Sufficient That He Doesn't Need Us Advertising His Minor Scholastic Achievements on the Bumper of Our Car.'
GEORGE CARLIN

The Chrysler Stratus looks like Pamela Anderson – a silicone sham with no real depth.
JEREMY CLARKSON

Men are superior to women. For one thing, men can urinate from a speeding car.
WILL DURST

(*on the launch of the Model T Ford in 1909*) Any customer can have a car painted any colour that he wants so long as it is black.
HENRY FORD

Men drive too fast, we were told, because the car is an extension of the penis. But if it were, men would surely not drive too fast; they would just back in and out of the garage. Or maybe just polish it all the time.
JEREMY HARDY

They think they can make fuel from horse manure. Now I don't know if your car will be able to get thirty miles to the gallon, but it's sure gonna put a stop to siphoning.
BILLIE HOLIDAY

Gas is so expensive guys are dating Monica Lewinsky just for her siphoning skills.
JAY LENO

Signs Your Car Won't Be Breaking the Land Speed Record:
You're often passed by guys riding mowers.
Mechanic tells you it won't survive another car wash.
Getting your car to start involves the fire department and a catapult.
Every time you fill the gas tank, the car doubles in value.
It's hard to gain speed with all those kids waving you down to buy ice cream.
It goes from 0 to 60 in nine days.
DAVID LETTERMAN, *The Late Show*

My licence plate says PMS. Nobody cuts me off!
WENDY LIEBMAN

The best car safety device is a rear-view mirror with a cop in it.
DUDLEY MOORE

When a man opens the car door for his wife, it's either a new car or a new wife.
PRINCE PHILIP, DUKE OF EDINBURGH

What's with the squeegee kids? I mean, they don't really wash the windshield, do they? They simply redistribute the dirt.
KEN SCOTT

No one needs an off-road vehicle, unless you are going off-road. If you want to drive a 4x4, then go and live in a field.
WILL SELF

Car trouble: when the engine won't start and the payments won't stop.

Children in back seats cause accidents. Accidents in back seats cause children.

The wheel was man's greatest invention until he sat behind it.

If all the cars in the United States were placed end to end, it would probably be Labor Day Weekend.

Awards

I don't deserve this award, but I have arthritis and I don't deserve that either.
JACK BENNY

(*on winning a Golden Globe, 2003*) You've no idea how many men I've had to sleep with to win this.
KIM CATTRALL

(*on winning a magazine poll to find women's favourite role model*) I am totally gobsmacked. I demand a recount.
DAWN FRENCH

(*hosting the 2002 Oscars*) So much mud has been thrown this year, all the nominees look black.
WHOOPI GOLDBERG

Awards are like piles. Sooner or later, every bum gets one.
MAUREEN LIPMAN

(*at the 2001 Oscars*) Hosting the Oscars is like making love to a beautiful woman – it's something I only get to do when Billy Crystal's out of town.
STEVE MARTIN

Getting an award from TV is like being kissed by someone with bad breath.
MASON WILLIAMS

This is my forty-eighth award this year. Apparently when I reach fifty I can trade them in for a kettle.
ROBBIE WILLIAMS

B

Babies

The baby is fine. The only problem is that he looks like Edward G. Robinson.
WOODY ALLEN

I've been breastfeeding for two years. I could light the gas ring with my nipples.
JO BRAND

Dressing a baby is like putting an octopus into a string bag, making sure none of the arms hang out. CHRIS EVANS

The worst feature of a new baby is its mother's singing. KIN HUBBARD

A baby is a loud noise at one end and no sense of responsibility at the other. RONALD KNOX

Bill Gates and his wife just had their third child, Bill Gates 3.0. JAY LENO

I always wondered why babies spend so much time sucking their thumbs. Then I tasted baby food. ROBERT ORBEN

I love being a grandmother. It's great to finally be greeted by someone who's bald, drooling, and wearing a diaper who's not my date. JOAN RIVERS

Another reason girls talk earlier than boys is breastfeeding. Boys would rather breastfeed than talk because they know they won't be getting that close again for another fifteen years. PAUL SEABURN

My friend has a baby boy. I'm recording all the noises he makes so later I can ask him what he meant. STEVEN WRIGHT

A baby is something that gets you down in the daytime and up at night.

Out of the mouths of babes – usually when you've got your best suit on.

Babysitters

I don't have a baby, but I still book a babysitter. I tell her to check on the kid after a half-hour or so. Then when I return I go, 'Escaped?' Well, give me fifty bucks and we'll call it even. HARRY HILL

A babysitter is a teenager acting like an adult while the adults are out acting like teenagers.

Bachelors

There comes a time in every bachelor's life when he must say, 'No more beans on toast' – and mean it. MEL CALMAN

The only time a bachelor's bed is made is when it's in the factory.
P.J. O'ROURKE

A bachelor never quite gets over the idea that he is a thing of beauty and a boy forever.
HELEN ROWLAND

As far as I know, a single man has never vacuumed behind a couch.
RITA RUDNER

A bachelor is one who enjoys the chase but does not eat the game.

A bachelor is a man who is footloose and fiancée free.

A bachelor is a man whose marriage vow is never to take one.

Bachelor: a man who can take women or leave them – and prefers to do both.

Bagpipes

The bagpipes sound exactly the same when you have finished learning them as when you start.
THOMAS BEECHAM

The best thing I can say about bagpipes is that they don't smell too.
BRENDAN BEHAN

The Irish gave the bagpipes to the Scots as a joke, but the Scots haven't seen the joke yet.
OLIVER HERFORD

Ballet

The Mafia once moved in and took over the New York Ballet. During a performance of *Swan Lake*, there was a lot of money on the swan to live.
WOODY ALLEN

I got kicked out of ballet class because I pulled a groin muscle. It wasn't mine.
RITA RUDNER

Ballet: men wearing pants so tight that you can tell what religion they are.
ROBIN WILLIAMS

Ballerinas are always on their toes. Why don't they just get taller ballerinas?
STEVEN WRIGHT

Banking

It's funny to me that I have to prove to the banks that *I'm* honest.
SCOTT ADAMS

I went downstairs. There was a letter from the bank. I could tell it was from the bank – it was pinned to the front door with a wreath. Les Dawson

Banking may well be a career from which no man really recovers. J.K. Galbraith

A bank is a place that will lend you money if you can prove that you don't need it. Bob Hope

If you owe your bank a hundred pounds, you have a problem; but if you owe it a million, it has. John Maynard Keynes

A financier is a pawnbroker with imagination. Arthur Wing Pinero, *The Second Mrs Tanqueray*

They usually have two tellers in my local bank, except when it's very busy, when they have one. Rita Rudner

A banker is a fellow who lends you his umbrella when the sun is shining and wants it back the minute it begins to rain. Mark Twain

If bankers can count, how come they have eight windows and only four tellers?

There is a way of transferring funds that is even faster than electronic banking. It's called marriage.

Barbecue

Things You Don't Want To Hear At Your Family Barbecue:
'Which do you want first, kids? Ice cream or the name of your real father?'
'I made the potato salad three weeks ago. It's naturally red, white and blue.'
'Somebody keep the cops busy while dad buries the knife.'
'It's me, Aunt Susan. You remember me from last year as Uncle Jeff.'
'And now cousin Dave will show us slides of his quintuple bypass.'
'If you don't wash your hands, it gives the burgers more flavour.'
'By the way, your wife is an excellent kisser.'
'Pick up your pants, grandpa. That's not how you put out a barbecue.'
'Dude, that firecracker really did a number on your eye.'
 David Letterman

Men like to barbecue. Men will cook if danger is involved. Rita Rudner

How is it that one careless match can start a forest fire, but it takes a whole box to start a barbecue?

Bargains

Garage sale shoppers have little trouble finding bargains, but lots of trouble finding a use for them later.   SAM EWING

One of the most difficult things in the world is to convince a woman that even a bargain costs money.   EDGAR WATSON HOWE

A bargain is something you don't need at a price you can't resist.
                                        FRANKLIN P. JONES

Bars

A man walked into a bar – ouch! – it was an iron bar.   TOMMY COOPER

I was at a bar nursing a beer. My nipple was getting quite soggy.
                                        EMO PHILIPS

Norm Peterson (George Wendt): I want something light and cold.
Carla Tortelli (Rhea Perlman): Sorry, it's Diane's day off.   *Cheers*

Baseball

Whoever wants to know the heart and mind of America had better learn baseball.   JACQUES BARZUN

A hot dog at the ball park is better than steak at the Ritz.
                                        HUMPHREY BOGART

Baseball is accused of being too slow. Here's something that would not only speed up the game but also provide a welcome opportunity for serious injuries. Like most good ideas, it's uncomplicated: if the pitcher hits the batter with the ball, the batter is out. That's it. A simple idea, but it would make quite a difference.   GEORGE CARLIN

Frasier Crane (Kelsey Grammer): Have you any idea of appropriate baseball-watching attire?
Niles Crane (David Hyde Pierce): Obviously you failed to detect the subtle diamond pattern in my tie.   *Frasier*

Magic Johnson bought a share of the Dayton, Ohio, Dragons, a minor-league baseball team. 'If their season goes up in smoke,' warns Steve Abney of San Francisco, 'the headline is going to be: "Puff Go Magic's Dragons."'
                                        TOM FITZGERALD

Baseball is drama with an endless run and an ever-changing cast.

JOE GARAGIOLA

A great catch is like watching girls go by – the last one you see is always the prettiest.   BOB GIBSON

I'm throwing twice as hard as I ever did. It's just not getting there as fast.

LEFTY GOMEZ

Baseball is very big with my people. It figures. It's the only time we can get to shake a bat at a white man without starting a riot.   DICK GREGORY

I wish I could play Little League now. I'd be way better than before.

MITCH HEDBERG

Baseball has been good to me since I quit trying to play it.   WHITEY HERZOG

Do you know what I love most about baseball? The pine tar, the resin, the grass, the dirt. And that's just in the hot dogs.   DAVID LETTERMAN

I'm one of those people who's not really turned on by baseball. My idea of a relief pitcher is one that's filled with martinis.   DEAN MARTIN

Baseball is a game where a curve is an optical illusion, a screwball can be a pitch or a person, stealing is legal and you can spit anywhere except in the umpire's eye or on the ball.   JIM MURRAY

I had only one superstition. I made sure to touch all the bases when I hit a home run.   BABE RUTH

Baseball has the great advantage over cricket of being sooner ended.

GEORGE BERNARD SHAW

The secret of managing is to keep the guys who hate you away from the guys who are undecided.   CASEY STENGEL

Baseball is almost the only orderly thing in a very unorderly world. If you get three strikes, even the best lawyer in the world can't get you off.

BILL VEECK

Baseball is the favourite American sport because it's so slow. Any idiot can follow it. And just about any idiot can play it.   GORE VIDAL

Baseball is like church. Many attend but few understand.   WES WESTRUM

Baseball, it is said, is only a game. True. And the Grand Canyon is only a hole in Arizona. Not all holes, or games, are created equal.   GEORGE F. WILL

Baseball is the only field of endeavour where a man can succeed three times out of ten and be considered a good performer.   TED WILLIAMS

For the parents of a Little Leaguer, a baseball game is simply a nervous breakdown in innings.   EARL WILSON

If at first you don't succeed, try playing second base.

Basketball

As long as [Larry] Bird's around, I'll only be the second-worst defensive player in basketball.   CHARLES BARKLEY

(*on the nose piercings of Dennis Rodman*) He has so many fish hooks in his nose, he looks like a piece of bait.   BOB COSTAS

Frasier Crane (Kelsey Grammer): It [basketball] is the archetypal male-bonding ritual.
Niles Crane (David Hyde Pierce): Couldn't we just go into the woods, kill something and have done with it?   *Frasier*

Beards

Why do beards stop at the neck? I spend a lot of time wondering that.   SCOTT ADAMS

All the men in my family were bearded, and most of the women.   W.C. FIELDS

(*on growing a beard*) I've been the nice guy in the kitchen too long. Now I'm the stranger on the porch.   TOM HANKS

You know it's hard to hear what a bearded man is saying. He can't speak above a whisker.   HERMAN J. MANKIEWICZ

The Beatles

As far as I'm concerned, there won't be a Beatles reunion as long as John Lennon remains dead.   GEORGE HARRISON, 1995 interview

We live in a country where John Lennon takes six bullets in the chest. Yoko Ono is standing right next to him. Not one fucking bullet. Explain that to me!
DENIS LEARY

If the Beatles or the Sixties had a message, it was 'Learn to swim. And once you've learned – swim!'
JOHN LENNON

Ringo wasn't even the best drummer in the Beatles.
JOHN LENNON

(*asked in 1977 if the Beatles would reform*) You cannot reheat a souffle.
PAUL MCCARTNEY

Beauty

Beauty is only skin deep, and the world is full of thin-skinned people.
RICHARD ARMOUR

They used to photograph Shirley Temple through gauze. They should photograph me through linoleum.
TALLULAH BANKHEAD

Today's beauty ideal, strictly enforced by the media, is a person with the same level of body fat as a paper clip. By today's beauty standards, Marilyn Monroe was an oil tanker.
DAVE BARRY

Sam Malone (Ted Danson): Oh my God, Woody, is it me or is that woman gorgeous?
Woody Boyd (Woody Harrelson): You look nice, Sam, but I'm gonna have to go with the woman.
Cheers

It has been said that a pretty face is a passport. But it's not, it's a visa, and it runs out fast.
JULIE BURCHILL

It's a good thing beauty is only skin deep, or I'd be rotten to the core.
PHYLLIS DILLER

Plain women know more about men than beautiful ones do.
KATHARINE HEPBURN

A bit of lusting after someone does wonders for the skin.
ELIZABETH HURLEY

I'm tired of all this nonsense about beauty being only skin-deep. That's deep enough. What do you want – an adorable pancreas?

JEAN KERR, *The Snake Has All the Lines*

She got her good looks from her father – he's a plastic surgeon.

GROUCHO MARX

Looks count! Forget 'inner beauty'. If a man wants inner beauty, he'll take X-rays.

JOAN RIVERS

Gwyneth Paltrow is quite pretty in a British, horsy sort of way.

JULIA ROBERTS

Beauty is the first present nature gives to a woman and the first it takes away.

FAY WELDON

A woman wants to be pretty rather than intelligent, because men generally see better than they think.

JEWISH PROVERB

Beauty parlour: a place where women curl up and dye.

Beauty products

Face creams are rubbish, aren't they? They're supposed to make you look younger, but they don't. You might as well slap flour, water and an egg on your face, mix it up and go out in the sun and lie down for an hour. At least you'll have a cake to show for it.

JO BRAND

I spent seven hours in a beauty shop – and that was just for the estimate.

PHYLLIS DILLER

I will never understand how women can take boiling hot wax, pour it on to their upper thigh, rip the hair out by the root, and still be afraid of a spider.

JERRY SEINFELD

They still haven't got round to my dream invention – a stretch mark removing cream that actually works.

KATE WINSLET

Victoria Beckham

She gives all her old clothes to starving children, you know. Well, who else are they going to fit?

PAULINE CALF

She can't even chew gum and walk in a straight line, let alone write a book.

LIAM GALLAGHER

Bed

A husband and wife who have separate bedrooms have either drifted apart or found happiness.

HONORÉ DE BALZAC

I defy you to put any blissfully happy married couple under an electric blanket with a single control and have them speaking to one another in the cold light of morning.

ERMA BOMBECK

No civilised person goes to bed the same day he gets up.

RICHARD HARDING DAVIS

Nothing was happening in my marriage. I nicknamed our water bed Lake Placid.

PHYLLIS DILLER

Do you wake up in the morning feeling sleepy and grumpy? Then you must be Snow White.

DAVID FROST

I like to wake up each morning feeling a new man.

JEAN HARLOW

I shave one leg so when I'm in bed I think I'm with a woman.

GARRY SHANDLING

Our bed's only MFI – it won't take multiple orgasm.

VICTORIA WOOD

If I'm not in bed by eleven at night, I go home.

HENNY YOUNGMAN

If you think women are the weaker sex, try pulling the blankets back to your side.

Beer

Without question, the greatest invention in the history of mankind is beer. Oh, I grant you that the wheel was also a fine invention, but the wheel doesn't go nearly as well with pizza.

DAVE BARRY

In a study, scientists report that drinking beer can be good for the liver. I'm sorry, did I say 'scientists?' I meant 'Irish people'.

TINA FEY

American beer is a lot like making love on a row boat – it's fucking close to water.

ERIC IDLE

Woody Boyd (Woody Harrelson): Pour you a beer, Mr Peterson?
Norm Peterson (George Wendt): Alright, but stop me at one. Make that one-thirty.   *Cheers*

Now, son, you don't want to drink beer. That's for Daddys, and kids with fake IDs.   HOMER SIMPSON, *The Simpsons*

Begging

When people ask me if I have any spare change, I tell them I have it at home in my spare wallet.   NICK ARNETTE

A bum asked me, 'Give me $10 till payday.' I said, 'When's payday?' He said, 'I don't know, you're the one who's working.'   HENNY YOUNGMAN

Belgium

Belgium is a country invented by the English to annoy the French.
                                                          CHARLES DE GAULLE

Belgium is known affectionately to the French as 'the gateway to Germany' and just as affectionately to the Germans as 'the gateway to France.'
                                                               TONY HENDRA

Bestiality

Zeus performed acts with swans and heifers that would debar him from every London club except the Garrick or possibly the Naval and Military.
                                                    STEPHEN FRY, *Paperweight*

I think people should be free to engage in any sexual practices they choose; they should draw the line at goats though!   ELTON JOHN

A guy in Wisconsin was caught having sex with a cow. The cow said, 'You don't remember me?' And the guy replied, 'Sorry, it doesn't ring a bell.'   JAY LENO

Bestiality: a poke in a pig.

Bigamy

Bigamists seldom look capable of getting one woman to marry them, let alone two.   MONICA DICKENS, *My Turn to Make the Tea*

Bigamy is one way of avoiding the painful publicity of divorce and the expense of alimony.   OLIVER HERFORD

(*asked what he would consider a proper punishment for bigamy*) Two mothers-in-law.
LORD JOHN RUSSELL

A bigamist is one who makes a second mistake before correcting the first.

Bigotry

Bigot: one who is obstinately and zealously attached to an opinion that you do not share.
AMBROSE BIERCE, *The Devil's Dictionary*

The bigot is another man who abuses the privilege of being stupid.

Osama Bin Laden

This Osama Bin Laden guy. I have three words for him: Anna Nicole Smith. We send her over there, she'll get his money, he'll be dead in a week.
JAY LENO

What we know about Osama Bin Laden is this: he's worth $300 million, he has five wives and twenty-six kids – and he hates Americans for their 'excessive' lifestyle.
DAVID LETTERMAN

It was reported today that Osama Bin Laden has fifty brothers and sisters, which absolutely shocked me because I had no idea he was Catholic.
CONAN O'BRIEN

Biography

In our rampantly secular world, biography is now the only certain form of life after death.
DAVID CANNADINE

Biography is a very definite region bordered on the north by history, on the south by fiction, on the east by obituary, and on the west by tedium.
PHILIP GUEDALLA

Every great man nowadays has his disciples, and it is always Judas who writes the biography.
OSCAR WILDE, *The Critic as Artist*

Birds

Here are instructions for being a pigeon:
1. Walk around aimlessly for a while, pecking at cigarette butts and other inappropriate items.
2. Take fright at someone walking along the platform and fly off to a girder.
3. Have a shit.
4. Repeat.
BILL BRYSON, *Notes From a Small Island*

When turkeys mate, they think of swans.   JOHNNY CARSON

The Dodo never had a chance. He seems to have been invented for the sole purpose of becoming extinct.   WILL CUPPY

Golden eagles have an interesting way of mating, where they connect in the air while flying at 80mph and then they start dropping and they don't stop dropping until the act is completed. So it's not uncommon that they both fall all the way to the ground, hit the ground and both of them die. That's how committed they are to this. I thought to myself, 'Boy, don't we feel like wimps for stopping to answer the phone?' I don't know about you, but if I'm one of these two birds, you're getting close to the ground . . . I would seriously consider faking it.
                    ELLEN DEGENERES

I *swan* about the place, I *duck* flying objects, I *goose* a lady friend. What is it about aquatic birds that lend themselves to the doing words?   HARRY HILL

Before birds get sucked into jet engines, do they ever think, 'Is that Rod Stewart in first class?'   EDDIE IZZARD

I saw a robin redbreast in Central Park today, but it turned out to be a sparrow with an exit wound.   DAVID LETTERMAN

Said the mother Tern
To her baby Tern
Would you like a brother?
Said baby Tern
To mother Tern
Yes
One good Tern deserves another.   SPIKE MILLIGAN, *The Terns*

There is an unseen force which lets birds know when you've just washed your car.   DENIS NORDEN, *Oh, My Word*

I am a conscientious man. When I throw rocks at seabirds, I leave no tern unstoned.   OGDEN NASH

Every day, the hummingbird eats its own weight in food. You may wonder how it weighs the food. It doesn't. It just eats another hummingbird.
                    STEVEN WRIGHT

Imagine if birds were tickled by feathers . . .   STEVEN WRIGHT

How can birds flock any way other than together?

Birth

(*on giving birth*) It was easier than having a tattoo. NICOLE APPLETON

People are giving birth underwater now. They say it's less traumatic for the baby because it's in water, then it comes out into water. I guess it probably would be less traumatic for the baby, but certainly more traumatic for the other people in the pool. ELAYNE BOOSLER

They say men can never experience the pain of childbirth. They can if you hit them in the goolies with a cricket bat – for fourteen hours. JO BRAND

Watching a baby being born is a little like watching a wet St Bernard coming in through the cat door. JEFF FOXWORTHY

My first words as I was being born . . . I looked up at my mother and said, 'That's the last time I'm going up one of those!' STEPHEN FRY

Amnesia is a condition that enables a woman who has gone through labour to have sex again. FRAN LEBOWITZ

I'm not interested in being Wonder Woman in the delivery room. Give me drugs. MADONNA

To enter life by way of the vagina is as good a way as any. HENRY MILLER

Don't tell your kids you had an easy birth or they won't respect you. For years I used to wake up my daughter and say, 'Melissa you ripped me to shreds. Now go back to sleep.' JOAN RIVERS

When I was born my father spent three weeks trying to find a loophole in my birth certificate. JACKIE VERNON

Who are these women in birth that say, 'I want to feel the pain'? Do you go to the dentist and say, 'Pull out my root canal. I want to get in touch with my gum'? RUBY WAX

By doing a bit of breathing and panting, men have this image that they're sharing the birthing experience. Not unless they're passing a bowling ball, they're not. ROBIN WILLIAMS

Having a baby is like watching two very inefficient removal men trying to get a very large sofa through a very small doorway, only in this case you can't say, 'Oh sod it, bring it through the French windows.'   VICTORIA WOOD

Birthdays

There comes a time when you should stop expecting other people to make a big deal about your birthday. That time is age eleven.   DAVE BARRY

Frasier Crane (Kelsey Grammer): I remember your fourth birthday party, when grandmother took us to the park to ride the carousel, and you made all those children wait while you wiped off your painted pony.
Niles Crane (David Hyde Pierce): I was wearing Bermuda shorts and that saddle was slick with toddler sweat.   *Frasier*

I had a friend bought a castle up in Scotland. Very nice. When his daughter had a birthday party, he hired a bouncy council estate.   HARRY HILL

George Michael turned thirty-seven today. A beautiful woman popped out of a cake and said, 'I must be at the wrong party.'   CRAIG KILBORN

George Hamilton turned sixty-one today. His skin is 350.   JAY LENO

Will Truman (Eric McCormack): It's the perfect time to tell your mother you're gay, on your thirtieth birthday.
Jack McFarland (Sean Hayes): Oh no, you're not telling my mother I'm thirty.   *Will and Grace*

I'm getting sick of pretending to be excited every time it's somebody's birthday. What is the big deal? How many times do we have to celebrate that someone was born? Every year, over and over . . . All you did was not die for twelve months.   JERRY SEINFELD

For my sister's fortieth birthday, I sent her a singing mammogram.   STEVEN WRIGHT

Birthdays are good for you; the more you have, the longer you live.

It's a sad birthday when the cake collapses under the weight of the candles.

The most effective way to remember your wife's birthday is to forget it . . . just once.

Mr Blackwell (*views of the U.S. fashion designer*)

Brigitte Bardot: A buxom milkmaid reminiscent of a cow wearing a girdle, and both have the same amount of acting talent.

Cameron Diaz looks like she was dressed by a colour-blind circus clown.

Britney Spears: Her bra-topped collection of Madonna rejects are pure fashion overkill. Relax. Help is on the way.

Roseanne Barr is a bowling ball looking for an alley.

Anne Robinson: Looks like Harry Potter in drag. A Hogwarts horror!

Diane Keaton: Dowdy, dumpy and frumpy. It could be Queen Victoria on jury duty.

Cher: Any attempt to look more masculine and she will need the operation.

Barbra Streisand: She looks like the masculine Bride of Frankenstein.

Elizabeth Taylor looks like two small boys fighting underneath a thick blanket.

Dustin Hoffman: Better as a woman. If I were him, I'd never get out of drag.

Madonna and Sandra Bernhard: The Mutt and Jeff of MTV.

Kelly Osbourne: A fright-wigged baby doll, stuck in a Goth prom gown.

Anne Rice looks like a cross between Queen Victoria and the vampire Lestate.

(*on André Agassi, 1990*) Looks like he missed the last train to Woodstock. He's tennis's flower-child gone to seed.

Martina Navratilova: The 'Tootsie' of tennis.

Melanie Griffith: A botox'd cockatoo in a painting by Dali.

Celine Dion: Half sequined scarecrow, half gaudy scrobat. Is it Abe Lincoln in drag?

Paris Hilton: From cyber disgrace to red carpet chills, she's the vapid Venus of Beverly Hills.

Tony Blair

He's got this habit of phoning you and playing his guitar at the same time.
ALASTAIR CAMPBELL

He's done more U-turns than a dodgy plumber. IAIN DUNCAN SMITH

They call him Teflon Tony because nothing sticks to him. WILL SELF

He is in danger of destroying his legacy as he becomes increasingly obsessed by his place in history. CLARE SHORT

Blame

To err is human. To blame it on someone else is politics. HUBERT HUMPHREY

(*on being investigated by the FBI*) They went down a list of every known charge conceivable to man: racketeering, skimming, kickback, ticket scalping, fixing fights, pre-ordaining fights, vitiating officials, corrupting judges, all the way down to laundering money. Everything but the Lindbergh baby. DON KING

You can't keep blaming yourself. Just blame yourself once, and move on.
HOMER SIMPSON, *The Simpsons*

Teamwork is essential. It allows you to blame someone else.

The man who smiles when things go wrong has thought of someone he can blame it on.

It is easier to fix the blame than to fix the problem.

I wish the buck stopped here as I could use a few.

Blondes

It is great to be a blonde. With low expectations it's very easy to surprise people.
PAMELA ANDERSON

She was a brunette by birth but a blonde by habit. ARTHUR BAER

She was what we used to call a suicide blonde – dyed by her own hand.
SAUL BELLOW

It was a blonde. A blonde to make a bishop kick a hole in a stained-glass window.   RAYMOND CHANDLER, *Farewell My Lovely*

Gentlemen prefer blondes, but marry brunettes.   ANITA LOOS

I'm not offended by all the dumb blonde jokes because I know I'm not dumb . . . and I also know that I'm not blonde.   DOLLY PARTON

She was a blonde . . . with a brunette past.   GWYN THOMAS

Going blonde is the only thing I've ever done that has got 100 per cent approbation.   ANN WIDDECOMBE

Blonde jokes are short so that men can remember them.

Blood

Remember, blood is not only thicker than water, it's much more difficult to get off the carpet.   PHYLLIS DILLER

Rhesus? They're monkeys, aren't they? How dare you! What are you implying? I didn't come here to be insulted by a legalised vampire.
          TONY HANCOCK, *Hancock's Half-Hour*

I came here in all good faith to help my country. I don't mind giving a reasonable amount, but a pint . . . why, that's very nearly an armful. I'm sorry, but I'm not walking around with an empty arm for anybody.
          TONY HANCOCK, *Hancock's Half-Hour*

Blood is thicker than water – but it makes lousy lemonade.

Body

Man consists of two parts, his mind and his body, only the body has more fun.
          WOODY ALLEN

It is a well-documented fact that guys will not ask for directions. This is a biological thing. This is why it takes several million guy sperm cells, each one wriggling in its own direction, totally confident it knows where it is going, to locate a female egg, despite the fact that the egg is, relative to them, the size of Wisconsin.   DAVE BARRY

The useless piece of flesh at the end of a penis is a man.   JO BRAND

I get goose pimples. Even my goose pimples get goose pimples.
WALLY CAMPBELL (BOB HOPE), *The Cat and the Canary*

I think men are very funny. If I had one of those dangly things stuffed down the front of my pants, I'd sit at home all day laughing at myself.
DAWN FRENCH

A couple of hanging glands have nothing to do with making someone a man.
MIRANDA HOBBES (CYNTHIA NIXON), *Sex and the City*

Of course men have names for their penis. Would you want to be bossed around by someone you don't even know?
MAGGIE PALEY

Blanche Devereaux (Rue McClanahan): I treat my body like a temple.
Sophia Petrillo (Estelle Getty): Yeah, open to everyone. Day or night.
The Golden Girls

I went into Gus's artificial organ and taco stand. I said, 'Give me a bladder.' The guy said, 'Is that to go?' I said, 'Well, what else would I want it for?'
EMO PHILIPS

I hate it when my foot falls asleep during the day because that means it's going to be up all night.
STEVEN WRIGHT

If your feet smell and your nose runs, you're built upside down.

Body piercing

I think the amount of metal a person has stuck in them is in inverse proportion to their intelligence.
RORY MCGRATH

Body piercing is a powerful, compelling visual statement that says, 'In today's competitive job market, what can I do to make myself less employable?'
DENNIS MILLER

Boots

Oh wellies they are wonderful,
Oh wellies they are swell;
'Cause they keep out the water
And they keep in the smell.
BILLY CONNOLLY

Boredom

The great advantage of being in a rut is that when one is in a rut, one knows exactly where one is.
ALAN BENNETT

I do not object to people looking at their watches when I am speaking. But I strongly object when they start shaking them to make certain they are still going.
NORMAN BIRKETT

The only difference between a rut and a grave is their dimensions.
ELLEN GLASGOW

Few men ever drop dead from overwork, but many quietly curl up and die because of undersatisfaction.
SYDNEY HARRIS

(*on Danville, Virginia*) It was one of those towns where you could do one of two things on a Friday night: drive round and get drunk, or get drunk and drive round.
MOJO NIXON

Boredom is rage spread thin.
PAUL TILLICH

Bores

Percy, you would bore the leggings off a village idiot.
EDMUND BLACKADDER (ROWAN ATKINSON), *Blackadder*

(*on Lana Turner*) She's a nice girl, but it's like sitting in a room with a beautiful vase.
JUDY GARLAND

(*to a small thin man who was boring him*) Sir, you are like a pin, but without either its head or its point.
DOUGLAS WILLIAM JERROLD

Bores can be divided into two classes; those who have their own particular subject, and those who do not need a subject.
A.A. MILNE

(*on Anthony Eden*) He is not only a bore, but he bores for England.
MALCOLM MUGGERIDGE

I only drink to make other people seem more interesting.
GEORGE JEAN NATHAN

There's nothing more boring than a really beautiful person who has nothing to say.
GWYNETH PALTROW

A bore is a man who, when you ask him how he is, tells you.

BERT LESTON TAYLOR

A healthy male adult bore consumes one and a half times his own weight in other people's patience.

JOHN UPDIKE, *Assorted Prose*

Bosses

Smithers: Sir, I'm afraid we have a bad image. People see you as a bit of an ogre.
Montgomery Burns: I ought to club them and eat their bones!

The Simpsons

When someone wins an argument with the boss, the argument isn't really over.

SAM EWING

The way to deal with a boss who steals credit for what you've done is to do inferior work.

AL FRANKEN

No man goes before his time – unless the boss leaves early.

GROUCHO MARX

Rebecca Howe (Kirstie Alley): You're not letting your employees take advantage of you, are you?
Norm Peterson (George Wendt): Yeah, maybe a little bit. Yesterday afternoon the guys decided just to knock off early and go bowling.
Rebecca: So what did you do?
Norm: I broke 200. Personal high.

Cheers

Kill my boss? Do I dare live out the American dream?

HOMER SIMPSON, *The Simpsons*

People at the top of the tree are those without qualifications to detain them at the bottom.

PETER USTINOV

A boss is someone who delegates all the authority, shifts all the blame, and takes all the credit.

Blessed is he who talks in circles, for he shall become a big wheel.

Tell your boss what you really think about him and the truth shall set you free.

Boston

Boston's freeway system is insane. It was clearly designed by a person who had spent his childhood crashing toy trains.

BILL BRYSON, *The Lost Continent: Travels in Small Town America*

I guess God made Boston on a wet Sunday. RAYMOND CHANDLER

This is a town where there are three pastimes: politics, sports, and revenge.

LAWRENCE C. MOULTER

Boxing

It's just a job. Grass grows, birds fly, waves pound the sand. I beat people up.

MUHAMMAD ALI

(*before a fight with Floyd Patterson*) I'll beat him so bad he'll need a shoehorn to put his hat on. MUHAMMAD ALI

There are no pleasures in a fight but some of my fights have been a pleasure to win. MUHAMMAD ALI

(*on Sonny Liston*) He's so ugly that when he cries the tears run down the back of his head. MUHAMMAD ALI

I've seen George Foreman shadow boxing, and the shadow won.

MUHAMMAD ALI

Boxing's just show business with blood. FRANK BRUNO

Undisputed heavyweight champion? Well, if it is undisputed, what's all the fighting about? To me, 'undisputed' means we all agree. Here you have two men beating the shit out of one another over something they apparently agree on. Makes no sense. GEORGE CARLIN

Don't you think it's funny that all those tough-guy boxers are fighting over a purse? GEORGE CARLIN

Boxers don't have sex before a fight. Do you know why? — They don't fancy each other. JIMMY CARR

I got into the ring with Muhammad Ali once and I had him worried for a while. He thought he'd killed me! TOMMY COOPER

(*on promoter Bob Arum*) When Bob Arum pats you on the back, he's just looking for a spot to stick the knife.
CUS D'AMATO

I was a hopeless boxer. I had handles sewn into my shorts so that they could carry me out of the ring easily.
LES DAWSON

Me and Jake LaMotta grew up in the same neighbourhood. You wanna know how popular Jake was? When we played hide-and-seek, nobody ever looked for LaMotta.
ROCKY GRAZIANO

To me, boxing is like a ballet, except there's no music, no choreography and the dancers hit each other.
JACK HANDEY

All fighters are prostitutes and all promoters are pimps.
LARRY HOLMES

Don King doesn't care about black or white. He just cares about green.
LARRY HOLMES

I was called 'Rembrandt' Hope in my boxing days, because I spent so much time on the canvas.
BOB HOPE

The ability to witness two men stand toe to toe in the spirit of sportsmanship and pummel each other into insensibility is what separates us from the animals.
'REVEREND' JIM IGNATOWSKI (CHRISTOPHER LLOYD), *Taxi*

A boxing match is like a cowboy movie. There's got to be good guys and there's got to be bad guys. And that's what people pay for – to see the bad guys get beat.
SONNY LISTON

No physical activity is so vain as boxing. A man gets into the ring to attract admiration. In no sport, therefore, can you be more humiliated.
NORMAN MAILER, *The Fight*

When Mike Tyson gets mad you don't need a referee, you need a priest.
JIM MURRAY

For ageing boxers, first your legs go, then your reflexes go, then your friends go.
WILLIE PEP

Everybody's got a plan – until he gets hit.
MIKE TYSON

Of course I don't mind the fight being at three in the morning. Everyone in Glasgow fights at three in the morning.
JIM WATT

Brains

Look, there's thick George, he's got a brain the size of a weasel's wedding tackle.
EDMUND BLACKADDER (ROWAN ATKINSON), *Blackadder*

Your brain's so minute, Baldrick, that if a hungry cannibal cracked your head open, there wouldn't be enough to cover a small water biscuit.
EDMUND BLACKADDER (ROWAN ATKINSON), *Blackadder*

Your brain is like the four-headed man-eating haddock-fish beast of Aberdeen. It doesn't exist.
EDMUND BLACKADDER (ROWAN ATKINSON), *Blackadder*

The eyes are open, the mouth moves, but Mr Brain has long since departed.
EDMUND BLACKADDER (ROWAN ATKINSON), *Blackadder*

If brains were lard, Jethro couldn't grease a pan.
JED CLAMPETT (BUDDY EBSEN), *The Beverly Hillbillies*

The brain is like a TV set; when it goes blank, it's a good idea to turn off the sound.
SAM EWING

The brain is a wonderful organ. It starts working the moment you get up in the morning and does not stop until you get into the office.
ROBERT FROST

Mallory Keaton (Justine Bateman): I'm glad Nick and I are so compatible. It's like we have one mind, you know? Like we share one brain.
Alex P. Keaton (Michael J. Fox): Who's using it tonight?   *Family Ties*

It only took me one night to realise if brains were dynamite you couldn't blow your nose.
DEBBIE MEDWAY (CANDY CLARK), *American Graffiti*

It has to be admitted that we English have sex on the brain, which is a very unsatisfactory place to have it.
MALCOLM MUGGERIDGE

I used to think that the brain was the most wonderful organ in my body. Then I realised who was telling me this.
EMO PHILIPS

Men's brains are like the prison system — not enough cells per man.

The best substitute for brains is silence.

Marlon Brando

I don't enjoy actors who seek to commune with their armpits.   GREER GARSON

Most of the time he sounds like he has a mouth full of toilet paper.

REX REED

He has preserved the mentality of an adolescent. When he doesn't try and someone's speaking to him, it's like a blank wall. In fact it's even less interesting because behind a blank wall you can always suppose that there's something interesting there.

BURT REYNOLDS

Brass bands

Brass bands are all very well in their place – outdoors and several miles away.

THOMAS BEECHAM

Breakfast

Do you *know* what breakfast cereal is made of? It's made of all those little curly wooden shavings you find in pencil sharpeners.

ROALD DAHL, *Charlie and the Chocolate Factory*

The critical period in matrimony is breakfast-time.

A.P. HERBERT, *Uncommon Law*

All happiness depends on a leisurely breakfast.

Breasts

In junior high a boy poured water down my shirt and yelled, 'Now maybe they'll grow!'

PAMELA ANDERSON

Scientists now believe that the primary biological function of breasts is to make males stupid.

DAVE BARRY

I've had my nipples pierced. Why? Because I was sick of losing my car keys. The only trouble is that I have got this really elongated nipple from shoving the keys in the ignition.

JENNY ECLAIR

(*on TV fashion guru Susannah Constantine*) For a woman with breasts half-way down her body, Susannah should stop slagging off the helpless public and invest in a new, sturdier bra.

PEACHES GELDOF

(*on Jane Russell*) There are two good reasons why men go to see her. Those are enough.

HOWARD HUGHES

Working with Sophia Loren was like being bombed with watermelons.

ALAN LADD

(*during pregnancy*) My breasts were so huge they needed their own postcode.

KATHY LETTE

Pamela Anderson Lee released a statement confirming that she has had her breast implants removed. Doctors say that Pamela is doing fine and that her old implants are now dating Charlie Sheen.   CONAN O'BRIEN

Director (at a Katharine Hepburn play): Don't you think it would be better if we made her wear a brassiere?
Dorothy Parker: Good God, no. At least something in the play is moving.

My feet are small for the same reason my waist is small – things don't grow in the shade.   DOLLY PARTON

I have no bosoms. I can iron my blouse while it's on me.   JOAN RIVERS

Looking at cleavage is like looking at the sun. You don't stare at it. You get a sense and then look away.   JERRY SEINFELD

If God had meant breasts to be lifted and separated, he would have put one on each shoulder.   VICTORIA WOOD

Without nipples, breasts would be pointless.

Cleavage is something you can look down on and approve at the same time.

Women's breasts are like train sets: they're meant for kids, but usually it's the fathers who wind up playing with them.

Bribery

Never underestimate the effectiveness of a straight cash bribe.

CLAUD COCKBURN, *In Time of Trouble*

Murray, lend me twenty dollars or I'll call your wife and tell her you're in Central Park wearing a dress!   OSCAR MADISON (WALTER MATTHAU), *The Odd Couple*

Sir, I will have you know that I cannot be bought, and I cannot be threatened, but you put the two together and I'm your man.

NORM PETERSON (GEORGE WENDT), *Cheers*

Bridge

Bridge is a game that separates the men from the boys. It also separates husbands and wives. GEORGE BURNS

When my bridge partner excused himself to go to the bathroom, it was the only time all night I knew what he had in his hand. GEORGE S. KAUFMAN

Bureaucracy

Well Minister, if you ask me for a straight answer, then I shall say that, as far as we can see, looking at it by and large, taking one thing with another in terms of the average of departments, then in the final analysis it is probably true to say, that at the end of the day, in general terms, you would probably find that, not to put too fine a point on it, there probably wasn't very much in it one way or the other, as far as one can see, at this stage.
SIR HUMPHREY APPLEBY (NIGEL HAWTHORNE), *Yes, Minister*

What the world really needs is more love and less paperwork. PEARL BAILEY

Bureaucracy defends the status quo long past the time when the quo has lost its status. LAURENCE J. PETER

(*on the Civil Service*) A difficulty for every solution. HERBERT SAMUEL

Britain has invented a new missile. It's called the civil servant – it doesn't work and it can't be fired. WALTER WALKER

Information deteriorates upwards through bureaucracies.

George Bush

(*asked in 2002 whether she still considered her husband to be the most handsome man in the world*) Yes. But my eyesight is getting bad. BARBARA BUSH

We need a President who's fluent in at least one language. BUCK HENRY

If ignorance goes to forty dollars a barrel, I want drilling rights to George Bush's head. JIM HIGHTOWER

(*on his verbal blunders*) Poor George, he can't help it – he was born with a silver foot in his mouth. ANN RICHARDS

George W. Bush

Bush is like McDonald's: pre-packaged, filled with empty calories and controlled by corporate interests.

PAUL BEGALA

In the Clinton administration we worried the President would open his zipper. In the Bush administration, they worry the President will open his mouth.

JAMES CARVILLE

Bush is like if Reagan and Quayle had a kid.

WILL DURST

Israeli Prime Minister Ariel Sharon arrived in Washington Sunday night to give President Bush a 91-page book proving that Yasser Arafat funded terrorists. White House sources say that President Bush has the book and is almost done colouring it.

TINA FEY

This is a guy who could not find oil in Texas.

AL FRANKEN

I know that if you are the leader of planet Earth, you should be smarter than me. You just get the feeling in the Oval Office that Dick Cheney is working behind the big desk. And then off to the right there is a little collapsible card table where George has airplanes and stuff. Then every once in a while he looks up and says, 'I've discovered that if I shut my eyes, I can disappear.'

DARREL HAMMOND

He has achieved the unusual feat of being simultaneously sinister and ridiculous.

ROY HATTERSLEY

Bush is unusually incurious, abnormally unintelligent, amazingly inarticulate, fantastically uncultured, extraordinarily uneducated, and apparently quite proud of all these things.

CHRISTOPHER HITCHENS

George W. Bush spoke for fifty-eight minutes at the Republican Convention. That's the longest speech he's ever made that didn't start, 'You see, Officer . . .'

CRAIG KILBORN

The Weakest Link is a fascinating programme. They ask a bunch of people questions and they keep getting rid of the dumbest person, so just the smartest person is left. It's kind of the opposite way we elect a President.

JAY LENO

This Monday President Bush will be celebrating his 100th day in office. When asked about it, Bush said, 'Gosh, 100 days? Has it been a year already?'

JAY LENO

I read today that President Bush was interrupted seventy-three times by applause and seventy-five times by really big words.   JAY LENO

George W. Bush went into a think-tank this week and almost drowned.
                                                                   JAY LENO

Saddam Hussein challenged President Bush to a debate. The Butcher of Baghdad versus the Butcher of the English language.   JAY LENO

Today, President Bush announced he's been mispronouncing the name of Iraq all along. He said it's actually pronounced Syria.   JAY LENO

Bush reiterated his stand to conservatives opposing his decision on stem cell research. He said today he believes life begins at conception and ends at execution.   JAY LENO

Sometimes when you look in his eyes you get the feeling that someone else is driving.   DAVID LETTERMAN

George W. Bush had a colonoscopy last week. They found 300 Al Gore ballots.
                                                             DAVID LETTERMAN

The Dalai Lama visited the White House and told the President that he could teach him to find a higher state of consciousness. Then after talking to George W. Bush for a few minutes, he said, 'You know what? Let's just grab lunch.'
                                                                 BILL MAHER

Bush has surrounded himself with smart people the way a hole surrounds itself with a doughnut.   DENNIS MILLER

U.S. soldiers in Iraq say that one of the things that's keeping them going and inspiring them is all the letters they're receiving from schoolchildren around the country. Then someone explained that those letters are actually from President George W. Bush.   CONAN O'BRIEN

President Bush is in trouble. His approval rating has never been lower. Bush says he hasn't had numbers this low since he took his SATs.
                                                              CONAN O'BRIEN

When President Bush went to Russia, they asked him if he wanted to see Lenin's tomb. He said he didn't — he wasn't really a Beatles fan.   JOAN RIVERS

These days, to find an American president, you have to scour the country for a mental defective who will do what he is told by the petrochemical industry.

JOHN SESSIONS

George W. Bush is like a bad comic working the crowd.   MARTIN SHEEN

When the world is going nuts, you want a guy who is nuttier than them.

GENE SIMMONS

When the media ask him a question, he answers, 'Can I use a lifeline?'

ROBIN WILLIAMS

The mentally retarded are treated equally in Texas – some executed, some elected.

Bushisms (*the wisdom of George W. Bush*)

The problem with the French is that they don't have a word for entrepreneur.

More and more of our imports come from overseas.

The war on terror involves Saddam Hussein because of the nature of Saddam Hussein, the history of Saddam Hussein, and his willingness to terrorise himself.

I hope the ambitious realise that they are more likely to succeed with success as opposed to failure.

A tax cut is really one of the anecdotes to coming out of an economic illness.

I am mindful not only of preserving executive powers for myself, but for pre-decessors as well.

(*on the Kyoto accord, 2001*) First, we would not accept a treaty that would not have been ratified, nor a treaty that I thought made sense for the country.

My trip to Asia begins here in Japan for an important reason. It begins here because for a century and a half now, America and Japan have formed one of the great and enduring alliances of modern times.

Families is where our nation takes hope, where wings take dream. I know how hard it is to put food on your family.

And so, in my State of the – my State of the Union – or State – my speech to the nation, whatever you want to call it, speech to the nation – I asked Americans to give 4,000 years – 4,000 hours over the next – the rest of your life – of service to America. That's what I asked – 4,000 hours.

Redefining the role of the United States from enablers to keep the peace to enablers to keep the peace from peacekeepers is going to be an assignment.

We need an energy bill that encourages consumption.

(*on education*) Rarely is the question asked, 'Is our children learning?'

The thing that's important for me is to remember what's the most important thing.

Business

Every company is better than your own. It's a rule of the universe.

SCOTT ADAMS

I never touched a gun in my life. That and that alone forever doomed me to middle management.   VINCE ANTONELLI (STEVE MARTIN), *My Blue Heaven*

What is a crook but a businessman without an office?   BRENDAN BEHAN

I'll keep it short and sweet. Family, Religion, Friendship. These are the three demons you must slay if you wish to succeed in business.

MONTGOMERY BURNS, *The Simpsons*

In the business world an executive knows something about everything, a technician knows everything about something and the switchboard operator knows everything.   HAROLD COFFIN

Integrity is like oxygen. The higher you go, the less there is of it.

PAUL DICKSON

There's no such thing as a free lunch.   MILTON FRIEDMAN

Any organisation is like a septic tank. The really big chunks rise to the top.

JOHN IMHOFF

(*to British businessmen*) When you are skinning your customers, you should leave some skin on to grow so that you can skin them again.

NIKITA KHRUSHCHEV

Revitalising General Motors is like teaching an elephant to tap dance. You find the sensitive spots and start poking. H. ROSS PEROT

The people who really run organisations are usually found several levels down, where it's still possible to get things done. TERRY PRATCHETT, *Small Gods*

Running a company on market research is like driving while looking in the rear-view mirror. ANITA RODDICK

Agent 99 (Barbara Feldon): Sometimes I wish you were just an ordinary businessman.
Maxwell Smart (Don Adams): Well, 99, we are what we are. I'm a secret agent, trained to be cold, vicious, and savage. Not enough to be a businessman.
Get Smart

The toughest thing in business is minding your own.

A business is too big when it takes a week for gossip to go from one end of the office to the other.

C

California

California is a fine place to live – if you happen to be an orange.
FRED ALLEN

Beverly Hills is so exclusive that even the police have an unlisted number.
MOREY AMSTERDAM

In California everyone thinks fat is something you can catch, and therefore is to be avoided. ROSEANNE BARR

California, the department-store state. The most of everything and the best of nothing. RAYMOND CHANDLER, *The Little Sister*

I'd move to Los Angeles if Australia and New Zealand were swallowed by a huge tidal wave, if there was a bubonic plague in Europe, and if Africa disappeared from some Martian attack. RUSSELL CROWE

Los Angeles, the city of angels. We've got O.J., the Menendez brothers and the Hillside Strangler. There are hardly enough halos to go around.

NICK DIPAOLO

If a tidal wave hits LA, just grab a fake boob for safety.

SARAH MICHELLE GELLAR

A great many people in Los Angeles are on strict diets that restrict their intake of synthetic foods. The reason for this appears to be a widely held belief that organically grown fruit and vegetables make the cocaine work faster.

FRAN LEBOWITZ, *Social Studies*

Fall is my favourite season in Los Angeles, watching the birds change colour and fall from the trees.

DAVID LETTERMAN

Nothing is wrong with Southern California that a rise in the ocean level wouldn't cure.

ROSS MACDONALD

In Los Angeles everyone has perfect teeth. It's crocodile land.

GWYNETH PALTROW

In California, handicapped parking is for women who are frigid.   JOAN RIVERS

I love Los Angeles. I love Hollywood. They're beautiful. Everybody's plastic, but I love plastic. I want to be plastic.   ANDY WARHOL

To a New Yorker, the only Californian houses on the market for less than a million dollars are those on fire.

Calm

Don't torture yourself, Gomez. That's my job.

MORTICIA ADDAMS (ANJELICA HUSTON), *The Addams Family*

Be like a duck, my mother used to tell me. Remain calm on the surface and paddle like hell underneath.   MICHAEL CAINE

Show me a man with both feet on the ground and I'll show you a man who can't get his pants on.   JOE E. LEWIS

Many people lose their tempers merely from seeing you keep yours.

Camping

Camping is nature's way of promoting the motel business.   DAVE BARRY

Some national parks have long waiting lists for camping reservations. When you have to wait a year to sleep next to a tree, something is wrong.
                                                                 GEORGE CARLIN

Putting up a tent is like making love to a beautiful woman. First you've got to lay her out, put up your pole and slip into the old bag.
                                         SWISS TONI (CHARLIE HIGSON), *The Fast Show*

Canada

If the natural mental illness of the United States is megalomania, that of Canada is paranoid schizophrenia.   MARGARET ATWOOD

Canada: a country so square that even the female impersonators are women.
                                                                 RICHARD BRENNER

You have to know a man awfully well in Canada to know his surname.
                                                                 JOHN BUCHAN

I don't even know what street Canada is on.   AL CAPONE

In any world menu, Canada must be considered the vichyssoise of nations – it's cold, half-French, and difficult to stir.   STUART KEATE

In Pierre Elliott Trudeau, Canada has at last produced a political leader worthy of assassination.   IRVING LAYTON

The Canadian Prime Minister said Canada would lend the US its full military support. You know what that means: both tanks.   JAY LENO

Canada is a country without a cuisine. When's the last time you went out for a Canadian?   MIKE MYERS

In Canada a gay marriage is one in which the husband doesn't watch hockey.
                                                                 CONAN O'BRIEN

Very little is known of the Canadian country since it is rarely visited by anyone but the Queen and illiterate sport fishermen.   P.J. O'ROURKE

Canada is an entire country named Doug.   GREG PROOPS

Canada is all right really, though not for the whole weekend.   SAKI

(*on Edmonton, Alberta*) It's not the end of the world, but you can see it from there.   PIERRE TRUDEAU

Cannibalism

I believe that if ever I had to practise cannibalism, I might manage if there were enough tarragon around.   JAMES BEARD

People were saying there's not enough food and too many people. Cannibalism is obviously the answer.   BILLY CONNOLLY

Two cannibals eating a clown. One says to the other, 'Does this taste funny to you?'   TOMMY COOPER

I do wish we could chat longer. But I'm having an old friend for dinner.
DR HANNIBAL LECTER (ANTHONY HOPKINS),
The Silence of the Lambs

A census taker once tried to test me. I ate his liver with some fava beans and a nice Chianti.   DR HANNIBAL LECTER (ANTHONY HOPKINS),
The Silence of the Lambs

(*of Joan Crawford*) I'd rather have a cannibal for a co-star.   ANTHONY PERKINS

Cannibal: someone who is fed up with people.

Cannibals won't eat divorced women – they're too bitter.

Career

I've had so many rebirths, I should come with my own midwife.   CHER

Dynasty was the opportunity to take charge of my career rather than walking around like a library book waiting to be loaned out.   JOAN COLLINS

I'm always making a comeback but nobody ever tells me where I've been.
BILLIE HOLIDAY

Of course I'm over the hill, but I'm up the next one.   JOHN LYDON

A career is wonderful, but you can't curl up with a career on a cold night.
MARILYN MONROE

A career is a job that has gone on too long.

Jimmy Carter

Jimmy's basic problem is that he's super cautious. He looks before and after he leaps.
JOEY ADAMS

(*on Jimmy and Billy*) Sometimes when I look at my children, I say to myself, 'Lillian, you should have stayed a virgin.'
LILLIAN CARTER

I wouldn't put Jimmy Carter in charge of snake control in Ireland.
EUGENE MCCARTHY

Cartoons

A lot of politicians seem glad even if you've done them as a gob of phlegm – it means they've arrived.
GERALD SCARFE

A cartoonist is someone who does the same thing every day without repeating himself.
CHARLES SCHULZ

Castles

When I first came here, this was all swamp. Everyone said I was daft to build a castle on a swamp, but I built it all the same, just to show them. It sank into the swamp, so I built a second one. And that one sank into the swamp. So I built a third. That burned down, fell over, and then sank into the swamp. But the fourth one stayed up. And that's what you're going to get, son, the strongest castle in all of England.
KING OF THE SWAMP (MICHAEL PALIN), *Monty Python and the Holy Grail*

Cats

Cat names are more for human benefit. They give one a certain degree more confidence that the animal belongs to you.
ALAN AYCKBOURN, *Table Manners*

To bathe a cat takes brute force, perseverance, courage of conviction, and a cat. The last ingredient is usually hardest to come by.
STEPHEN BAKER

Cats' hearing apparatus is built to allow the human voice to go easily in one ear and out the other.
STEPHEN BAKER

A man who was loved by 300 women singled me out to live with him. Why? I was the only one without a cat.
ELAYNE BOOSLER

A cat isn't fussy – just so long as you remember he likes his milk in the shallow, rose-patterned saucer and his fish on the blue plate, from which he will take it and eat it off the floor.

ARTHUR BRIDGES

A dog will sit beside you while you work. A cat will sit on the work.

PAM BROWN

Guys are like dogs. They keep coming back. Ladies are like cats. Yell at a cat one time, they're gone.

LENNY BRUCE

I had been told that the training procedure with cats was difficult. It's not. Mine had me trained in two days.

BILL DANA

Some people say that cats are sneaky, evil and cruel. True, and they have many other fine qualities as well.

MISSY DIZICK

Women and cats will do as they please, and men and dogs should relax and get used to the idea.

ROBERT A. HEINLEIN

I have noticed that what cats most appreciate in a human being is not the ability to produce food, which they take for granted – but his or her entertainment value.

GEOFFREY HOUSEHOLD, *Rogue Male*

Some people say man is the most dangerous animal on the planet. Obviously those people have never met an angry cat.

LILLIAN JOHNSON

Cats are intended to teach us that not everything in nature has a function.

GARRISON KEILLOR

True story. In China a healthy cat has been born with three heads. Here, kitty, kitty, kitty!

CRAIG KILBORN

Cats seem to go on the principle that it never does any harm to ask for what you want.

JOSEPH WOOD KRUTCH, *Twelve Seasons*

I found out why cats drink out of the toilet. My mother told me it's because the water is cold in there. And I'm like: how did my mother know that?

WENDY LIEBMAN

I gave my cat a bath the other day. They love it. He just sat there and enjoyed it. It was fun for me. The fur kept sticking to my tongue, but other than that . . .

STEVE MARTIN

A tomcat hijacked a plane, stuck a pistol into the pilot's ribs and demanded: 'Take me to the canaries.' Bob Monkhouse

Cats are mean for the fun of it. P.J. O'Rourke

A cat pours his body on the floor like water. William Lyon Phelps

The problem with cats is that they get the exact same look on their face whether they see a moth or an axe-murderer. Paula Poundstone

Many Real cats are instantly recognisable. For example, all cats with faces that look as though they had been put in a vice and hit repeatedly by a hammer with a sock round it are Real cats. Terry Pratchett, *The Unadulterated Cat*

We have two cats. They're my wife's cats, Mischa and Alex. Women always give cats sensitive names: Muffy, Fluffy, Buffy. Guys name cats things like Tuna Breath or Fur Face. They're nice cats. They've been neutered and they've been declawed. So they're like pillows that eat. Larry Reeb

You can tell a dog to do something. You can put to a cat a reasonable proposition. Michael Stevens

One is never sure, watching two cats washing each other, whether it's affection, the taste, or a trial run for the jugular. Helen Thomson

If it's raining at the back door, every cat is convinced there's a good chance that it won't be raining at the front door. William Toms

A man who carries a cat by the tail learns something he can learn in no other way. Mark Twain

A dog is a man's best friend. A cat is a cat's best friend. Robert J. Vogel

If a dog jumps onto your lap it is because he is fond of you; but if a cat does the same thing it is because your lap is warmer. A.N. Whitehead, *Dialogues*

The phrase 'domestic cat' is an oxymoron. George F. Will

Do radioactive cats have eighteen half-lives? Steven Wright

Dogs come when they're called; cats take a message and get back to you.

Cat's motto: no matter what you've done wrong, always try to make it look like the dog did it.

Do not meddle in the affairs of cats, for they are subtle and will piss on your computer.

The cat that looks poorly and sad has just stolen a carton of cream and is about to be sick in the hall.

The cat that is kissing you lovingly has just devoured a rabbit and has left the entrails under the bed.

There is no snooze button on a cat who wants breakfast.

You can tell your cat is overweight when the last hairball it coughed up was your dog.

You can tell your cat is overweight when it lands on its belly before it lands on its feet.

You can tell your cat is overweight when it's run over by a car and the car comes off worse.

You can tell your cat is overweight when you need oxygen after it sits on your chest.

You can tell your cat is overweight when mice point at it and snigger.

Caution

Anything that is worth doing has been done frequently. Things hitherto undone should be given, I suspect, a wide berth. MAX BEERBOHM

Don't take the bull by the horns, take him by the tail; then you can let go when you want to. JOSH BILLINGS

Hold it, El Guapo! Or I'll pump you so full of lead you'll be using your dick for a pencil. LUCKY DAY (STEVE MARTIN), *Three Amigos!*

When you jump for joy, beware that no one moves the ground from beneath your feet. STANISLAW LEC

I wonder why it is that young men are always cautioned against bad girls. Anyone can handle a bad girl. It's the good girls men should be warned against.
DAVID SLATER (DAVID NIVEN), *The Moon is Blue*

Be careful when reading health books; you may die of a misprint.
MARK TWAIN

Never entrust your life to a surgeon with more than three Band Aids on his fingers.

Celebrity

A celebrity is a person who works hard all his life to become well known, then wears dark glasses to avoid being recognised.
FRED ALLEN, *Treadmill to Oblivion*

A sign of celebrity is that his name is often worth more than his services.
DANIEL J. BOORSTIN

Being a personality is not the same as having a personality.   ALAN COREN

Celebrity is death. It's the worst thing that can happen to an actor.
JOHN CUSACK

I find the cult of celebrity absolutely astonishing. It used to be that if you were a celebrity, you had achieved something. Now you can be a celebrity for a single dress.
P.D. JAMES

A celebrity is any well-known TV or movie star who looks like he spends more than two hours working on his hair.   STEVE MARTIN.

I think we've gorged on celebrity and we're soon going to be sick. And I'll probably be one of the first to be vomited out.   MELINDA MESSENGER

Sure, I am one of the biggest stars in Finland. But we don't have that many.
KIMI RAIKKONEN

Cemeteries

The fence around a cemetery is foolish, for those inside can't get out and those outside don't want to get in.   ARTHUR BRISBANE

I get no respect. I bought a cemetery plot. The guy said, 'There goes the neighbourhood!'   RODNEY DANGERFIELD

Do cemetery workers prefer the graveyard shift?

Censorship

The British Board of Censors will not pass any seduction scene unless the seducer has one foot on the floor. Apparently sex in England is something like snooker. FRED ALLEN

I'm all in favour of free expression provided it's kept rigidly under control.
ALAN BENNETT, *Forty Years On*

(*on UK movie censor ratings*) Oh, I get it. It's simple. PG means the hero gets the girl, 15 means that the villain gets the girl, and 18 means everybody gets the girl. MICHAEL DOUGLAS

I dislike censorship. Like an appendix it is useless when inert and dangerous when active. MAURICE EDELMAN

I seriously object to seeing on the screen what belongs in the bedroom.
SAM GOLDWYN

Censorship is like demanding that grown men live on skim milk because the baby can't eat steak. ROBERT A. HEINLEIN

(*on the threat of censorship to one of his films*) They can't censor the gleam in my eye. CHARLES LAUGHTON

The censors say they're protecting the family unit in America, when the reality is, if you suck a tit, you're an X, but if you cut it off with a sword, you're a PG.
JACK NICHOLSON

I believe in censorship. After all, I made a fortune out of it. MAE WEST

Blessed are the censors; they shall inhibit the earth.

Champagne

Champagne has the taste of an apple peeled with a steel knife.
ALDOUS HUXLEY

There comes a time in every woman's life when the only thing that helps is a glass of champagne.
KATHERINE 'KIT' MARLOWE (BETTE DAVIS), *Old Acquaintance*

I'll stick with gin. Champagne is just ginger ale that knows somebody.
'HAWKEYE' PIERCE (ALAN ALDA), *M*A*S*H*

Champions

Champions aren't made in the gyms. Champions are made from something they have deep inside them – a desire, a dream, a vision. MUHAMMAD ALI

Champions keep playing until they get it right. BILLIE JEAN KING

Change

The main dangers in this life are the people who want to change everything – or nothing. NANCY ASTOR

I guess some people never change. Or, they quickly change and then quickly change back. HOMER SIMPSON, *The Simpsons*

Change is inevitable, except from a vending machine.

Charlie Chaplin

I find his films about as funny as getting an arrow through the neck and discovering there's a gas bill tied to it.
EDMUND BLACKADDER (ROWAN ATKINSON), *Blackadder*

Baldrick, in the Amazonian rain forests there are tribes of Indians as yet untouched by civilisation who have developed more convincing Charlie Chaplin impressions than yours. EDMUND BLACKADDER (ROWAN ATKINSON), *Blackadder*

When he found a voice to say what was on his mind, he was like a child of eight writing lyrics for Beethoven's Ninth. BILLY WILDER

Character

No one can be exactly like me. Sometimes even I have trouble doing it.
TALLULAH BANKHEAD

There's terrific merit in having no sense of humour, no sense of irony, practically no sense of anything at all. If you're born with these so-called defects you have a very good chance of getting to the top. PETER COOK

You can judge the character of others by how they treat those who can do nothing to them or for them. MALCOLM FORBES

Ability may get you to the top but it's character that will keep you there.
ABRAHAM LINCOLN

You get to know more of the character of a man in a round of golf than in six months of political experience.   DAVID LLOYD GEORGE

Kevin Costner has personality-minus.   MADONNA

(*on political activist Abbie Hoffman*) He had a charisma that must have come out of an Immaculate Conception between Fidel Castro and Groucho Marx. They went into his soul and he came out looking like an ethnic milkshake — Jewish revolutionary, Puerto Rican lord, Italian street kid, Black Panther with the old Afro haircut, even a glint of Irish gunman in the mad, green eyes.
                                        NORMAN MAILER

(*on Conservative Party leader Iain Duncan Smith*) I cannot stay in a Tory party led by a man who thinks that charisma is December 25.   DAVID MELLOR

I am the most anti-social person I know. But of course, I don't know anyone because I'm so anti-social.   DEREK NEITZEL

I have always had some difficulty in distinguishing between charisma and after-shave.   OLIVER PRITCHETT

You can tell a lot about a fellow's character by his way of eating jelly beans.
                                        RONALD REAGAN

Jean-Claude Van Damme exudes the charisma of a packet of Cup-a-Soup.

Character is like a fence — it cannot be strengthened by whitewash.

Charity

Charity is taking an ugly girl to lunch.   WARREN BEATTY

Charity begins at home: at about 6.30 when they call and interrupt your dinner.
                                        JOHN WAGNER, *Crabby Road*

I know that there are people in this world who do not love their fellow man, and I hate people like that!   TOM LEHRER

Charm

If you have charm, you don't need to have anything else; and if you don't have it, it doesn't much matter what else you have.   J.M. BARRIE

You know what charm is: a way of getting the answer yes without having asked any clear question.
ALBERT CAMUS

[John] McEnroe was as charming as always, which means that he was as charming as a dead mouse in a loaf of bread.
CLIVE JAMES

It's innocence when it charms us, ignorance when it doesn't.
MIGNON MCLAUGHLIN

A beauty is a woman you notice; a charmer is one who notices you.
ADLAI STEVENSON

Cheese

Cheese: milk's leap toward immortality.
CLIFTON FADIMAN, *Any Number Can Play*

Chefs

(*on Antony Worrall Thompson*) He has more chips on his shoulder than McDonald's. His biggest hang-up is he hasn't won a Michelin star.
GORDON RAMSAY

(*on Ainsley Harriott*) He is a comedian, not a chef.
GORDON RAMSAY

(*on Raymond Blanc*) He has a temperament like a rottweiller.
GORDON RAMSAY

Chemicals

Not all chemicals are bad. Without chemicals such as hydrogen and oxygen, for example, there would be no way to make water, a vital ingredient in beer.
DAVE BARRY

Cher

Working with Cher was like being in a blender with an alligator.
PETER BOGDANOVICH

Cher performed at a private party for the President. She was mortified when another woman showed up wearing the same ass.
CRAIG KILBORN

For $39.95 you can buy the new Cher action figure. It's so lifelike the breasts, lips, nose and buttocks are sold separately.
JAY LENO

Cher knew she was going to win a Grammy. A week ago she had her plastic surgeon put a surprised look on her face.   JAY LENO

One of Cher's wigs has been stolen. Cher has issued a plea to turn the wig in to the nearest heterosexual.   CONAN O'BRIEN

If Cher has another face-lift she'll be wearing a beard.   JENNIFER SAUNDERS

Chess

I failed to make the chess team because of my height.   WOODY ALLEN

Because of the level of my chess game, I was able – even against a weak opponent, such as my younger brothers or the dog – to get myself checkmated in under three minutes. I challenge any computer to do it faster.
                    DAVE BARRY

Life's too short for chess.   HENRY JAMES BYRON, *Our Boys*

Chess is the most elaborate waste of human intelligence that you can find outside an advertising agency.   RAYMOND CHANDLER

It is impossible to win gracefully at chess. No man has yet said 'Mate!' in a voice which failed to sound to his opponent bitter, boastful and malicious.
                    A.A. MILNE, *Not That It Matters*

A computer once beat me at chess, but it was no match for me at kick boxing.
                    EMO PHILIPS

I had lunch with a chess champion the other day. I knew he was a chess champion because it took him twenty minutes to pass the salt.   ERIC SYKES

Chicago

Loving Chicago is like loving a woman with a broken nose.
                    NELSON ALGREN

Chicago is an October sort of city even in spring.   NELSON ALGREN

Sharks are as tough as those football fans who take their shirts off during games in Chicago in January, only more intelligent.   DAVE BARRY

This is virgin territory for whorehouses   AL CAPONE

That's great advertising when you can turn Chicago into a city you'd want to spend more than three hours in.   JERRY DELLA FEMINA

There's only one thing for Chicago to do, and that's move to a better neigh-bourhood.   HERMAN FETZER

I think that's how Chicago got started. A bunch of people in New York said, 'Gee, I'm enjoying the crime and the poverty but it just ain't cold enough. Let's go west!'   RICHARD JENI

It's one of the most progressive cities in the world. Shooting is only a sideline.
                                                                        WILL ROGERS

Childhood

When I was born I was so surprised I didn't talk for a year and a half.
                                                                       GRACIE ALLEN

I wasn't an athletic boy. I was once lapped in the long jump.
                                                                     RONNIE CORBETT

My father confused me. From the ages of one to seven, I thought my name was Jesus Christ.   BILL COSBY

I had plenty of pimples as a kid. One day I fell asleep in the library. When I woke up, a blind man was reading my face.   RODNEY DANGERFIELD

I was coming home from kindergarten – well they told me it was kindergarten. I found out later I had been working in a factory for ten years. It's good for a kid to know how to make gloves.   ELLEN DEGENERES

I grew up in the Sixties, well, not really, because I grew up in Milwaukee, Wisconsin, and we didn't get the Sixties until 1974. We got the Sixties and disco in the same week.   WILL DURST

I was born at the age of twelve on a Metro-Goldwyn-Mayer lot.
                                                                      JUDY GARLAND

I grew up with six brothers. That's how I learned to dance – waiting for the bathroom.   BOB HOPE

You want to know what the best thing about childhood is? At some point it stops.   MALCOLM (FRANKIE MUNIZ), *Malcolm in the Middle*

I'd the upbringing a nun would envy and that's the truth. Until I was fifteen I was more familiar with Africa than my own body.

JOE ORTON, *Entertaining Mr Sloane*

People don't believe I was a fat kid, but I really was. When I got off the carousel, the horse limped.

JOAN RIVERS

I had a rough childhood. When I was born, the doctor advised me of my rights.

SCOTT ROEBEN

When I was a kid, I had two friends, and they were imaginary and they would only play with each other.

RITA RUDNER

Children

It was no wonder that people were so horrible when they started life as children.

KINGSLEY AMIS, *One Fat Englishman*

Raising kids is part joy and part guerrilla warfare.

ED ASNER

One of the first things you notice about a backward country is the way children obey their parents.

ERMA BOMBECK

When my kids become wild and unruly, I use a nice safe playpen. When they're finished, I climb out.

ERMA BOMBECK

Have you any idea how many kids it takes to turn off one light in the kitchen? Three. It takes one to say, 'What light?' and two more to say, 'I didn't turn it on.'

ERMA BOMBECK

All of us have moments in our lives that test our courage. Taking children into a house with a white carpet is one of them.

ERMA BOMBECK

A child develops individuality long before he develops taste. I have seen my kids straggle into the kitchen in the morning with outfits that need only one accessory: an empty gin bottle.

ERMA BOMBECK

In general my children refused to eat anything that hadn't danced on TV.

ERMA BOMBECK

It puzzles me how a child can see a dairy bar three miles away, but cannot see a four by six rug that has scrunched up under his feet and has been dragged through two rooms.

ERMA BOMBECK

One thing they never tell you about child raising is that for the rest of your life, at the drop of a hat, you are expected to know your child's name and how old he or she is.
ERMA BOMBECK

Being a child is horrible. It is slightly better than being a tree or a piece of heavy machinery but not half as good as being a domestic cat.
JULIE BURCHILL, *Damaged Goods*

Smithers: There is a small boy on the grounds.
Montgomery Burns: Release the hounds.
The Simpsons

Children really brighten up a household. They never turn the lights off.
RALPH BUS

Never raise your hands to your kids. It leaves your groin unprotected.
RED BUTTONS

Learning to dislike children at an early age saves a lot of expense and aggravation later in life.
ROBERT BYRN

Personally, Vita's convinced me that alligators have the right idea – they eat their young.
IDA CORWIN (EVE ARDEN), *Mildred Pierce*

Always end the name of your child with a vowel, so that when you yell the name will carry.
BILL COSBY

Nothing separates the generations more than music. By the time a child is eight or nine, he has developed a passion for his own music that is even stronger than his passions for procrastination and weird clothes.
BILL COSBY

The trouble with children is that they are not returnable.
QUENTIN CRISP, *The Naked Civil Servant*

Why do parents always take their children to supermarkets to smack them?
JACK DEE

People who are pro smacking children say, 'It's the only language they understand.' You could apply that to tourists.
JACK DEE

I'm a godmother. That's a great thing to be, a godmother. She calls me god for short. That's cute – I taught her that.
ELLEN DEGENERES

We spend the first twelve months of our children's lives teaching them to walk and talk and the next twelve years telling them to sit down and shut up.

PHYLLIS DILLER

Most children threaten at times to run away from home. This is the only thing that keeps some parents going.

PHYLLIS DILLER

Always be nice to your children because they are the ones who will choose your rest home.

PHYLLIS DILLER

I want my children to have all the things I couldn't afford. Then I want to move in with them.

PHYLLIS DILLER

I don't believe in smacking children – I just use a cattle prod.

JENNY ECLAIR

There's no such thing as a tough child. If you parboil them first for seven hours, they always come out tender.

W.C. FIELDS

Having one child makes you a parent; having two you are a referee.

DAVID FROST

The face of a child can say it all, especially the mouth part of the face.

JACK HANDEY

Most people don't realise that large pieces of coral, which have been painted brown and attached to the skull by common wood screws, can make a child look like a deer.

JACK HANDEY

The moment you have children yourself, you forgive your parents everything.

SUSAN HILL

Children are unpredictable. You never know what inconsistency they're going to catch you in next.

FRANKLIN P. JONES

The real menace in dealing with a five-year-old is that in no time at all you begin to sound like a five-year-old.

JEAN KERR, *Please Don't Eat the Daisies*

What is the advantage of having a kid at forty-nine? So you can both be in diapers at the same time?

SUE KOLINSKY

If you want your children to listen, try talking softly – to someone else.

ANN LANDERS

There are many things you can learn from children – like how much patience you have.
FRAN LEBOWITZ

There is nobody who is thirstier than a four-year-old who has just gone to bed.
FRAN LEBOWITZ

If thine enemy offend thee, give his child a drum.
FRAN LEBOWITZ

Even when freshly washed and relieved of all obvious confections, children tend to be sticky.
FRAN LEBOWITZ

Your responsibility as a parent is not as great as you might imagine. You need not supply the world with the next conqueror of disease or major motion picture star. If your child simply grows up to be someone who does not use the word 'collectible' as a noun, you can consider yourself an unqualified success.
FRAN LEBOWITZ

Children are the emotional glue in most marriages.
KATHY LETTE

Kids. They're not easy. But there has to be some penalty for sex.
BILL MAHER

I've got seven kids. The three words you hear most around my house are 'hello', 'goodbye', and 'I'm pregnant'.
DEAN MARTIN

Adorable children are considered to be the general property of the human race. Rude children belong to their mothers.
JUDITH MARTIN

She was growing up, and that was the direction I wanted her to take. Who wants a daughter that grows sideways?
SPIKE MILLIGAN, *Indefinite Articles*

I love children. Especially when they cry – for then someone takes them away.
NANCY MITFORD

Even very young children need to be informed about dying. Explain the concept of death very carefully to your child. This will make threatening him with it much more effective.
P.J. O'ROURKE

Everybody knows how to raise children except the people who have them.
P.J. O'ROURKE

Humans are the only animals that have children on purpose with the exception of guppies, who like to eat theirs.　　　　　　　　P.J. O'ROURKE

You know your children are growing up when they stop asking you where they came from and refuse to tell you where they're going.　　　　P.J. O'ROURKE

The best way to keep children home is to make the home atmosphere pleasant and let the air out of the tyres.　　　　　　　　DOROTHY PARKER

Adopted kids are such a pain – you have to teach them how to look like you.
　　　　　　　　　　　　　　　　　　　GILDA RADNER

I'm trying to decide whether or not to have children. My time is running out. I know I want to have children while my parents are still young enough to take care of them.　　　　　　　　　　　　RITA RUDNER

That's the thing about independently minded children. You bring them up teaching them to question authority, and you forget that the very first authority they question is you.　　　　　　　　　　　　SUSAN SARANDON

A two-year-old is like having a blender, but you don't have a top for it.
　　　　　　　　　　　　　　　　　　JERRY SEINFELD

I'm getting to the age where I'm thinking about having little stepkids of my own. Maybe a thirteen-year-old daughter to bond with. Take her out, get her tattooed or something. I don't care, she's not my kid.　　　　TRACY SMITH

There are only two things a child will share willingly – communicable diseases and his mother's age.　　　　　　　　DR BENJAMIN SPOCK

A three-year-old child is a being who gets almost as much fun out of a $300 set of swings as it does out of finding a small green caterpillar.
　　　　　　　　　　　　　　　　　　BILL VAUGHAN

Children begin by loving their parents; as they grow older they judge them; sometimes they forgive them.　　OSCAR WILDE, *The Picture of Dorian Gray*

Children used to ask their parents where they came from; now they tell them where to go.

There are three ways to get something done: do it yourself, hire someone, or forbid your kids to do it.

Chocolate

I wouldn't give anybody my last Rolo, even if they were in a diabetic coma.
JO BRAND

Anything is good if it's made of chocolate.
JO BRAND

Don't wreck a sublime chocolate experience by feeling guilty. Chocolate isn't like premarital sex. It will not make you pregnant. And it always feels good.
LORA BRODY

Chocolate-covered raisins? I'd like to meet the idiot who came up with these. Take a grape, let it shrivel into a disgusting little wart, cover it with perfectly good chocolate. What the hell, I'll just suck the chocolate off.
ROZ DOYLE (PERI GILPIN), *Frasier*

There are only two kinds of women in this world — those who love chocolate, and complete bitches.
DAWN FRENCH

I think I've scratched the surface after twenty years of marriage. Women want chocolate and conversation.
MEL GIBSON

There's nothing better than a good friend, except a good friend with chocolate.
LINDA GRAYSON

It's not that chocolates are a substitute for love. Love is a substitute for chocolate. Chocolate is, let's face it, far more reliable than a man.
MIRANDA INGRAM

Researchers have discovered that chocolate produced some of the same reactions in the brain as marijuana. The researchers also discovered other similarities between the two, but can't remember what they are.
MATT LAUER

All I really need is love, but a little chocolate now and then doesn't hurt.
CHARLES SCHULZ, *Peanuts*

Strength is the capacity to break a chocolate bar into four pieces with your bare hands, and then eat just one of the pieces.
JUDITH VIORST

Chocolate is cheaper than therapy and you don't need an appointment.

A chocolate in the mouth is worth two on the plate.

If not for chocolate, there would be no need for control top pantyhose. An entire garment industry would be devastated.

Christmas

There's nothing sadder in this world than to awake Christmas morning and not be a child.
ERMA BOMBECK

Oh, joy, Christmas Eve. By this time tomorrow, millions of Americans, knee-deep in tinsel and wrapping paper, will utter those heartfelt words: 'Is this all I got?'
FRASIER CRANE (KELSEY GRAMMER), *Cheers*

Christmas at my house is always at least six or seven times more pleasant than anywhere else. We start drinking early. And while everyone else is seeing only one Santa Claus, we'll be seeing six or seven.
W.C. FIELDS

Next to a circus there ain't nothing that packs up and tears out of town any quicker than the Christmas spirit.
KIN HUBBARD

The day after Christmas is like the day after the senior prom, everybody asking each other, 'What did you get?'
JAY LENO

The best stocking stuffer is a human leg.
NORM MACDONALD

Why is it that when snooty department stores put their Christmas decorations out just after the 4th of July it's 'elegant foresight', but when I leave my Christmas lights up until April, my neighbours think I'm just tacky?
ALISA MEADOWS

The one thing women do not want to find in their stockings on Christmas morning is their husband.
JOAN RIVERS

Aren't we forgetting the true meaning of Christmas? You know, the birth of Santa.
BART SIMPSON, *The Simpsons*

From a commercial point of view, if Christmas did not exist it would be necessary to invent it.
KATHARINE WHITEHORN

I love Christmas. I receive a lot of wonderful presents I can't wait to exchange.
HENNY YOUNGMAN

A puppy isn't just for Christmas – if you're lucky, there should be some left over for Boxing Day dinner as well.

Church

I have no objections to churches so long as they do not interfere with God's work.
BROOKS ATKINSON

Sir, you are one of the most foul, disgusting, immoral, perverted men that I have ever known. Have you considered a career in the church?
BABY-EATING BISHOP of BATH AND WELLS, *Blackadder*

As for the British churchman, he goes to church as he goes to the bathroom, with the minimum of fuss and no explanation if he can help it.
RONALD BLYTHE, *The Age of Illusion*

The secret of a good sermon is to have a good beginning and a good ending, then having the two as close together as possible.
GEORGE BURNS

While people may not be a great deal wiser after my sermons, they are always a great deal older.
WILLIAM RALPH INGE

A good sermon should be like a woman's skirt: short enough to arouse interest but long enough to cover the essentials.
RONALD KNOX

I still say a church steeple with a lightning rod on top shows a lack of confidence.
DOUG MCLEOD

Whatever happened to the separation of church and hate? Everybody take it easy. I'm pretty sure God's registered as an independent.
DENNIS MILLER

Going to church does not make you a Christian any more than going to the garage makes you a car.
LAURENCE J. PETER

I'm not a bad guy. I work hard and I love my kids. So why should I spend half my Sunday hearing about how I'm going to Hell?
HOMER SIMPSON, *The Simpsons*

Winston Churchill

I thought he was a young man of promise, but it appears he is a young man of promises.
ARTHUR JAMES BALFOUR

He would rather make love to a word than to a woman.
INGRID BERGMAN

The mediocrity of his thinking is concealed by the majesty of his language.
ANEURIN BEVAN

When I am right, I get angry. Churchill gets angry when he is wrong. We are angry at each other much of the time.   CHARLES DE GAULLE

He would make a drum out of the skin of his mother in order to sound his own praises.   DAVID LLOYD GEORGE

Cinema

For some reason, I'm more appreciated in France than I am at home. The subtitles must be incredibly good.   WOODY ALLEN

(*on his penchant for making soft-porn movies*) I put two big balls and a big cock between the legs of Italian cinema.   TINTO BRASS

I've yet to be convinced that the film business is a profession for adults.
FREDERICK FORSYTH

I love British cinema like a doctor loves his dying patient.   BEN KINGSLEY

Circle

A circle is the longest distance to the same point.
TOM STOPPARD, *Every Good Boy Deserves Favour*

Class

Put three Englishmen on a desert island and within an hour they'll have invented a class system.   ALAN AYCKBOURN

I've met a better class of person in the gutter than I have in the drawing-room.
JEFFREY BERNARD, *Low Life*

There's the aristocracy, the upper class, middle class, working class, dumb animals, waiters, creeping things, head lice, people who eat packaged soup, and then you.   GARETH BLACKSTOCK (LENNY HENRY), *Chef!*

Sex you can get anywhere in the world. But class, I mean, real class, you can only get in Britain.   MALCOLM BRADBURY, *Love on a Gunboat*

We must be crooked but never common.
'COLONEL' HARRY HARRINGTON (CHARLES COBURN), *The Lady Eve*

The essence of a class system is not that the privileged are conscious of their privileges, but that the deprived are conscious of their deprivation.

CLIVE JAMES, *Unreliable Memoirs*

Britain is the society where the ruling class does not rule, the working class does not work and the middle class is not in the middle.

GEORGE MIKES, *English Humour for Beginners*

I have changed. I no longer keep coal in the bath, I keep it in the bidet.

JOHN PRESCOTT

I have to live for others and not for myself; that's middle class morality.

GEORGE BERNARD SHAW, *Pygmalion*

(*on his working class roots*) If I had the choice between smoked salmon and tinned salmon, I'd have it tinned. With vinegar.   HAROLD WILSON

Bill Clinton

The prince of sleaze.   JERRY BROWN

Clinton is a man who thinks international affairs means dating a girl from out of town.   TOM CLANCY

A hard dog to keep on the porch.   HILLARY RODHAM CLINTON

When I was President, I said I was a Ford, not a Lincoln. Well what we have now is a convertible Dodge.   GERALD FORD

(*on the fall of Saddam Hussein's statue in Baghdad, 2003*) Did you see the statue topple? Bill Clinton got nostalgic seeing something that big in a beret go down.   CRAIG KILBORN

Bill Clinton was in Arizona today visiting the Virgin River. He didn't go in. He just stood at the mouth.   JAY LENO

Can you believe there's only two days left in the Clinton administration? Boy, time flies when you're having sex.   JAY LENO

Former President Bill Clinton will not be hosting a talk show here at NBC. I believe this marks the first time that Clinton has ever turned down a desk job.

JAY LENO

On Friday the 13th Bill Clinton won't have sex under a ladder.

DAVID LETTERMAN

Monica Lewinsky turns thirty-one today. It seems like only yesterday she was crawling around on all fours in the Oval Office.   DAVID LETTERMAN

(*on hearing that the Clintons were to give away White House cat Socks*) It's the first time Clinton has ever rejected pussy in his life.   G. GORDON LIDDY

The Republican Party always believed Clinton would bring the country to its knees – they just didn't think he'd do it one person at a time.

BOB MONKHOUSE

Last time I saw Clinton he was swinging on the chandelier in the Oval Office with a brassiere around his head, Viagra in one hand and a Bible in the other, and he was torn between good and evil.   JAMES TRAFICANT

Clinton is most comfortable when thinking about little things – school uniforms, the minimum wage and, above all, himself.   GEORGE F. WILL

Hillary Rodham Clinton

I always feel a genuine bond whenever I see Senator Clinton. She's the only person who's at the centre of more conspiracy theories than I am.

DICK CHENEY

(*on the prospect of Hillary Clinton baring her rear in a magazine*) They don't have a page that broad.   GENNIFER FLOWERS

Hillary Clinton said in her book it was a challenge to forgive Bill, but she figured if Nelson Mandela could forgive, she could give it a try. Isn't that amazing? I didn't know Clinton hit on Mandela's wife.   JAY LENO

Hillary Clinton officially announced her Senate candidacy in front of two hundred of the faithful, plus her husband.   JAY LENO

When they swore her in, she used the Clinton family Bible. You know, the one with only seven commandments.   DAVID LETTERMAN

A raisin-eyed, carrot-nosed, twig-armed, straw-stuffed mannequin trundled on a go-kart by the mentally bereft powerbrokers of the Democratic Party.

CAMILLE PAGLIA

Clothes

My dad's pants kept creeping up on him. By sixty-five he was just a pair of pants and a head.
JEFF ALTMAN

Can young people wear their pants any lower? Their waistbands are now at approximately knee level. Where will this trend end? The shins? The feet? Will young people eventually detach themselves from their pants altogether and just drag them along behind, connected to their ankles by a belt?
DAVE BARRY

Dress simply. If you wear a dinner jacket, don't wear anything else on it — like lunch or dinner.
GEORGE BURNS

Why do women wear tights? Haven't they seen what they do to a bank raider's face?
JASPER CARROTT

My wife met me at the door wearing a see-through negligee. Unfortunately she was just coming home.
RODNEY DANGERFIELD

That's a nice top. There must be a Cortina going about without seat covers.
JIM DAVIDSON

In my day, hot pants were something we had, not wore.
BETTE DAVIS

Don't spend two pounds on dry cleaning a shirt. Donate it to the Salvation Army instead. They'll clean it and put it on a hanger, and then you can buy it back for fifty pence.
JACK DEE

According to a new survey, women say they feel more comfortable undressing in front of men than they do undressing in front of other women. They say that women are too judgmental, whereas, of course, men are just grateful.
ROBERT DE NIRO

I don't care whether I am seen in a T-shirt and jeans and whether I have make-up. Once a burger and chips addict, always a burger and chips addict.
CAMERON DIAZ

I dress for women and undress for men.
ANGIE DICKINSON

I have an *Alice in Wonderland* White Rabbit costume in a wardrobe. I had it for a school play when I was nine. I can't get into it now but if I'm feeling very low, I sometimes put on the polystyrene ears to watch TV.
HUGH GRANT

Your dresses should be tight enough to show you're a woman and loose enough to show you're a lady.   EDITH HEAD

This shirt is dry clean only, which means . . . it's dirty.   MITCH HEDBERG

No boy should have a $95 shirt unless he is on stage with his four brothers.
                                    CLIFF HUXTABLE (BILL COSBY), *The Cosby Show*

People used to complain to me all the time, 'I can't even hear you sing because your clothes are so loud.'   CYNDI LAUPER

(*on the 1970s*) There we were in the middle of a sexual revolution wearing clothes that guaranteed we wouldn't get laid!   DENIS LEARY

A woman's dress should be like a barbed wire fence: serving its purpose without obstructing the view.   SOPHIA LOREN

Today a man can see practically the whole woman at a single glance. It's swallowing a meal at one mouthful.   SOPHIA LOREN

(*on Christina Aguilera*) She couldn't be in the band [Atomic Kitten], no way. Not with those outfits. Her stylist wants to have a word.   LIZ MCLARNON

Is there anything worn under the kilt? No, it's all in perfect working order.
                                                                SPIKE MILLIGAN

Nice outfit. I can really see what you were trying to do.
                                    TWIST MORGAN (KATY CARMICHAEL), *Spaced*

That's quite a dress you almost have on.
                                    JERRY MULLIGAN (GENE KELLY), *An American in Paris*

You ought to get out of those wet clothes and into a dry Martini.
                                    PEACHES O'DAY (MAE WEST), *Every Day's a Holiday*

Never wear anything that panics the cat.   P.J. O'ROURKE

(*on Cherie Blair's dress sense*) Off the top of my head, I cannot think of a single reason why anyone over the age of thirty-five would contemplate wearing powder blue.   ANNE ROBINSON

Every time a woman leaves off something she looks better, but every time a man leaves off something he looks worse.   WILL ROGERS

Some women hold up dresses that are so ugly and they always say the same thing: 'This looks much better on.' On what? On fire?   RITA RUDNER

When a woman tries on clothing from her closet that feels tight, she will assume she has gained weight. When a man tries something from his closet that feels tight, he will assume the clothing has shrunk.   RITA RUDNER

A dress has no meaning unless it makes a man want to take it off.

FRANÇOISE SAGAN

Women dress alike all over the world: they dress to be annoying to other women.

ELSA SCHIAPARELLI

I once had a leather jacket that got ruined in the rain. Why does moisture ruin leather? Aren't cows outside a lot of the time? When it's raining, do cows go up to the farmhouse: 'Let us in! We're all wearing leather! Open the door! We're going to ruin the whole outfit here!'   JERRY SEINFELD

Clothes make the man. Naked people have little or no influence in society.

MARK TWAIN

I went to buy some camouflage trousers the other day but I couldn't find any.

TIM VINE

Brains are never a handicap to a girl if she hides them under a see-through blouse.   BOBBY VINTON

Blanche Devereaux (Rue McClanahan): What do you think of my new dress? Is it me?
Sophia Petrillo (Estelle Getty): It's too tight, it's too short, and shows too much cleavage for a woman your age.
Dorothy Zbornak (Bea Arthur): Yes, Blanche. It's you.   *The Golden Girls*

A woman knows she's wearing the right dress when her man wants to take it off.

Just because it's your size, doesn't mean you have to wear it.

Clowns

I once made love to a female clown. It was weird, because she twisted my penis into a poodle.   DAN WHITNEY

If ever you're about to be mugged by a pair of clowns, don't hesitate: go for the juggler.

Clubs

So have you heard about the oyster who went to a disco and pulled a mussel?
BILLY CONNOLLY

I believe in clubs for women, but only if every other form of persuasion fails.
W.C. FIELDS

(*on being barred from a Californian beach club on racial grounds*) Since my daughter is only half-Jewish, could she go in the water up to her knees?
GROUCHO MARX

To be an Englishman is to belong to the most exclusive club there is.
OGDEN NASH, *England Expects*

Coffee

English coffee tastes like water that has been squeezed out of a wet sleeve.
FRED ALLEN

Like any drug, caffeine can have serious side effects if we ingest too much. This fact was noticed in Ancient Egypt when a group of workers, who were supposed to be making a birdbath, began drinking Egyptian coffee, which is very strong, and wound up constructing the Pyramids.
DAVE BARRY

In Seattle you haven't had enough coffee until you can thread a sewing machine while it's running.
JEFF BEZOS

Coffee in England always tastes like a chemistry experiment.
AGATHA CHRISTIE

I'll have a double cappuccino, half-caf, non-fat milk, with enough foam to be aesthetically pleasing but not to leave me with a moustache.
NILES CRANE (DAVID HYDE PIERCE), *Frasier*

I wouldn't have coffee enemas. Aren't they horrible? I suppose you go into Starbucks and ask for the screens to be put around. Anyway, who wants part of their anatomy awake all night?
DAME EDNA EVERAGE

I like my coffee like I like my women – in a plastic cup.
EDDIE IZZARD

I never drink coffee at lunch – I find it keeps me awake for the afternoon.

RONALD REAGAN

I put instant coffee in a microwave oven and almost went back in time.

STEVEN WRIGHT

If men were more like coffee, they'd all be rich, warm and keep you up all night.

You can tell you're drinking too much coffee when the only time you're standing still is during an earthquake.

You can tell you're drinking too much coffee when you have to watch videos in fast-forward.

You can tell you're drinking too much coffee when you chew on other people's fingernails.

You can tell you're drinking too much coffee when you don't sweat, you percolate.

You can tell you're drinking too much coffee when instant coffee takes too long.

You can tell you're drinking too much coffee when you ski uphill.

You can tell you're drinking too much coffee when you answer the door before people knock.

You can tell you're drinking too much coffee when you help your dog chase its tail.

You can tell you're drinking too much coffee when Starbucks owns the mortgage on your house.

College

I believe that we parents must encourage our children to become educated, so they can get into a good college that we cannot afford.   DAVE BARRY

College is a place to keep warm between high school and an early marriage.

GEORGE GOBEL

A telephone survey says that 51 per cent of college students drink until they pass out at least once a month. The other 49 per cent didn't answer the phone.

CRAIG KILBORN

Things You Don't Want To Hear From Your New College Roommate:
'I'm studying viruses . . . Wanna see my West Nile mosquitos?'
'Hope you like toothless drifters . . .'
'Good news! Everything we do will be broadcast live on the Internet.'
'Sorry this plastic bubble I live in takes up so much space.'
'Do you want to be on the top or the bottom and I know we don't have bunkbeds?'
'Me no like room-mate . . . Me wait till room-mate sleeps, then no more room-mate.'
DAVID LETTERMAN

American students are like American colleges — each has half-dulled faculties.
JAMES THURBER

College athletes used to get a degree in bringing your pencil.
RUBY WAX

You're a college student if your trash is overflowing and your bank account isn't.

You're a college student if it takes a shovel to find the floor of your room.

Comedians

(*on Milton Berle*) He's done everybody's act. He's a parrot with skin on.
FRED ALLEN

(*on Milton Berle*) He's been on TV for ages and I finally figured out the reason for his success. He never improved.
STEVE ALLEN

Bob Monkhouse's jokes will live on . . . as long as Jim Davidson has a career.
JIMMY CARR

Chevy Chase couldn't ad-lib a fart after a baked-bean dinner.
JOHNNY CARSON

I have a television set in every room of the house but one. There has to be some place you can go when Bob Monkhouse is on.
BENNY HILL

(*on Paul Merton*) An alien from Planet Stroppy.
IAN HISLOP

Sandra Bernhard is as much fun as barbed wire.
TOM HUTCHINSON

Jimmy Tarbuck doesn't tell gags — he just refreshes your memory.
BERNARD MANNING

(*on Jerry Lewis*) At some point he said to himself, I'm extraordinary, like Chaplin. From then on nobody could tell him anything. He knew it all.

DEAN MARTIN

People always say, 'You're a comedian, tell us a joke.' They don't say, 'You're an MP, tell us a lie.' BOB MONKHOUSE

Over the past fifty years Bob Hope employed eighty-eight joke-writers who supplied him with more than one million gags. And he still couldn't make me laugh. EDDIE MURPHY

(*on Frank Skinner*) The amount of money he's earned for not making me laugh is staggering. WILL SELF

(*on Robin Williams*) A fellow with the inventiveness of Albert Einstein but with the attention span of Daffy Duck. TOM SHALES

Many people are surprised to hear that we have comedians in Russia, but they are there. They are dead, but they are there. YAKOV SMIRNOFF

If Roseanne Barr is the new Lucille Ball, I'm the new Garbo! NANCY WALKER

It's tradition for female comics to put down their boyfriends, but I couldn't find a vet willing to do it. CAL WILSON

A comedian is someone who knows a good joke when he steals one.

Comedy

Comedy is a blood sport. It flays the truth and spurts twisted logic. In America, people become comics because we don't have bullfighting.

ELAYNE BOOSLER

Tragedy is if I cut my finger. Comedy is if you walk into an open sewer and die.

MEL BROOKS

Comedy equals tragedy plus distance. LENNY BRUCE

I think it's the duty of the comedian to find out where the line is drawn and cross it deliberately. GEORGE CARLIN

All I need to make comedy is a park, a policeman and a pretty girl.

CHARLIE CHAPLIN

Comedy, like sodomy, is an unnatural act.   MARTY FELDMAN

They say the seeds of what we will do are in all of us, but it always seemed
to me that in those who make jokes in life the seeds are covered with better
soil and with a higher grade of manure.   ERNEST HEMINGWAY

The difference between English and American humour is $150 a minute.
                                                            ERIC IDLE

Comedy is the art of making people laugh without making them puke.
                                                        STEVE MARTIN

Everything is funny as long as it is happening to somebody else.   WILL ROGERS

Humour is emotional chaos remembered in tranquillity.   JAMES THURBER

Comedy is simply a funny way of being serious.   PETER USTINOV

Commercials

Americans love the Home Shopping Network because it's commercial free.
                                                          WILL DURST

Seeing a murder on television . . . can help work off one's antagonisms. And if you
haven't any antagonisms, the commercials will give you some.   ALFRED HITCHCOCK

It is difficult to produce a television documentary that is both incisive and probing
when every twelve minutes one is interrupted by twelve dancing rabbits singing
about toilet paper.   ROD SERLING

Homer Simpson: Well, here we are. The whole family. All together, sharing,
getting to know each other, exchanging ideas, stories and laughs, snuggling up,
bonding together as only a tightly knit family can. Why, we're more than a . . .
Bart: Dad, you can stop now. The commercial's over. The show's back on.
Homer: Oh. Oh, yeah.   *The Simpsons*

The only reason I made a commercial for American Express was to pay for my
American Express bill.   PETER USTINOV

Commitment

'I'm sorry,' guys are always telling women, 'but I'm just not ready to make a
commitment.' Guys are in a permanent state of nonreadiness. If guys were turkey
breasts, you could put them in a 350-degree oven on July 4th, and they still
wouldn't be done in time for Thanksgiving.   DAVE BARRY

I can't get engaged because that requires calling people back.

CHARLIE GRANDY

I'm not just involved in tennis but committed. Do you know the difference between involvement and commitment? Think of ham and eggs. The chicken is involved. The pig is committed. MARTINA NAVRATILOVA

If you never want to see a man again, say: 'I love you, I want to marry you. I want to have children . . .' They leave skid marks. RITA RUDNER

Why is commitment such a big problem for a man? When a man is driving down that freeway of love, the woman he's involved with is like an exit. But he doesn't want to get out, he wants to keep driving. The woman is like, 'Look, gas, food, lodging, that's our exit, that's everything we need to be happy, get out, here, now!' But the man is focusing on the sign underneath. It says, 'Next exit, 27 miles.' And he thinks, 'I can make it!' JERRY SEINFELD

When women hold off from marrying men, we call it independence; when men hold off from marrying women, we call it fear of commitment.

Committees

A committee is a group that keeps the minutes and loses hours.

MILTON BERLE

A committee is a cul-de-sac down which ideas are lured and then quietly strangled. BARNETT COCKS

What is a committee? A group of the unwilling, picked from the unfit, to do the unnecessary. RICHARD HARKNESS

A committee is an animal with four back legs.

JOHN LE CARRÉ, *Tinker, Tailor, Soldier, Spy*

(*when writers complained of changes to their work*) The number one book of the ages was written by a committee, and it was called The Bible.

LOUIS B. MAYER

A committee should consist of three men, two of whom are absent.

HERBERT BEERBOHM TREE

Any committee that is the slightest use is composed of people who are too busy to want to sit on it for a second longer than they have to.

KATHARINE WHITEHORN

Common sense

Common sense is the collection of prejudices acquired by age eighteen.

ALBERT EINSTEIN

I've got plenty of common sense . . . I just choose to ignore it.

BILL WATTERSON, *Calvin and Hobbes*

Even a fish wouldn't get into trouble if it kept its mouth shut.

KOREAN PROVERB

Communication

Men and women belong to different species and communication between them is still in its infancy.

BILL COSBY

The world has seen many spectacular advances in communications with satellites and all, but the quickest is still the wink.

SAM EWING

The mobile phone, the fax machine, the e-mail . . . call me old-fashioned but what's wrong with a chain of beacons, eh?

HARRY HILL

Communism

I'm a Communist by day and a Catholic as soon as it gets dark.

BRENDAN BEHAN

Under capitalism, man exploits man. Under communism, it's just the opposite.

J.K. GALBRAITH

Communist: one who has nothing, and is eager to share it with others.

Company

For the single woman preparing for company means wiping the lipstick off the milk carton.

ELAYNE BOOSLER

When you lie down with dogs, you get up with fleas.

JEAN HARLOW

Excuse me while I brush the crumbs out of my bed. I'm expecting company.

GROUCHO MARX

My father used to go round in strange circles – one of his legs was shorter than the other.   RIK MAYALL

Two's company. Three's the result.

Competition

Competition brings out the best in products and the worst in people.
DAVID SARNOFF

Complacency

Nothing wilts faster than laurels that have been rested on.   CARL ROWAN

Compliments

Some people pay a compliment as if they expect a receipt.   KIN HUBBARD

When a man makes a woman his wife, it's the highest compliment he can pay her – and it's usually the last.   HELEN ROWLAND

I can live for two months on a good compliment.   MARK TWAIN

Composers

All Bach's last movements are like the running of a sewing machine.
ARNOLD BAX

Beethoven's last quartets were written by a deaf man and should only be listened to by a deaf man.   THOMAS BEECHAM

I have never heard any Stockhausen, but I do believe I have stepped in some.
THOMAS BEECHAM

Listening to the Fifth Symphony of Ralph Vaughan Williams is like staring at a cow for forty-five minutes.   AARON COPLAND

Berlioz says nothing in his music, but he says it magnificently.
JAMES G. HUNEKER

The problem with [Andrew] Lloyd Webber's music is not that it sounds as if it were written by other composers, but that it sounds as if it were written by Lloyd Webber.   GERALD KAUFMAN

I can't listen to that much Wagner. I start getting the urge to conquer Poland.

LARRY (WOODY ALLEN), *Manhattan Murder Mystery*

It is a sobering thought that when Mozart was my age he had been dead for two years.

TOM LEHRER

(*on Frederick Delius*) The musical equivalent of blancmange.

BERNARD LEVIN

(*of Igor Stravinsky*) Bach on the wrong notes.

SERGEY PROKOFIEV

One cannot judge Wagner's opera *Lohengrin* after a first hearing and I have no intention of sitting through it a second time.

GIOACCHINO ROSSINI

Beethoven always sounds to me like the upsetting of a bag of nails, with here and there an also dropped hammer.

JOHN RUSKIN

Sometimes I think, not so much am I a pianist, but a vampire. All my life I have lived off the blood of Chopin.

ARTUR RUBINSTEIN

Brahms is an extraordinary musician, with the brains of a third-rate village policeman.

GEORGE BERNARD SHAW

[Edward] Elgar is one of the Seven Humbugs of Christendom.

GEORGE BERNARD SHAW

(*on Grieg's* Peer Gynt) Two or three catch-penny phrases served up with plenty of orchestral sugar.

GEORGE BERNARD SHAW

[Arnold] Schoenberg would be better off shovelling snow.

RICHARD STRAUSS

(*on Sergei Rachmaninov*) A six-and-a-half-foot-tall scowl.

IGOR STRAVINSKY

[Richard] Wagner's music is better than it sounds.

MARK TWAIN

After Rossini dies, who will there be to promote his music?

RICHARD WAGNER

Compromise

A compromise is the art of dividing a cake in such a way that everyone believes he has the biggest piece.

LUDWIG ERHARD

The man who is willing to meet you halfway is usually a poor judge of distance.
LAURENCE J. PETER

You might as well fall flat on your face as lean over too far backward.
JAMES THURBER, *Fables For Our Time*

Computer programmers

A computer is a stupid machine with the ability to do incredibly smart things, while computer programmers are smart people with the ability to do incredibly stupid things. BILL BRYSON

Programming today is a race between software engineers striving to build bigger and better idiot-proof programs, and the universe trying to produce bigger and better idiots. So far, the universe is winning. RICH COOK

If builders built buildings the way programmers wrote programs, then the first woodpecker that came along would destroy civilisation.
HARRY WEINBERGER

Computers

Part of the inhumanity of the computer is that, once it is completely programmed and working smoothly, it is completely honest. ISAAC ASIMOV

If you asked me to name the three scariest threats facing the human race, I would give the same answer that most people would: nuclear war, global warming and Windows. DAVE BARRY

The word 'user' is the word used by the computer professional when they mean idiot. DAVE BARRY

Software: These programs give instruction to the CPU, which processes billions of tiny facts called bytes, and within a fraction of a second it sends you an error message that requires you to call the customer-support hot line and be placed on hold for approximately the life-span of a caribou. DAVE BARRY

The computer was working fine when Rob (my son) started; after several hours of installation, it was a totally dysfunctional, muttering, potentially violent thing, and we had to take it outside and shoot it. DAVE BARRY

In the Computer Revolution everything changes way too fast for the human brain to comprehend. That is why only fourteen-year-olds really understand what is going on. DAVE BARRY

The other day I called my computer helpline, because I needed to be made to feel ignorant by someone much younger than me.

BILL BRYSON, *Notes from a Big Country*

Computers are like Old Testament gods; lots of rules and no mercy.

JOSEPH B. CAMPBELL

Reading computer manuals without the hardware is as frustrating as reading sex manuals without the software.   ARTHUR C. CLARKE, *The Odyssey File*

The question of whether computers can think is like the question of whether submarines can swim.   EDSGAR DIJKSTRA

To err is human, but to really foul things up you need a computer.

PAUL EHRLICH

The perfect computer has been developed. You just feed in your problems and they never come out again.   AL GOODMAN

That's what's cool about working with computers. They don't argue, they remember everything and they don't drink all your beer.   PAUL LEARY

I stare at the key marked HELP on my keyboard. If only it could.

DAVID LODGE, *Therapy*

A debugged program is one for which you have not yet found the conditions that make it fail.   JERRY OGDIN

To err is human – and to blame it on a computer is even more so.

ROBERT ORBEN

You could use your old computer to shop for a new computer online. But that seems kind of cruel, doesn't it? Like asking your dying spouse if he or she has any cute friends.   SCOTT OSTLER

Imagine if every Thursday your shoes exploded if you tied them the usual way. This happens to us all the time with computers, and nobody thinks of complaining.

JEFF RASKIN

A computer lets you make more mistakes faster than any invention in human history – with the possible exceptions of hand guns and tequila.

MITCH RATLIFFE

Computers make it easier to do a lot of things, but most of the things they make it easier to do don't need to be done. ANDY ROONEY

Maybe some things *do* improve with age, but no matter how long I wait, my Commodore 64 just won't run Windows 95. KEITH SULLIVAN

We used to have lots of questions to which there were no answers. Now, with the computer, there are lots of answers to which we haven't thought up the questions. PETER USTINOV

There is only one satisfying way to boot a computer.

Failure is not an option. It's included in the software.

Home computers are being called upon to perform many new functions, including the consumption of homework formerly eaten by the dog.

A television may insult your intelligence, but nothing rubs it in like a computer.

A patch is a piece of software which replaces old bugs with new bugs.

A printer consists of three parts: the case, the jammed paper tray and the blinking red light.

Concentration

Nothing interferes with my concentration. You could put on an orgy in my office and I wouldn't look up. Well, maybe once. ISAAC ASIMOV

Conference

A conference is a meeting held to decide when the next meeting will take place.

There is no crisis to which academics will not respond with a conference.

Confidence

We have no faith in ourselves. I have never met a woman who, deep down in her core, really believes she has great legs. And if she suspects that she might have great legs, then she's convinced that she has a shrill voice and no neck. CYNTHIA HEIMEL

Men are self-confident because they grow up identifying with superheroes. Women have bad self-images because they grow up identifying with Barbie.

RITA RUDNER

All you need is ignorance and confidence; then success is sure.

MARK TWAIN

Confidence is the feeling a person has before he fully understands the situation.

Congress

What's the difference between a whore and a congressman? A congressman makes more money.   EDWARD ABBEY

The only way to get elected to Congress is to raise a bunch of campaign money, and pretty much the only way to do that is to already be a member of Congress.

DAVE BARRY

(*on ex-husband Sonny Bono's entry to Congress*) Sonny is perfectly at home there. Politicians are one step below used-car salesmen.   CHER

Senate office hours are from twelve to one with an hour off for lunch.

GEORGE S. KAUFMAN

The reason there are two senators for each state is so that one can be the designated driver.   JAY LENO

Earlier this week the Senate voted for tougher regulations. For example, when corporations buy a senator, they must now get a receipt.   JAY LENO

There ought to be one day – just one – when there is open season on senators.

WILL ROGERS

Conscience

What do you get in place of a conscience? Don't answer, I know: a lawyer.
JIM MCLEOD (KIRK DOUGLAS), *Detective Story*

Conscience is the inner voice which warns us that someone may be looking.
H.L. MENCKEN

Most people sell their souls, and live with a good conscience on the proceeds.
LOGAN PEARSALL SMITH, *Afterthoughts*

A guilty conscience needs no accuser. ENGLISH PROVERB

A clear conscience is usually the sign of a bad memory.

A conscience is what hurts when all your other parts feel so good.

Conscience gets a lot of credit that belongs to cold feet.

Conservatism

A conservative is a man who is too cowardly to fight and too fat to run.
ELBERT HUBBARD

Liberals feel unworthy of their possessions. Conservatives feel they deserve everything they've stolen. MORT SAHL

A conservative is someone who believes in reform. But not now.
MORT SAHL

A conservative is a man who sits and thinks, mostly sits.
WOODROW T. WILSON

A conservative is someone who admires radicals a century after they're dead.

Conservative Party

Tories are not always wrong, but they are always wrong at the right moment.
LADY ASQUITH

(*on Michael Howard's appointment as Conservative Party leader, 2003*) The trouble with the Conservative Party is they are actually going backwards. They have now skipped a generation. At this rate the next leader will have to be exhumed. RORY BREMNER

Consistency

The only completely consistent people are the dead.
ALDOUS HUXLEY, *Do What You Will*

Consistency is the last refuge of the unimaginative. OSCAR WILDE

Consultants

Consultants have credibility because they are not dumb enough to work at your company. SCOTT ADAMS

Hiring consultants to conduct studies can be an excellent means of turning problems into gold: your problems into their gold.   NORMAN R. AUGUSTINE

A consultant is a person called in when nobody wants to take the blame for what's going wrong.   LEONARD ROSSITER, *The Devil's Bedside Book*

A consultant is a man sent in after the battle to bayonet the wounded.

Definition of a consultant: someone who borrows your watch, tells you the time and then charges you for the privilege.

Contraception

My husband and I found this great new method of birth control that really, really works. Every night before we go to bed, we spend an hour with the kids.   ROSEANNE BARR

Have you noticed that all the people in favour of birth control are already born?   BENNY HILL

In Ancient Egypt women used crocodile dung for birth control. Makes you wonder how many other types of dung they tried first.   JAY LENO

Contraceptives should be used on every conceivable occasion.   SPIKE MILLIGAN, *The Last Goon Show Of All*

Scientists have announced the invention of a woman's condom. It works by fitting snugly over a woman's wine glass.   KEVIN NEALON

A friend of mine confused her valium with her birth control pills. She had fourteen kids but didn't give a shit.   JOAN RIVERS

The best contraception is the word 'No' – repeated frequently.   MARGARET CHASE SMITH

(*on Marie Stopes*) I used to think it a pity that her mother rather than she had not thought of birth control.   MURIEL SPARK

A birth control pill for men, that's fair. It makes more sense to take the bullets out of the gun than to wear a bulletproof vest.   GREG TRAVIS

A woman who took the pill with a glass of pond water has been diagnosed three months stagnant.   *The Two Ronnies*

My father was a condom salesman with ten kids. MARLON WAYANS

When mom found my diaphragm, I told her it was a bathing cap for my cat.
LIZZ WINSTEAD

The best form of contraception is a pill – held firmly between the knees.

Did you hear about the new 'morning after' pill for men? It changes your blood type.

Conversation

It is all right to hold a conversation but you should let go of it now and then.
RICHARD ARMOUR

Intimacies between women often go backwards, beginning in revelations and ending in small talk. ELIZABETH BOWEN, *The Death of the Heart*

Seems ages since I had a natter with old Yoko Suji in Tokyo. I wonder how his wife is, what was her name? 'Radiant Flower of the Divine Heavens'. I wonder if her feet are still playing her up. TONY HANCOCK, *Hancock's Half-Hour*

Conversation is the enemy of good wine and food. ALFRED HITCHCOCK

Women speak because they wish to speak, whereas a man speaks only when driven to speech by something outside himself – like, for instance, he can't find any clean socks. JEAN KERR

Polite conversation is rarely either. FRAN LEBOWITZ

That's how conversations go in this family. I tell them my needs, they say no, and dad reveals another cartoon character he's afraid of.
MALCOLM (FRANKIE MUNIZ), *Malcolm in the Middle*

Most conversation are simply monologues delivered in the presence of witnesses.
MARGARET MILLAR

Beware of the conversationalist who adds 'in other words'. He is merely starting afresh. ROBERT MORLEY

(*of Aldous Huxley*) You could always tell by his conversation which volume of the *Encyclopedia Britannica* he'd been reading. One day it would be Alps, Andes and Apennines, and the next it would be the Himalayas and the Hippocratic Oath.
BERTRAND RUSSELL

I just use my muscles as a conversation piece, like someone walking a cheetah down 42nd Street.
ARNOLD SCHWARZENEGGER

If you talk about yourself, he'll think you're boring. If you talk about others, he'll think you're a gossip. If you talk about him, he'll think you're a brilliant conversationalist.
LINDA SUNSHINE

A dialogue is a good monologue spoiled by somebody else talking.
PETER USTINOV

The intelligence of any discussion diminishes with the square of the number of participants.
ADAM WALINSKY

You know, until I met you Rose, I didn't know that people actually talked back to their Rice Krispies.
DOROTHY ZBORNAK (BEA ARTHUR), *The Golden Girls*

Cookery

This recipe is certainly silly. It says to separate two eggs, but it doesn't say how far to separate them.
GRACIE ALLEN

Who bothers to cook TV dinners? I suck them frozen.
WOODY ALLEN

I don't like to say that my kitchen is a religious place, but I would say that if I were a voodoo princess, I would conduct my rituals there.
PEARL BAILEY

When you cook it should be an act of love. To put a frozen bag in the microwave for your child is an act of hate.
RAYMOND BLANC

When it comes to cooking, five years ago I felt guilty 'just adding water'. Now I want to bang the tube against the countertop and have a five-course meal pop out. If it comes with plastic silverware and a plate that self-destructs, all the better.
ERMA BOMBECK

(*on husband David*) He doesn't cook or shop or do anything. Not because he's a rock star, but because I wouldn't trust him. He can't even boil water.
IMAN BOWIE

I don't even butter my bread; I consider that cooking. KATHERINE CEBRIAN

Life is too short to stuff a mushroom. SHIRLEY CONRAN, *Superwoman*

Do not taste food while you're cooking. You may lose your nerve to serve it. PHYLLIS DILLER

If it looks like a duck, walks like a duck, talks like a duck, it probably needs a little more time in the microwave. LORI DOWDY

I cook with wine. Sometimes I even add it to the food. W.C. FIELDS

There is one thing more exasperating than a wife who can cook and won't, and that's the wife who can't cook and will. ROBERT FROST

My husband says I feed him like a god: every meal is a burnt offering. RHONDA HANSOME

I'm such a lousy cook my cat only has three lives left. JOE HICKMAN

(*to Edina*) You've only ever used the cooker to light your fags off. SAFFRON MONSOON (JULIA SAWALHA), *Absolutely Fabulous*

I can't cook. I use a smoke alarm as a timer. JOAN RIVERS

I can never understand why they cook on TV. I can't smell it. Can't eat it. Can't taste it. At the end of the show they hold it up to the camera. 'Well here it is. You can't have any. Thanks for watching. Goodbye.' JERRY SEINFELD

The only premarital thing girls don't do these days is cooking. OMAR SHARIF

I prefer Hostess fruit pies to pop-up toaster tarts because they don't require so much cooking. CARRIE SNOW

While it may be true that a watched pot never boils, the one you don't keep an eye on can make an awful mess of your stove. EDWARD STEVENSON

(*on Grandad's cooking*): Tough? Tough? It's the toughest chicken I've ever known. It's asked me for a fight in the car park twice! DEL TROTTER (DAVID JASON), *Only Fools and Horses*

Cooking is like love. It should be entered into with abandon or not at all. HARRIET VAN HORNE

I'm not saying my wife is a terrible cook, but our garbage disposal has developed an ulcer.
                                                                    HENNY YOUNGMAN

You know you're a bad cook when you consider it a culinary success if the pop-tart stays in one piece.

You know you're a bad cook when your dog goes to the neighbours' to eat.

You know you're a bad cook when it takes a hammer and chisel to remove a casserole from the dish.

You know you're a bad cook when your gravy doesn't move.

You know you're a bad cook when your salad dressing burns a hole in the carpet.

You know you're a bad cook when your family buy indigestion tablets in bulk.

If at first you don't succeed, order pizza.

Calvin Coolidge

Calvin Coolidge's perpetual expression was that of someone smelling something burning on a stove.
                                                                    SHERWIN L. COOK

His one really notable talent . . . he slept more than any other President, whether by day or by night. Nero fiddled, but Coolidge only snored.   H.L. MENCKEN

(*on learning that Coolidge had died*) How can they tell?   DOROTHY PARKER

Calvin Coolidge didn't say much, and when he did he didn't say much.
                                                                    WILL ROGERS

Corruption

I either want less corruption, or more chance to participate in it.
                                                                    ASHLEIGH BRILLIANT

Cosmetic surgery

If I want to wear my tits on my back, that's my business!   CHER

Phyllis Diller's had so many facelifts, there's nothing left in her shoes.
                                                                    BOB HOPE

I don't suggest that her face has been lifted, but there's a possibility that her body has been lowered.
CLIVE JAMES

Joan Rivers' face hasn't just had a lift, it's taken the elevator all the way to the top floor without stopping.
CLIVE JAMES

A study shows breast implants can cause nausea and dizziness – from all the free drinks.
CRAIG KILBORN

Within two years women will be able to get breast enhancement done in their lunch hour. You get turned down for a raise in the morning. In the afternoon you can go in and try again.
JAY LENO

A Beverly Hills plastic surgeon says his patented procedure can make a woman a 'born-again virgin'. I think he's pulling those faces way too tight!
JAY LENO

The thing you notice here after America is how refreshingly ordinary people look because they haven't had their chin wrapped around the back of their ears.
IAN MCKELLEN

My husband said 'show me your boobs' and I had to pull up my skirt . . . so it was time to get them done!
DOLLY PARTON

Plastic surgeons are always making mountains out of molehills.
DOLLY PARTON

I lent a friend of mine $10,000 for plastic surgery and now I don't know what he looks like.
EMO PHILIPS

Not all plastic surgeons are good. My cousin went to one and told him she wanted to turn back the hands of time. Now she has a face that could stop a clock.
JOAN RIVERS

Joan Collins told a reporter that she hasn't had plastic surgery. Come on! She's had more tucks than a motel bedsheet!
JOAN RIVERS

Have I had a facelift? Does Jonathan Ross have difficulty rolling his Rs? Does Michael Winner eat out a lot?
ANNE ROBINSON

I don't plan to grow old gracefully. I plan to have facelifts until my ears meet.
RITA RUDNER

One of the most popular procedures today is the nose job. The technical term for the nose job is rhinoplasty. Rhino? I mean, do we really need to insult the person at this particular moment in their life? They know they have a big nose, that's why they're coming in. Do they really need the abuse of being compared to a rhinoceros on top of everything else?   JERRY SEINFELD

(*on Demi Moore*) I suspect that most men would prefer to see a bosom that turns and moves when the rest of its owner does.   CHRISTOPHER TOOKEY

(*on Demi Moore*) Her remarkably expressionless face stands as an awful warning that plastic surgery can do everything except give you acting ability.
                                                                 CHRISTOPHER TOOKEY

A plastic surgeon's office is the only place where no one gets offended when you pick your nose.

Courage

Corporal Perkins: I must say, Captain, I've got to admire your balls.
Edmund Blackadder (Rowan Atkinson): Perhaps later.
                                                              Blackadder Goes Forth

Bravery is the capacity to perform properly even when scared half to death.
                                                                    OMAR BRADLEY

Courage is grace under pressure.   ERNEST HEMINGWAY

It is better to die on your feet than to live on your knees.   DOLORES IBÁRRURI

Bravery is being the only one who knows you're afraid.
                                                                FRANKLIN P. JONES

The only courage that matters is the kind that gets you from one moment to the next.   MIGNON MCLAUGHLIN

No man in the world has more courage than the man who can stop after eating one peanut.   CHANNING POLLOCK

Cowardice

Coward: one who in a perilous emergency thinks with his legs.
                                              AMBROSE BIERCE, *The Devil's Dictionary*

A team is where a boy can prove his courage on his own. A gang is where a coward goes to hide.   MICKEY MANTLE

Courage is often lack of insight, whereas cowardice in many cases is based on good information.
PETER USTINOV

Joan Crawford

I'm a little repulsed by her shining lips, like balloon tyres in wet weather.
JOHN BETJEMAN

Joan always cries a lot. Her tear ducts must be close to her bladder.
BETTE DAVIS

Why am I so good at playing bitches? I think it's because I'm not a bitch. Maybe that's why Miss Crawford always plays ladies.
BETTE DAVIS

The best time I ever had with Joan Crawford was when I pushed her down the stairs in *Whatever Happened to Baby Jane?*
BETTE DAVIS

She had perfect posture, but it was rather intimidating. She looked as if she'd swallowed a yardstick.
GLENN FORD

She should have puppies, not children.
OSCAR LEVANT

A mean, tipsy, powerful, rotten-egg lady.
MERCEDES McCAMBRIDGE

Joan Crawford would have made an exemplary prison matron, possibly at Buchenwald. She had the requisite sadism, paranoia and taste for violence.
HARRIET VAN HORNE

Creativity

Creativity is allowing yourself to make mistakes. Art is knowing which ones to keep.
SCOTT ADAMS, *The Dilbert Principle*

The act of creating is as integral a part of life as going to the lavatory.
DAVID BOWIE

Creativity varies inversely with the number of cooks involved in the broth.
BERNICE FITZ-GIBBON

Destruction leads to a very rough road, but it also breeds creation.
ANTHONY KIEDIS

Creativity can be described as letting go of certainties.

Creativity is great, but plagiarism is faster.

Credit cards

As a child, a library card takes you to exotic, faraway places. When you're grown up, a credit card does it.
SAM EWING

I was feeling very irritable. It was that difficult time of the month when the credit card statement arrives.
JULIE WALTERS

My wife lost all her credit cards, but I'm not going to report it. Whoever found them spends less than she does.
HENNY YOUNGMAN

I gave my wife plastic surgery – I cut up her credit cards.
HENNY YOUNGMAN

Cricket

A cut so late as to be positively posthumous.
JOHN ARLOTT

The umpire at cricket is like the geyser in the bathroom; we cannot do without it, yet we notice it only when it is out of order.
NEVILLE CARDUS

A Test Match is like a painting. A one-day match is like a Rolf Harris painting.
IAN CHAPPELL

Cricket – a game which the English, not being a spiritual people, have invented in order to give themselves some conception of eternity.
LORD MANCROFT, *Bees in Some Bonnets*

I want to play cricket. It doesn't seem to matter if you win or lose.
MEAT LOAF

I am to cricket what Dame Sybil Thorndike is to non-ferrous welding.
FRANK MUIR

It's a funny kind of month, October. For the really keen cricket fan it's when you discover that your wife left you in May.
DENIS NORDEN

(*comparing baseball unfavourably with cricket*) I don't think I can be expected to take seriously any game which takes less than three days to reach its conclusion.
TOM STOPPARD

(*asked why he bowled slow left-arm*) You can't smoke twenty a day and bowl fast.
PHIL TUFNELL

I cannot for the life of me see why the umpires, the only two people on a cricket field who are not going to get grass stains on their knees, are the only two people allowed to wear dark trousers.
KATHARINE WHITEHORN

Cricket is baseball on valium.
ROBIN WILLIAMS

Crime

I think crime pays. The hours are good, you travel a lot.
WOODY ALLEN

I'd like to get away as quick as possible. I've left my Mercedes parked downstairs and you know what they're like on this estate. They'd have the wheels off a Jumbo if it flew too low.
BOYCIE (JOHN CHALLIS), *Only Fools and Horses*

Good mornin', ladies and gentlemen, this is a robbery. Now if no one loses their head, no one will lose their head.
THELMA DICKINSON (GEENA DAVIS), *Thelma and Louise*

Woman: Is this some kind of bust?
Detective Frank Drebin (Leslie Nielsen): Yes, ma'am, it's very impressive, but we need to ask you a few questions.
Police Squad

Crime in the cities is very discouraging. Apartment house dwellers have locks, bolts, chains, and bars on their doors. It takes a tenant longer to get out than a burglar to get in.
SAM EWING

Disturbing the peace? I got thrown out of a window! What's the fuckin' charge for getting pushed out of a moving car, huh? Jaywalking?
AXEL FOLEY (EDDIE MURPHY), *Beverly Hills Cop*

The cure for crime is not the electric chair, but the high chair.
J. EDGAR HOOVER

A man who worked in a mortuary stole 157lbs of body parts. Bail cost him an arm and a leg.
JAY LENO

On my first day in New York a guy asked me if I knew where Central Park was. When I told him I didn't, he said, 'Do you mind if I mug you here?'
PAUL MERTON

A hijacker at Kennedy Airport stole an armoured car with $1.2 million. He used the money to fill up the truck with gas.   CONAN O'BRIEN

Inside every hardened criminal beats the heart of a ten-year-old boy.
BART SIMPSON, *The Simpsons*

A mugger jumped out on an old lady and searched her for cash. He patted her all over but couldn't find a thing. 'Where's the money?' he snarled. 'I don't have any on me right now,' said the old lady, 'but if you pat me like that for another five minutes, I'll damn sure write you a cheque!'   FLIP WILSON

Crisis

I'm not concerned about all hell breaking loose, but that a *part* of hell will break loose – it'll be much harder to detect.   GEORGE CARLIN

There cannot be a crisis next week. My schedule is already full.
HENRY KISSINGER

Saffron Monsoon (Julia Sawalha): Mum, you've absolved yourself of responsibility. You live from self-induced crisis to self-induced crisis. Someone chooses what you wear. Someone does your brain. Someone tells you what to eat and, three times a week, someone sticks a hose up your bum and flushes it all out for you.
Edina Monsoon (Jennifer Saunders): It's called colonic irrigation, darling, and it's not to be sniffed at.   *Absolutely Fabulous*

Midlife crisis is that moment you realise your children and your clothes are about the same age.

Critics and criticism

A critic is to an author as a fungus to an oak.   EDWARD ABBEY

Literary critics, like a herd of cows or a school of fish, always face in the same direction, obeying that love for unity that every critic requires.
EDWARD ABBEY

I approach reading reviews the way some people anticipate anal warts.
ROSEANNE BARR

(*on critic Clive Barnes*) Giving Clive Barnes his CBE for services to the theatre is like giving Goering the DFC for services to the RAF.   ALAN BENNETT

A good writer is not, per se, a good book critic. No more so than a good drunk is automatically a good bartender.
JIM BISHOP

(*on writer Ford Madox Ford*) His mind was like a Roquefort cheese, so ripe that it was palpably falling to pieces.
VAN WYCK BROOKS

The biggest critics of my books are people who never read them.
JACKIE COLLINS

(*of Julie Burchill*) I cannot take seriously the criticism of someone who doesn't know how to use a semicolon.
SHIRLEY CONRAN

I love criticism, just so long as it is unqualified praise.
NOËL COWARD

(*on Carroll Baker*) More bomb than bombshell.
JUDITH CRIST

(*on Robert Mitchum in* The Winds of War) Nowadays Mitchum doesn't so much act as point his suit at people.
RUSSELL DAVIES

Television criticism is like describing an accident to an eye-witness.
JACKIE GLEASON

(*on Jean Harlow*) Her technique was the gangster's technique – she toted a breast like a man totes a gun.
GRAHAM GREENE

The only thing that bugs me is critics. It's like shooting at a flying saucer as it tries to land, without giving the occupants a chance to identify themselves.
JIMI HENDRIX

A good review from the critics is just another stay of execution.
DUSTIN HOFFMAN

Honest criticism is hard to take, particularly from a relative, a friend, an acquaintance, or a stranger.
FRANKLIN P. JONES

(*on Greer Garson*) One of the most richly syllabled queenly horrors of Hollywood.
PAULINE KAEL

(*on Richard Harris*) He hauls his surly carcass from movie to movie, being dismembered. I'd just as soon wait till he's finished.
PAULINE KAEL

(*on Candice Bergen*) As an actress her only flair is her nostrils.
PAULINE KAEL

(*on Cecil B. De Mille*) He made small-minded pictures on a big scale.

PAULINE KAEL

An actor can remember his briefest notice well into senescence and long after he has forgotten his phone number and where he lives.   JEAN KERR

When it comes to acting, Joan Rivers has the range of a wart.

STEWART KLEIN

(*on coping with hostile criticism*) I cried all the way to the bank.   LIBERACE

My first short story was harshly denounced by one particular critic. I brooded and made caustic remarks about the man. Then one day I reread the story and realised he had been correct. It was shallow and badly constructed. I never forgot the incident and years later, when the Luftwaffe were bombing London, I shone a light on the critic's house.   W. SOMERSET MAUGHAM

Raquel Welch is one of the few actresses in Hollywood history who looks more animated in still photographs than she does on the screen.

MICHAEL MEDVED

Farrah Fawcett is uniquely suited to play a woman of limited intelligence.

MICHAEL MEDVED

If I kept all my bad notices, I'd need two houses.   ROGER MOORE

[George Bernard] Shaw writes his plays for the ages – the ages between five and twelve.   GEORGE JEAN NATHAN

Critics? I love every bone in their heads.   EUGENE O'NEILL

Asking a working writer what he feels about critics is like asking a lamp-post what it feels about dogs.   JOHN OSBORNE

A critic is a legless man who teaches running.   CHANNING POLLOCK

No degree of dullness can safeguard a work against the determination of critics to find it fascinating.   HAROLD ROSENBERG

You stick your head above the crowd and attract attention, and sometime, maybe somebody, will throw a rock at you. That's the territory. You buy the land, you get the Indians.   DAVID LEE ROTH

A drama critic is a man who leaves no turn unstoned.

GEORGE BERNARD SHAW

(*telephoning a critic from the bathroom*) I have your review in front of me and soon it will be behind me.

GEORGE BERNARD SHAW

Pay no attention to what the critics say. Remember, a statue has never been set up in honour of a critic.

JEAN SIBELIUS

(*on Diane Keaton*) An acting style that's really a nervous breakdown in slow motion.

JOHN SIMON

I never read a book before reviewing it; it prejudices a man so.

REV. SYDNEY SMITH

A bad review is like baking a cake with all the best ingredients and having someone sit on it.

DANIELLE STEEL

Critics search for ages for the wrong word which, to give them credit, they eventually find.

PETER USTINOV

Having the critics praise you is like having the hangman say you've got a pretty neck.

ELI WALLACH

Every actor in his heart believes everything bad that's printed about him.

ORSON WELLES

(*on Charlotte Church*) She seems to want to turn herself into a pre-pubescent Shirley Bassey and it's grotesque. It makes my stomach churn.

MICHAEL WHITE

Has anybody ever seen a dramatic critic in the daytime? Of course not. They come out after dark, up to no good.

P.G. WODEHOUSE

Richard Chamberlain is a man with the sex appeal of a sheep and the comic timing of a manatee.

After Arnold Schwarzenegger, Dolph Lundgren is a bit of a disappointment. At least Arnold looks as if he comes supplied with batteries.

Cult

What's a cult? It just means not enough people to make a minority.

ROBERT ALTMAN

Father Dougal McGuire (Ardal O'Hanlon): God, I've heard about those cults, Ted. People dressing up in black and saying Our Lord's going to come back and save us all.
Father Ted Crilly (Dermot Morgan): No, Dougal, that's us. That's Catholicism.
Dougal: Oh, right.

Father Ted

A cult is a religion with no political power.

TOM WOLFE

Curtains

There are some lace curtains popular nowadays that are gathered up for some reason in the middle. They look to me like a woman who's been to the lav and got her underskirt caught up behind her.

ALAN BENNETT, *Talking Heads*

Cynicism

A cynic is just a man who found out when he was about ten that there wasn't any Santa Claus, and he's still upset.

JAMES GOULD COZZENS

A cynic is not merely one who reads bitter lessons from the past; he is one who is prematurely disappointed in the future.

SYDNEY HARRIS

Cynicism is an unpleasant way of telling the truth.

LILLIAN HELLMAN, *The Little Foxes*

The power of accurate observation is commonly called cynicism by those who have not got it.

GEORGE BERNARD SHAW

No matter how cynical you get, you can never keep up.

LILY TOMLIN

Cynicism is humour in ill-health.

H.G. WELLS

The cynic knows the price of everything and the value of nothing.

OSCAR WILDE, *Lady Windermere's Fan*

D

Dance

Dance partners should be changed often, like nappies.

JILLY COOPER, *Jolly Marsupial*

Fred Astaire danced himself so thin, I could almost spit through him.

BING CROSBY

I could dance with you till the cows come home. On second thought, I'd rather dance with the cows and you come home.

RUFUS T. FIREFLY (GROUCHO MARX), *Duck Soup*

(*on* Oh, Calcutta!) The trouble with nude dancing is that not everything stops when the music does.

ROBERT HELPMAN

He makes you feel more danced against than with.

SALLY POPLIN

I did everything Fred Astaire did – except backwards and in high heels.

GINGER ROGERS

Dancing is a perpendicular expression of a horizontal desire.

GEORGE BERNARD SHAW

I got kicked out of *Riverdance* for using my arms.

GARY VALENTINE

My father originated the limbo dance – trying to get into a pay toilet.

SLAPPY WHITE

Darkness

My wife insists on turning off the lights when we make love. That doesn't bother me. It's the hiding that seems so cruel.

JEFF ALTMAN

Younger men are coming on to me. I was flattered when a really cute one asked me to spend the night – until I realised it was because he was afraid of the dark.

JOAN RIVERS

Dating

I was unable to get a date on only six weeks' notice.

WOODY ALLEN, *Getting Even*

I'm a practising heterosexual, but bisexuality immediately doubles your chances for a date on Saturday night.
WOODY ALLEN

When you're dating you're so insecure. My last relationship, I was always there for her and she dumped me. I told her about it. I said, 'Remember when your grandma died? I was there. Remember when you flunked out of school? I was there. Remember when you lost your job? I was there!' She said, 'I know — you're bad luck!'
TOM ARNOLD

Monica Geller (Courteney Cox): It's not a date; it's just two people going out to dinner and not having sex.
Chandler Bing (Matthew Perry): Sounds like a date to me.
Friends

(*on boyfriends*) They were a convenience, something you had to wear when you went to school functions, like a bra.
RITA MAE BROWN, *Rubyfruit Jungle*

Courtship to marriage, as a very witty prologue to a very dull play.
WILLIAM CONGREVE, *The Old Bachelor*

For me to ask a woman out, I've got to get into a mental state like the karate guys before they break the bricks.
GEORGE COSTANZA (JASON ALEXANDER), *Seinfeld*

Roz Doyle (Peri Gilpin): Is there no place I can go without running into some guy I've dated?
Niles Crane (David Hyde Pierce): I was reading about a trappist monastery in the Amazon that they somehow built into the treetops . . .
Frasier

I once had three dates on a single Saturday and still had time to defrost my refrigerator and rotate my tyres.
ROZ DOYLE (PERI GILPIN), *Frasier*

Wise people will say Daniel should like me just as I am, but I am a child of *Cosmopolitan* culture, have been traumatised by supermodels and too many quizzes and know that neither my personality nor my body is up to it if left to its own devices. I can't take the pressure. I am going to cancel and spend the evening eating doughnuts in a cardigan with egg on it.
HELEN FIELDING, *Bridget Jones's Diary*

As you get older, the pickings get slimmer, but the people don't.
CARRIE FISHER

My favourite type of girl was always one that would go out with me. Twice.
JOE HICKMAN

I can't go on any more bad dates. I would rather be home alone than out with some guy who sells socks on the Internet.

MIRANDA HOBBES (CYNTHIA NIXON), *Sex and the City*

Samantha Jones (Kim Cattrall): A guy could just as easily dump you if you fuck him on the first date as he can if you wait until the tenth.
Miranda Hobbes (Cynthia Nixon): When have you ever been on a tenth date?
Sex and the City

My grandmother's ninety. She's dating. He's about ninety-three. It's going great. They never argue. They can't hear each other. CATHY LADMAN

Signs You're on a Bad Date:
He seems to know an awful lot about your shower routine.
His multiple personalities begin arguing after dinner about splitting the check.
You find yourself spending an inordinate amount of time lifting his head out of the soup.
After two beers he starts calling you 'mommy'.
Every place you suggest for dinner, he says, 'Nah – there might be cops there.'
DAVID LETTERMAN, *The Late Show*

I've been on so many blind dates, I should get a free dog.

WENDY LIEBMAN

I still remember sitting in a darkened movie theatre with my arm around 17-year-old Mary Jo Ramussen, trying to get to first base. I can even remember the name of the film: *The Lion King*. STEVE MARTIN

Finding a man is like finding a job; it's easier to find one when you already have one. PAIGE MITCHELL

Scientific studies have shown that in these sexually confused days pulling is the third most terrifying thing any man can do after chucking girlfriends and bringing overdue books back to the library.
SIMON NYE, *The A–Z of Behaving Badly*

Going out with a girl is like entering a new town. Either you get lucky and go straight through onto the next or you get unlucky and end up on the ring-road heading for the industrial estate. SIMON NYE, *The A–Z of Behaving Badly*

I was dating an older guy. He said, 'Do you want to meet my parents?' I said, 'Sure.' He took me to the cemetery. JOAN RIVERS

You know your date is old when you find out that his recreational vehicle is a Lazy Boy recliner.
JOAN RIVERS

I have no luck with women. I once went on a date and asked the woman if she'd bought any protection. She pulled a switchblade on me.
SCOTT ROEBEN

I once dated a girl on the track team. It didn't work out. She kept giving me the runaround.
SCOTT ROEBEN

The closest I ever came to a *ménage à trois* was when I dated a schizophrenic.
RITA RUDNER

How about the doggie bag on a date? That's a good move for a guy, huh? Let me tell you something: if you're a guy and you ask for the doggie bag on a date, you might as well have them just wrap up your genitals too. You're not going to be needing those for a while either.
JERRY SEINFELD

It is assumed that the woman must wait, motionless, until she is wooed. That is how the spider waits for the fly.
GEORGE BERNARD SHAW

There's someone out there for everyone – even if you need a pickaxe, a compass, and night goggles to find them.
HARRIS TELEMACHER (STEVE MARTIN), *L.A. Story*

I saw a bloke chatting up a cheetah. I thought, 'He's trying to pull a fast one.'
TIM VINE

Employees make the best dates. You don't have to pick them up and they're always tax-deductible.
ANDY WARHOL

Courtship: a period during which a girl decides whether or not she can do better.

Dating is when you pretend you're someone you're not, to impress someone you don't even know.

Bette Davis

Surely nobody but a mother could have loved Bette Davis at the height of her career.
BRIAN AHERNE

Bette Davis and I are good friends. There's nothing I wouldn't say to her face – both of them.
TALLULAH BANKHEAD

I don't see how she built a career out of a set of mannerisms instead of acting ability. Take away the pop eyes, the cigarette and those funny clipped words, and what have you got? She's a phoney. JOAN CRAWFORD

I saw Bette Davis in a hotel in Madrid once and went up to her and said, 'Miss Davis, I'm Ava Gardner and I'm a great fan of yours.' 'Of course you are, my dear,' she said, 'of course you are.' And then she swept on. AVA GARDNER

I can't imagine any guy giving her a tumble. CARL LAEMMLE

(*on working with Bette Davis*) I was never so scared in my life. And I was in the war! JOHN MILLS

Doris Day

I knew Doris Day before she was a virgin. OSCAR LEVANT

Doris Day is as wholesome as a bowl of cornflakes and at least as sexy. DWIGHT MACDONALD

The only real talent Miss Day possesses is that of being absolutely sanitary: her personality untouched by human emotions, her brow unclouded by human thought, her form unsmudged by the slightest evidence of femininity. JOHN SIMON

Death

My grandfather was killed at Custer's last stand. He was camping in the next field and went over to complain about the noise. JOEY ADAMS

It's not that I'm afraid to die, I just don't want to be there when it happens. WOODY ALLEN, *Without Feathers*

Sex is like death, only after death you don't feel like a pizza. WOODY ALLEN

Death is a wonderful way of cutting down on your expenses. WOODY ALLEN

If the doctor told me I had six minutes to live, I'd type a little faster. ISAAC ASIMOV

When I die I want to go to *Vogue*. DAVID BAILEY

I like the dead – they're so uncritical.   TOM BAKER

What a disgusting verdict: he choked on his own vomit. You never hear of anyone choking on someone else's vomit.   JEFFREY BERNARD

Death comes along like a gas bill one can't pay.   ANTHONY BURGESS

He was so crooked that when he died they had to screw him into the ground.
WALLY CAMPBELL (BOB HOPE), *The Cat and the Canary*

I am ready to meet my Maker. Whether my Maker is prepared for the great ordeal of meeting me is another matter.   WINSTON CHURCHILL

The only way you can become a legend is in your coffin.   BETTE DAVIS

(*hearing rumours of her impending death*) With the newspaper strike on, I wouldn't consider dying.   BETTE DAVIS

(*on facing death at 101*) My dear, I'm always nervous about doing something for the first time.   GWEN FFRANGCON-DAVIES

When I die, I want it to be on my 100th birthday, in my beach house on Maui and I want my husband to be so upset he has to drop out of college.
ROZ DOYLE (PERI GILPIN), *Frasier*

If the guest isn't singing 'Oh What a Beautiful Morning', I don't immediately think, 'Oh there's another snuffed it in the night. Another name in the Fawlty Towers Book of Remembrance.' I mean this is a hotel, not the Burma Railway.
BASIL FAWLTY (JOHN CLEESE), *Fawlty Towers*

(*on his deathbed*) I have spent a lot of time searching through the Bible for loopholes.   W.C. FIELDS

Once you're dead, you're made for life.   JIMI HENDRIX, 1968

Death will be a great relief. No more interviews.   KATHARINE HEPBURN

Some die young, some die old. The harsh truth is that the cause of death is birth.   DAVID HOCKNEY

When a man knows he is to be hanged in a fortnight, it concentrates his mind wonderfully.   SAMUEL JOHNSON

Dying is easy, it's living that scares me to death.   Annie Lennox

A 98-year-old *Titanic* survivor has just died. It's a pity. They were *this* close to pulling her out of the water.   Jay Leno

They announced on US TV that Patrick Magee, star of *The Avengers*, had died. So they rang up my daughter in Palm Springs. 'Sorry to hear that your father's dead.' She said: 'But I was talking to him twelve minutes ago in Australia.' They said, 'No, he's dead – it's just the time difference.'   Patrick Macnee

Those who welcome death have only tried it from the ears up.   Wilson Mizner

Sex and death. Two things that come once in a lifetime. Only after death, you're not so nauseous.   Miles Monroe (Woody Allen), *Sleeper*

I could never bear to be buried with people to whom I had not been introduced.   Norman Parkinson

My cousin just died. He was only nineteen. He got stung by a bee – the natural enemy of a tightrope walker.   Emo Philips

Dozens of people spontaneously combust each year. It's just not widely reported.   David St Hubbins (Michael McKean), *This is Spinal Tap*

The proof that we don't understand death is that we give dead people a pillow.   Jerry Seinfeld

Don't let Krusty's death get you down, boy. People die all the time, just like that. Why, you could wake up dead tomorrow! Well, good night.   Homer Simpson, *The Simpsons*

A single death is a tragedy, a million deaths is a statistic.   Josef Stalin

(*unveiling a plaque to the late Harry Secombe*) Harry is going to have to read it upside down.   Eric Sykes

Geraldine Granger (Dawn French): Don't people deal with death in strange ways?
Alice Tinker (Emma Chambers): Oh, they certainly do. When my father died, my mum cracked open a bottle of champagne and went straight to Majorca. But that was probably because she hated him.   *The Vicar of Dibley*

(*cable to Associated Press, 1897*) The reports of my death are greatly exaggerated.
MARK TWAIN

(*joking about the death of Spike Milligan*) It sounds like attention-seeking behaviour to me.   PAUL WHITEHOUSE

Death is nature's way of saying, 'Your table's ready.'   ROBIN WILLIAMS

I wouldn't mind being dead – it would be something new.
ESTELLE WINWOOD, at the age of 100

In India when a man dies, his widow throws herself on the funeral pyre. Over here, she says, 'Fifty ham baps, Connie – you slice, I'll butter.'
VICTORIA WOOD

If your time ain't come, not even a doctor can kill you.   AMERICAN PROVERB

Debt

I'm not the man I used to be, so why should I have to pay off his debts?
GARY APPLE

Creditors have better memories than debtors.   BENJAMIN FRANKLIN

Blessed are the young, for they will inherit the national debt.
HERBERT HOOVER

If you think nobody cares whether you are alive or dead, try missing a couple of car payments.   ANN LANDERS

Deceit

(*on the search for weapons of mass destruction in Iraq, 2003*) You can put up a sign on the door 'beware of the dog' without having a dog.   HANS BLIX

Decision

Indecision may, or may not, be my problem.   JIMMY BUFFETT

No good decision was ever made in a swivel chair.   GEORGE S. PATTON

I was going to buy a copy of *The Power of Positive Thinking*, and then I thought, what good would that do?   RONNIE SHAKES

Delegation

Delegating is a sign of weakness: let someone else do it.

If a job's worth doing, make sure you delegate it to the right person.

Democracy

Democracy means government by discussion, but it is only effective if you can stop people talking.   CLEMENT ATTLEE

The best argument against democracy is a five-minute conversation with the average voter.   WINSTON CHURCHILL

Democracy is a process by which the people are free to choose the man who will get the blame.   LAURENCE J. PETER

Democrats

You get fifteen Democrats in a room, and you get twenty opinions.
                                          PATRICK LEAHY

My grandmother's brain was dead, but her heart was still beating. It was the first time we ever had a Democrat in the family.   EMO PHILIPS

You might be a Democrat if you think fidelity means not cheating on your mistress.

You might be a Democrat if you've filed for unemployment within two weeks of getting out of high school.

Dentists

The English language may hold a more disagreeable combination of words than 'The dentist will see you now.' I am willing to concede something to the question: 'Have you anything to say before the current is turned on?' That may be worse for the moment but it doesn't last so long.

ROBERT BENCHLEY, *One Minute Please*

I'm always amazed to hear of air crash victims so badly mutilated that they have to be identified by their dental records. What I can't understand is, if they don't know who you are, how do they know who your dentist is?

PAUL MERTON

I go to a woman dentist. It's a relief to be told to open my mouth instead of shut it.   BOB MONKHOUSE

You know it's time to start using mouthwash when your dentist leaves the room and sends in a canary.   JOAN RIVERS

To the person with a toothache, even if the world is tottering, there is nothing more important than a visit to a dentist.   GEORGE BERNARD SHAW

Most dentists' chairs go up and down, don't they? The one I was in went back and forward. I thought, 'This is unusual.' Then the dentist said to me, 'Mr Vine, get out of the filing cabinet.'   TIM VINE

Depression

What may seem depressing or even tragic to one person may seem like an absolute scream to another person, especially if he has had between four and seven beers.   DAVE BARRY

When women are depressed they either eat or go shopping. Men invade another country.   ELAYNE BOOSLER

You know it's a bad day when you wake up and the birds are singing Leonard Cohen numbers.   JENNY ECLAIR

It's brilliant, being depressed; you can behave as badly as you like.
                                                    NICK HORNBY, *High Fidelity*

People who drink to drown their sorrow should be told that sorrow knows how to swim.   ANN LANDERS

Whenever I get depressed, I raise my hemlines. If things don't change, I am bound to be arrested.   ALLY MCBEAL (CALISTA FLOCKHART), *Ally McBeal*

Only have a nervous breakdown if you've got loads of money, and then you can really enjoy it.   PHILIP OAKEY

I'm so fat and I'm so depressed about it. Last night I tried to hang myself – but the rope broke.   JOAN RIVERS

I was depressed . . . I was suicidal. As a matter of fact, I would have killed myself but I was in analysis with a strict Freudian and if you kill yourself they make you pay for the sessions you miss.

ALVY SINGER (WOODY ALLEN), *Annie Hall*

When you're feeling down, at least make sure it's eider.

Desire

I have an intense desire to return to the womb. Anybody's. WOODY ALLEN

Desire is in men a hunger, in women only an appetite.

MIGNON MCLAUGHLIN, *The Neurotic's Notebook*

Diamonds

Diamonds never leave you – men do! SHIRLEY BASSEY

I never hated a man enough to give him his diamonds back.

ZSA ZSA GABOR

Kissing your hand may make you feel very good but a diamond and sapphire bracelet lasts forever. ANITA LOOS, *Gentlemen Prefer Blondes*

I wouldn't have you if you were hung with diamonds – upside down!

LYNN MARKHAM (JOAN CRAWFORD), *The Female on the Beach*

Diaries

It's the good girls keep diaries. The bad girls never have the time.

TALLULAH BANKHEAD

I do not keep a diary. Never have. To write a diary every day is like returning to one's own vomit. ENOCH POWELL

I always say, keep a diary and some day it'll keep you. MAE WEST

Dice

Dice are small polka-dotted cubes of ivory, constructed like a lawyer to lie on any side. AMBROSE BIERCE, *The Devil's Dictionary*

Dictatorship

I believe in benevolent dictatorships, provided I am the dictator.

RICHARD BRANSON

The General Pinochet game show. It was called *The Generation Game*: you had to guess which member of your family wasn't coming home that night.

PAUL MERTON

Dictatorship: a place where public opinion can't even be expressed privately.

WALTER WINCHELL

Diet and dieting

The first law of dietetics seems to be: if it tastes good, it's bad for you.

ISAAC ASIMOV

What you eat standing up doesn't count.

BETH BARNES

I'm already two years ahead on my daily fat allowance. I'm looking for skinny people to see if I can borrow theirs.

JO BRAND

Niles Crane (David Hyde Pierce): (of Maris) Just remember that she can't have shellfish, poultry, red meat, saturated fats, nitrates, wheat, starch, sulphates, MSG or herring. Did I say nuts?
Frasier Crane (Kelsey Grammer): Oh, I think that's implied.   *Frasier*

I don't diet. I just don't eat as much as I'd like to.

LINDA EVANGELISTA

A diet is when you watch what you eat and wish you could eat what you watch.

HERMIONE GINGOLD

The second day of a diet is always easier than the first. By the second day you're off it.

JACKIE GLEASON

I refuse to spend my life worrying about what I eat. There's no pleasure worth foregoing just for an extra three years in the geriatric ward.   JOHN MORTIMER

My friend lost five inches on the Slim Fast plan. Now he has no penis at all.

ROB MUNDA

A new study shows that going on the Atkins Diet can turn you into a crabby person with serious mood swings. On the other hand, the study says that always happens when you take doughnuts away from a fat person.   CONAN O'BRIEN

Keeping off a large weight loss is a phenomenon about as common in American medicine as an impoverished dermatologist. CALVIN TRILLIN

My doctor told me to stop having intimate dinners for four, unless there are three other people. ORSON WELLES

I never worry about diets. The only carrots that interest me are the number you get in a diamond. MAE WEST

A balanced diet is a biscuit in each hand.

A diet is when you go to some length to change your width.

Diets are for women who not only kept their girlish figure but doubled it.

The best way to lose weight is by skipping . . . snacks and dessert.

A diet is what you go on when not only can't you fit into the store's dresses, you can't fit into the changing room.

The biggest drawback to fasting for seven days is that it makes one weak.

Nothing arouses more false hopes than the first four hours of a diet.

Dignity

It is only people of small stature who need to stand on their dignity. ARNOLD BENNETT

I know of no case where a man added to his dignity by standing on it. WINSTON CHURCHILL

Dinner

Monica Geller (Courteney Cox): Okay, I've got a leg, three breasts, and a wing.
Chandler Bing (Matthew Perry): How do you find clothes that fit?
Friends

Meal time is the only time in the day when children resolutely refuse to eat. FRAN LEBOWITZ

If a man prepares dinner for you and the salad contains three or more types of lettuce, he is serious. RITA RUDNER

For thirty years my mother served the family nothing but leftovers. The original meal has never been found.　　　　　TRACEY ULLMAN

Diplomacy

In diplomacy an ultimatum is the last demand before resorting to concessions.
　　　　　AMBROSE BIERCE, *The Devil's Dictionary*

A diplomat is a man who always remembers a woman's birthday but never remembers her age.　　　　　ROBERT FROST

Diplomacy – lying in state.　　　　　OLIVER HERFORD

Diplomacy: the art of jumping into troubled waters without making a splash.
　　　　　ART LINKLETTER

If an ambassador says yes, it means perhaps; if he says perhaps, it means no; if he ever said no, he would cease to be an ambassador.　　　　　K.M. PANNIKAR

Diplomacy is letting someone else have your way.　　　　　LESTER PEARSON

In archaeology you uncover the unknown. In diplomacy you cover the known.
　　　　　THOMAS PICKERING

Sincere diplomacy is no more possible than dry water or a wooden iron.
　　　　　JOSEF STALIN

A diplomat these days is nothing but a head waiter who's allowed to sit down occasionally.　　　　　PETER USTINOV, *Romanoff and Juliet*

Diplomacy is about surviving till the next century. Politics is about surviving until Friday afternoon.

Disappointment

I crave disappointment. That's why I buy Kinder Surprise eggs – crap chocolate, crap toy.　　　　　BILL BAILEY

I couldn't remember when I had been so disappointed. Except perhaps the time I found out that M&Ms really do melt in your hand.　　　　　PETER OAKLEY

You know Moe, my mom once said something that really stuck with me. She said, 'Homer, you're a big disappointment', and God bless her soul, she was really onto something. HOMER SIMPSON, *The Simpsons*

Discretion

Discretion is the salt, and fancy the sugar of life; the one preserves, the other sweetens it. CHRISTIAN NESTELL BOVEE

Discretion is the better part of indiscretion.

Disease

We live in an age where illness and deformity are commonplace and yet you are without a doubt the most repulsive individual I have ever met. I would shake your hand but I fear it would come off.
  EDMUND BLACKADDER (ROWAN ATKINSON), *Blackadder*

My friend has chickenpox. He's running a high temperature and his chest looks like a bad Matisse. NOËL COWARD

A fever is like a sunburn. Only it's on the inside. DENNIS THE MENACE

I had measles so quickly on top of chickenpox that the spots were fighting each other for space. HARRY SECOMBE

I got food poisoning today. I don't know when I'll use it. STEVEN WRIGHT

Disguise

(*to Bob*) You are a girl. And you're a girl with as much talent for disguise as a giraffe in dark glasses trying to get into a polar bears-only golf club.
  EDMUND BLACKADDER (ROWAN ATKINSON), *Blackadder*

Disorders

I have obsessive-compulsive disorder. I have to do things in threes. That's how I got my reputation as a slut.
  MIMI BOBECK (KATHY KINNEY), *The Drew Carey Show*

When you think about it, attention deficit disorder makes a lot of sense. In this country, there isn't a lot worth paying attention to. GEORGE CARLIN

I really must run. I'm conducting a seminar for multiple personality disorders and it takes me forever to fill out the name tags.

NILES CRANE (DAVID HYDE PIERCE), *Frasier*

All those disorders. When I was a kid we just had crazy people.

ELLEN DEGENERES

Divorce

My toughest fight was with my first wife.

MUHAMMAD ALI

It was partially my fault that we got divorced . . . I tended to place my wife under a pedestal.

WOODY ALLEN

My wife got the house, the car, the bank account, and if I marry again and have children, she gets them too.

WOODY ALLEN

A divorce is like an amputation; you survive, but there's less of you.

MARGARET ATWOOD

(*on the break-up of her marriage to Tom Arnold*) I'm not upset about my divorce. I'm only upset I'm not a widow.

ROSEANNE BARR

There is no fury like an ex-wife searching for a new lover.

CYRIL CONNOLLY, *The Unquiet Grave*

You never really know a man until you've divorced him.

ZSA ZSA GABOR

I am a marvellous housekeeper. Every time I leave a man, I keep his house.

ZSA ZSA GABOR

It's a sad fact that fifty per cent of marriages in this country end in divorce. But hey, the other half end in death. You could be one of the lucky ones!

RICHARD JENI

I can't believe I have had three marriages. Two is one thing, but three is like someone who goes on the Jerry Springer show.

PATSY KENSIT

Being divorced is like being hit by a Mack truck. If you live through it, you start looking very carefully to the right and to the left.

JEAN KERR

Angelina Jolie has filed for divorce. It's never good when a guy named Billy Bob marries someone to whom he's not related.

JAY LENO

Signs You Should Get A Divorce:
The only thing you have in common is your hatred for one another.
You ask the guy at Hallmark where the 'Controlling Bitch' section is.
You keep finding receipts for the guys she's hired to kill you.
She brings a date to couples counselling.
You sleep in separate beds in separate bedrooms in separate houses in separate states.
DAVID LETTERMAN

(*on the divorce of baseball star Joe DiMaggio from Marilyn Monroe*) It proves that no man can be a success in two national pastimes. OSCAR LEVANT

My husband and I had our best sex during our divorce. It was like cheating on our lawyers. PRISCILLA LOPEZ, *Cheaper to Keep Her*

If you made a list of reasons why any couple got married, and another list of the reasons for their divorce, you'd have a lot of overlapping.
MIGNON MCLAUGHLIN

(*on the divorce from one of his eleven wives*) She cried, and the judge wiped her tears with my chequebook. TOMMY MANVILLE

People ask me how short I am. Since my last divorce, I'm about $100,000 short.
MICKEY ROONEY

Why do Jewish divorces cost so much? Because they're worth it.
HENNY YOUNGMAN

A wife lasts only for the length of the marriage, but an ex-wife is there for the rest of your life.

It takes just a few words mumbled in church to get married and just a few words mumbled in your sleep to get divorced.

Doctors

My doctor is wonderful. Once when I couldn't afford an operation, he touched up the X-rays. JOEY BISHOP

Doctors are just the same as lawyers; the only difference is that lawyers merely rob you, whereas doctors rob you and kill you, too. ANTON CHEKHOV

A man went to the doctor with a strawberry growing out of his head. The doctor said, 'I'll give you some cream to put on it.' TOMMY COOPER

I went to see my doctor. I said, 'Doctor, every morning when I get up and I look in the mirror I feel like throwing up. What's wrong with me?' He said, 'I don't know, but your eyesight is perfect.'   RODNEY DANGERFIELD

I went to my doctor and asked for something for persistent wind. He gave me a kite.   LES DAWSON

God heals and the doctor takes the fee.   BENJAMIN FRANKLIN

I don't believe the kindliest of men ever learned about the death of his doctor without a feeling of smugness.   RICHARD GORDON, *Bedside Manners*

A doctor who isn't a hypochondriac is as rare as a teetotal pub-keeper.   RICHARD GORDON, *Doctor in the Swim*

An apple a day keeps the doctor away. So does not having health insurance.   JOE HICKMAN

I'm not feeling very well – I need a doctor immediately. Ring the nearest golf course.   GROUCHO MARX

Doctorship – the art of getting one up on the patient without actually killing him.   STEPHEN POTTER, *One-Upmanship*

Kerry Weaver (Laura Innes): Did you ever take the Hippocratic Oath?
Robert Romano (Paul McCrane): I had my fingers crossed.   *ER*

I hate the waiting room. Because it's called the waiting room, there's no chance of not waiting. It's built, designed, and intended for waiting. Why would they take you right away when they've got this room all set up?   JERRY SEINFELD

A man goes to the doctor and says, 'Doctor, I have a ringing in my ears.' The doctor says, 'Don't answer!'   HENNY YOUNGMAN

Doctors say that a sneeze travels at 100 miles an hour. Who can sneeze that long?

The mark of a real doctor is usually illegible.

Virus is a Latin word translated by doctors to mean, 'Your guess is as good as mine.'

Dogs

When a man's best friend is his dog, that dog has a problem.

EDWARD ABBEY

You can say any foolish thing to a dog, and the dog will give you this look that says, 'My God, you're right! I would never have thought of that!'

DAVE BARRY

Dogs feel very strongly that they should always go with you in the car, in case the need should arise for them to bark violently at nothing right in your ear.

DAVE BARRY

You will find that the woman who is really kind to dogs is always one who has failed to inspire sympathy in men.   MAX BEERBOHM, *Zuleika Dobson*

A dog teaches a boy fidelity, perseverance, and to turn around three times before lying down.   ROBERT BENCHLEY

Dachshunds are ideal dogs for small children, as they are already stretched and pulled to such a length that the child cannot do much harm one way or the other.   ROBERT BENCHLEY

I have never stretched myself on a beach for an afternoon's nap that a dog, fresh from a swim, did not take up a position just to the left of my tightly closed eyes, and shake himself.

ROBERT BENCHLEY, *Around the World Backwards and Sideways*

Two guys were watching a log lick himself, and one said, 'I wish I could do that.' The other replied, 'Maybe you should pet him first.'   DOUG BENSON

A dog is the only thing on earth that loves you more than you love yourself.

JOSH BILLINGS

I'm looking for an attack dog. One who likes the sweet gamey tang of human flesh. Mmmm, why here's the fellow! Wiry, fast, firm, proud buttocks. Reminds me of me.   MONTGOMERY BURNS, *The Simpsons*

Montgomery Burns: Dogs are idiots. Think about it, Smithers. If I came into your house and started sniffing at your crotch and slobbering all over you, what would you say?
Smithers: If *you* did it, sir?   *The Simpsons*

My dog is half Labrador, half pit bull. She bites off my leg and then brings it back to me.
FRANK CARSON

You call to a dog and a dog will break its neck to get to you. Dogs just want to please. Call to a cat and its attitude is, 'What's in it for me?'
LEWIS GRIZZARD

I hope if dogs take over the world, and they choose a king, they don't just go by size, because I bet there are some chihuahuas with good ideas.
JACK HANDEY

People teach their dogs to sit — it's a trick. I've been sitting my whole life, and a dog has never looked at me as though he thought I was tricky.
MITCH HEDBERG

Why do dogs always race to the door when the doorbell rings, because it's hardly ever for them?
HARRY HILL

The trees in Siberia are miles apart — that's why the dogs are so fast.
BOB HOPE

To his dog, every man is Napoleon.
ALDOUS HUXLEY

They never talk about themselves but listen to you while you talk about yourself, and keep up an appearance of being interested in the conversation.
JEROME K. JEROME

Anybody who doesn't know what soap tastes like never washed a dog.
FRANKLIN P. JONES

Don't accept your dog's admiration as conclusive evidence that you are wonderful.
ANN LANDERS

A dog who thinks he is man's best friend is a dog who obviously has never met a tax lawyer.
FRAN LEBOWITZ

I don't like big dogs. They always come and sniff you in the crotch. Little dogs are even worse because you have to kneel down for them to do it.
BOB MONKHOUSE

No one appreciates the very special genius of your conversation as your dog does.
CHRISTOPHER MORLEY

The censure of a dog is something no man can stand.
CHRISTOPHER MORLEY, *The Haunted Bookshop*

A door is what a dog is perpetually on the wrong side of.   OGDEN NASH

The noblest of all dogs is the hot-dog; it feeds the hand that bites it.
LAURENCE J. PETER

I wonder if other dogs think poodles are members of a weird religious cult.
RITA RUDNER

We've begun to long for the pitter-patter of little feet – so we bought a dog.
Well, it's cheaper and you get more feet.   RITA RUDNER

Dogs are the leaders of the planet. If you see two life forms, one of them's making a poop, the other's carrying it for him, who would you assume is in charge?   JERRY SEINFELD

My dog is half pit bull, half poodle. Not much of a guard dog, but a vicious gossip.   CRAIG SHOEMAKER

A dog is not intelligent. Never trust an animal that's surprised by its own farts.
FRANK SKINNER

I loathe people who keep dogs. They're cowards who have not got the guts to bite people themselves.   AUGUST STRINDBERG

There is no psychiatrist in the world like a puppy licking your face.
BEN WILLIAMS

I got a new dog. He's a paranoid retriever. He brings back everything because he's not sure what I threw him.   STEVEN WRIGHT

My dog was my only friend. I told my wife that a man needs at least two friends so she bought me another dog.   HENNY YOUNGMAN

You know you're a dog lover when poop has become a topic of conversation.

A dog at a flea circus is likely to steal the show.

Doubt

Live so that you can at least get the benefit of the doubt.   KIN HUBBARD

Doubt comes in at the window when inquiry is denied at the door.

BENJAMIN JOWETT

When in doubt, I take everything for a compliment, and this rule does a great deal of good to my self-esteem.   GEORGE MIKES

I respect faith, but doubt is what gets you an education.   WILSON MIZNER

Four be the things I'd been better without:
Love, curiosity, freckles, and doubt.   DOROTHY PARKER

Kirk Douglas

I'm here to speak about his wit, his charm, his warmth, his talent . . . At last, a real acting job!   BURT LANCASTER

Kirk would be the first to tell you that he's a difficult man; I would be the second.

BURT LANCASTER

Drag

Dressing up is a way of disguising that you have got no personality. I could meet an old lady at a bus stop and have a more interesting conversation than I could with a drag queen.   BOY GEORGE

Look, you don't know me from Adam. But I was a better man with you as a woman than I ever was with a woman as a man. Know what I mean?

MICHAEL DORSEY (DUSTIN HOFFMAN), *Tootsie*

I guess a drag queen's like an oil painting; you gotta stand back from it to get the full effect.   HARVEY FIERSTEIN

Frank Burns (Larry Linville): Klinger! I want to see you out of that dress!
Maxwell Klinger (Jamie Farr): Never on a first date, sir!

M*A*S*H

B.J. Hunnicutt (Mike Farrell): Some guys'd shoot themselves in the foot to get sent home.
Klinger (Jamie Farr): Not me. I'd ruin a perfectly good pair of nylons.

M*A*S*H

The only really firm rule of taste about cross dressing is that neither sex should ever wear anything they haven't yet figured out how to get to the bathroom in.

P.J. O'ROURKE, *Modern Manners*

I cut down trees, I skip and jump,
I like to press wild flowers.
I put on women's clothing
And hang around in bars.

> Michael Palin, 'The Lumberjack Song', *Monty Python's Flying Circus*

I've got a soft spot for Klinger. He looks a little like my son, and he dresses a lot like my wife.
> Colonel Potter (Henry Morgan), *M*A*S*H*

Drama

What is drama but life with the dull bits cut out?
> Alfred Hitchcock

Dreams

The trouble with dreams, of course, is that other people's are so boring.
> W.H. Auden

I had a dream last night, I was eating a 10lb marshmallow. I woke up this morning and the pillow was gone.
> Tommy Cooper

I don't use drugs; my dreams are frigtening enough.
> M.C. Escher

My lifelong dream has always been to own a little bakery in a remote provincial French town, something small and quaint. Then I'd close all the windows and watch pornography all day long. A man can dream, can't he?
> LeMel Hebert-Williams

I dream of a rural life – raising cheques.
> Dorothy Parker

In a dream you are never eighty.
> Anne Sexton

I was trying to daydream but my mind kept wandering.
> Steven Wright

Quantum mechanics: the dreams stuff is made of.
> Steven Wright

Drink

Ah, 7 Up – Snow White's favourite drink.
> Dave Allen

Jane Spencer (Priscilla Presley): Would you like a nightcap?
Lt Frank Drebin (Leslie Nielsen): No thank you, I don't wear them.
> *Naked Gun*

The only way that I could figure they could improve upon Coca-Cola, one of life's most delightful elixirs, which studies prove will heal the sick and occasionally raise the dead, is to put rum or bourbon in it.   LEWIS GRIZZARD

Driving

I know some people are against drunk driving, but you know, sometimes you've just got no choice. Those kids gotta get to school . . .   DAVE ATTELL

The one thing that unites all human beings, regardless of age, gender, religion, economic status, or ethnic background, is that, deep down inside, we all believe that we are above-average drivers.   DAVE BARRY

The British motorist likes to fight, to give no quarter, to arrive at his destination in the certain knowledge that he has given to all other road users as good as, if not better than, he got.   PATRICK CAMPBELL, *All Ways on Sundays*

Have you ever noticed? Anybody going slower than you is an idiot, and anyone going faster than you is a moron.   GEORGE CARLIN

Somebody actually complimented me on my driving today. They left a little note on the windscreen. It said, 'Parking Fine'.   TOMMY COOPER

It's funny how a wife can spot a blonde hair at twenty yards yet miss the garage doors.   RODNEY DANGERFIELD

(*on speeding fines*) I always get out of it. The cop ends up giving me his business card and saying, 'Let's go to dinner.'   PARIS HILTON

When I'm driving and I see a sign that says, 'CAUTION: SMALL CHILDREN PLAYING', I slow down. And then it occurs to me, I'm not afraid of small children.   JONATHAN KATZ

If your wife wants to learn to drive, don't stand in her way.   SAM LEVENSON

I sit in the traffic trying to get out of the centre of Killarney. It's a slow business. If aliens landed, you'd be hard pressed to explain to them the difference between Killarney traffic, and parking.

          PETE MCCARTHY, *McCarthy's Bar*

There are two things no man will admit he cannot do well: drive and make love.

          STIRLING MOSS

So, I'm not the best behind the wheel. But if you don't like the way I drive, stay off the sidewalk!   JOAN RIVERS

I like to drive with my knees. Otherwise, how can I put on my lipstick and talk on the phone?   SHARON STONE

Half the motorists can't drive fast enough to please their girlfriends, while the other half can't drive slow enough to appease their wives.   BILL VAUGHAN

I like to pick up hitchhikers. When they get in the car I say, 'Put on your seat belt. I want to try something. I saw it once in a cartoon, but I think I can do it.'
                                                                       STEVEN WRIGHT

Drive slow and enjoy the scenery; drive fast and join the scenery.

It is the overtakers who keep the undertakers busy.

Drive carefully. It's not only cars that can be recalled by their maker.

The young man who stands on his own two feet has probably failed his driving test.

Drugs

Cocaine isn't habit-forming. I should know – I've been using it for years.
                                                                   TALLULAH BANKHEAD

You find out so many interesting things when you're not on drugs.
                                                                       BOY GEORGE

They're selling crack in my neighbourhood. Finally.   KEVIN BRENNAN

(*on his drug addiction*) I'll die young, but it's like kissing God.
                                                                       LENNY BRUCE

There are drugs tests everywhere in sport now. Even the old guys who play crown green bowls, they've been giving urine samples. They don't mean to . . .
                                                                     JASPER CARROTT

Never take ecstasy, beer, bacardi, weed, pepto bismol, vivarin, turns, tagamet hb, xanax, and valium in the same day. It makes it difficult to sleep at night.
                                                                         EMINEM

Stay away from Ecstasy. This is a drug so strong it makes white people think they can dance.
LENNY HENRY

The trouble with heroin is that apparently it's so moreish
HARRY HILL

(*on a tour of troops in Vietnam*) I believe a lot of you are into gardening – security officers said you were growing your own grass.
BOB HOPE

'Reverend' Jim Ignatowski (Christopher Lloyd): Yeah, I did some drugs, though probably not as many as you think. How many drugs do you think I did?
Elaine Nardo (Marilu Henner): A lot.
Ignatowski: Wow! Right on the nose!
Taxi

It's very easy to get into America if you've hit an old lady over the head, but it's very difficult to get in if someone says you've smoked a joint.
MICK JAGGER, 1973 interview

It's amazing how low you go to get high.
JOHN LENNON

So many Olympic athletes are failing their drug tests. Maybe those drug tests are just too darned hard!
JAY LENO

Dan Quayle said that when teenagers see Ozzy Osbourne, it sends them the right message about drugs. Think about it. Dan Quayle never did drugs, he's middle-aged and unemployed. Ozzy did drugs for thirty years, lives in a ten million-dollar house, has his own TV show and a three million-dollar book deal. What's the message?
JAY LENO

Drugs have nothing to do with the creation of music. In fact, they are dumb and self-indulgent. Kind of like sucking your thumb!
COURTNEY LOVE

I don't like people who take drugs . . . customs men for example.
MICK MILLER

Drugs have taught an entire generation of American kids the metric system.
P.J. O'ROURKE

I've never had any problems with drugs, only policemen.
KEITH RICHARDS

(*asked to autograph a fan's school chemistry book, 1990s*) Sure thing, man, I used to be a laboratory myself once.
KEITH RICHARDS

Saffron Monsoon (Julia Sawalha): I thought they didn't let people with drug convictions into America.
Patsy Stone (Joanna Lumley): It's not so much a conviction, darling. It's more of a strong belief. *Absolutely Fabulous*

Customs officer: The white powder we found was a perfectly harmless, innocent substance. You are all free to go.
Patsy Stone (Joanna Lumley): Just hang on there. I demand you retest it. Come back here. I paid a huge amount of money for that. Don't you tell me it's talcum powder. *Absolutely Fabulous*

I hate to advocate drugs, alcohol, violence, or insanity to anyone, but they've always worked for me. HUNTER S. THOMPSON

I heard that your brain stops growing when you start doing drugs. Let's see, I guess that makes me nineteen. STEVEN TYLER

Cocaine is God's way of saying you're making too much money.
ROBIN WILLIAMS

I can't understand why anybody would want to devote their life to a cause like dope. It's the most boring pastime I can think of. It ranks a close second to television. FRANK ZAPPA

Drugs may lead to nowhere, but at least it's the scenic route.

Drunkenness

You know you drank too much the night before when you wake up with crop circles in your pubes. DOUG BENSON

What on earth was I drinking last night? My head feels like there's a Frenchman living in it. EDMUND BLACKADDER (ROWAN ATKINSON), *Blackadder*

It takes only one drink to get me drunk. The trouble is, I can't remember if it's the thirteenth or the fourteenth. GEORGE BURNS

I've never been drunk, but I've often been overserved. GEORGE GOBEL

A Coarse Drinker is a man who blames his hangover on the tonic water and not the gin. MICHAEL GREEN, *The Art of Coarse Drinking*

Always do sober what you said you'd do drunk. That will teach you to keep your mouth shut.
ERNEST HEMINGWAY

You're not drunk if you can lie on the floor without holding on.
DEAN MARTIN

I'd hate to be a teetotaller. Imagine getting up in the morning and knowing that's as good as you're going to feel all day.
DEAN MARTIN

The reason I drink is because when I'm sober I think I'm Eddie Fisher.
DEAN MARTIN

The proper behaviour all through the holiday season is to be drunk. This drunkenness culminates in New Year's Eve, when you get so drunk you kiss the person you're married to.
P.J. O'ROURKE

When I was a practising alcoholic, I was unbelievable. One side effect was immense suspicion. I'd come off tour like Inspector Clouseau on acid: 'Where's this cornflake? It wasn't here before.'
OZZY OSBOURNE

I can honestly say all the bad things that ever happened to me were directly attributed to drugs and alcohol. I mean, I would never urinate at the Alamo at nine o'clock in the morning dressed in a woman's evening dress, sober.
OZZY OSBOURNE

People wonder why they can't understand him [Ozzy]. Well, you'd be hard to understand too if you drank two vats of coffee, two vats of wine, and took twenty-five Vicodin a day.
SHARON OSBOURNE

What, when drunk, one sees in other women, one sees in [Greta] Garbo sober.
KENNETH TYNAN

You can learn a lot about a woman by getting smashed with her.
TOM WAITS

Maybe there isn't a devil; perhaps it's just God when he's drunk.
TOM WAITS

The problem with some people is that when they aren't drunk, they're sober.
W.B. YEATS

A hangover is the wrath of grapes.

To be intoxicated is to feel sophisticated, but not be able to say it.

A hangover is something to fill a head that was empty the night before.

Duct tape

Duct tape is like the Force. It has a light side, a dark side, and it holds the universe together.

You need only two tools in life: WD-40 and duct tape. If it doesn't move and it should, use WD-40. If it moves and it shouldn't, use the tape.

Dyslexia

Old MacDonald was dyslexic IEIEO.

BILLY CONNOLLY

Andy Warhol may have been dyslexic. That's great news. We all get fifty-one minutes of fame.

JAY LENO

I wasn't that great a student. I was disappointed to find out I *wasn't* dyslexic.

LUKE WILSON

Dyslexia means never having to say you're syrro.

E

Eating

A fork is an instrument used chiefly for the purpose of putting dead animals into the mouth.

AMBROSE BIERCE, *The Devil's Dictionary*

Man is the only animal that can remain on friendly terms with the victims he intends to eat, until he eats them.

SAMUEL BUTLER, *Notebooks*

It's important to watch what you eat. Otherwise, how are you going to get it into your mouth?

MATT DIAMOND

I can eat a man, but I'm not sure of the fibre content.

JENNY ECLAIR

Anybody'll agree with you if you've been eatin' onions.

KIN HUBBARD, *New Sayings by Abe Martin*

Statistics show that of those who contract the habit of eating, very few survive.
                                                    WALLACE IRWIN

I'm a light eater. When it gets light, I start eating.   TOMMY JOHN

I'm sorry, what was the question? I was distracted by that half-masticated cow rolling around in your wide open trap.
                    VICTOR MELLING (MICHAEL CAINE), *Miss Congeniality*

Chopsticks are one of the reasons the Chinese never invented custard.
                                                    SPIKE MILLIGAN

The next time you feel like complaining, remember that your garbage disposal probably eats better than thirty per cent of the people in the world.
                                                    ROBERT ORBEN

Never eat more than you can lift.   MISS PIGGY

Men who can eat anything they want and not gain weight should do it out of sight of women.   RITA RUDNER

To eat is human, to digest, divine.   MARK TWAIN

It's not the minutes spent at the table that put on weight, it's the seconds.

Chickens are the only creatures you can eat before they are born and after they are dead.

Eccentricity

The English like eccentrics. They just don't like them living next door.
                                                    JULIAN CLARY

Eccentricity, to be socially acceptable, had still to have at least four or five generations of inbreeding behind it.   OSBERT LANCASTER

Economics

No real English gentleman, in his secret soul, was ever sorry for the death of a political economist.   WALTER BAGEHOT

Slumps are like soft beds. They're easy to get into and hard to get out of.
                                                    JOHNNY BENCH

There are three kinds of economist. Those who can count and those who can't.
EDDIE GEORGE

Please find me a one-armed economist so we will not always hear, 'On the other hand . . .'
HERBERT HOOVER

(*to J.K. Galbraith*) Did you ever think, Ken, that making a speech on economics is a lot like pissing down your leg? It seems hot to you, but it never does to anyone else.
LYNDON B. JOHNSON

George W. Bush's economic plan will create 2.5 million new jobs. The bad news, they are all for Iraqi soldiers.
CRAIG KILBORN

I'm not worried about the deficit. It is big enough to take care of itself.
RONALD REAGAN

An economist's guess is as good as anybody else's.
WILL ROGERS

If all economists were laid end to end, they would not reach a conclusion.
GEORGE BERNARD SHAW

A study of economics usually reveals that the best time to buy anything was last year.

Isn't it strange that the same people who laugh at fortune-tellers take economists seriously?

Education

I read Shakespeare and the Bible and I can shoot dice. That's what I call a liberal education.
TALLULAH BANKHEAD

Genitals are a great distraction to scholarship.
MALCOLM BRADBURY, *Cuts*

Education is a progressive discovery of our own ignorance.
WILL DURANT

He that teaches himself hath a fool for a master.
BENJAMIN FRANKLIN

Education makes machines which act like men, and produces men who act like machines.
ERICH FROMM

Education isn't everything. For a start it isn't an elephant.
SPIKE MILLIGAN

Getting an education was a bit like a communicable sexual disease. It made you unsuitable for a lot of jobs and then you had the urge to pass it on.

TERRY PRATCHETT, *Hogfather*

Instead of giving money to found colleges to promote learning, why not pass a constitutional amendment prohibiting anybody from learning anything? If it works as good as Prohibition, in five years we would have the smartest race of people on earth.

WILL ROGERS

How is education supposed to make me feel smarter? Besides, every time I learn something new, it pushes some old stuff out of my brain. Remember when I took that home winemaking course, and I forgot how to drive?

HOMER SIMPSON, *The Simpsons*

Education has produced a vast population able to read but unable to distinguish what is worth reading.

G.M. TREVELYAN

Education: the path from cocky ignorance to miserable uncertainty.

MARK TWAIN

British education is probably the best in the world, if you can survive it. If you can't, there is nothing left for you but the diplomatic corps.

PETER USTINOV

Education is an admirable thing, but it is well to remember from time to time that nothing that is worth knowing can be taught.

OSCAR WILDE, *The Critic as Artist*

Egotism

Egotism is the anaesthetic given by a kindly nature to relieve the pain of being a damned fool.

BELLAMY BROOKS

The graveyards are full of indispensable men.

CHARLES DE GAULLE

You know how fragile men's egos are: one little mistake like screaming out the wrong name and they go all to pieces.

BLANCHE DEVEREAUX (RUE MCCLANAHAN), *The Golden Girls*

When I read something saying I've not done anything as good as *Catch-22* I'm tempted to reply, 'Who has?'

JOSEPH HELLER

Egotism is the anaesthetic that dulls the pain of stupidity.

FRANK LEAHY

I'm fond of Steve Allen, but not so much as he is. JACK PAAR

Egotism – usually just a case of mistaken non-entity. BARBARA STANWYCK

[James] Whistler has always spelt art with a capital I. OSCAR WILDE

(*on Mrs Patrick Campbell*) She has an ego like a raging tooth. W.B. YEATS

An egotist is someone who is usually me-deep in conversation.

One nice thing about egotists: they don't talk about other people.

Dwight D. Eisenhower

It's hard to play [golf with] a guy who rattles his medals when you're putting.
BOB HOPE

Eisenhower is the only living unknown soldier. ROBERT S. KERR

Once he makes up his mind, he's full of indecision. OSCAR LEVANT

This fellow doesn't know any more about politics than a pig knows about Sunday.
HARRY S. TRUMAN

Elections

Folk who don't know why America is the Land of Promise should be here during an election campaign. MILTON BERLE

Hell, I never vote *for* anybody. I always vote *against*. W.C. FIELDS

(*on the 2000 Presidential election*) You know you win some, lose some, and then there's that little-known third category. AL GORE

A straw vote only shows which way the hot air blows. O. HENRY

(*reading out a message supposedly from his father, 1958*) Don't buy a single vote more than necessary. I'll be damned if I'm going to pay for a landslide.
JOHN F. KENNEDY

Opinion poll: a survey which claims to show what voters are thinking but which only succeeds in changing their minds. MILES KINGTON (*on a pre-election poll*) One day the don't-knows will get in, and then where will we be?　　　　　　　　　　　　　　　　　　　　　SPIKE MILLIGAN

Montgomery Burns: This anonymous clan of slack-jawed troglodytes has cost me the election, and yet if I were to have them killed, I would be the one to go to jail. That's democracy for you.
Smithers: You are noble and poetic in defeat, sir.　　　　　*The Simpsons*

Those who cast the votes decide nothing. Those who count the votes decide everything.　　　　　　　　　　　　　　　　　　　　　JOSEF STALIN

It is not enough to have every intelligent person in the country voting for me –
I need a majority.　　　　　　　　　　　　　　　　　　ADLAI STEVENSON

Elections are when people find out what politicians stand for and politicians find out what people will fall for.

Electricity

We believe that electricity exists, because the electric company keeps sending us bills for it, but we cannot figure out how it travels inside wires.
　　　　　　　　　　　　　　　　　　　　　　　　　　　　DAVE BARRY

Electricity is actually made up of extremely tiny particles called electrons, which you cannot see with the naked eye unless you have been drinking.
　　　　　　　　　　　　　　　　　　　　　　　　　　　　DAVE BARRY

Electricity is really just organised lightning.　　　　　GEORGE CARLIN

When Thomas Edison worked late into the night on the electric light, he had to do it by gas lamp or candle. I'm sure it made the work seem that much more urgent.　　　　　　　　　　　　　　　　　　　　　GEORGE CARLIN

Her own mother lived the latter years of her life in the horrible suspicion that electricity was dripping invisibly all over the house.　　　JAMES THURBER

Elevators

Certain people in this life are natural lift-button pressers. Should you presume to take on the function yourself, they will press the button anyway, after you have done so.　　　　　　　　　　　　　　　　　　OLIVER PRITCHETT

When I was little, my grandfather used to make me stand in a closet for five minutes without moving. He said it was elevator practice.　　STEVEN WRIGHT

Elopement

If it were not for the presents, an elopement would be preferable to a wedding.
GEORGE ADE, *Forty Modern Fables*

Woody Boyd (Woody Harrelson): What can I do for you, Mr Peterson?
Norm Peterson (George Wendt): Elope with my wife.

Cheers

Eloquence

Eloquence is the art of saying as little as possible but making it sound as much as possible.
EVAN ESAR

An eloquent male is one who can describe Dolly Parton without using his hands.
JOAN RIVERS

Embarrassment

To my embarrassment, I was born in bed with a lady.   WILSON MIZNER

Blanche Devereaux (Rue McClanahan): I've never been so humiliated in my life.
Dorothy Zbornak (Bea Arthur): What about the time you lost the key to your handcuffs and had to go with that guy on his mail route?

The Golden Girls

You don't know real embarrassment until your hip sets off a metal detector.

Emotions

The nerve of that man saying I have an emotional problem. I'd like to meet him in a dark alley with a cleaver.   REBECCA HOWE (KIRSTIE ALLEY), *Cheers*

Men are emotional bonsai. You have to whack the fertilizer on to get any feelings out of them.   KATHY LETTE

Men are like mascara — they tend to run at the first sign of emotion.

Enemies

The lion and the calf shall lie down together, but the calf won't get much sleep.
WOODY ALLEN, *Without Feathers*

When my enemies stop hissing, I shall know I'm slipping.   MARIA CALLAS

An intimate friend and a hated enemy have always been indispensable to my emotional life.   SIGMUND FREUD

We English are good at forgiving our enemies; it releases us from the obligation of liking our friends.   P.D. JAMES

Forgive your enemies, but never forget their names.   JOHN F. KENNEDY

Be careful to choose your enemies well. Friends don't much matter. But the choice of enemies is very important.   OSCAR WILDE

Always forgive your enemies – nothing annoys them so much.   OSCAR WILDE

Friends may come and go, but enemies accumulate.

Energy

My vigour, vitality and cheek repel me. I am the kind of woman I would run away from.   NANCY ASTOR

Cecil Hardwicke had the personality and drive of an old tortoise hunting for lettuce.   RACHEL ROBERTS

Many Americans are trying to conserve energy as never before – they're now burning their morning toast only on one side.

England and the English

The English instinctively admire any man who has no talent and is modest about it.   JAMES AGATE

One has no great hopes from Birmingham. I always say there is something direful in the sound.   JANE AUSTEN, *Emma*

I like the English. They have the most rigid code of immorality in the world.   MALCOLM BRADBURY

The English are polite by telling lies. The Americans are polite by telling the truth.   MALCOLM BRADBURY, *Stepping Westward*

The English never draw a line without blurring it.   WINSTON CHURCHILL

(*on the differences between England and America*) When we have a world series, we ask other countries to participate.   JOHN CLEESE

Sometimes I wonder if we don't actually prefer things a little crap.   BEN ELTON

A lot of my countrymen say rude things about England because it has the lowest standard of living in the world, and I don't think that's fair. I think that's mean and horrid. Because I know England will rise again. It will – say, to the level of Sicily or Ethiopia.   DAME EDNA EVERAGE (BARRY HUMPHRIES)

My roles play into a certain fantasy of what people want English people to be, whereas half the time we're vomiting beer and beating people up.
HUGH GRANT

From every Englishman emanates a kind of gas, the deadly choke-lamp of boredom.   HEINRICH HEINE

I've always felt England was a great place to work in. It's an island and the audience can't run very far.   BOB HOPE

When I first came to England I couldn't speak a word of English, but my sex life was perfect. Now my English is perfect, but my sex life is rubbish.
JULIO IGLESIAS

We do not regard Englishmen as foreigners. We look on them only as rather mad Norwegians.   HALVARD LANGE

England is the only country where food is more dangerous than sex.
JACKIE MASON

If an Englishman gets run down by a truck, he apologises to the truck.
JACKIE MASON

On the Continent people have good food; in England people have good table manners.   GEORGE MIKES, *How to be an Alien*

Continental people have sex lives; the English have hot-water bottles.
GEORGE MIKES, *How to be an Alien*

An Englishman, even if he is alone, forms an orderly queue of one.
GEORGE MIKES, *How to be an Alien*

English humour resembles the Loch Ness Monster in that both are famous but there is a strong suspicion that neither exists. Here the similarity ends. The Loch Ness Monster seems to be a gentle beast and harms no one; English humour is cruel.   GEORGE MIKES, *English Humour for Beginners*

Whenever I call an Englishman rude he takes it as a compliment.

GEORGE MIKES, *How to be Inimitable*

Nothing unites the English like war. Nothing divides them like Picasso.

HUGH MILLS, *Prudence and the Pill*

The English have three vegetables and two of them are cabbage.

WALTER PAGE

An Englishman thinks he is moral when he is only uncomfortable.

GEORGE BERNARD SHAW, *Man and Superman*

The Englishwoman is so refined,
She has no bosom and no behind.

STEVIE SMITH, *This Englishwoman*

I know why the sun never set on the British Empire: God wouldn't trust an Englishman in the dark.

DUNCAN SPAETH

English people apparently queue up as a sort of hobby. A family man might pass a mild autumn evening by taking the wife and kids to stand in the cinema queue for a while and then leading them over for a few minutes in the sweetshop queue and then, as a special treat for the kids, saying, 'Perhaps we've time to have a look at the No. 31 bus queue before we turn in.'

CALVIN TRILLIN

I did a picture in England one winter and it was so cold I almost got married.

SHELLEY WINTERS

Enthusiasm

A mediocre idea that generates enthusiasm will go further than a great idea that inspires no one.

MARY KAYE ASH

Zeal: a certain nervous disorder affecting the young and inexperienced.

AMBROSE BIERCE

Men who never get carried away should be.

MALCOLM FORBES

Nothing dispels enthusiasm like a small admission fee.

KIN HUBBARD

Son, I wanna apologise. I just got so caught up trying to encourage you I was blinded to your stinky performance. If you forgive me, I promise I'll never encourage you again.

HOMER SIMPSON, *The Simpsons*

Envy

Love looks through a telescope; envy, through a microscope.   JOSH BILLINGS

I envy people who drink. At least they have something to blame everything on.
OSCAR LEVANT, *Humoresque*

I will do anything to look like him — except, of course, exercise or eat right.
STEVE MARTIN

To jealousy, nothing is more frightful than laughter.   FRANÇOISE SAGAN

Jealousy, the great exaggerator.   FRIEDRICH VON SCHILLER

Epitaphs

No flowers please, I'm allergic.   GOODMAN ACE

(*suggested*) I've played everything but the harp.   LIONEL BARRYMORE

(*suggested*) Did you hear about my operation?   WARNER BAXTER

When I am dead, I hope it may be said,
'His sins were scarlet, but his books were read.'   HILAIRE BELLOC

(*suggested*) Do not disturb.   CONSTANCE BENNETT

(*suggested*) On the whole, I'd rather be in Philadelphia.   W.C. FIELDS

At last — I get top billing.   WALLACE FORD

(*suggested*) Back to the silents.   CLARK GABLE

He practised no religion, which is why he died laughing.   BENNY GREEN

(*suggested*) Here's something I want to get off my chest.   WILLIAM HAINES

(*suggested*) Pardon me for not getting up.   ERNEST HEMINGWAY

(*suggested*) I'm involved in a plot.   ALFRED HITCHCOCK

(*suggested*) Over my dead body!   GEORGE S. KAUFMAN

Here lies Groucho Marx
and Lies and Lies and Lies
P.S. He never kissed an ugly girl.   GROUCHO MARX (*suggested*)

(*suggested*) I told you I was sick.   SPIKE MILLIGAN

(*suggested*) Excuse my dust.   DOROTHY PARKER

Her name, cut clear upon this marble cross,
Shines as it shone when she was still on earth;
While tenderly the mild, agreeable moss
Obscures the figures of her date of birth.
                        DOROTHY PARKER (*on an actress's tombstone*)

(*in the event of falling victim to cannibals, Schweitzer hoped that his tombstone
would read*) We have eaten Dr Schweitzer. He was good to the end.
                                              ALBERT SCHWEITZER

Equality

I began wearing hats as a young lawyer because it helped me to establish my
professional identity. Before that, whenever I was at a meeting, someone would
ask me to get coffee.   BELLA ABZUG

Women who seek to be equal with men lack ambition.   TIMOTHY LEARY

The vote, I thought, means nothing to women. We should be armed.
                                                            EDNA O'BRIEN

(*defending his demand for equal billing with Katharine Hepburn*) This is a movie,
not a lifeboat.   SPENCER TRACY

Women's liberation will not be achieved until a woman can become paunchy
and bald and still think she's attractive to the opposite sex.   EARL WILSON

Eternity

Eternity is a terrible thought. I mean, where's it going to end?
                        TOM STOPPARD, *Rosencrantz and Guildenstern are Dead*

If you are killing time, are you damaging eternity?   STEVEN WRIGHT

Etiquette

Etiquette means behaving yourself a little better than is absolutely essential.
WILL CUPPY

Social etiquette means making visitors feel at home even though you wish they were.

Eunuchs

Eunuch: a man who has had his works cut out for him.

Euphemisms

Euphemisms are unpleasant truths wearing diplomatic cologne.
QUENTIN CRISP, *Manners From Heaven*

In order to avoid the embarrassment of calling a spade a spade, newspapermen have agreed to talk about the credibility gap. This is a polite euphemism for deception.
WALTER LIPPMANN

Those comfortably padded lunatic asylums which are known, euphemistically, as the stately homes of England.
VIRGINIA WOOLF, *The Common Reader*

Evil

Infamy, infamy, they've all got it in for me.
JULIUS CAESAR (KENNETH WILLIAMS), *Carry On Cleo*

May the forces of evil become confused on the way to your house.
GEORGE CARLIN

Constantly choosing the lesser of two evils is still choosing evil.
JERRY GARCIA

It is a sin to believe evil of others, but it is seldom a mistake.
H.L. MENCKEN

Unfortunately, evil is perversely compelling. It always has been. Let's face it, the Bible is duller than the operating instructions for a hinge until the snake shows up.
DENNIS MILLER

Exaggeration

I never exaggerate. I just remember big.
CHI CHI RODRIGUEZ

Excess

Excess on occasion is exhilarating. It prevents moderation from acquiring the deadening effect of a habit.   W. SOMERSET MAUGHAM

Too much of a good thing can be wonderful.   MAE WEST

Life is like an overnight bag: if you try to cram too much into it, something has got to give.

Exchanges

Jim Hacker (Paul Eddington): Sometimes I suspect that the budget is all you really care about.
Sir Humphrey Appleby (Nigel Hawthorne): It is rather important. If nobody cares about the budget we could end up with a Department so small that even a Minister could run it.   *Yes, Minister*

Jean Harlow: Is the 't' in 'Margot' pronounced?
Margot Asquith: No. The 't' is silent – as in 'Harlow'.

Katharine Hepburn: Thank God I don't have to act with you anymore.
John Barrymore: I didn't realise you ever had, darling.

Oscar Wilde: Do you mind if I smoke?
Sarah Bernhardt: I don't care if you burn.

Arthur Schlesinger Jr: I liked your book, Liz. Who wrote it for you?
Liz Carpenter: I'm glad you like it, Arthur. Who read it to you?

Nancy Astor: Winston, if you were my husband, I should flavour your coffee with poison.
Winston Churchill: Madam, if I were your husband I should drink it.

Niles Crane (David Hyde Pierce): It seems like only yesterday that Dad moved in with you.
Frasier Crane (Kelsey Grammer): Isn't it interesting that two people can have completely opposite impressions of the same event?   *Frasier*

Producer: Would you like to play golf with me?
W.C. Fields: No thanks. If I ever want to play with a prick, I'll play with my own.

Charlie McCarthy: Say, Mr Fields, I read in the paper where you consumed two quarts of liquor a day. What would your father think about that?
W.C. Fields: He'd think I was a sissy.

Reporter: How many husbands have you had?
Zsa Zsa Gabor: You mean, apart from my own?

(*on Mahatma Gandhi's arrival at Southampton, 1930*)
Reporter: Mr Gandhi, what do you think of Western civilisation?
Gandhi: I think it would be a very good idea.

Mary Anderson: What do you think is my best side?
Alfred Hitchcock: My dear, you're sitting on it.

Steve McCroskey (Lloyd Bridges): Jacobs, what have you got on Elaine Dickinson?
Controller Jacobs (Stephen Stucker): Well, I'm two inches taller, a better dancer, and much more fun to be with.   *Airplane II: The Sequel*

Reporter: Tell me, how did you find America?
John Lennon: Turned left at Greenland.   *A Hard Day's Night*

George Melly: How come you've got more lines on your face than me?
Mick Jagger: They're laughter lines.
Melly: Surely nothing's that funny.

Edina Monsoon (Jennifer Saunders): What you don't understand is that inside of me, sweetie, inside of me, there's a thin person just screaming to get out.
Mother (June Whitfield): Just the one, dear?   *Absolutely Fabulous*

Austin Powers (Mike Myers): How do you get into those pants?
Felicity Shagwell (Heather Graham): Well, you can start by buying me a drink.   *Austin Powers: The Spy Who Shagged Me*

Lisa: Dad, we did something very bad!
Homer: Did you wreck the car?
Bart: No.
Homer: Did you raise the dead?
Lisa: Yes.
Homer: But the car's okay?
Bart and Lisa: Uh-huh.
Homer: All right then.   *The Simpsons*

Katharine Hepburn: I'm afraid that I'm a little tall for you, Mr Tracy.
Spencer Tracy: Not to worry, Miss Hepburn, I'll soon cut you down to size.

Oscar Wilde: I wish I had said that.
James McNeill Whistler: You will, Oscar, you will.

Excuse

He that is good for making excuses is seldom good for anything else.
BENJAMIN FRANKLIN

Excuses are like assholes, Taylor — everybody got one.
SGT O'NEILL (JOHN MCGINLEY), *Platoon*

It isn't what you know that counts, it's what you think of in time.

People who are always making allowances for themselves soon go bankrupt.

Exercise

If it weren't for the fact that the TV set and the refrigerator are so far apart, some of us wouldn't get any exercise at all.   JOEY ADAMS

My favourite machine at the gym is the vending machine.   JO BRAND

Fitness: if it came in a bottle everyone would have a great body.   CHER

When I run marathons, my goal isn't to win or to place, or even to finish it under a certain time. It's to catch that cute guy with the nice butt in the little shorts running in front of me.   ANN DANTSUKA

Weight-lifting apparatus is a curious phenomenon — machines invented to replicate the back-breaking manual labour the industrial revolution relieved us of.
SUE GRAFTON

If God had wanted us to run, instead of a belly button, he'd have given us a fast-forward button.   JOE HICKMAN

I swim a lot. It's either that or buy a new golf ball.   BOB HOPE

I have a punishing workout regimen. Every day I do three minutes on a treadmill, then I lie down, drink a glass of vodka and smoke a cigarette.
ANTHONY HOPKINS

Whenever I feel like exercise, I lie down until the feeling passes.
ROBERT M. HUTCHINS

I'm not into working out. My philosophy: No pain, no pain.   CAROL LEIFER

The only exercise I get these days is walking behind the coffins of my friends who take exercise.   PETER O'TOOLE

Do I lift weights? Sure. Every time I stand up.   DOLLY PARTON

I ran three miles today. Finally I said, 'Lady, take your purse.'   EMO PHILIPS

I'm Jewish. I don't work out. If God had wanted us to bend over, he'd have put diamonds on the floor.   JOAN RIVERS

I burned sixty calories. That should take care of the peanut I ate in 1962.
RITA RUDNER

I usually last about ten minutes on the stairmaster. Unless, of course, there's someone stretching in front of me in a leotard, then I can go an hour. That's why they call it the stairmaster. You get up there and you stare.
JERRY SEINFELD

Exercise? I get it on the golf course. When I see my friends collapse, I run for the paramedics.   RED SKELTON

As a nation we are dedicated to keeping physically fit — and parking as close to the stadium as possible.   BILL VAUGHAN

Here's a reason to smile: every seven minutes of every day, someone in an aerobics class pulls a hamstring.   ROBIN WILLIAMS

(*on taking up exercise*) I reckoned if my boobs got any lower I would have to buy them their own pair of shoes.   JEANETTE WINTERSON

The only good thing about leotards is that they're a very effective deterrent against any sort of unwanted sexual attention. If you're wearing stretch knickers, stretch tights, and a stretch Lycra leotard, you might as well try and sexually harass a trampoline.   VICTORIA WOOD

A doctor says to a man: 'You want to improve your love life? You need to get some exercise. Run ten miles a day.' Two weeks later the man called the doctor. The doctor says, 'How is your love life since you've been running?' The man says, 'I don't know, I'm 140 miles away!'　HENNY YOUNGMAN

How do you get a man to do sit-ups? – Put the remote control between his toes.

Experience

Experience teaches you that the man who looks you straight in the eye, particularly if he adds a firm handshake, is hiding something.

CLIFTON FADIMAN, *Enter, Conversing*

Experience is a good teacher, but her fees are very high.　WILLIAM RALPH INGE

Experience is that marvellous thing that enables you to recognise a mistake when you make it again.　FRANKLIN P. JONES

Experience is what you get when you don't get what you wanted.

ANN LANDERS

Experience is a hard teacher because she gives the test first, the lesson afterwards.　VERNON SANDERS

Education is when you read the fine print. Experience is what you get if you don't.　PETE SEEGER

We learn from experience that men never learn anything from experience.

GEORGE BERNARD SHAW

Experience is the name everyone gives to their mistakes

OSCAR WILDE, *Lady Windermere's Fan*

Experience is the comb that Nature gives us when we are bald.

BELGIAN PROVERB

Experts

Often the experts make the worst possible ministers in their own fields. In this country we prefer rule by amateurs.　CLEMENT ATTLEE

An expert is a man who has made all the mistakes which can be made in a very narrow field.　NIELS BOHR

Where facts are few, experts are many.   DONALD R. GANNON

Always listen to experts. They'll tell you what can't be done, and why. Then do it.   ROBERT A. HEINLEIN

Expression

He gave her a look you could have poured on a waffle.
RING LARDNER, *The Big Town*

Listen, I got three expressions: looking left, looking right and looking straight ahead.   ROBERT MITCHUM

Extravagance

An extravagance is anything you buy that is of no earthly use to your wife.
FRANKLIN P. ADAMS

Anyone with money to burn will always find himself surrounded by people with matches.   JOE RYAN

Marge Simpson: I thought we agreed to consult each other before any major purchases.
Homer Simpson: Well, you bought all those smoke alarms, and we haven't had a single fire.   *The Simpsons*

Marge: This chair is $2000! We could buy a whole living room set for that.
Homer: Marge, there's an empty spot I've always had inside me. I tried to fill it with family, religion, community service, but those were dead ends. I think this chair is the answer.   *The Simpsons*

F

Facts

It's a little known fact that the tan became popular in what is known as the Bronze Age.   CLIFF CLAVIN (JOHN RATZENBERGER), *Cheers*

Facts are meaningless. You can use facts to prove anything that's remotely true!
HOMER SIMPSON, *The Simpsons*

Get the facts first. You can distort them later. MARK TWAIN

Failure

Failure is the condiment that gives success its flavour. TRUMAN CAPOTE

A man may fail many times but he isn't a failure until he begins to blame somebody else. J. PAUL GETTY

He was a self-made man who owed his lack of success to nobody.
JOSEPH HELLER, *Catch-22*

If there is something you must do and you cannot do it, you cannot do anything else. MIGNON McLAUGHLIN, *The Neurotic's Notebook*

Failure is regarded in Hollywood as practically a contagious disease; people will literally cross the road to avoid someone who is tainted with it.
BARRY NORMAN, *The Film Greats*

The thing that we call 'failure' is not the falling down, but the staying down.
MARY PICKFORD

Flops are a part of life's menu and I've never been a girl to miss out on any of the courses. ROSALIND RUSSELL

Success is a public affair. Failure is a private funeral. ROSALIND RUSSELL

You tried your best and you failed miserably. The lesson is 'never try'.
HOMER SIMPSON, *The Simpsons*

Trying is the first step towards failure. HOMER SIMPSON, *The Simpsons*

Success has many parents, but failure is an orphan. AMERICAN PROVERB

Fairness

My grandmother had a way of saying one thing *for* a person and ten things against, a formula which maintained her reputation for fairness.
RICHARD ARMOUR, *Pills, Potions – and Granny*

Expecting the world to treat you fairly because you are good is like expecting the bull not to charge because you are a vegetarian. DENNIS WHOLEY

Fame

Five minutes of stardom means another SIXTY-FIVE years of emptiness.
MARC ALMOND

When someone follows you all the way to the shop and watches you buy toilet roll, you know your life has changed.
JENNIFER ANISTON

It's bloody tough being a legend.
RON ATKINSON

Any idiot can get laid when they're famous. That's easy. It's getting laid when you're not famous that takes some talent.
KEVIN BACON

I have enemies I've never even met – that's fame.
TALLULAH BANKHEAD

The final test of fame is to have a crazy person imagine he is you.
MEL BROOKS

Fame means when your computer modem is broken, the repair guy comes out to your house a little faster.
SANDRA BULLOCK

Fame is only good for one thing – they will cash your cheque in a small town.
TRUMAN CAPOTE

When you live in New York and people are looking at you all the time, the first instinct is that you're going to be mugged – or wondering if my flies were undone.
TOM CRUISE

Fame is like a bad tattoo, it's hard to get rid of once you've got it.
DIDO

Being noticed can be a burden. Jesus got himself crucified because he got himself noticed. So I disappear a lot.
BOB DYLAN

Fame usually comes to those who are thinking about something else.
OLIVER WENDELL HOLMES

I'm afraid of losing my obscurity. Genuineness only thrives in the dark. Like celery.
ALDOUS HUXLEY, *Those Barren Leaves*

The best fame is a writer's fame: it's enough to get a table at a good restaurant, but not enough that you get interrupted when you eat.
FRAN LEBOWITZ

You're not famous until my mother has heard of you. JAY LENO

I may be a living legend, but that sure don't help when I've got to change a tyre. ROY ORBISON

For years I could walk the streets unrecognised except by people who thought I was Dustin Hoffman. AL PACINO

The other day a woman came up to me and said, 'Didn't I see you on television?' I said, 'I don't know. You can't see out the other way.' EMO PHILIPS

It makes you feel permanently like a girl walking past construction workers. BRAD PITT

The legend part is easy. It's the living that's hard. KEITH RICHARDS

Often celebrity is a lead weight around your neck. It's like you pointing at the moon, but people are looking at your finger. STING

You can't get spoiled if you do your own ironing. MERYL STREEP

The fame you earn has a different taste from the fame that is forced upon you. GLORIA VANDERBILT

Everyone wants to ride with you in the limo, but what you need is someone who will take the bus with you when the limo breaks down. OPRAH WINFREY

Family

I'm very proud of my gold pocket watch. My grandfather, on his deathbed, sold me this watch. WOODY ALLEN

Richard, you know I love my family, but that is no reason why I need to acknowledge them in public. HYACINTH BUCKET (PATRICIA ROUTLEDGE), *Keeping Up Appearances*

The greater part of every family is always odious. If there are one or two good ones in a very large family it is as much as can be expected. SAMUEL BUTLER, *The Way of All Flesh*

The first half of our lives is ruined by our parents, and the second half by our children. CLARENCE DARROW

I took my mother-in-law to Madame Tussaud's Chamber of Horrors and one of the attendants said, 'Keep her moving sir, we're stocktaking.'

LES DAWSON

I saw six men kicking and punching the mother-in-law. My neighbour said, 'Are you going to help?' I said, 'No, six should be enough.'   LES DAWSON

My husband's granny is eighty-seven, and she just got two new hearing aids, and cataracts removed from both eyes. I tell her we're going to fix her up just a little more and then sell her.

TINA FEY

Secretary: It must be hard to lose your mother-in-law.
W.C. Fields: Yes, it is, very hard. It's almost impossible.

(*on being shown the Grand Canyon*) What a marvellous place to drop one's mother-in-law!

MARSHAL FOCH

My Hungarian grandfather was the kind of man that could follow someone into a revolving door and come out first.

STEPHEN FRY

Sure I love [my brother] Liam – but not as much as I love Pot Noodle.

NOEL GALLAGHER

We all have rosy memories of a simpler, happy time – a time of homemade apple pie and gingham curtains, a time when Mom understood everything and Dad could fix anything. 'Let's get those traditional family values back,' we murmur to each other. Meanwhile, in a simultaneous universe, everyone I know, and every celebrity I don't know, is coming out of the closet to talk about how miserable they are because they grew up in dysfunctional families.

CYNTHIA HEIMEL

Distant relatives are the best kind, and the further the better.   KIN HUBBARD

The simplest toy, one which even the youngest child can operate, is called a grandparent.

SAM LEVENSON

If you want to know how your girl will treat you after marriage, just listen to her talking to her little brother.   SAM LEVENSON

My wife said, 'Can my mother come down for the weekend?' I said, 'Why?' She said, 'Well, she's been up on the roof two weeks already.'

BOB MONKHOUSE

Having a family is like having a bowling alley installed in your brain.

MARTIN MULL

A family is a unit composed not only of children but of men, women, an occasional animal, and the common cold.　　　OGDEN NASH

Family love is messy, clinging, and of an annoying and repetitive pattern, like bad wallpaper.　　　P.J. O'ROURKE

My grandmother was a very tough woman. She buried three husbands and two of them were just napping.　　　RITA RUDNER

Big sisters are the crab grass in the lawn of life.

CHARLES SCHULZ, *Peanuts*

It's not easy to juggle a pregnant wife and a troubled child, but somehow I managed to fit in eight hours of TV a day.

HOMER SIMPSON, *The Simpsons*

Now, remember. As far as anyone knows, we're a nice, normal family.

HOMER SIMPSON, *The Simpsons*

The family — that dear octopus from whose tentacles we never quite escape.

DODIE SMITH, *Dear Octopus*

Adam was the luckiest man: he had no mother-in-law.　　　MARK TWAIN

Relations never lend one any money, and won't give one credit, even for genius. They are a sort of aggravated form of the public.　　　OSCAR WILDE

Relations are a tedious lot of people who don't know how to live or when to die.　　　OSCAR WILDE

I wanted to do something nice, so I bought my mother-in-law a chair. Now they won't let me plug it in.　　　HENNY YOUNGMAN

Families are like fudge — mostly sweet, with a few nuts.

Be good to your family: you never know when you are going to need them to empty your bedpan.

Mother-in-law: a woman who destroys her son-in-law's peace of mind by giving him a piece of hers.

Why is it better to fight with a rottweiller than your mother-in-law? — The rottweiller eventually lets go.

Fanaticism

A fanatic is one who can't change his mind and won't change the subject.

WINSTON CHURCHILL

A fanatic is one who sticks to his guns whether they're loaded or not.

FRANKLIN P. JONES

Fanaticism consists in redoubling your effort when you have forgotten your aim.

GEORGE SANTAYANA

Fans

I don't get sent anything strange like underwear. I get sent cookies.

JENNIFER ANISTON

A fan club is a group of people who tell an actor he is not alone in the way he feels about himself.

JACK CARSON

Latins are tenderly enthusiastic. In Brazil they throw flowers at you. In Argentina they throw themselves.

MARLENE DIETRICH

Larry, what I like to do is have a huge slumber party with all my obsessed fans. We break out the sleeping bags, order pizza, watch everything I've ever done on video, and then spend hours and hours talking about me. It's great.

PHIL HARTMAN, *The Larry Sanders Show*

The fact is that I am sixty years old — and 20-year-old chicks are still throwing their pants at me. It's ridiculous really.

KEITH RICHARDS

(*on the strangest thing he's ever received from a fan*) Herpes.

ROBBIE WILLIAMS

Fantasies

A man will fantasise that he's having sex with someone else; a woman will fantasise that she's having sex with *anyone* else.

JO BRAND

You fantasize about a man with a Park Avenue apartment and a nice big stock portfolio. For me, it's a fireman with a nice big hose.

SAMANTHA JONES (KIM CATTRALL), *Sex and the City*

I have low self-esteem. When we were in bed together, I would fantasise that *I* was someone else.　RICHARD LEWIS

The fantasy of every Australian man is to have two women – one cleaning and the other dusting.　MAUREEN MURPHY

In sex I like to role play. I like to pretend I'm not paying for it.
　DAN NATURMAN

Farce

Farce is tragedy played at a thousand revolutions per minute.
　JOHN MORTIMER

Fashion

I never cared for fashion much, amusing little seams and witty little pleats: it was the girls I liked.　DAVID BAILEY

The trick of wearing mink is to look as though you are wearing a cloth coat. The trick of wearing a cloth coat is to look as though you are wearing a mink.
　PIERRE BALMAIN

Art produces ugly things which frequently become beautiful with time. Fashion, on the other hand, produces beautiful things which always become ugly with time.　JEAN COCTEAU

When someone says that lime green is the new black for this season, you just want to tell them to get a life.　BRUCE OLDFIELD

(*on fashion gurus Trinny Woodall and Susannah Constantine*) My business sense has been insulted by the amount of money they are making.
　GRIFF RHYS JONES

The fashion magazines are suggesting that women wear clothes that are 'age appropriate'. For me, that would be a shroud.　JOAN RIVERS

They should put expiration dates on clothing so we men will know when they go out of style.　GARRY SHANDLING

Fashion is a form of ugliness so intolerable that we have to alter it every six months.　OSCAR WILDE

Fashion is something that goes in one year and out the other.

The only man who can fool all the women all the time is a fashion designer.

Fast food

What is it with McDonald's staff who pretend they don't understand you unless you insert the 'Mc' before the item you are ordering? It has to be a McChicken Burger – just a chicken burger gets blank looks. Well I'll have a McStraw and jam it in your McEyes, you fucking McTosser!   BILLY CONNOLLY

(*of Ronald McDonald*) I know he's a fictional character but if such a man existed, it would be the duty of social services to warn the local parents that he had come to live in the area.   JEREMY HARDY

I went into a McDonald's yesterday and said, 'I'd like some fries.' The girl at the counter said, 'Would you like some fries with that?'   JAY LENO

Why do they sell hot dogs in packs of ten and buns in packs of eight?

Fathers

Fatherhood is pretending the present you love most is soap-on-a-rope.
   BILL COSBY

I remember the time I was kidnapped and they sent a piece of my finger to my father. He said he wanted more proof.   RODNEY DANGERFIELD

To be a successful father . . . there's one absolute rule: when you have a kid, don't look at it for the first two years.   ERNEST HEMINGWAY

I never got along with my dad. Kids used to come up to me and say, 'My dad can beat up your dad.' And I'd say, 'Yeah? When?'   BILL HICKS

My father only hit me once – but he used a Volvo.   BOB MONKHOUSE

A man's desire for a son is usually nothing but the wish to duplicate himself in order that such a remarkable pattern may not be lost to the world.
   HELEN ROWLAND

The fundamental defect of fathers is that they want their children to be a credit to them.   BERTRAND RUSSELL

Growing up, my father told me I could be whomever I wanted. What a cruel hoax that was! I'm still his son.   KENNY SMITH

A father is someone who carries pictures where his money used to be.

Fear

There is no terror in a bang, only in the anticipation of it.

ALFRED HITCHCOCK

I discovered I scream the same way whether I'm about to be devoured by a Great White or if a piece of seaweed touches my foot.   KEVIN JAMES

I like terra firma – the more firma, the less terra.   GEORGE S. KAUFMAN

The man who is not afraid of danger is not a hero, but a psychopath.

GEORGE MIKES, *How To Be a Guru*

All men are afraid of eyelash curlers. They don't understand them and they don't want to be near them. I sleep with one under my pillow, instead of a gun.

RITA RUDNER

Vercotti (Michael Palin): Doug. I was terrified of him. Everyone was terrified of Doug. I've seen grown men pull their own heads off rather than see Doug. Even Dinsdale was frightened of Doug.
Interviewer: What did he do?
Vercotti: He used sarcasm. He knew all the tricks, dramatic irony, metaphor, bathos, puns, parody, litotes and satire.   *Monty Python's Flying Circus*

Fear is just excitement in need of an attitude adjustment.

What happens if you get scared half to death twice?

Feminism

If a woman insists on being called Ms, ask her if it stands for miserable.

RUSSELL BELL

I've no time for broads who want to rule the world alone. Without men, who'd do up the zipper on the back of your dress?   BETTE DAVIS

Where else but in America could the women's liberation movement take off their bras, then go on TV to complain about their lack of support?

BOB HOPE

Feminism is just a way for ugly women to get into the mainstream of America.
RUSH LIMBAUGH

I'm furious about the Women's Liberationists. They keep getting up on soapboxes and proclaiming that women are brighter than men. That's true, but it should be kept very quiet or it ruins the whole racket. ANITA LOOS

Leaving sex to the feminists is like letting your dog vacation at the taxidermist.
CAMILLE PAGLIA

A man can be called ruthless if he bombs a country to oblivion. A woman can be called ruthless if she puts you on hold. GLORIA STEINEM

(*of feminist Mary Wollstonecraft*) A philosophising serpent . . . that hyena in petticoats. HORACE WALPOLE

Fertility

Chinese men aren't considered sex symbols and it's so unfair. We're obviously fertile. Give us a country, we'll fill it. RAYBON KAN

W.C. Fields

The only thing I can say about W.C. Fields, whom I have admired since the day he advanced upon Baby LeRoy with an ice pick, is this: any man who hates dogs and babies can't be all bad. LEO ROSTEN

(*when Fields arrived drunk on set*) Pour him out of here! MAE WEST

Fighting

I'm not a fighter, I have bad reflexes. I was once run over by a car being pushed by two guys. WOODY ALLEN

A man may fight for many things. His country, his friends, his principles, the glistening tear on the cheek of a golden child. But personally, I'd mud-wrestle my own mother for a ton of cash, an amusing clock and a sack of French porn.
EDMUND BLACKADDER (ROWAN ATKINSON), *Blackadder*

Whenever women catfight, men think it's going to turn to sex.
YASMINE BLEETH

Fighting is essentially a masculine idea; a woman's weapon is her tongue.
HERMIONE GINGOLD

Gentlemen, you can't fight in here. This is the war room!
President Muffley (Peter Sellers), *Dr Strangelove: Or How I Learned to Stop Worrying and Love the Bomb*

I thoroughly disapprove of duels. If a man should challenge me, I would take him kindly and forgivingly by the hand and lead him to a quiet place and kill him.
Mark Twain

Never pick a fight with an ugly person – they've got nothing to lose.
Robin Williams

Anything worth fighting for is worth fighting dirty for.

Figure

I had no intention of giving her my vital statistics. 'Let me put it this way,' I said. 'According to my girth, I should be a 90ft redwood.'
Erma Bombeck

The first time someone said, 'What are your measurements?' I answered, '37, 24, 38 – but not necessarily in that order.'
Carol Burnett

After forty a woman has to choose between losing her figure or her face. My advice is to keep your face, and stay sitting down.
Barbara Cartland

(*on Sarah Ferguson, Duchess of York*) She is a lady short on looks, absolutely deprived of any dress sense, and has a figure like a Jurassic monster.
Nicholas Fairbairn

I wouldn't change anything but I could do with my sharing my bottom and thighs with at least two other people.
Christine Hamilton

I have everything now I had twenty years ago – except now it's all lower.
Gypsy Rose Lee

Jennifer Lopez has started the big-butt look. But take my advice, guys. Don't show the article to your wife and say, 'Look, honey, you're a trend setter.'
Jay Leno

I have a million dollar figure . . . but it's all loose change.
Joan Rivers

(*of Marilyn Monroe*) She had curves in places other women don't even have places.
Cybill Shepherd

Miss [Judy] Garland's figure resembles the giant-economy-size tube of tooth-paste in girls' bathrooms. Squeezed intemperately at all points, it acquires a shape that defies definition by the most resourceful solid geometrician.

John Simon

You've been a fabulous mother. You've let them ruin your figure, your stomach's stretched beyond recognition, you've got tits down to your knees – and what for, for God's sake? Patsy Stone (Joanna Lumley), *Absolutely Fabulous*

(*to Rose*): So you're five years older, so am I, so is Blanche. Alright, so you have a few more wrinkles, so do I, so does Blanche. Okay, so you're a little thicker around the middle, so is Blanche.

Dorothy Zbornak (Bea Arthur), *The Golden Girls*

Women and greyhounds should have thin waists.

Spanish proverb

Film-making

Making a funny film provides all the enjoyment of getting your leg caught in the blades of a threshing machine. As a matter of fact, it's not even that pleas-urable; with the threshing machine the end comes much quicker.

Woody Allen

Good producers are as rare as rocking horse doo-doo.

Jon Amiel

I suppose I'm the boy who stood on the burning deck whence all but he had fled. The trouble is I don't know whether the boy was a hero or a bloody idiot.

Lindsay Anderson

It is the business of turning money into light and then back into money again.

John Boorman

I only direct in self-defence.

Mel Brooks

Cecil B. DeMille was De phony and De hypocrite of all time.

Yul Brynner

(*on Otto Preminger*) I don't think he could direct his nephew to the bathroom.

Dyan Cannon

Louis B. Mayer's arm around your shoulder meant his hand was closer to your throat.

Jules Dassin

The movie business is macabre. Grotesque. It is a combination of a football game and a brothel. FEDERICO FELLINI

A producer shouldn't get ulcers — he should give them. SAM GOLDWYN

It took longer to make one of Mary Pickford's contracts than it did to make one of Mary's pictures. SAM GOLDWYN

You can't direct a [Charles] Laughton picture. The best you can hope for is to referee. ALFRED HITCHCOCK

Up until now, I thought Monsters Inc. was a documentary about the Weinstein brothers. NATHAN LANE

(on Louis B. Mayer) He charms the birds out of the trees, then shoots 'em. HERMAN J. MANKIEWICZ

Sidney Lumet is the only director who could double-park in front of a whorehouse. He's that fast. PAUL NEWMAN

The only time I use women [in films], they're either naked or dead. JOEL SILVER

(on Die Hard) I want to make this movie so much I'd stab *myself* in the back. JOEL SILVER

The most expensive habit in the world is celluloid, not heroin, and I need a fix every few years. STEVEN SPIELBERG

(on Star Wars *director George Lucas*) He reminded me a little of Walt Disney's version of a mad scientist. STEVEN SPIELBERG

I thank God that neither I nor any member of my family will ever be so hard up that we have to work for Otto Preminger. LANA TURNER

(on Roman Polanski) The four-foot Pole you wouldn't want to touch with a ten-foot pole. KENNETH TYNAN

I have ten commandments. The first nine are, thou shalt not bore. The tenth is, thou shalt have the right of final cut. BILLY WILDER

Steven Spielberg is so powerful he had final cut at his own circumcision. ROBIN WILLIAMS

A team effort is a lot of people doing what I say. Michael Winner

Fire

You know, men and women are a lot alike in certain situations. Like when they're both on fire. Dave Attell

The very existence of flame-throwers proves that some time, somewhere, someone said to themselves, 'You know, I want to set those people over there on fire, but I'm just not close enough to get the job done.'
George Carlin

(*at fire drill*) Right. Well obviously if there was a fire you would all be standing down here like this, right here in the lobby, wouldn't you? I don't know why we bother! We should let you all burn.
Basil Fawlty (John Cleese), *Fawlty Towers*

I was at this casino minding my own business, and this guy came up to me and said, 'You're gonna have to move, you're blocking a fire exit.' As though if there was a fire, I wasn't gonna run. If you're flammable and have legs, you are never blocking a fire exit. Mitch Hedberg

My dad used to say 'always fight fire with fire', which is probably why he got thrown out of the fire brigade. Harry Hill

In elementary school, in case of fire you have to line up quietly in single file from the smallest to the tallest. What was the logic? Do tall people burn slower?
Warren Hutcherson

Build a man a fire and he'll be warm for a day. Set a man on fire and he'll be warm for the rest of his life. Terry Pratchett

Beverly Hills is very exclusive. For instance their fire department won't make house calls. Mort Sahl

Last week the candle factory burned down. Everyone just stood around and sang 'Happy Birthday'. Steven Wright

Fireworks

Sparklers are the gay cousins of the fireworks family. Dave Attell

(*on a neighbour's firework display*) It was like listening to someone else having sex – deeply irritating, unless you are doing it yourself. Amanda Platell

Fish

Dried fish is a staple food in Iceland. It varies in toughness. The tougher kind tastes like toenails, and the softer kind like the skin off the soles of one's feet.

W.H. AUDEN

I'm afraid of sharks — but only in a water situation. DEMETRI MARTIN

A baby Sardine
Saw her first submarine:
She was scared and watched through a peephole.
'Oh, come, come, come,'
Said the Sardine's mum,
'It's only a tin full of people.' SPIKE MILLIGAN

You don't have to swim faster than the shark. You only have to swim faster than the person you're with. KEVIN NEALON

Fish is the only food that is considered spoiled once it smells like what it is.

P.J. O'ROURKE

In Mexico, we have a word for sushi: bait. JOSÉ SIMON

Fishing

Give a man a fish and he will eat for a day. Teach him how to fish, and he will sit in a boat and drink beer all day. GEORGE CARLIN

I had no idea how much I liked fishing until I realised all the shopping involved.

NILES CRANE (DAVID HYDE PIERCE), *Frasier*

Anglers think they are divining some primeval natural force by outwitting a fish, a creature that never even got out of the evolutionary starting gate.

RICH HALL

On fishing shows they always throw the fish back. They don't want to eat them. They just want to make them late for something. MITCH HEDBERG

There are only two occasions when Americans respect privacy, especially in presidents. Those are prayer and fishing. HERBERT HOOVER

A fishing rod is a stick with a worm at one end and a fool at the other.

SAMUEL JOHNSON

Dr Strabismus (Whom God Preserve) of Utrecht is carrying out research work with a view to crossing salmon with mosquitoes. He says it will mean a bite every time for fishermen.   J.B. MORTON, ('BEACHCOMBER')

Give a man a fish and he has food for a day; teach him how to fish and you can get rid of him for the entire weekend.   ZENNA SCHAFFER

Last year I went fishing with Salvador Dali. He was using a dotted line. He caught every other fish.   STEVEN WRIGHT

Flattery

Flattery is like a cigarette – it's all right so long as you don't inhale.
                ADLAI STEVENSON

Flatterer: one who says things to your face that he wouldn't say behind your back.

Flattery is telling other people exactly what they think of themselves.

Flirting

I'll flirt with anyone from garbagemen to grandmothers.   MADONNA

Flirt: a woman who thinks it's every man for herself.

There are times not to flirt. When you're sick. When you're with children. When you're on the witness stand.

Florida

We humans do not need to leave Earth to get to a hostile, deadly, alien environment; we already have Miami.   DAVE BARRY

We never look outside [in Miami] on Christmas morning to discover that the landscape has been magically transformed by a blanket of white, unless a cocaine plane has crashed on our lawn.   DAVE BARRY

Miami Beach is where neon goes to die.   LENNY BRUCE

My parents didn't want to move to Florida, but they turned sixty, and that's the law.   JERRY SEINFELD

Errol Flynn

His life was a fifty-year trespass against good taste.   LESLIE MALLORY

You knew where you were with Errol — he always let you down.

DAVID NIVEN

Folly

Every man has his follies — and often they are the most interesting things he has got.

JOSH BILLINGS

Food

I will not eat oysters. I want my food dead. Not sick. Not wounded. Dead.

WOODY ALLEN

Appetizers are little things you keep eating until you lose your appetite.

RICHARD ARMOUR

I never eat on an empty stomach.

TALLULAH BANKHEAD

In Spain, attempting to obtain a chicken salad sandwich, you wind up with a dish whose name, when you look it up in your Spanish-English dictionary, turns out to mean: eel with big abscess.

DAVE BARRY

A gourmet who thinks of calories is like a tart who looks at her watch.

JAMES BEARD

Anytime a person goes into a delicatessen and orders a pastrami on white bread, somewhere a Jew dies.

MILTON BERLE

I'm a man
More dined against than dining.

MAURICE BOWRA

I personally stay away from natural foods. At my age I need all the preservatives I can get.

GEORGE BURNS

There are some foods that just sound too funny to eat. Like guacamole. It sounds like something you yell when you're on fire. 'Holy guacamole! My ass is burnin'!' Or . . . when you can't remember the name of something: 'Hey Ed, where's that little guacamole that plugs into the lamp?'

GEORGE CARLIN

Leftovers make you feel good twice. First, when you put them away, you feel thrifty and intelligent: 'I'm saving food!' Then a month later when blue hair is growing out of the ham, and you throw it away, you feel *really* intelligent: 'I'm saving my life!'

GEORGE CARLIN

My favourite food is Guinness. It's the only food that doesn't have to be cooked or kept in a refrigerator.   QUENTIN CRISP

Won't you have some cake, Father? It's got cocaine in it. Oh no, hang on, it's not cocaine, is it? What do I mean now? – The little things . . . raisins.
                                        MRS DOYLE (PAULINE MCLYNN), *Father Ted*

What a clever man invented sun-dried tomatoes! Went into the garden and said, 'Look at these shrivelled, maggot-infested things. I'll sell them for more than real tomatoes.'   DAME EDNA EVERAGE

(*of Howard Hughes*) One day when he was eating a cookie he offered me a bite. Don't underestimate that. The poor guy's so frightened of germs, it could darn near have been a proposal.   JEAN HARLOW

I think Pringles' intention was to make tennis balls. But the day the rubber was supposed to show up, they got a big load of potatoes instead.
                                                              MITCH HEDBERG

Rice is great when you're hungry and want two thousand of something.
                                                              MITCH HEDBERG

On a traffic light green means go and yellow means yield, but on a banana it's just the opposite. Green means hold on, yellow means go ahead, and red means where the heck did you get that banana?   MITCH HEDBERG

I like vending machines, because snacks are better when they fall. If I buy a candy bar at the store, oftentimes I will drop it, so that it achieves its maximum flavour potential.   MITCH HEDBERG

As life's pleasures go, food is second only to sex. Except for salami and eggs. Now that's better than sex, but only if the salami is thickly sliced.
                                                                 ALAN KING

Bread that must be sliced with an axe is bread that is too nourishing.
                                                              FRAN LEBOWITZ

Everything you see, I owe to spaghetti.   SOPHIA LOREN

(*on having matzo balls for dinner for a third time at Arthur Miller's parents*) Isn't there any other part of a matzo you can eat?   MARILYN MONROE

Anything you have to acquire a taste for was not meant to be eaten.

EDDIE MURPHY

I don't eat grapes out of sympathy for the migrant farm workers. And I don't eat raisins out of respect for the older migrant farm workers.

GENE PAMPA

I've eaten a river of liver and an ocean of fish! I've eaten so much fish, I'm ready to grow gills! I've eaten so much liver, I can only make love if I'm smothered in bacon and onions.   'HAWKEYE' PIERCE (ALAN ALDA), *M*A*S*H*

After all the trouble you go to, you get about as much actual 'food' out of eating an artichoke as you would from licking thirty or forty postage stamps.

MISS PIGGY

The frozen pea was a landmark in the development of convenience food. It is important to remember that word 'convenience' as you wrestle the strong plastic packet with numb fingers before finally tearing it open with your teeth.

OLIVER PRITCHETT

There is no love sincerer than the love of food.   GEORGE BERNARD SHAW

Donuts . . . is there anything they can't do?

HOMER SIMPSON, *The Simpsons*

Red meat is *not* bad for you. Now blue-green meat, *that's* bad for you.

TOMMY SMOTHERS

Get yer haggis right here! Chopped heart and lungs, boiled in a wee sheep's stomach! Tastes as good as it sounds!

GROUNDSKEEPER WILLIE, *The Simpsons*

You can say this for ready-mixes: the next generation isn't going to have any trouble making pies exactly like mother used to make.   EARL WILSON

Why do people who work in health food shops always look so unhealthy?

VICTORIA WOOD

A sandwich is an unsuccessful attempt to make both ends meat.

Why do croutons come in airtight packages? Aren't they just stale bread?

Why does a round pizza come in a square box?

Fools

A common mistake people make when trying to design something completely foolproof is to underestimate the ingenuity of complete fools.
DOUGLAS ADAMS

If fifty million people say a foolish thing it is still a foolish thing.
ANATOLE FRANCE

He may look like an idiot and talk like an idiot, but don't let that fool you. He really is an idiot.
GROUCHO MARX

One disadvantage of being a hog is that at any moment some blundering fool may try to make a silk purse out of your wife's ear.
J.B. MORTON

I'm all in favour of keeping dangerous weapons out of the hands of fools. Let's start with typewriters.
FRANK LLOYD WRIGHT

It is a foolish sheep that makes the wolf its confessor.
ITALIAN PROVERB

Football (American)

Losing the Super Bowl is worse than death. With death you don't have to get up next morning.
GEORGE ALLEN

If me and King Kong went into an alley, only one of us would come out. And it wouldn't be the monkey.
LYLE ALZADO

(*on a religious linebacker*) He knocks the hell out of people, but in a Christian way.
SAMMY BAUGH

Thanksgiving dinners take eighteen hours to prepare. They are consumed in twelve minutes. Half-times take twelve minutes. This is not coincidence.
ERMA BOMBECK

Football is not a contact sport. It's a collision sport. Dancing is a good example of a contact sport.
DUFFY DAUGHERTY

The reason women don't play football is because eleven of them would never wear the same outfit in public.
PHYLLIS DILLER

Pro football is like nuclear warfare. There are no winners, only survivors.
FRANK GIFFORD

A good coach needs a patient wife, a loyal dog and a great quarterback, but not necessarily in that order.   BUD GRANT

Kicking is very important in [American] football. In fact, some of the more enthusiastic players even kick the football, occasionally.   ALFRED HITCHCOCK

American football makes rugby look like a Tupperware party.

SUE LAWLEY

The quarterback's spending so much time behind the center that he may jeopardise his right to lead a Boy Scout troop.   DENNIS MILLER

I've seen women pee standing up with better aim.   DENNIS MILLER

When we won the league championship, all the married guys on the club had to thank their wives for putting up with all the stress and strain all season. I had to thank all the single broads in New York.   JOE NAMATH

(*asked if he preferred Astroturf to grass*) I don't know. I've never smoked Astroturf.   JOE NAMATH

It isn't necessary to see a good tackle. You can hear it.   KNUTE ROCKNE

Football combines the two worst things about America: it is violence punctuated by committee meetings.   GEORGE F. WILL

Gerald Ford

Nixon impeached himself. He gave us Gerald Ford as his revenge.

BELLA ABZUG

He looks like the guy in a science fiction movie who is the first to see the Creature.   DAVID FRYE

Gerald Ford – the most dangerous driver since Ben Hur – has made golf a contact sport. It's not hard to find him on a golf course – just follow the wounded.   BOB HOPE

Alan Shepard walking on the moon found a golf ball with Gerald Ford's initials on it.   BOB HOPE

In the Bob Hope Golf Classic, the participation of President Gerald Ford was more than enough to remind you that the nuclear button was at one stage at the disposal of a man who might have either pressed it by mistake or else pressed it deliberately in order to obtain room service.   CLIVE JAMES

Gerry Ford is so dumb he can't fart and chew gum at the same time.
LYNDON B. JOHNSON

Gerry Ford is a nice guy but he played too much football with his helmet off.
LYNDON B. JOHNSON

Intervening in Gerald Ford's re-election campaign is like rearranging the deck chairs on the *Titanic*.   ROGERS MORTON

Foreplay

A study shows the average guy burns sixty calories in thirty minutes of foreplay. Listen, if he gives thirty minutes of foreplay, he's not the average guy.
JAY LENO

Want to know why women don't blink during foreplay? Not enough time.
JOAN RIVERS

Foreplay is like beefburgers – three minutes each side.   VICTORIA WOOD

For the man, driving back to her place is considered part of foreplay.

Forgiveness

You'll have to forgive Hank. His heart's in the right place but he keeps his brain in a box at home.   ARTIE (RIP TORN), *The Larry Sanders Show*

It is easier to get forgiveness than permission.

To err is human; to forgive, unusual.

France and the French

The first thing that strikes a visitor to Paris is a taxi.   FRED ALLEN

We hate the French! We fight wars against them! Did all those men die in vain on the field of Agincourt? Was the man who burnt Joan of Arc simply wasting good matches?   EDMUND BLACKADDER (ROWAN ATKINSON), *Blackadder*

I've lived in England for thirty years and I'm a much better Frenchman for it.
RAYMOND BLANC

(*on the French*) They are short, blue-vested people who carry their own onions when cycling abroad, and have a yard which is 3.37 inches longer than other people's.   ALAN COREN, *The Sanity Inspector*

The French will only be united under the threat of danger. Nobody can simply bring together a country that has 246 kinds of cheese.
                                                        CHARLES DE GAULLE

It is unthinkable for a Frenchman to arrive at middle age without having both syphilis and the Cross of the Legion of Honour.   ANDRÉ GIDE

The best thing I know between France and England is . . . the sea.
                                                DOUGLAS WILLIAM JERROLD

French is the language that turns dirt into romance.   STEPHEN KING

Frenchmen drink wine just like we used to drink water before Prohibition.
                                                          RING LARDNER

In France, they're having trouble translating a lot of Internet terms into French. In France the law is you have to use French words. For example, there are no French words for 'surfing the Web', there aren't any French words for 'chat session', and there aren't any French words for 'hacker'. Of course, a lot of other words don't translate to French either: military victory, deodorant . . .
                                                              JAY LENO

A Frenchman dreams of a smart funeral. He works hard throughout a lifetime to be able to die above his station.   GEORGE MIKES

The overall impression from the British is that they love France but would prefer it if the French didn't live there.   JOHN MORTIMER

Going to war without France is like going duck hunting without your accordion.
                                                        DONALD RUMSFELD

I can never forgive God for creating the French.   PETER USTINOV

Anyone who tries to be funny in France is met with machine-gun fire.
                                                        FRANCIS VEBER

France is a country where the money falls apart in your hands and you can't tear the toilet paper.   BILLY WILDER

The French invented the only known cure for dandruff. It is called the guillotine.

P.G. WODEHOUSE

A fighting Frenchman runs away from even a she-goat.   RUSSIAN PROVERB

Free speech

The right to be heard does not automatically include the right to be taken seriously.

HUBERT HUMPHREY

It is by the goodness of God that in our country we have those three unspeakably precious things: freedom of speech, freedom of conscience, and the prudence never to practise either of them.   MARK TWAIN, *Following the Equator*

Freedom

My husband said he needed more space. So I locked him outside.

ROSEANNE BARR

The freedom women were supposed to have found in the Sixties largely boiled down to easy contraception and abortion: things to make life easier for men, in fact.   JULIE BURCHILL, *Damaged Goods*

Give a man a free hand and he'll try to put it all over you.

FRISCO DOLL (MAE WEST), *Klondike Annie*

There's nothing wrong with being cut from the herd. It makes you the one buffalo that isn't there when the Indians run the rest of them off the cliff.

LOIS (JANE KACZMAREK), *Malcolm in the Middle*

The only man who is really free is the one who can turn down an invitation to dinner without giving an excuse.   JULES RENARD

All men are born free and equal, but some of them get married.

Giving a man space is like giving a dog a computer: the chances are he will not use it wisely.

Friendship

A friend in power is a friend lost.   HENRY ADAMS

The best time to make friends is before you need them.   ETHEL BARRYMORE

I lost closer friends than 'darling Georgie' the last time I was deloused.
EDMUND BLACKADDER (ROWAN ATKINSON), *Blackadder*

A friend doesn't go on a diet because you are fat.   ERMA BOMBECK

A friend will tell you she saw your old boyfriend — and he's a priest.
ERMA BOMBECK

No man can be friends with a woman he finds attractive. He always wants to have sex with her. Sex is always out there. Friendship is ultimately doomed.
HARRY BURNS (BILLY CRYSTAL), *When Harry Met Sally . . .*

A man's friendships, like his will, are invalidated by his marriage.
SAMUEL BUTLER, *The Way of All Flesh*

It's hard when you don't like someone a friend marries . . . It means that even a simple flat inquiry like 'How's Helen?' is taken amiss, since your friend always thinks that what you hope he's going to say is 'Dead.'
NORA EPHRON, *Heartburn*

A false friend and a shadow attend only when the sun shines.
BENJAMIN FRANKLIN

A friend that ain't in need is a friend indeed.   KIN HUBBARD

Friends are God's apology for relatives.   HUGH KINGSMILL

A friend is one who has the same enemies you have.   ABRAHAM LINCOLN

Money can't buy you friends, but you can get a better class of enemy.
SPIKE MILLIGAN, *Puckoon*

Love demands infinitely less than friendship.   GEORGE JEAN NATHAN

I've tried to have women friends, but they always end up pregnant.
NATHAN (WOODY HARRELSON), *Will and Grace*

Awards become corroded, friends gather no dust.   JESSE OWENS

I was the kid next door's imaginary friend.   EMO PHILIPS

My friends tell me I have an intimacy problem, but they don't really know me.
GARRY SHANDLING

You know what really kicks a great friendship into high gear? Expensive gifts.
CYBILL SHERIDAN (CYBILL SHEPHERD), *Cybill*

I do not believe that friends are necessarily the people you like best, they are merely the people who got there first.   PETER USTINOV, *Dear Me*

Whenever a friend succeeds, a little something in me dies.
GORE VIDAL

We cherish our friends not for their ability to amuse us, but for ours to amuse them.   EVELYN WAUGH

When you are down and out something always turns up – and it is usually the noses of your friends.   ORSON WELLES

A real friend is one who walks in when the rest of the world walks out.
WALTER WINCHELL

(*on Burt Lancaster*) I know we were buddies because he threatened to kill me on no fewer than three occasions, and he did that only to his friends.
MICHAEL WINNER

Before borrowing money from a friend, decide which you need most.
AMERICAN PROVERB

Friends are like fiddle-strings and they must not be screwed too tightly.
IRISH PROVERB

It's what people don't know about each other that makes them such good friends.

Friends are like condoms: they protect you when things get hard.

Fun

Most of the time I don't have much fun. The rest of the time I don't have any fun at all.   WOODY ALLEN

Fun stuff: walk into a gun store, buy three guns and a bunch of ammunition, then ask them if they have any ski masks.   GEORGE CARLIN

Sometimes you've got to specifically go out of your way to get into trouble. It's called fun.   ADRIAN CRONAUER (ROBIN WILLIAMS), *Good Morning, Vietnam*

Funerals

In the city a funeral is just an interruption of traffic; in the country it is a form of popular entertainment. GEORGE ADE

My grandfather was a very insignificant man. At his funeral his hearse *followed* the other cars. WOODY ALLEN

(*to a fellow pallbearer at the funeral of escapologist Harry Houdini*) I bet you a hundred bucks he ain't in here. CHARLES BANCROFT DILLINGHAM

(*after Louis B. Mayer's funeral*) The only reason so many people showed up was to make sure he was dead. SAM GOLDWYN

Everything has its drawbacks, as the man said when his mother-in-law died, and they came down upon him for the funeral expenses.
JEROME K. JEROME, *Three Men in a Boat*

Movie actors wear dark glasses to funerals to conceal the fact that their eyes are not red from weeping. NUNNALLY JOHNSON

They say such nice things about people at their funerals that it makes me sad to realise that I'm going to miss mine by just a few days. GARRISON KEILLOR

Memorial services are the cocktail parties of the geriatric set.
HAROLD MACMILLAN

The show which, alas, every actor has to miss is his own memorial service.
ROBERT MORLEY

Everything is drive-through. In California they even have a burial service called Jump-in-the-Box. WIL SHRINER

(*on the large crowd attending the funeral of Hollywood mogul Harry Cohn*) It proves what they always say: give the public what they want to see, and they'll come out for it. RED SKELTON

The Future

Always remember that the future comes one day at a time.
DEAN ACHESON

Make love and be merry for tomorrow you may catch some disgusting skin disease. EDMUND BLACKADDER (ROWAN ATKINSON), *Blackadder*

The day after tomorrow is the third day of the rest of your life.

GEORGE CARLIN

Well, what if there is no tomorrow? There wasn't one today.

PHIL CONNORS (BILL MURRAY), *Groundhog Day*

Let's face facts, shall we? There is a very real possibility that this could also be the *last* day of the rest of your life.

DAVE HENRY

Don't worry about the world coming to an end today. It is already tomorrow in Australia.

CHARLES SCHULZ

Why should I care about posterity? What's posterity ever done for me?

GROUCHO MARX

How does a man show he's planning for the future? – He buys two cases of beer instead of one.

G

Zsa Zsa Gabor

Zsa Zsa Gabor got married as a one-off and it was so successful she turned it into a series.

BOB HOPE

You can calculate Zsa Zsa Gabor's age by the rings on her fingers.

BOB HOPE

The only person who ever left the Iron Curtain wearing it.

OSCAR LEVANT

Zsa Zsa Gabor has been married so many times she has rice marks on her face.

HENNY YOUNGMAN

Gadgets

My father worked for the same firm for twelve years. They fired him. They replaced him with a tiny gadget this big. It does everything that my father does, only it does it much better. The depressing thing is my mother ran out and bought one.

WOODY ALLEN

Electric can openers are the perfect thing for people who want absolutely no arm muscles at all.   *Crabby Road*

One of the universal rules of happiness is: always be wary of any helpful item that weighs less than its operating manual.   TERRY PRATCHETT

Real men don't use instructions, son. Besides, this is just the manufacturer's opinion on how to put this together.

TIM TAYLOR (TIM ALLEN), *Home Improvement*

Gaffes

He dribbles a lot and the opposition doesn't like it — you can see it all over their faces.   RON ATKINSON

Right now I feel that I've got my feet on the ground as far as my head is concerned.   BO BELINSKY

Baseball is ninety per cent mental. The other half is physical.   YOGI BERRA

It seems like déjà vu all over again.   YOGI BERRA

When you come to a fork in the road, take it.   YOGI BERRA

For seven and a half years I've worked alongside President Reagan. We've had triumphs, made some mistakes. We've had some sex . . . uh . . . setbacks.

GEORGE BUSH

(*at the 1977 University Boat Race*) Ah, isn't that nice! The wife of the Cambridge president is kissing the cox of the Oxford crew.   HARRY CARPENTER

You read what Disraeli had to say. I don't remember what he said. He said something. He's no longer with us.   BOB DOLE

I intend to open this country up to democracy, and anyone who is against that, I will jail.   JOAO BAPTISTA FIGUEIREDO

I've got ten pairs of training shoes — one for every day of the week.

SAMANTHA FOX

We must have had 99 per cent of the game. It was the other three per cent that cost us the match.   RUUD GULLIT

You can't just let nature run wild.   WALLY HICKEL

I cannot tell you how grateful I am — I am filled with humidity.
                                                                          GIB LEWIS

Sure, there have been injuries and deaths in boxing — but none of them serious.
                                                                        ALAN MINTER

Republicans understand the importance of bondage between a mother and child.
                                                                        DAN QUAYLE

It isn't pollution that's harming the environment. It's the impurities in our air and
water that are doing it.   DAN QUAYLE

I believe we are on an irreversible trend toward more freedom and democracy.
But that could change.   DAN QUAYLE

I am happy when our fans are happy, when our players are happy and our
chairman is on the moon.   CLAUDIO RANIERI

And now the sequence of events in no particular order.   DAN RATHER

(*on being asked a political question at a 'Just Say No' rally*) I didn't intend for
this to take on a political tone. I'm just here for the drugs.
                                                                      NANCY REAGAN

(*after a 1982 tour of Latin America*) I didn't go down there with any plan for the
Americas, or anything. I went down to find out from them. You'd be surprised.
They're all individual countries.   RONALD REAGAN

I think that gay marriage should be between a man and a woman.
                                                              ARNOLD SCHWARZENEGGER

(*on the attraction of fame*) I get to go to lots of overseas places, like Canada.
                                                                     BRITNEY SPEARS

If history repeats itself, I should think we can expect the same thing again.
                                                                     TERRY VENABLES

We are launching this innovation for the first time.   JIMMY WALKER

The lead car is absolutely unique, except for the one behind it, which is identical.
                                                                     MURRAY WALKER

Patrick Tambay's hopes, which were nil before, are absolutely zero now.

MURRAY WALKER

With half the race gone, there is half the race still to go.

MURRAY WALKER

Do my eyes deceive me, or is Senna's Lotus sounding a bit rough?

MURRAY WALKER

I've just stopped my startwatch . . .   MURRAY WALKER

And Helena got six inches during the night . . . Helena, Montana, that is.

U.S. TV weatherman

Gambling

One way to stop a runaway horse is to bet on him.   JEFFREY BERNARD

A sucker's groan is music to a gambler's ear.

SGT ERNEST T. BILKO (PHIL SILVERS), *The Phil Silvers Show*

At gambling, the deadly sin is to mistake bad play for bad luck.

IAN FLEMING, *Casino Royale*

I love blackjack, but I'm not addicted to gambling. I'm addicted to sitting in a semi-circle.   MITCH HEDBERG

The only man who makes money following the races is one who does it with a broom and shovel.   ELBERT HUBBARD

If you're playing a poker game and you look around the table and can't tell who the sucker is, it's you.   PAUL NEWMAN

There are few things in this world more reassuring than an unhappy Lottery winner.   TONY PARSONS

The race is not always to the swift, nor the battle to the strong, but that's the way to bet.   DAMON RUNYON

Nobody has ever bet enough on a winning horse.   RICHARD SASULY

Gambling promises the poor what property performs for the rich – something for nothing.   GEORGE BERNARD SHAW

Homer Simpson: Your mother has this crazy idea that gambling is wrong. Even though they say it's okay in the Bible.
Lisa: Really? Where?
Homer: Uh . . . somewhere in the back.   *The Simpsons*

Slot machines are like crack for old people.   KEENAN IVORY WAYANS

I backed a great horse the other day – it took seven horses to beat him.
HENNY YOUNGMAN

Why don't you ever see the headline: 'Psychic Wins Lottery'?

Games

Snooker is chess with balls.   CLIVE JAMES

I suspect that the game 'Rock, Paper, Scissors, Pavement-Saw' would generally end in a tie.   TOM KELLEHER

Children are the most desirable opponents at Scrabble as they are both easy to beat and fun to cheat.   FRAN LEBOWITZ

(*watching Kramer and Newman*): It's Risk. It's a game of world domination being played by two guys who can barely run their own lives.
JERRY SEINFELD, *Seinfeld*

Greta Garbo

Boiled down to essentials, she is a plain mortal girl with large feet.
HERBERT KRETZMER

Co-starring with Garbo hardly constituted an introduction.   FREDRIC MARCH

Gardening

Mrs Bryson has outlined a big, ambitious programme of gardening. Worse, she's wearing what I nervously call her Nike expression – the one that says 'Just do it.'   BILL BRYSON, *Notes from a Big Country*

What is a weed? A plant whose virtues have not been discovered.
RALPH WALDO EMERSON, *Fortune of the Republic*

My neighbour asked if he could use my lawnmower. I told him of course he could as long as he didn't take it out of my garden.   ERIC MORECAMBE

If I were to choose where to die, it would be in the herbaceous border.

MIRIAM STOPPARD

Perennials are the ones that grow like weeds, biennials are the ones that die this year instead of next, and hardy annuals are the ones that never come up at all.

KATHARINE WHITEHORN

Garlic

There is no such thing as a little garlic.

ARTHUR BAER

There are five elements: earth, air, fire, water, and garlic.

LOUIS DIAT

Gays

My hope is that gays will be running the world, because then there would be no war – just a greater emphasis on military apparel.

ROSEANNE BARR

I was a man trapped in a woman's body. That was before I was born, of course.

MIKE BENT

The world dictates that heteros make love, while gays have sex.   BOY GEORGE

They say you can't tell guys are gay just by looking. But if two guys are kissing, you can figure at least one of them's gay.

BILL BRAUDIS

My lesbianism is an act of Christian charity. All those women out there are praying for a man, and I'm giving them my share.

RITA MAE BROWN

I think that the longer I look good, the better gay men feel.

CHER

I started being really proud of the fact that I was gay even though I wasn't.

KURT COBAIN

The worst part of being gay in the 20th century is all that damn disco music to which one has to listen.

QUENTIN CRISP

I became one of the stately homos of England.

QUENTIN CRISP, *The Naked Civil Servant*

Paige Clark (Joely Fisher): I still can't believe that Ellen is gay!

Spence Kovak (Jeremy Piven): Well, I always thought for a while she might be. I mean, she could always run faster than I could, throw a ball farther, climb a tree faster . . .

Joe Farrell (David Anthony Higgins): Did you ever think maybe YOU were gay?

Ellen

You can get gay anything now. Gay coffee, gay lager – it's like straight lager, it just goes down much easier.   GRAHAM NORTON

Today in the Oval Office, President Bush said he's 'troubled' by all the gay weddings that have been going on in San Francisco. Bush says he's also troubled by Bert and Ernie's relationship on *Sesame Street*.   CONAN O'BRIEN

Rock Hudson let his gay agent marry him off to his secretary because he didn't want people to get the right idea.   ANTHONY PERKINS

I am not gay. I am, however, thin, single and neat.   JERRY SEINFELD

Gay people should be allowed to get married. Just because somebody's gay doesn't mean he shouldn't suffer like the rest of us.   JEFF SHAW

Homosexuality in Russia is a crime and the punishment is seven years in prison, locked up with other men. There is a three-year waiting list.

YAKOV SMIRNOFF

If homosexuality is a disease, let's all call in queer to work: 'Hello. Can't work today, still queer.'   ROBIN TYLER

I think you're missing the silver lining here. When you're old and in diapers, a gay son will know how to keep you away from chiffon and backlighting.

KAREN WALKER (MEGAN MULLALLY), *Will and Grace*

We had gay burglars the other night. They broke in and rearranged the furniture.   ROBIN WILLIAMS

(*on Samantha*): I don't think she's a lesbian, I think she just ran out of men.

CHARLOTTE YORK (KRISTIN DAVIS), *Sex and the City*

You might just be gay if you can be in a crowded bar and still spot a toupee from fifty yards away.

You might just be gay if you know the difference between a latte, a cappuccino, café au lait and a macchiato, and if you don't you know how to fake it.

You might just be gay if you never hold a grudge for longer than a decade.

Genius

Geniuses are like ocean liners: they should never meet.   Louis Aragon

The guy who invented the first wheel was an idiot. The guy who invented the other three, he was a genius.   Sid Caesar

Genius is one per cent inspiration and ninety nine per cent perspiration.   Thomas Alva Edison

Intellectuals solve problems; geniuses prevent them.   Albert Einstein

We are all geniuses up to the age of ten.   Aldous Huxley

There is no off position on the genius switch.   David Letterman

There's a fine line between genius and insanity. I have erased this line.   Oscar Levant

Men of genius are often dull and inert in society, as a blazing meteor, when it descends to earth, is only a stone.   Henry Wadsworth Longfellow

To some, I'm a junkie madman who should be dead, and to others, I'm a mythical genius.   Keith Richards

(*on Andy Warhol*) The only genius with an IQ of sixty.   Gore Vidal

The public is wonderfully tolerant. It forgives everything except genius.   Oscar Wilde

Gentlemen

A gentleman is any man who wouldn't hit a woman with his hat on.   Fred Allen

Gentlemen prefer blondes, but take what they can get.   Don Herold

A gentleman need not know Latin, but he should at least have forgotten it.   Brander Matthews

Hotel manager: Do you have a gentleman in your room?
Dorothy Parker: Just a minute. I'll ask him.

A gentleman is simply a patient wolf.   Lana Turner

Germany

She is famous for having the worst personality in Germany. And as you can imagine, that's up against some pretty stiff competition.

EDMUND BLACKADDER (ROWAN ATKINSON), *Blackadder*

My husband's German. Every night I get dressed up as Poland and he invades me.
BETTE MIDLER

You can always reason with a German. You can always reason with a barnyard animal, too, for all the good it does.
P.J. O'ROURKE, *Holidays in Hell*

My sister married a German. He complained he couldn't get a good bagel back home. I said, 'Well, whose fault is that?'
EMO PHILIPS

Ghosts

More women believe in ghosts than men. They've had experience. They have sex with a guy. They turn around, and he's vanished.
JAY LENO

Ghosts can walk through walls; how come they don't fall through the floor?
STEVEN WRIGHT

Gifts

The worst gift is a fruitcake. There is only one fruitcake in the world and people keep sending it to each other.
JOHNNY CARSON

I don't accept flowers. I take nothing perishable.
PAULETTE GODDARD

The other day I sent my girlfriend a huge pile of snow. I rang up and said, 'Did you get my drift?'
PETER KAY

(*on ex-husband Rod Stewart*) What do you give the man who's had everyone?
ALANA STEWART

A woman may race to get a man a gift but it always ends in a tie.
EARL WILSON

If you are sending someone some Styrofoam, what do you pack it in?
STEVEN WRIGHT

William Ewart Gladstone

He has not a single redeeming defect.
BENJAMIN DISRAELI

(*quantifying disaster*) A misfortune is if Gladstone fell into the Thames; a calamity would be if someone pulled him out.   BENJAMIN DISRAELI

He speaks to me as if I was a public meeting.   QUEEN VICTORIA

Glamour

Glamour: the indefinable something about a girl with a big bosom.
ABE BURROWS

Glamour is what Julie Andrews doesn't have. She does her duties efficiently but mechanically, like an airline stewardess.   PAULINE KAEL

Glamour is just sex that got civilised.   DOROTHY LAMOUR

Glass

It is a curious fact that good glass cracks at a touch, while cheap stuff can be hurled about with perfect safety.   MONICA DICKENS, *One Pair of Hands*

Gluttony

I am not a glutton – I am an explorer of food.   ERMA BOMBECK

Gluttony is a great fault; but we do not necessarily dislike a glutton. We only dislike the glutton when he becomes a gourmet – that is, we only dislike him when he not only wants the best for himself, but knows what is best for other people.   G.K. CHESTERTON

Signs You've Eaten Too Much:
Hundreds of volunteers have started to stack sandbags around you.
Doctor tells you your weight would be perfect for a man 17 feet tall.
You are responsible for a slight but measurable shift in the earth's axis.
Getting off your couch requires help from the fire department.
Every escalator you step on immediately grinds to a halt.
You're sweatin' gravy.   DAVID LETTERMAN

By six years of age I ate so much I had stretch marks around my mouth
JOAN RIVERS

God

Not only is there no God, but try getting a plumber on weekends.
WOODY ALLEN, *Getting Even*

How can I believe in God when just last week I got my tongue caught in the roller of an electric typewriter? WOODY ALLEN, *Without Feathers*

As the poet said, 'Only God can make a tree' – probably because it's so hard to figure out how to get the bark on. WOODY ALLEN

God made man in his own image, and it would be a sad lookout for Christians around the globe if God looked anything like you, Baldrick. EDMUND BLACKADDER (ROWAN ATKINSON), *Blackadder*

God don't make no mistakes. That's how he got to be God. ARCHIE BUNKER (CARROLL O'CONNOR), *All in the Family*

In the beginning there was nothing. God said, 'Let there be light!' And there was light. There was still nothing, but you could see it a whole lot better. ELLEN DEGENERES

What if God's a woman? Not only am I going to hell, I'll never know why! ADAM FERRARA

God not only plays dice, He sometimes throws the dice where they cannot be seen. STEPHEN HAWKING

If there is no God, who pops up the next Kleenex? ART HOPPE

God writes a lot of comedy. The trouble is, he's stuck with so many bad actors who don't know how to play funny. GARRISON KEILLOR

And God said, 'Let there be light', and there was light, but the Electricity Board said He would have to wait until Thursday to be connected. SPIKE MILLIGAN

They say God has existed from the beginning and will exist beyond the end of time. Can you imagine trying to sit through his home movies? SCOTT ROEBEN

Men don't get cellulite. God might just be a man. RITA RUDNER

You know why God is a man? Because if God was a woman she would have made sperm taste like chocolate. CARRIE SNOW

Cliff Clavin (John Ratzenberger): I'm ashamed God made me a man.
Carla Tortelli (Rhea Perlman): I don't think God's doing a lot of bragging
about it either.   *Cheers*

Goldwynisms (the thoughts of film producer Sam Goldwyn)

The next time I want to send an idiot on some errand, I'll go myself.

A verbal contract isn't worth the paper it's written on.

I don't want any yes-men around me. I want everybody to tell me the truth even
if it costs them their jobs.

(*on* The Best Years of Our Lives) I don't care if it doesn't make a nickel. I just
want every man, woman and child in America to see it!

What we want is a story that starts with an earthquake and works its way up
to a climax.

Let's have some new clichés.

In two words – impossible!

Golf

It took me seventeen years to get 3,000 hits in baseball. I did it in one afternoon on the golf course.   HANK AARON

If you break 100, watch your golf. If you break eighty, watch your business.
                                                                  JOEY ADAMS

G is for Green, that's constructed to roll
In every direction away from the hole.
                                RICHARD ARMOUR, *Golf is a Four-Letter Word*

Although golf was originally restricted to wealthy Protestants, today it's open
to anybody who owns hideous clothing.   DAVE BARRY

Give me golf clubs, fresh air and a beautiful partner, and you can keep the clubs
and the fresh air.   JACK BENNY

Golf is a game where guts and blind devotion will always net you absolutely
nothing but an ulcer.   TOMMY BOLT

I regard golf as an expensive way of playing marbles. G.K. CHESTERTON

Golf is an ineffectual attempt to direct an uncontrollable sphere into an inaccessible hole with instruments ill-adapted to the purpose.

WINSTON CHURCHILL

Golf and sex are the only two things you can enjoy without being good at either of them. JIMMY DEMARET

The difference in golf and government is that in golf you can't improve your lie.

GEORGE DEUKMEJIAN

They say golf is like life, but don't believe them. Golf is more complicated than that. GARDNER DICKINSON

The reason the pro tells you to keep your head down is so you can't see him laughing. PHYLLIS DILLER

When the wind blows at St Andrews, even the seagulls walk. NICK FALDO

They call it golf because all the other four-letter words were taken.

RAYMOND FLOYD

If there is any larceny in man, golf will bring it out. PAUL GALLICO

The only time my prayers are never answered is on the golf course.

BILLY GRAHAM

Golf balls are attracted to water as unerringly as the eye of a middle-aged man to a female bosom. MICHAEL GREEN, *The Art of Coarse Golf*

The secret of missing a tree is to aim straight at it.

MICHAEL GREEN, *The Art of Coarse Golf*

I played golf. I did not get a hole in one, but I did hit a guy. That's way more satisfying. MITCH HEDBERG

Golf is the hardest game in the world to play, and the easiest to cheat at.

DAVE HILL

Reverse every natural instinct and do the opposite of what you are inclined to do, and you will probably come very close to having a perfect golf swing.

BEN HOGAN

If you watch a game, it's fun. If you play it, it's recreation. If you work at it, it's golf.
BOB HOPE

Golf is my profession. Show business is just to pay the green fees.
BOB HOPE

I never kick my ball in the rough or improve my lie in a sand trap. For that I have a caddy.
BOB HOPE

If I'm on the course and lightning starts, I get inside fast. If God wants to play through, let him.
BOB HOPE

I don't want to play golf. When I hit a ball, I want someone else to go chase it.
ROGERS HORNSBY

If profanity had an influence on the flight of the ball, the game of golf would be played far better than it is.
HORACE G. HUTCHINSON

Competitive golf is played mainly on a five-and-a-half-inch course, the space between your ears.
BOBBY JONES

Alaska would be an ideal place for a golf course – mighty few trees and damn few ladies' foursomes.
REX LARDNER

The easiest shot in golf is the fourth putt.
RING LARDNER

Golf may be played on Sunday, not being a game within view of the law, but being a form of moral effort.
STEPHEN LEACOCK

Show me a man who is a good loser and I'll show you a man who is playing golf with his boss.
JIM MURRAY

The older you get the stronger the wind gets – and it's always in your face.
JACK NICKLAUS

I tee the ball high because through years of experience I have found that the air offers less resistance than dirt.
JACK NICKLAUS

Golf combines two favourite American pastimes: taking long walks and hitting things with a stick.
P.J. O'ROURKE

I have a tip that can take five strokes off anyone's golf game. It's called an eraser.
ARNOLD PALMER

Golf is a marriage. If I had to choose between my wife and my putter, well, I'd miss her.
GARY PLAYER

The only useful putting advice I ever got from my caddy was to keep the ball low.
CHI CHI RODRIGUEZ

I have never been depressed enough to take up the game, but they say you get so sore at yourself you forget to hate your enemies.
WILL ROGERS

Anyone who likes golf on television would enjoy watching the grass grow on the greens.
ANDY ROONEY

(*on Winged Foot Golf Club, New York*) The greens are harder than a whore's heart.
SAM SNEAD

Some of us worship in churches, some in synagogues, some on golf courses.
ADLAI STEVENSON

Columbus went around the world in 1492. That isn't a lot of strokes when you consider the course.
LEE TREVINO

The meek will inherit the earth, but they won't make the green in two.
LEE TREVINO

If there's a thunderstorm on a golf course, walk down the middle of the fairway, holding a one-iron over your head. Even God can't hit a one-iron.   LEE TREVINO

Real pressure in golf is playing for $10 when you've only got $5 in your pocket.
LEE TREVINO

It's good sportsmanship not to pick up lost golf balls while they are still rolling.
MARK TWAIN

Don't play too much golf. Two rounds a day are plenty.   HARRY VARDON

Sudden success in golf is like the sudden acquisition of wealth. It is apt to unsettle and deteriorate the character.
P.G. WODEHOUSE

Golf, like measles, should be caught young.   P.G. WODEHOUSE

All is fair in love and golf.   AMERICAN PROVERB

Golf vocabulary: a Lorena Bobbitt — a nasty slice.

Golfers

I had a wonderful experience on the golf course today. I had a hole in nothing. Missed the ball and sank the divot.   DON ADAMS

Love and putting are mysteries for the philosopher to solve. Both subjects are beyond golfers.   TOMMY ARMOUR

Putting allows the touchy golfer two to four opportunities to blow a gasket in the short space of two to forty feet.   TOMMY BOLT

Being left-handed is a big advantage. No one knows enough about your swing to mess you up with advice.   BOB CHARLES

When male golfers wriggle their feet to get their stance right, they look exactly like cats preparing to pee.   JILLY COOPER

The only time Nick Faldo opens his mouth is to change feet.

DAVID FEHERTY

I know I'm getting better at golf because I'm hitting fewer spectators.

GERALD FORD

I would like to deny all allegations by Bob Hope that during my last game of golf, I hit an eagle, a birdie, an elk and a moose.   GERALD FORD

A coarse golfer is one who has to shout 'fore' when he putts.

MICHAEL GREEN, *The Art of Coarse Golf*

Sammy Davis Jr hits the ball 130 yards and his jewellery goes 150.

BOB HOPE

(*on playing golf with President Ford and his security men*) It's fun to run down the fairway and have the trees run with you.   BOB HOPE

Arnold Palmer is the biggest crowd-pleaser since the invention of the portable sanitary facility.   BOB HOPE

I've done as much for golf as Truman Capote has for Sumo wrestling.

BOB HOPE

(*asked to explain the difference between amateur and professional golfers*)
When a pro hits it left to right, it's called a fade. When an amateur hits it left
to right, it's called a slice.   PETER JACOBSEN

(*on the colourful attire of a fellow golfer*) Doug Sanders' outfit has been described
as looking like the aftermath of a direct hit on a pizza factory.
                                                                  DAVE MARR

When [Jack] Nicklaus plays well he wins, when he plays badly he comes second.
When he's playing terribly, he's third.   JOHNNY MILLER

I'm playing like Tarzan, but scoring like Jane.   CHI CHI RODRIGUEZ

What a terrible round of golf! I only hit two good balls all day and that was
when I stood on a rake.   JIMMY TARBUCK

Amie [Palmer] would go for the flag from the middle of an alligator's back.
                                                                  LEE TREVINO

I'm not saying my golf game went bad, but if I grew tomatoes they'd come up
sliced.   LEE TREVINO

The other day I broke seventy. That's a lot of clubs.   HENNY YOUNGMAN

Gossip

The most powerful force in the universe is gossip.   DAVE BARRY

I won't stand for gossip! No, I sit down and make myself comfortable for gossip.
                                                                  Crabby Road

It isn't what they say about you, it's what they whisper.   ERROL FLYNN

Gossip columnists are diseases, like 'flu. Everyone is subject to them.
                                                                  JAMES GOLDSMITH

There isn't much to be seen in a little town, but what you hear makes up for
it.   KIN HUBBARD

It's really difficult to get out of gossip columns once you've got in.
                                                                  MICK JAGGER

Men have always detested women's gossip because they suspect the truth: their measurements are being taken and compared.   ERICA JONG

Gossip has got a bad name. Politicians dismiss it as tittle-tattle, particularly when it's true.   JOHN MORTIMER

Some people will believe anything if you whisper it to them.
                    LOUIS B. NIZER

Dorothy Zbornak (Bea Arthur): You know, sometimes I can't believe my ears.
Sophia Petrillo (Estelle Getty): I know. I should've taped them back when you were seven.   *The Golden Girls*

Gossip is just news running ahead of itself in a red satin dress.
                    LIZ SMITH

There is only one thing in the world worse than being talked about, and that is not being talked about.   OSCAR WILDE, *The Picture of Dorian Gray*

Gossip is the art of saying nothing in a way that leaves practically nothing unsaid.   WALTER WINCHELL

The reason a dog has so many friends is that he wags his tail instead of his tongue.

The difference between gossip and news is whether you hear it or tell it.

Gossip: a person who will never tell a lie if the truth will do more damage.

Wild horses couldn't drag a secret out of most women. However women seldom have lunch with wild horses.

Government

The government is unresponsive to the needs of the little man. Under 5' 7", it is impossible to get your congressman on the phone.   WOODY ALLEN

Jim Hacker (Paul Eddington): Opposition is about asking awkward questions.
Sir Humphrey Appleby (Nigel Hawthorne): And government is about not answering them.   *Yes, Minister*

There are two ways to get into government – one is to crawl in and the other is to kick your way in.   ANEURIN BEVAN

It may be true that you can't fool all the people all the time, but you can fool enough of them to rule a large country.
                                                                    WILL DURANT

In government, a 'highly placed source' is the person who started the rumour.
                                                                    SAM EWING

An interim government was set up in Afghanistan. It included two women, one of whom was Minister of Women's Affairs. Man, who'd she have to show her ankles to in order to get that job?
                                                                    TINA FEY

The government solution to a problem is usually as bad as the problem.
                                                                    MILTON FRIEDMAN

A government that is big enough to give you all you want is big enough to take it all away.
                                                                    BARRY GOLDWATER

It [the government] treats people as goods and then gets upset when they arrive in containers on the back of lorries.
                                                                    JEREMY HARDY

I don't know what people have got against the government – they've done nothing.
                                                                    BOB HOPE

Giving money and power to government is like giving whisky and car keys to teenage boys.
                                                    P.J. O'ROURKE, *Parliament of Whores*

Whatever it is that the government does, sensible Americans would prefer that the government does it to somebody else. This is the idea behind foreign policy.
                                                    P.J. O'ROURKE, *Parliament of Whores*

The mystery of government is not how Washington works but how to make it stop.
                                                                    P.J. O'ROURKE

One way to make sure crime doesn't pay would be to let the government run it.
                                                                    RONALD REAGAN, 1967

Today, if you invent a better mousetrap, the government comes along with a better mouse.
                                                    RONALD REAGAN, campaigning in 1976

A government is the only known vessel that leaks from the top.
                                                                    JAMES RESTON

Trying to make things work in government is sometimes like trying to sew a button on a custard pie.
                                                                    HYMAN G. RICKOVER

Two kinds of chair correspond with the two kinds of minister: one sort folds up instantly and the other sort goes round and round in circles.

BERNARD WOOLLEY (DEREK FOWLDS), *Yes, Minister*

Graduation

A graduation ceremony is an event where the commencement speaker tells thousands of students dressed in identical caps and gowns that individuality is the key to success.   ROBERT ORBEN

Graffiti

The following have been spotted on walls around the world:

Abstinence is the thin end of the pledge.

Adam came first, but men always do.

Add some variety to your sex life: use the other hand.

Aibohphobia: the fear of palindromes.

Alcohol: the cause of, and solution to, all of life's problems.

Alimony: bounty after the mutiny.

All this beer drinking will be the urination of me.

Alzheimer's advantage: new friends every day.

A man without a woman is like a neck without a pain.

American Indian driver – smoke signals only.

Anarchy, no rules, OK?

A seminar on time travel will be held two weeks ago.

A vasectomy means never having to say you're sorry.

A woman's word is never done.

Back in a minute – Godot.

Bad spellers of the world – Untie!

Beanz Meanz Fartz.

(*in a ladies' toilet*) Better to have loved and lost than to have spent your whole damn life with him.

Birth control: copulation without population.

British trees rule. Oak, eh?

Buggery is boring. Incest is relatively boring. Necrophilia is dead boring.

But for Venetian blinds, it would be curtains for us all.

Camel: a horse designed by a committee.

Chastity is curable, if detected early.

Coffee (n.), a person who is coughed upon.

Cole's Law: Thinly sliced cabbage.

Coup de grâce: lawnmower.

Dead owls don't give a hoot.

Death is nature's way of telling you to slow down.

Deja moo: the feeling that you've heard this bullshit before.

Disembowelling takes some guts.

Don't accuse me of being anti-semantic. Some of my best friends are words.

Down with gravity.

Dust: mud with the juice squeezed out.

Dwn wth vwls.

Earn cash in your spare time – blackmail friends.

Eat right. Stay fit. Die anyway.

Everyone has a price: mine is chocolate.

Every time I lose weight, it finds me again.

(*sign over urinal*) Express lane: five beers or less.

Flabbergasted (adj.), appalled over how much weight you have gained.

For the man who has everything . . . Penicillin.

42.7 per cent of all statistics are made up on the spot.

Free the Heinz 57.

Gasoline and alcohol don't mix – but try drinking them straight.

Geography is everywhere.

Good girls go to heaven, bad girls go everywhere.

Gravity always gets me down.

Handkerchief: cold storage.

Help wanted: Telepath. You know where to apply.

How can you tell when a man's had an orgasm? – You can hear him snoring.

How do you get a man to do sit-ups? – Put the remote control between his feet.

How does Bob Marley like his donuts? Wi' jammin'.

I am a nobody, and nobody is perfect; therefore I am perfect.

I could give up chocolate, but I'm not a quitter.

I'd give my right hand to be ambidextrous.

I earn a seven-figure salary. Unfortunately there's a decimal point involved.

I enjoy driving. It takes my mind off the road.

If a thing is worth doing, wouldn't it have been done already?

If Bill Gates had a dime for every time Windows crashed . . . Oh, wait a minute, he already does.

If God had wanted me to touch my toes, he would have put them on my knees.

If men had periods, they'd brag about the size of their tampons.

If we are what we eat, I'm cheap, fast and easy.

If you feel strongly about graffiti, sign a partition.

I'm a fairy. My name is Nuff. Fairynuff.

I'm an apathetic sociopath — I'd kill you if I cared.

I'm not tense, just terribly, terribly alert.

I'm not 30. I'm $29.95 plus shipping and handling.

I'm pink, therefore I'm spam.

I'm young at heart. Slightly older in other places.

Indecision is the key to flexibility.

I need my sinuses like I need a hole in the head.

IN GOD WE TRUST. All others pay cash.

Is a lady barrister without her briefs a solicitor?

Is 'tired old cliché' one?

It's not easy having dyslexia. Last week I went to a toga party as a goat.

It's not the pace of life that concerns me, it's the sudden stop at the end.

I've lost my faith in nihilism.

I've never had premonitions, but I think one day I might.

I've told you a hundred thousand times, stop exaggerating.

JESUS IS COMING: everybody look busy.

Just think what the speed of lightning would be if it didn't zigzag.

Just when I was used to yesterday, along came today.

Laugh and the world laughs with you, snore and you sleep alone.

Laughing stock: cattle with a sense of humour.

Love is grand; divorce is a hundred grand.

Money can't buy happiness, but it can rent it.

My daughter thinks I'm nosy. At least that's what she says in her diary.

My imaginary friend thinks you have serious mental problems.

My income seems to be the only thing I can't live without or within.

My inferiority complexes aren't as good as yours.

My mother was the travel agent for guilt trips.

Negligent (adj.), describes a condition in which you absentmindedly answer the door in your nightie.

99 per cent of lawyers give the rest a bad name.

No man is an island. But then, neither is a potato salad.

Nuts just take up space where chocolate ought to be.

Old fishermen never die, they just smell that way.

Old movie stars never die, they just keep Faye Dunaway.

Old professors never die, they just lose their faculties.

Only Robinson Crusoe had everything done by Friday.

Pedants rule, OK — or, more accurately, exhibit certain of the trappings of traditional leadership.

Perforation is a rip-off.

Polynesia: memory loss in parrots.

Procrastinate now!

Queensberry Rules, KO.

Saliva drools, OK.

Start a new movement — eat a prune.

Streakers beware: your end is in sight.

Sycophancy rules — if it's OK by you.

Talk is cheap because supply exceeds demand.

Time flies like an arrow; fruit flies like a banana.

Time is never wasted when you're wasted all the time.

2B or not 2B? That is the pencil.

Two in every one people in Britain are schizophrenic.

Variety is the life of spies.

Veni, Vidi, Velcro: I came, I saw, I stuck around.

What is E.T. short for? — Because he's got no legs.

What makes me tick? I don't know, but the noise is driving me mad.

When blondes have more fun, do they know it?

Whenever I feel blue, I start breathing again.

Whoever said that talk was cheap never hired a lawyer.

Why do black widow spiders kill their males after mating? To stop the snoring before it starts.

You're never alone with schizophrenia.

Grammar

When I split an infinitive, God damn it, I split it so it stays split.

RAYMOND CHANDLER

I adore adverbs; they are the only qualifications I really much respect.

HENRY JAMES

I was once in a spelling bee, but I lost because the other contastents cheeted.

PAUL PATERNOSTER

Remember, double negatives are a complete no-no.

Greatness

The street to obscurity is paved with athletes who perform great feats before friendly crowds. Greatness in major league sports is the ability to win in a stadium filled with people who are pulling for you to lose.

GEORGE ALLEN

Greed

Why do people say, 'Oh you just want to have your cake and eat it too'? Dead right! What good is a cake if you can't eat it?   BILLY CONNOLLY

Greed is envy with its sleeves rolled up.   GEORGE F. WILL

You can't have everything. I mean, where would you put it?

STEVEN WRIGHT

Groping

No man has ever stuck his hand up your dress looking for a library card.

JOAN RIVERS

Grudges

I bear no grudges. I have a mind that retains nothing.   BETTE MIDLER

When [Maria] Callas carried a grudge, she planted it, nursed it, fostered it, watered it, and watched it grow to sequoia size.   HAROLD C. SCHONBERG

(*on movie mogul Jack L. Warner*) He never bore a grudge against anyone he had wronged.   SIMONE SIGNORET

To carry a grudge is like being stung to death by one bee.

Guests

A satisfied customer. We should have him stuffed.
BASIL FAWLTY (JOHN CLEESE), *Fawlty Towers*

Some people can stay longer in an hour than others can in a week.
WILLIAM DEAN HOWELLS

Fish and guests stink after three days.   GREEK PROVERB

Guilt

There's only one difference between Catholics and Jews. Jews are born with guilt and Catholics have to go to school to learn it.   ELAYNE BOOSLER

I have great respect for someone from a strict Catholic upbringing who can climax without reservation.   ROBERT DOWNEY

Show me a woman who doesn't feel guilt and I'll show you a man.
ERICA JONG

Each snowflake in an avalanche pleads not guilty.   STANISLAW LEC

What is guilt? Guilt is the reason they put the articles in *Playboy*.
DENNIS MILLER

In the elaborate wardrobe of human emotions, guilt is the itchy wool turtleneck that's three sizes too small.   DENNIS MILLER

Guilt is simply God's way of letting you know that you're having too good a time.   DENNIS MILLER

My mother could make anybody feel guilty. She used to get letters of apology from people she didn't even know.   JOAN RIVERS

Oh no! What have I done? I smashed open my little boy's piggy bank, and for what? A few measly cents, not even enough to buy one beer. Wait a minute, lemme count and make sure.   HOMER SIMPSON, *The Simpsons*

A guilty conscience is the mother of invention.

Guns

You can get much further with a kind word and a gun than you can with a kind word alone.   AL CAPONE

In writing a novel, when in doubt, have two guys come through the door with guns.   RAYMOND CHANDLER

Actually, I'm a biochemical superfreak, but I still need a gun.
                    DR STANLEY GOODSPEED (Nicolas Cage), *The Rock*

Don't move. I've got a gun. Not here, but I got one.
                    RYAN HARRISON (LESLIE NIELSEN), *Wrongfully Accused*

They say that 'guns don't kill people, people kill people.' Well, I think the gun helps. If you just stood there and yelled BANG, I don't think you'd kill too many people.   EDDIE IZZARD

My, my. Such a lot of guns around town and so few brains.
                    PHILIP MARLOWE (HUMPHREY BOGART), *The Big Sleep*

I will not carry a gun, Frank. When I got thrown into this war I had a clear understanding with the Pentagon: no guns. I'll carry your books, I'll carry a torch, I'll carry a tune, I'll carry on, carry over, carry forward, Cary Grant, cash and carry, carry me back to Old Virginia, I'll even 'hari-kari' if you show me how, but I will not carry a gun!   'HAWKEYE' PIERCE (ALAN ALDA), *M*A*S*H*

Be careful what you shoot at. Most things in here don't react too well to bullets.
                    CAPTAIN MARKO RAMIUS (SEAN CONNERY), *The Hunt for Red October*

Gynaecology

I've always wanted to date a gynaecologist. I wanna *know* I'm special.
                    JANE CHRISTIE (GINA BELLMAN), *Coupling*

My body is falling so fast, my gynaecologist wears a hard hat.
                                    JOAN RIVERS

Going to a male gynaecologist is like going to a mechanic who doesn't own his own car.

CARRIE SNOW

H

Habits

My habits are not my own, I only rent them, which is why I probably can't afford to break them.

DAVID ADDISON (BRUCE WILLIS), *Moonlighting*

Happily a woman told her neighbour, 'At last! I've finally cured my husband of biting his nails.' 'How?' asked the neighbour. 'I hide his teeth.'

SAM EWING

Hair

I feel old when I see mousse in my opponent's hair.

ANDRE AGASSI

I refuse to think of them as chin hairs. I think of them as stray eyebrows.

JANETTE BARBER

My pubic hair is going grey. In a certain light you'd swear it was Stewart Granger down there.

BILLY CONNOLLY

Grey hair is God's graffiti.

BILL COSBY

Hey, believe me, baldness will catch on. When the aliens come, who do you think they're gonna relate to? Who do you think's gonna be the first ones getting a tour of the ship?

GEORGE COSTANZA (JASON ALEXANDER), *Seinfeld*

When others kid me about being bald, I simply tell them that the way I figure it, the good Lord only gave men so many hormones, and if others want to waste theirs on growing hair, that's up to them.

JOHN GLENN

The most expensive haircut I ever had cost £10 – and £9 went on the search fee!

WILLIAM HAGUE

I got my hair highlighted because I felt some strands were more important than others.

MITCH HEDBERG

Good to see a lot of bald men. Did you first notice it, sir, when it took longer and longer to wash your face? Flannels not quite lasting as long as they should?

HARRY HILL

A man is usually bald four or five years before he knows it.

EDGAR WATSON HOWE

And you should see the bush on him. I need a weedwacker just to find his dick.

SAMANTHA JONES (KIM CATTRALL), *Sex and the City*

Things To Consider Before Buying A Hairpiece:
Will I be able to handle all the women?
Am I easily offended by smart-ass teenagers?
Should I wait for the after-Christmas hairpiece sales?
Will it appreciate in value?
What hairpiece would Jesus wear?
Have I explored all my comb-over options?
Should I spend the extra twenty bucks for the sideburns?   DAVID LETTERMAN

(*on Paul McCartney*) His hair dye is so obvious that, when he last played at the Oscars, it received an unofficial award as the evening's best special effect.

PHILIP NORMAN

(*on Joan Collins*) She looks like she combs her hair with an eggbeater.

LOUELLA PARSONS

I love bald men. Just because you've lost your fuzz don't mean you ain't a peach.

DOLLY PARTON

(*when asked how long it took to do her hair*) I don't know. I'm never there.

DOLLY PARTON

Did you know that a single strand of hair grows for about 1500 days? And it's usually on your chin!   JOAN RIVERS

She dyes her hair so much, her driver's licence has a colour wheel.

JOAN RIVERS

I don't consider myself bald. I'm simply taller than my hair.   TOM SHARPE

(*on Cecil B. De Mille*) He wore baldness like an expensive hat, as if it were out of the question for him to have hair like other men.

GLORIA SWANSON

If Dracula can't see his reflection in a mirror, how come his hair is always so neatly combed?
STEVEN WRIGHT

What was God thinking when he came up with the idea of pubic hair?

Why do hair shampoo instructions say, 'Lather. Rinse. Repeat?' If you did this, would you ever be able to stop?

Hallowe'en

Could it be that all those trick-or-treaters wearing sheets aren't going as ghosts but as mattresses?
GEORGE CARLIN

I learned that Jehovah's Witnesses will not participate in Hallowe'en. I don't know if it's part of their religion. I guess they just don't like it when strangers go up to their doors and bother them.
BRUCE CLARK

I bet living in a nudist colony takes all the fun out of Hallowe'en.
STEVEN WRIGHT

Two men at Hallowe'en with burned faces. What happened? They were bobbing for French fries.
HENNY YOUNGMAN

Happiness

It isn't necessary to be rich and famous to be happy. It's only necessary to be rich.
ALAN ALDA

Happiness is like a cat — if you coax it or call it, it will avoid you; it won't come. But if you pay no attention to it and go about your business, you will find it rubbing against your legs and jumping into your lap.
WILLIAM J. BENNETT

Happiness: an agreeable sensation arising from contemplating the misery of another.
AMBROSE BIERCE

My Zen teacher also said: the only way to true happiness is to live in the moment and not worry about the future. Of course, he died penniless and single.
CARRIE BRADSHAW (SARAH JESSICA PARKER), *Sex and the City*

Happiness is having a large, loving, caring, close-knit family in another city.
GEORGE BURNS

Happiness is your dentist telling you it won't hurt and then having him catch his hand in the drill.
JOHNNY CARSON

Happiness makes up in height what it lacks in length.   ROBERT FROST

Whoever said you can't buy happiness forgot about puppies.   GENE HILL

The search for happiness is one of the chief sources of unhappiness.
ERIC HOFFER

Happiness is like coke – something you get as a by-product in the process of making something else.   ALDOUS HUXLEY, *Point Counter Point*

Happy is the man with a wife to tell him what to do and a secretary to do it.
LORD MANCROFT

Happiness is the interval between periods of unhappiness.   DON MARQUIS

Real happiness is when you marry a girl for love and find out later she has money.   BOB MONKHOUSE

Happiness is having a scratch for every itch.   OGDEN NASH

Happiness isn't a goal, it's a by-product.   ELEANOR ROOSEVELT

What do you think is the meaning of true happiness? Is it money, cars and women? Or is it just money and cars?
BILL WATTERSON, *Calvin and Hobbes*

Some cause happiness wherever they go; others, whenever they go.
OSCAR WILDE

Being happy doesn't mean everything's perfect: it means you've decided to see beyond the imperfections.

Money can't buy happiness, but it helps you look for it in a lot more places.

Happiness is merely the remission of pain.

Hard work

Hard work spotlights the character of people: some turn up their sleeves, some turn up their noses, and some don't turn up at all.   SAM EWING

If hard work were such a wonderful thing, surely the rich would have kept it to themselves.   LANE KIRKLAND

Nobody ever drowned in his own sweat. ANN LANDERS

Hard work is damn near as overrated as monogamy. HUEY LONG

If you really want something in life, you have to work for it. Now quiet, they're about to announce the lottery numbers.

HOMER SIMPSON, *The Simpsons*

Hate

Just because I cut the heads off dolls, they say I must hate babies. But it's not true. I just hate dolls. ALICE COOPER

I am free of all prejudices. I hate everyone equally. W.C. FIELDS

I'm not mad at you! I hate you! I despise you! I loathe the ground under which you burrow! MADDIE HAYES (CYBILL SHEPHERD), *Moonlighting*

(*on Harry Cohn*) You had to stand in line just to hate him. HEDDA HOPPER

I'm a controversial figure. My friends either dislike me or hate me.

OSCAR LEVANT

Frank Burns (Larry Linville): Why do people take an instant dislike to me?
'Trapper' John McIntyre (Wayne Rogers): It saves time, Frank.

*M*A*S*H*

Hats

There are very few moments in a man's existence when he experiences so much ludicrous distress . . . as when he is in pursuit of his own hat.

CHARLES DICKENS, *Pickwick Papers*

A cowboy actor needs only two changes of expression — hat on and hat off.

FRED MACMURRAY

Hats divide generally into three classes: offensive hats, defensive hats, and shrapnel. KATHARINE WHITEHORN, *Shouts and Murmurs*

Health

Women complain about PMS, but I think of it as the only time of the month when I can be myself. ROSEANNE BARR

I liked it better when my only medical responsibility was to stick my tongue out.
DAVE BARRY

I used to eat a lot of natural foods until I learned that most people die of natural causes.
JO BRAND

I am so psychosomatic it makes me sick just thinking about it.
GEORGE COSTANZA (JASON ALEXANDER), *Seinfeld*

The English find ill-health not only interesting but respectable, and often experience death in the effort to avoid a fuss.
PAMELA FRANKAU

Health is an illusion. Somewhere in my old body the auto destruct mechanism is just waiting to be activated.
GERMAINE GREER

My aunt used to tell me, 'What you can't see, can't hurt you.' Well, she died of radiation poisoning a few months back . . .
HARRY HILL

Some people are so sensitive they feel snubbed if an epidemic overlooks them.
KIN HUBBARD

A study in Italy showed that people who eat a lot of pizza are less likely to get colon cancer. And another study says masturbation reduces risk of prostate cancer. It's what I've always said, diet and exercise.
JAY LENO

(*after an operation for cancer*) Well, better a semi-colon than a full stop!
JAMES MCAULEY

It's no longer a question of staying healthy. It's a question of finding a sickness you like.
JACKIE MASON

(*asked what advice doctors had given him after having a heart pacemaker fitted*) Keep paying the electricity bill.
ROGER MOORE

Quit worrying about your health. It'll go away.
ROBERT ORBEN

Woody Boyd (Woody Harrelson): What's up?
Norm Peterson (George Wendt): The warranty on my liver.
Cheers

Every man who feels well is a sick man neglecting himself.
JULES ROMAINS

Health food makes me sick.
CALVIN TRILLIN

Definition of man flu: a cold.

There must be something to acupuncture because you never see any sick porcupines.

Health plans are like hospital gowns: you only think you're covered.

Heaven and hell

Maybe there is no actual place called hell. Maybe hell is just having to listen to our grandparents breathe through their noses when they're eating sandwiches.
JIM CARREY

There have been many definitions of hell, but for the English the best definition is that it is the place where the Germans are the police, the Swedish are the comedians, the Italians are the defence force, Frenchmen dig the roads, the Belgians are the pop singers, the Spanish run the railways, the Turks cook the food, the Irish are the waiters, the Greeks run the government, and the common language is Dutch.
DAVID FROST

If I'm going to hell, I'm going there playing the piano.
JERRY LEE LEWIS

(on her idea of heaven) Just silence and me dusting. I do like a good dust.
KYLIE MINOGUE

Hell has been described as a pocket edition of Chicago.
ASHLEY MONTAGU

Hell is an all-male black tie dinner of chartered accountants which goes on for eternity.
JOHN MORTIMER

We may be surprised at the people we find in heaven. God has a soft spot for sinners. His standards are quite low.
DESMOND TUTU

Hecklers (replies to)

Why don't you talk to the wall? That's plastered as well.
JASPER CARROTT

Don't clap on your own. Someone will throw you a fish.
JULIAN CLARY

Is that your face or has your neck just vomited?
JULIAN CLARY

When they put teeth in your mouth, they spoiled a perfectly good bum!
BILLY CONNOLLY

Shut up. Do I come to work and tell you how to sweep up?   BILLY CONNOLLY

You'd make a good burglar – your arse would rub your footprints out.
JIM DAVIDSON

There he is, folks, the poster child for Planned Parenthood.   BOB DEHNHARDT

The outpatients are out in force tonight, I see.   TOM LEHRER

Woman heckler: I wouldn't vote for you if you were the Archangel Gabriel.
Robert Menzies: If I were the Archangel Gabriel, madam, I'm afraid you would
not be in my constituency.   ROBERT MENZIES

I'm paid to make an idiot out of myself. Why do you do it for free?
HENNY YOUNGMAN

Those two are a fastidious couple – she's fast and he's hideous.
HENNY YOUNGMAN

This man used to go to school with his dog. Then they were separated. His dog
graduated!   HENNY YOUNGMAN

I would engage in a battle of wits with you, but I never duel with an unarmed
person.

Save your breath: you'll need it to blow up your date.

I'm impressed: I've never met such a small mind inside such a big head before.

I can't believe that out of 100,000 sperm, *you* were the quickest one.

If you want to be on stage we'll switch places – you come up here and be
funny, I'll go down there and act like an asshole.

If stupidity was painful, you'd be in agony.

What holds your ears apart?

I think your problem is low self-esteem. It's very common among losers.

Anything preying on your mind would starve to death.

What's on your mind – if you'll excuse the exaggeration?

What's wrong, don't you get any attention back home?

If you stand close enough to him, you can hear the ocean.

Keep talking. I always yawn when I'm interested.

Let's play horse. I'll be the front end and you be yourself.

I don't know what makes you so stupid, but it really works!

Don't you realise that there are enough people to hate in the world already without your working so hard to give us another?

Did your parents ever ask you to run away from home?

Hedgehogs

It is statistically proven,
In chapter and in verse,
That in a car-and-hedgehog fight
The hedgehog comes off worse.

PAM AYRES

Height

Why did Napoleon behave in the way he did? First of all, by all accounts, he was a bit of a short-arse and you know what they say about small men. They only come up to your Adam's apples and don't like it, so they have to compensate by becoming Emperor of France.

JO BRAND

I'm so short I'm the only citizen in the UK with a full-length picture in my passport.

RONNIE CORBETT

I used to be a lumberjack on a mushroom farm.

RONNIE CORBETT

Mickey Rooney's favourite exercise is climbing tall people.

PHYLLIS DILLER

Like a midget at a urinal, I was going to have to stay on my toes.

LT. FRANK DREBIN (LESLIE NIELSEN), *Naked Gun 33⅓: The Final Insult*

(*on his diminutive stature*) The worst thing that happened to me was when platforms went out of style.

JOHN OATES

I'm too tall to be a girl. I'm between a chick and a broad.   JULIA ROBERTS

It's better to have loved a short man than never to have loved a tall.

Katharine Hepburn

She has a cheekbone like a death's head allied to a manner as sinister and aggressive as crossbones.   JAMES AGATE

Katharine Hepburn isn't really stand-offish. She ignores everyone equally.
LUCILLE BALL

She sounds more and more like Donald Duck.   BETTE DAVIS

She ran the whole gamut of emotions from A to B.   DOROTHY PARKER

Heroism

Heroes are people who rise to the occasion and slip quietly away.
TOM BROKOW

A hero is no braver than an ordinary man, but he is braver five minutes longer.
RALPH WALDO EMERSON

Every hero becomes a bore at last.
RALPH WALDO EMERSON, *Representative Men*

I'm a hero with coward's legs.   SPIKE MILLIGAN, *Puckoon*

I'm not the heroic type. I was beaten up by Quakers.
MILES MONORE (WOODY ALLEN), *Sleeper*

Being a hero is one of the shortest-lived professions on earth.
WILL ROGERS

Hindsight

Hindsight is always twenty-twenty.   BILLY WILDER

Hippies

A hippie wears his hair long like Tarzan, walks like Jane, and smells like Cheeta.
BUSTER CRABBE

History

History is the sum total of things that could have been avoided.

KONRAD ADENAUER

Bonnie Prince Charlie was the only man ever to be named after three sheep-dogs.

BILLY CONNOLLY

History does not repeat itself; historians merely repeat each other.

PHILIP GUEDALLA

History is a set of lies agreed upon.

NAPOLEON BONAPARTE

Historians have now definitely established that Juan Cabrillo, discoverer of California, was not looking for Kansas, thus setting a precedent that continues to this day.

WAYNE SHANNON

Any event, once it has occurred, can be made to appear inevitable by a competent historian.

LEE SIMONSON

Adolf Hitler

The moustache of Hitler
Could hardly be littler
Was the thought that kept recurring
To Field Marshal Goering.

EDMUND CLERIHEW BENTLEY

Adolf Hitler was the first pop star. I think he was quite as good as [Mick] Jagger.

DAVID BOWIE

One is reminded of the exquisite pre-war comment on Hitler: 'If the fellow's going to raise his right arm so much, he really ought to go to a decent tailor.'

JILLY COOPER, *Jolly Marsupial*

Hobbies

There is a very fine line between 'hobby' and 'mental illness'.

DAVE BARRY

Only a man could think that getting a miniature plane off the ground was time well spent.

LUCY ELLMANN

Hockey

A puck is a hard rubber disc that hockey players strike when they can't hit one another.

JIMMY CANNON

The hardest thing for me has always been that I've been compared to myself.

WAYNE GRETZKY

Hockey is murder on ice.   JIM MURRAY

Ross Geller (David Schwimmer): You know what? I'd better pass on the game. I'm just gonna go home and think about my ex-wife and her lesbian lover.
Joey Tribbiani (Matt LeBlanc): The hell with hockey. Let's all do that.

Friends

Hollywood

I went out there for a thousand a week, and I worked Monday, and I got fired Wednesday. The guy that hired me was out of town Tuesday.

NELSON ALGREN

You can take all the sincerity in Hollywood, place it in the navel of a fruit fly and still have room for three caraway seeds and a producer's heart.

FRED ALLEN

Hollywood is not only dog eat dog, it's dog doesn't return other dog's phone calls.   WOODY ALLEN

There are only three ages for women in Hollywood – babe, District Attorney and Driving Miss Daisy.

ELISE ELIOT ATCHISON (GOLDIE HAWN), *First Wives Club*

Hollywood is the only place where an amicable divorce means each one gets fifty per cent of the publicity.   LAUREN BACALL

When a girl marries in Hollywood she throws the bridegroom away before she throws the bouquet.   BRENDAN BEHAN

To survive in Hollywood, you need the ambition of a Latin American revolutionary, the ego of a grand opera tenor, and the physical stamina of a cow pony.

BILLIE BURKE

If my books had been any worse, I should not have been invited to Hollywood and if they had been any better, I should not have come.

RAYMOND CHANDLER

Giving your book to Hollywood is like turning your daughter over to a pimp.
TOM CLANCY

If you say what you mean in this town, you're an outlaw.   KEVIN COSTNER

The only place in the world where a man can get stabbed in the back while climbing a ladder.   WILLIAM FAULKNER

You can't find any true closeness in Hollywood, because everybody does the fake closeness so well.   CARRIE FISHER

They've great respect for the dead in Hollywood, but none for the living.
ERROL FLYNN

Working in Hollywood does give one a certain expertise in the field of prostitution.   JANE FONDA

Hollywood is the only place where you can wake up in the morning and hear the birds coughing in the trees.   JOE FRISCO

There's nothing the matter with Hollywood that a good earthquake couldn't cure.
MOSS HART

In Hollywood, a starlet is the name for any woman under thirty who is not actively employed in a brothel.   BEN HECHT

In Hollywood you can be forgotten while you're out of the room going to the toilet.   DUSTIN HOFFMAN

Hollywood: the only town where you can die of encouragement.
PAULINE KAEL

Hollywood — that's where they give Oscars to people like Charlton Heston for acting.   SHIRLEY KNIGHT

Given the choice of Hollywood or poking steel pins into my eyes, I'd prefer steel pins.   MIKE LEIGH

Strip the phoney tinsel off Hollywood and you'll find the real tinsel underneath.
OSCAR LEVANT

In Hollywood, if a guy's wife looks like a new woman, she probably is.
DEAN MARTIN

In Hollywood they have the decency not to brag if they've slept with me.

STEVE MARTIN

Ever since they found out that Lassie was a boy, the public has believed the worst about Hollywood.

GROUCHO MARX

Hollywood: where the stars twinkle until they wrinkle.

VICTOR MATURE

It's a trip through a sewer in a glass-bottomed boat.

WILSON MIZNER

I've had several years in Hollywood and I still think the movie heroes are in the audience.

WILSON MIZNER

Hollywood's a place where they'll pay you a thousand dollars for a kiss and fifty cents for your soul.

MARILYN MONROE

I look upon going to Hollywood as a mission behind enemy lines. You parachute in, set up the explosion, then fly out before it goes off.

ROBERT REDFORD

In Hollywood, if you don't have happiness, you send out for it.

REX REED

In Hollywood a marriage is a success if it outlasts milk.

RITA RUDNER

Hollywood: a place where the inmates are in charge of the asylum.

LAURENCE STALLINGS

The only way to be a success in Hollywood is to be as obnoxious as the next guy.

SYLVESTER STALLONE

There's an old saying in Hollywood: it's not the length of your film, it's how you use it.

BEN STILLER

Living in Hollywood is like wearing fibreglass underwear – interesting but painful.

ROBIN WILLIAMS

Disneyland restaged by Dante.

ROBIN WILLIAMS

Hollywood is a town that has to be seen to be disbelieved.

WALTER WINCHELL

Hollywood: a place where they shoot too many pictures and not enough actors.

WALTER WINCHELL

Home

A man's home is his coffin.
AL BUNDY (ED O'NEILL), *Married . . . With Children*

The hard part of this job is the travelling. This time I'm out for three and a half weeks without going home. It's hard to be gone three and a half weeks because then I have to ask my friends: 'Would you mind going to the house and watering the plants, turning the lights on to make it look like somebody's home and making sure the mobile over the crib doesn't get tangled in case the baby gets bored?'
ELLEN DEGENERES

Home is where you hang your head.
GROUCHO MARX

All I need is room enough to lay a hat and a few friends.
DOROTHY PARKER

Yes, I've got this nice little apartment in New York, one of those L-shaped ones. Unfortunately, it's a lower case l.
RITA RUDNER

Home is where you can say anything you like – because nobody listens to you anyway.

Home improvement

It takes only four men to wallpaper a house, but you have to slice them thinly.
JO BRAND

If you want something fixed right, get an ugly guy to do it.
AL BUNDY (ED O'NEILL), *Married . . . With Children*

If these walls could talk, they'd probably say, 'No! Not the nails again! Not the hammer!'
JENNIFER A. FORD

I was doing some decorating, so I got out my step-ladder. I don't get on with my real ladder.
HARRY HILL

In painting a ceiling a good rule of thumb is that there should be at least as much paint on the ceiling as on your hair.
P.J. O'ROURKE

Homelessness

I'm dating a homeless woman. After a date I can just drop her off anywhere.
TOM DRESSEN

When homeless people start walking south early, you know it's going to be a hard winter.   DUANE PERKINS

I'm dating a homeless woman. It was easier talking her into staying over.
                                                                    GARRY SHANDLING

If a turtle doesn't have a shell, is it homeless or naked?

Honesty

Honesty may be the best policy, but it's important to remember that apparently, by elimination, dishonesty is the second-best policy.   GEORGE CARLIN

The best measure of a man's honesty isn't his income tax return. It's the zero adjust on his bathroom scale.   ARTHUR C. CLARKE

Honesty is the best policy, but insanity is a better defence.
                                                                    STEVE LANDESBERG

Honesty is a good thing but it is not profitable to its possessor unless it is kept under control.   DON MARQUIS

A man's idea of honesty in a relationship is telling you his real name.
                                                                    RITA RUDNER

Honesty is the best policy – when there is money in it.   MARK TWAIN

Honesty is the best policy – there's less competition.

Honeymoon

(*on hearing that her editor had been trying to contact her while she was on honeymoon*) Tell him I've been too fucking busy – or vice versa.
                                                                    DOROTHY PARKER

We went to Chicago for a second honeymoon, to the same hotel where we got married, the same suite of rooms . . . only this time it was me who went in the bathroom and cried.   HENNY YOUNGMAN

A honeymoon couple are in the Watergate Hotel, Washington. The bride is concerned: 'What if the place is still bugged?' The groom says, 'I'll look for a bug.' He looks behind the drapes, behind the pictures, under the rug. Aha! Under the rug was a disc with four screws. He gets his Swiss army knife, unscrews the screws, throws them and the disc out the window. The next morning, the hotel manager asks the newlyweds: 'How was your room? How was the service? How was your stay at the Watergate Hotel?' The groom says, 'Why are you asking me all these questions?' The manager says, 'Well, the room under you complained of the chandelier falling on them.' HENNY YOUNGMAN

Honour

Remember, you're fighting for this woman's honour, which is probably more than she ever did. RUFUS T. FIREFLY (GROUCHO MARX), *Duck Soup*

There are people who observe the rules of honour as we observe the stars: from a distance. VICTOR HUGO

One thing you can give and still keep is your word.

J. Edgar Hoover

You should trust him as much as you would a rattlesnake with a silencer on its rattle. DEAN ACHESON

(*asked why he had kept Hoover at the FBI*) I'd much rather have that fellow inside my tent pissing out, than outside my tent pissing in.
  LYNDON B. JOHNSON

Hope

George Costanza (Jason Alexander): I don't want hope. Hope is killing me. My dream is to become hopeless. When you're hopeless you don't care. And when you don't care, that indifference makes you attractive.
Jerry Seinfeld: So, hopelessness is the key?
George: It's my only hope. *Seinfeld*

He that lives upon hope will die fasting.
  BENJAMIN FRANKLIN, *Poor Richard's Almanack*

Hope is the feeling that the feeling you have isn't permanent.
  JEAN KERR, *Finishing Touches*

Bob Hope

There is nothing in the world I wouldn't do for Hope, and there is nothing he wouldn't do for me. We spend our lives doing nothing for each other.
  BING CROSBY

Bob Hope has a beautiful short game. Unfortunately it's off the tee.

JIMMY DEMARET

Horror

True horror is seeing my stories turned into poor films.　CLIVE BARKER

(*to Vincent Price at the funeral of horror movie star Bela Lugosi*) Do you think we should drive a stake through his heart just in case?　PETER LORRE

Father Dougal McGuire (Ardal O'Hanlon): Can I stay up tonight to watch the scary film?
Father Ted Crilly (Dermot Morgan): Ah, no no no. The last time you stayed up to watch a scary film you ended up having to sleep in my bed. I wouldn't mind, but it wasn't even a scary film.
Dougal: Come on, Ted. A Volkswagen with a mind of its own. If that isn't scary, I don't know what is.　*Father Ted*

I've never been in a horror film – on purpose.　PETER O'TOOLE

Horse racing

(*on racehorse trainer Jenny Pitman*) She's about as cuddly as a dead hedgehog. The Alsatians in her yard would go around in pairs for protection.

JOHN FRANCOME

There are, they say, fools, bloody fools, and men who remount in a steeple-chase.　JOHN OAKSEY

In racing, to insult a man's horse is worse than insulting his wife.

JOHN OAKSEY

What do they say when they geld a racehorse? 'And they're off!'

CONAN O'BRIEN

Horses

You ride a horse rather less well than another horse would.

EDMUND BLACKADDER (ROWAN ATKINSON), *Blackadder*

If the world were a logical place, men would ride side-saddle.

RITA MAE BROWN

I'm lucky because I have an athlete between my legs.　WILLIE CARSON

Horse sense is a good judgement which keeps horses from betting on people.
W.C. FIELDS

Dangerous at both ends and uncomfortable in the middle.   IAN FLEMING

Emily, I've a little confession to make. I really am a horse doctor. But marry me, and I'll never look at another horse.
DR HACKENBUSH (GROUCHO MARX), *A Day at the Races*

Horses are what glue is made from, which is a bit odd because if you touch a horse, they're not sticky, are they?   HARRY HILL

Horseshoes are lucky. Horses have four bits of luck nailed to their feet. They should be the luckiest animals in the world. They should rule the country. They should win all their races.   EDDIE IZZARD

People on horses look better than they are. People in cars look worse than they are.   MARYA MANNES

Few girls are as well shaped as a good horse.   CHRISTOPHER MORLEY

There is nothing better for the inside of a man than the outside of a horse.
RONALD REAGAN

I always think better with a horse between my knees.   RONALD REAGAN

Hospital

I took my husband to the hospital yesterday to have seventeen stitches out — that'll teach him to buy me a sewing kit for my birthday.   JO BRAND

After two days in hospital, I took a turn for the nurse.   W.C. FIELDS

To nab a nurse for a bedpan outside regulation hours is an art compared with which catching a waiter's eye in a busy restaurant is simple.
RICHARD GORDON, *Bedside Manners*

One of the most difficult things to contend with in a hospital is that assumption on the part of the staff that because you have lost your gall bladder you have also lost your mind.   JEAN KERR

I had a temperature of 106. When I opened my eyes, the hospital people said, 'We can't believe you woke up. Here's your bill.'   MARTIN LAWRENCE

Did you ever notice it's usually sick people who end up in hospitals?
FATHER DOUGAL McGUIRE (ARDAL O' HANLON), *Father Ted*

A hospital bed is a parked taxi with the meter running.   GROUCHO MARX

Dr Rumack (Leslie Nielsen): You'd better tell the Captain we've got to land as soon as we can. This woman has to be gotten to a hospital.
Elaine Dickinson (Julie Hegarty): A hospital – what is it?
Dr Rumack: It's a big building with patients, but that's not important right now.
Airplane

Hotels

In a British hotel, the words 'Can I help you sir?' mean roughly 'What the hell do you want?'   KINGSLEY AMIS

A hotel is a place that keeps the manufacturers of 25-watt bulbs in business.
SHELLEY BERMAN

Mrs Richards (Joan Sanderson): When I pay for a view I expect something more interesting than that.
Basil Fawlty (John Cleese): That is Torquay, madam.
Mrs Richards: Well, it's not good enough.
Basil: Well . . . may I ask what you were hoping to see out of a Torquay hotel bedroom window? Sydney Opera House perhaps? The Hanging Gardens of Babylon? Herds of wildebeest sweeping majestically . . .
Fawlty Towers

When you want to take a bath, would you be so kind as to sign the little book you'll find inside the bathroom door . . . Hot water is only provided in the afternoons between the hours of half-past two and six.
HOTEL PROPRIETRESS (JOYCE GRENFELL), *Genevieve*

The landlady of a boarding-house is a parallelogram – that is, an oblong angular figure, which cannot be described, but which is equal to anything.
STEPHEN LEACOCK, *Literary Lapses*

I came into my hotel room one night and found a strange blonde in my bed. I would not stand for any of that nonsense. I gave her exactly 24 hours to get out.   GROUCHO MARX

Room service? Send me up a larger room.   GROUCHO MARX

I'm not very wild. I tried to trash hotel rooms when I was younger, but I just ended up making the bed and leaving a small chocolate on the pillow for the maid.
ARDAL O'HANLON

The Faces were banned from so many hotels, the entire Holiday Inn chain, that we had to check in as Fleetwood Mac lots of times.
RONNIE WOOD

My hotel room was so small, when I had a headache, the guy next door had to take the aspirin.
HENNY YOUNGMAN

Houses

This house has quite a long and colourful history. It was built on an ancient Indian burial ground, and was the setting of Satanic rituals, witch-burnings, and five John Denver Christmas specials.
MONTGOMERY BURNS, *The Simpsons*

What's the worst that can happen? So the tornado picks up our house and slams it down in a better neighborhood.
ROSEANNE CONNER (ROSEANNE BARR), *Roseanne*

Thou shalt not covet thy neighbour's house unless they have a well-stocked bar.
W.C. FIELDS

I want a house that has got over all its troubles. I don't want to spend the rest of my life bringing up a young and inexperienced house.
JEROME K. JEROME, *They and I*

Sammy's right. It's a BIG responsibility. You got lawns to mow, you got plumbing to fix, you got gutters to clean, then every couple of years you have to paint the entire thing from top to bottom. Honestly, I don't know where Vera gets the energy.
NORM PETERSON (GEORGE WENDT), *Cheers*

I told my mother-in-law that my house was her house, and she said, 'Get the hell off my property.'
JOAN RIVERS

Housework

I'm not going to vaccum till Sears makes one you can ride on.
ROSEANNE BARR

I'm a pretty good housekeeper. Ask anybody. No, wait: don't ask my wife. She and I disagree on certain housekeeping issues, such as whether it's OK for a house to contain dirt.
DAVE BARRY

Men – because of a tragic genetic flaw – cannot see dirt until there is enough of it to support agriculture.   DAVE BARRY

Housework is a treadmill from futility to oblivion with stop-offs at tedium and counter productivity.   ERMA BOMBECK

My theory on housework is, if the item doesn't multiply, smell, catch on fire or block the refrigerator door, let it be. No one cares. Why should you?
ERMA BOMBECK

My wife must think I'm an idiot! 'Separate the white clothes from the colours,' she says. Ha! Whether I separate them left-to-right or top-to-bottom, the washing machine will still mix them up anyway!   CHUCK BONNER

How do you know if it's time to wash the dishes and clean your house? Look inside your pants. If you find a penis in there, it's not time.   JO BRAND

I make no secret of the fact that I would rather lie on a sofa than sweep beneath it.   SHIRLEY CONRAN, *Superwoman*

There was no need to do any housework at all. After the first four years the dirt doesn't get any worse.   QUENTIN CRISP, *The Naked Civil Servant*

Housework can't kill you, but why take a chance?   PHYLLIS DILLER

Cleaning your house while your kids are still growing is like shovelling the walk before it stops snowing.   PHYLLIS DILLER

I'd like to marry a nice domesticated homosexual with a fetish for wiping down Formica and different vacuum-cleaner attachments.   JENNY ECLAIR

All the rudiments of success in life can be found in ironing a pair of trousers.
CHRIS EUBANK

(*on hearing that Mariah Carey claims to do her own housework*) Does Mariah know that polishing her American Music Award doesn't constitute housework?
KATHY GRIFFIN

The man has not been born for whom I will iron a shirt.   KATE O'MARA

How often does a house need to be cleaned? Just once every girlfriend. After that she can get to know the real you.   P.J. O'ROURKE

I hate housework. You make the beds, you do the dishes – and six months later you have to start all over again.
JOAN RIVERS

Some people's idea of housework is to sweep the room with a glance.

Human race

Nothing defines humans better than their willingness to do irrational things in the pursuit of phenomenally unlikely payoffs. This is the principle behind lotteries, dating, and religion.
SCOTT ADAMS

The first humans were short, hairy, tree-dwelling creatures that strongly resembled Danny DeVito.
DAVE BARRY

The ability to make love frivolously is the chief characteristic which distinguishes human beings from beasts.
HEYWOOD BROUN

The public is like a piano. You just have to know what keys to poke.
AL CAPP

All human beings connect sex and love . . . except for men.
ROSEANNE CONNER (ROSEANNE BARR), *Roseanne*

An anthropologist has just come back from a field trip to New Guinea with reports of a tribe so primitive that they have Tide but not new Tide with lemon-fresh Borax.
DAVID LETTERMAN

No human being believes that any other human being has a right to be in bed when he himself is up.
ROBERT LYND, *Rain, Rain Go To Spain*

Most human beings are quite likeable if you do not see too much of them.
ROBERT LYND, *The Peal of Bells*

A human being is an ingenious assembly of portable plumbing.
CHRISTOPHER MORLEY, *Human Being*

I finally know what distinguishes man from the other beasts: financial worries.
JULES RENARD

Humility

At home I am a nice guy; but I don't want the world to know. Humble people, I've found, don't get very far.
MUHAMMAD ALI

I've never had a humble opinion in my life. If you're going to have one, why bother to be humble about it?   JOAN BAEZ

When the meek inherit the earth, lawyers will be there to work out the deal.
                                                                        SAM EWING

The meek shall inherit the earth, but not the mineral rights.   J. PAUL GETTY

I feel very humble, but I think I have the strength of character to fight it.
                                                                        BOB HOPE

Humility is no substitute for a good personality.   FRAN LEBOWITZ

Only the untalented can afford to be humble.   SYLVIA MILES

If only I had a little humility, I'd be perfect.   TED TURNER

Hunger

I said I'm hungry enough to eat a horse. I didn't say nothin' about carrots.
                                                            DENNIS THE MENACE

(*on his early struggles*) I would not have had anything to eat if it wasn't for the stuff the audience threw at me.   BOB HOPE

I used to be a starving actor. Then one day I got a break. My landlady started putting real cheese in the traps.   BOB HOPE

I've known what it is to be hungry, but I always went right to a restaurant.
                                                                    RING LARDNER

Hunting

Men hunt because they have something wrong with their own equipment and they need something else to shoot.   PAMELA ANDERSON

Deer hunting would be a fine sport, if only the deer had guns.
                                                                WILLIAM S. GILBERT

I'm against hunting. In fact I'm a hunt saboteur. I go out the night before and shoot the fox.   PETER KAY

When a man wants to murder a tiger he calls it sport; when a tiger wants to murder him, he calls it ferocity.   GEORGE BERNARD SHAW

The world can be divided into people that read, people that write, people that think, and fox-hunters.　　　　　　　　　　　　　　WILLIAM SHENSTONE

One morning I shot an elephant in my pyjamas. How he got into my pyjamas I'll never know.

CAPTAIN JEFFREY SPAULDING (GROUCHO MARX), *Animal Crackers*

I am not a good shot. If people are interested in animal preservation, I am the person to invite on a shoot.　　　　　　　　　　　　　　DAVID STEEL

The English country gentleman galloping after a fox — the unspeakable in full pursuit of the uneatable.

OSCAR WILDE, *A Woman of No Importance*

Husbands

(*on her search for a third husband*) I can't have a conservative, and he can't be on psychotropic drugs. I want him to be from forty to sixty. He has to be very funny, very smart, and a children's rights activist. I would like it if he was married before, but single now. And I'd like somebody who has had children. But I don't want him to be a psychiatrist.　　　　　　　　　　　　　　KIRSTIE ALLEY

I never married because there was no need. I have three pets at home that answer the same purpose as a husband. I have a dog that growls every morning, a parrot that swears all afternoon and a cat that comes home late at night.

MARIE CORELLI

Any husband who says, 'My wife and I are completely equal partners,' is talking about either a law firm or a hand of bridge.　　　　　　　　　　BILL COSBY

I'd marry again — if I found a man who had $15 million, would sign over half to me, and guarantee that he'd be dead within a year.　　　　　BETTE DAVIS

Husbands are like fires. They go out when unattended.　　　　ZSA ZSA GABOR

Get a job, your husband hates you. Get a good job, your husband leaves you. Get a stupendous job, your husband leaves you for a teenager.

CYNTHIA HEIMEL, *If You Can't Live Without Me, Why Aren't You Dead Yet?*

Michael Douglas likes to have Catherine Zeta-Jones dress up in a French maid's outfit, complete with feather duster. How old is your husband when you have to dust him?　　　　　　　　　　　　　　　　　　CRAIG KILBORN

The husband who wants a happy marriage should learn to keep his mouth shut and his cheque book open.
GROUCHO MARX

Dullness is the first requisite of a good husband.
W. SOMERSET MAUGHAM, *Lady Frederick*

Husbands never become good; they merely become proficient.
H.L. MENCKEN

Husbands are chiefly good as lovers when they are betraying their wives.
MARILYN MONROE

(*on husband Douglas Fairbanks*) In his private life Douglas always faced a situation in the only way he knew, by running away from it.   MARY PICKFORD

Never trust a husband too far, nor a bachelor too near.
HELEN ROWLAND, *A Guide to Men*

There is a vast difference between the savage and the civilised man, but it is never apparent to their wives until after breakfast.
HELEN ROWLAND, *A Guide to Men*

A husband is what is left of a lover, after the nerve has been extracted.
HELEN ROWLAND, *A Guide to Men*

Hygiene

My grandmother took a bath every year, whether she needed it or not.
BRENDAN BEHAN

Baldrick, your breath comes straight from Satan's bottom.
EDMUND BLACKADDER (ROWAN ATKINSON), *Blackadder*

My kids always perceived the bathroom as a place where you wait it out until all the groceries are unloaded from the car.   ERMA BOMBECK

Bath twice a day to be really clean, once a day to be passably clean, once a week to avoid being a public menace.
ANTHONY BURGESS, *Inside Mr Enderby*

Don't you get discouraged each morning when you wake up and realise you have to wash again?
GEORGE CARLIN

Can someone please tell me what is the deal with B.O.? Everything in nature has a function, a purpose, except B.O. Doesn't make any sense. Do something good — hard work, exercise — smell very bad. That is the way the human being is designed: you move, you stink. Why don't our bodies help us? Why can't sweat smell good? Be a different world, wouldn't it? Instead of putting your laundry in the hamper, you'd put it in a vase. You'd have a dirty sock hanging from the rearview mirror of your car. And then on a really special night, maybe a little underwear coming out of your breast pocket, just to show her that she's important.   JERRY SEINFELD

(*on rock singer Patti Smith*) All I could think about her was B.O. She wouldn't be bad-looking if she would wash.   ANDY WARHOL

Why do British people have baths? It's just lying in your own dirt.
                                                                    RUBY WAX

Hypnosis

If hypnosis worked, wouldn't all the leaders be hypnotists? What if they are?
                                                                  SCOTT ADAMS

Hypochondria

Niles Crane (David Hyde Pierce): What's wrong with Maris?
Martin Crane (John Mahoney): I'll start. Frasier can jump in when I get hoarse.   *Frasier*

Health nuts are going to feel stupid someday, lying in hospitals dying of nothing.
                                                                    REDD FOXX

Hypochondria is Greek for 'men'.   KATHY LETTE

Everyone thinks I'm a hypochondriac. It makes me feel sick.
                           FELIX UNGAR (TONY RANDALL), *The Odd Couple*

I went to the doctor and he said, 'You've got hypochondria.' I said, 'Not that as well!'   TIM VINE

Hypocrisy

We're women. We have a double standard to live up to.
                          ALLY MCBEAL (CALISTA FLOCKHART), *Ally McBeal*

Hypocrisy is the most difficult and nerve-racking vice that any man can pursue; it needs an unceasing vigilance and a rare detachment of spirit. It cannot, like adultery or gluttony, be practised at spare moments; it is a whole-time job.

W. SOMERSET MAUGHAM, *Cakes and Ale*

Where there is no religion, hypocrisy becomes good taste.

GEORGE BERNARD SHAW

I

Ice cream

Now some women fantasise nightly
Of erotic adventures and steam
But without sounding drab, all I want to grab
Is a bucket or two of ice-cream.

PAM AYRES

I doubt the world holds for anyone a more soul-stirring surprise than the first adventure with ice cream.

HEYWOOD BROUN

I didn't get where I am today by selling ice cream tasting of bookends, pumice stone and West Germany.

CJ (JOHN BARRON), *The Fall and Rise of Reginald Perrin*

Idealism

Idealism increases in direct proportion to one's distance from the problem.

JOHN GALSWORTHY

An idealist is one who, on noticing that a rose smells better than a cabbage, concludes that it will also make better soup.

H.L. MENCKEN

Ideas

Maddie Hayes (Cybill Shepherd): I had an idea.
David Addison (Bruce Willis): That's OK, I got lots of 'em. I'll loan you one.

Moonlighting

Nothing is more dangerous than an idea when that's the only one you have got.

ALAIN, *Propos sur la religion*

I've got a plan so cunning, you could put a tail on it and call it a weasel.
EDMUND BLACKADDER (ROWAN ATKINSON), *Blackadder*

Baldrick, you wouldn't recognise a cunning plan if it painted itself purple and danced naked on top of a harpsichord singing 'Cunning plans are here again.'
EDMUND BLACKADDER (ROWAN ATKINSON), *Blackadder*

I think Kleenex ought to put a little bull's-eye right in the middle of the tissue. Wouldn't that be great? Especially when you're hangin' out with your buddies. 'Look Joey . . . an 85!'   GEORGE CARLIN

If at first an idea isn't totally absurd, there's no hope for it.
ALBERT EINSTEIN

I have an even better idea. I'm going to place him in an easily escapable situation involving an overly elaborate and exotic death.
DR EVIL (MIKE MYERS), *Austin Powers: International Man of Mystery*

The English approach to ideas is not to kill them, but to let them die of neglect.
JEREMY PAXMAN

(*on Jayne Mansfield*) I won't say she was dumb, but one time Jayne squealed out loud on the set and said she had a terrific idea. The director stared at her, then said, 'Treat it gently, dear. It's in a strange place.'   TONY RANDALL

A cold in the head causes less suffering than an idea.   JULES RENARD

Ideas are like rabbits. You get a couple, learn how to handle them and pretty soon you have a dozen.   JOHN STEINBECK

A man with a new idea is a crank, until the idea succeeds.   MARK TWAIN

Ideas are like beards: men do not have them until they grow up.   VOLTAIRE

Ideas are like umbrellas. If left lying about, they are likely to change ownership.

Ignorance

Every year education gets more expensive, but ignorance costs even more.
SAM EWING

What we call evil is simply ignorance bumping its head in the dark.
HENRY FORD

A person is never happy except at the price of some ignorance.

ANATOLE FRANCE

(*on Harold Ross, editor of the* New Yorker) His ignorance was an Empire State Building of ignorance. You had to admire it for its size.   DOROTHY PARKER

Everyone is ignorant, only on different subjects.   WILL ROGERS

If ignorance is bliss, why aren't more people happy?

LEONARD ROSSITER, *The Devil's Bedside Book*

He knows nothing; and he thinks he knows everything. That points clearly to a political career.   GEORGE BERNARD SHAW, *Major Barbara*

Stupidity has a certain charm – ignorance does not.   FRANK ZAPPA

Why do people who know the least know it the loudest?

Imagination

Imagination is the highest kite that one can fly.   LAUREN BACALL

Although I can accept talking scarecrows, lions and great wizards of emerald cities, I find it hard to believe there is no paperwork involved when your house lands on a witch.   DAVE JAMES

(*on John Dryden*) His imagination resembled the wings of an ostrich. It enabled him to run, though not to soar.   THOMAS BABINGTON MACAULAY

Falling in love consists merely in uncorking the imagination and bottling the common sense.   HELEN ROWLAND

Lisa, vampires are make-believe, like elves, gremlins, and Eskimos.

HOMER SIMPSON, *The Simpsons*

Immigration

The White House looked into a plan that would allow illegal immigrants to stay in the United States. The plan called for a million Mexicans to marry a million of our ugliest citizens.   DENNIS MILLER

All the problems we face in the United States today can be traced to an un-enlightened immigration policy on the part of the American Indian.

PAT PAULSEN

I'm in favour of liberalised immigration because of the effect it would have on restaurants. I'd let just about everybody in except the English.

CALVIN TRILLIN

Immortality

I don't want to achieve immortality through my work – I want to achieve it through not dying. WOODY ALLEN

If man were immortal, do you realise what his meat bills would be?

WOODY ALLEN

The only thing wrong with immortality is that it tends to go on forever.

HERB CAEN

Poets have said that the reason to have children is to give yourself immortality. Immortality? Now that I have five children, my only hope is that they are all out of the house before I die. BILL COSBY

Millions long for immortality who don't know what to do with themselves on a rainy Sunday afternoon. SUSAN ERTZ

He had decided to live for ever or die in the attempt.

JOSEPH HELLER, *Catch-22*

The key to immortality is first to live a life worth remembering. BRUCE LEE

Impotence

To succeed with the opposite sex, tell her you're impotent. She can't wait to disprove it. CARY GRANT

Monica Geller (Courteney Cox): Hey, Joey, what would you do if you were omnipotent?
Joey Tribbiani (Matt LeBlanc): Probably kill myself!
Monica: Excuse me?
Joey: Hey, if Little Joey's dead, then I got no reason to live! *Friends*

Impulse

When men attempt bold gestures, generally it's considered romantic. When women do it, it's often considered desperate or psycho.

CARRIE BRADSHAW (SARAH JESSICA PARKER), *Sex and the City*

Jumping to conclusions can be bad exercise.

Incest

What's wrong with a little incest? It's both handy and cheap.   JAMES AGATE

One should try everything once, except incest and folk-dancing.
ARNOLD BAX, *Farewell to My Youth*

The trouble with incest is that it gets you involved with relatives.
GEORGE S. KAUFMAN

Incompetence

This island is made mainly of coal and surrounded by fish. Only an organising genius could produce a shortage of coal and fish at the same time.
ANEURIN BEVAN

Most people don't know what they're doing. And a lot of them are really good at it.
GEORGE CARLIN

The English think that incompetence is the same thing as sincerity.
QUENTIN CRISP

(*on the phone*): Hallo, Mr O'Reilly, and how are you this morning? . . . Oh good, good, no rare diseases or anything? . . . Oh, I do beg your pardon, Basil Fawlty, you remember, the poor sod you do jobs for . . . Well now, how are things your end . . . Oh, good. Good, good, good. Well now, how would you like to hear about things my end? . . . Oh well, up to your usual standard I think I could say, a few holes in the wall, the odd door missing, but nothing you couldn't be sued for.   BASIL FAWLTY (JOHN CLEESE), *Fawlty Towers*

Independence

Men say they love independence in a woman, but they don't waste a second demolishing it brick by brick.   CANDICE BERGEN

I want to prove that I'm strong and independent, and I can't do that alone.
NILES CRANE (DAVID HYDE PIERCE), *Frasier*

Individuality

We boil at different degrees.
RALPH WALDO EMERSON, *Society and Solitude*

About the only sign of personal individuality that the average woman is allowed to retain after she marries is her toothbrush.

HELEN ROWLAND, *Reflections of a Bachelor Girl*

Industrial relations

I used to think that all the king's horses and all the king's men to fix one guy was a bit excessive. Then I realised they must have had a really strong union.

MARKO PERIC

Inferiority

Am I truly nothing? Could the neighbourhood children be right?

AL BUNDY (ED O'NEILL), *Married . . . With Children*

No one can make you feel inferior without your consent.

ELEANOR ROOSEVELT

I have an inferiority complex. But it's not a very good one.

STEVEN WRIGHT

Infidelity

To be with another woman, that is French. To be caught, that is American.

FREDDY BENSON (STEVE MARTIN), *Dirty Rotten Scoundrels*

Donny is seeing Daphne and I am not the kind who steals other people's boyfriends. Not friends' boyfriends. Not *good* friends'. Not again.

ROZ DOYLE (PERI GILPIN), *Frasier*

There is one thing I would break up over, and that is if she caught me with another woman. I wouldn't stand for that.

STEVE MARTIN

(*after his wife caught him kissing a chorus girl*) I wasn't kissing her. I was whispering in her mouth.

CHICO MARX

My girlfriend said she was seeing another man. I told her to rub her eyes.

EMO PHILIPS

Some people actually cheat on the people they're cheating with, which is like being in a hold-up and then turning to the robber next to you and going, 'All right, gimme everything you have, too.'

JERRY SEINFELD

Inflation

A man explained inflation to his wife thus: 'When we married you measured 36–24–36. Now you're 42–42–42. There's more of you, but you are not worth as much.'
LORD BARNETT

Inflation is when you pay fifteen dollars for the ten-dollar haircut you used to get for five dollars when you had hair.
SAM EWING

Inflation is the one form of taxation that can be imposed without legislation.
MILTON FRIEDMAN

One good thing about inflation is that the fellow who forgets his change nowadays doesn't lose half as much as he used to.
KIN HUBBARD

Americans are getting stronger. Twenty years ago, it took two people to carry ten dollars' worth of groceries. Today, a five-year-old can do it.
HENNY YOUNGMAN

Inflation: cutting money in half without damaging the paper.

Insanity

Insanity runs in my family. It practically gallops.
MORTIMER BREWSTER (CARY GRANT), *Arsenic and Old Lace*

There is only one difference between a madman and me. I am not mad.
SALVADOR DALI

Insanity: doing the same thing over and over again and expecting different results.
ALBERT EINSTEIN

That's the truest sign of insanity – insane people are always sure they're just fine. It's only the sane people who are willing to admit they're crazy.
NORA EPHRON

I don't buy temporary insanity as a murder defence. Breaking into someone's home and ironing all their clothes is temporary insanity.
SUE KOLINSKY

If someone ever catches you talking to yourself, the best thing to do is point at a chair and say, 'He started it!' That way they won't think you're crazy.
CRAIG STACEY

Let me see if I've got this straight: in order to be grounded, I've got to be crazy and I must be crazy to keep flying. But if I ask to be grounded, that means I'm not crazy any more and I have to keep flying.

YOSSARIAN (ALAN ARKIN), *Catch-22*

Insects

An ant colony is every bit as complex and organised as human society. In fact it is more organised, because there are no teenagers.   DAVE BARRY

I don't kill flies but I like to mess with their minds. I hold them above globes. They freak out and yell, 'Whoa, I'm way too high!'   BRUCE BAUM

Ants can carry twenty times their own body weight, which is useful information if you're moving out and need help getting a potato chip across town.

RON DARIAN

I suppose that when ants get stepped on, they have no idea what hit them. But I'll bet that hasn't stopped them from coming up with fancy names for it, like 'spontaneous compression' or 'vertical planar syndrome.'

LEMEL HEBERT-WILLIAMS

What did moths bump into before the electric light bulb was invented? Boy, the light bulb really screwed the moth up, didn't it? Are there moths on their way to the sun now, going: 'It's gonna be worth it!'   BILL HICKS

It's only when you look at an ant through a magnifying glass on a sunny day that you realise how often they burst into flames.   HARRY HILL

Look at that ugly little bee. Makes honey. I'm a nice-looking person and all I can do is make a little wax with my ears.   MILT KAMEN

The stick insect has sex for 79 days straight. If it's only been 77 days, is that a quickie? And you know that even after 79 days, the female goes, 'Oh, so close!' And the guy tells his buddies it was 158 days.   JAY LENO

When the insects take over the world, we hope they will remember with gratitude how we took them along on all our picnics.   BILL VAUGHAN

I wouldn't have wanted to be a fly on the wall when they invented fly spray.

TIM VINE

Insemination

Artificial insemination: copulation without representation.

Instinct

Women have a wonderful instinct about things. They can discover everything except the obvious. OSCAR WILDE, *An Ideal Husband*

Insult

They do say, Mrs M, that verbal insults hurt more than physical pain. They are, of course, wrong, as you will soon discover when I stick this toasting fork into your head. EDMUND BLACKADDER (ROWAN ATKINSON), *Blackadder*

The only gracious way to accept an insult is to ignore it; if you can't ignore it, top it; if you can't top it, laugh at it; if you can't laugh at it, it's probably deserved. J. RUSSELL LYNES

Women and elephants never forget an injury. SAKI, *Reginald*

A husband should not insult his wife publicly, at parties. He should insult her in the privacy of the home. JAMES THURBER, *Thurber Country*

If you can't say anything nice, say it about Diane.
CARLA TORTELLI (RHEA PERLMAN), *Cheers*

Insurance

I don't want to tell you how much insurance I carry with the Prudential, but all I can say is: when I go, they go too. JACK BENNY

The main object when selling fire insurance was to scare the hell out of the householder. I found that 'maimed' is a very powerful word. It's so permanent. If you break a leg, it eventually gets better but if it's maimed, you're stuck with it for life. JASPER CARROTT

The Act of God designation on all insurance policies . . . means roughly that you cannot be insured for the accidents that are most likely to happen to you. If your ox kicks a hole in your neighbour's Maserati, however, indemnity is instantaneous. ALAN COREN, *The Lady From Stalingrad Mansions*

I took a physical for some life insurance. All they would give me was fire and theft. HENNY YOUNGMAN

Intellect

An intellectual is a man who doesn't know how to park a bike.

SPIRO T. AGNEW

I've been called many things, but never an intellectual.

TALLULAH BANKHEAD

The stories about my intellectual capacity do get under my skin. You know for a while I even thought my staff believed it. There on my schedule first thing every morning it said, 'Intelligence briefing'.　　GEORGE W. BUSH

An intellectual is a man who takes more words than necessary to tell more than he knows.　　DWIGHT D. EISENHOWER

An intellectual is someone who has found something more interesting to think about than sex.　　ALDOUS HUXLEY

The trouble with Senator Long is that he is suffering from halitosis of the intellect. That's presuming Emperor Long has an intellect.

HAROLD L. ICKES

I know I've got a degree. Why does that mean I have to spend my life with intellectuals? I've got a life-saving certificate but I don't spend my evenings diving for a rubber brick with my pyjamas on.　　VICTORIA WOOD

Intelligence

I'm really smart. I know a whole lot, but I just can't think of it.

MOREY AMSTERDAM

Man forgives woman anything save the wit to outwit him.

MINNA ANTRIM

The dullard's envy of brilliant men is always assuaged by the suspicion that they will come to a bad end.　　MAX BEERBOHM, *Zuleika Dobson*

The object of opening the mind, as of opening the mouth, is to shut it again on something solid.　　G.K. CHESTERTON

We've all met people who are supposedly incredibly intelligent but don't know which way to sit on a lavatory.　　STEPHEN FRY

If dolphins are so intelligent, how come they ain't got Walkmans?

JOHN LYDON (aka Johnny ROTTEN)

An intelligence test sometimes shows a man how smart he would have been not to have taken it.

LAURENCE J. PETER

George Costanza (Jason Alexander): People think I'm smart, but I'm not smart.
Jerry Seinfeld: Who thinks you're smart? *Seinfeld*

I'm a very physical person. People don't credit me with much of a brain, so why should I disillusion them?

SYLVESTER STALLONE

Don't assume the other fellow has intelligence to match yours — he may have more!

TERRY-THOMAS

All the unhappy marriages come from the husband having brains. What good are brains to a man? They only unsettle him.

P.G. WODEHOUSE, *The Adventures of Sally*

Internet

The Internet is the most important single development in the history of human communication since the invention of call waiting.

DAVE BARRY

When I took office, only high energy physicists had ever heard of what is called the Worldwide Web. Now even my cat has its own page.

BILL CLINTON

The Internet is wonderful. You can find a whole book, select a chapter, and zoom in on a particular word — just like a library really.

BEN ELTON

The World Wide Web is fantasyland. There is no way that anyone can find anything on the Web without having to adopt the thought patterns of a weirdo.

GERMAINE GREER

Wonderbread has a Web site. How bored and lonely would you have to be to visit the Web site of a bakery? So I did.

DAVE HUGHES

America Online customers are upset because the company has decided to allow advertising in its chat rooms. I can see why: you got computer sex, you can download pornography, people are making dates with ten-year-olds. Hey, what's this? A Pepsi ad? They're ruining the integrity of the Internet.

JAY LENO

Did you see where eBay wouldn't let this guy auction off his soul? They said, 'If you want to sell your soul, you'll just have to run for President like everybody else.'
JAY LENO

The trouble with the Internet is that it's replacing masturbation as a leisure activity.
PATRICK MURRAY

(*on why he disconnected his home computer from the Internet*) There's so much darn porn there, I never got out of the house.
JACK NICHOLSON

How do you keep your husband from reading your e-mail? – Rename the folder 'Instruction manuals.'

You know you're addicted to the Internet when all of your friends have an @ in their names.

You know you're addicted to the Internet when your husband tells you he's had the beard for two months.

You know you're addicted to the Internet when your phone bill comes to your doorstep in a box.

Interrogation

What, no small-talk? No chit-chat? You know, that's the problem these days. No one bothers to take the time to give a really sinister interrogation.
JAMES BOND (Pierce Brosnan), *GoldenEye*

Interviews

When you go in for a job interview, I think a good thing to ask is if they ever press charges.
JACK HANDEY

Apparently some human resource managers don't appreciate having interview questions answered through interpretive dance.
MICHAEL HAYWARD

Intuition

When a naked man is chasing a woman through an alley with a butcher knife and a hard-on, I figure he isn't out collecting for the Red Cross.
HARRY CALLAHAN (Clint Eastwood), *Dirty Harry*

God made men stronger but not necessarily more intelligent. He gave women intuition and femininity and, used properly, that combination easily jumbles the brain of any men I ever met.   FARRAH FAWCETT

What passes for woman's intuition is often nothing more than man's transparency.   GEORGE JEAN NATHAN

There's just something I don't like about him. I can't put my finger on it, but if I did, I'd have to wash it.   SOPHIA PETRILLO (Estelle Getty), *The Golden Girls*

Inventions

I'm a wannabe inventor. I'm still working on my perpetual motion machine. Ironically, I can't seem to stop.
                                 SCOTT ADAMS, *Seven Years of Highly Defective People*

Who invented the brush they put next to the toilet? That thing hurts!
                                                                        ANDY ANDREWS

When the inventor of the drawing board messed things up, what did he go back to?   BOB MONKHOUSE

I genuinely try as hard as I can to buy British. So, in consequence, my house is full of a load of slightly second-rate crap. Imagine if there was no Japanese, and the British had invented the Walkman. It would be a teak box about that wide, covered in leatherette with the headphones out of a Lancaster bomber.
                                                                        ALEXEI SAYLE

Investment

Don't invest all your money in just one or two stocks. That's the danger. I know a man who put all his money in just two stocks – a paper-towel company and a revolving-door outfit. He was wiped out before he could turn around.
                                                                        DAVE ASTOR

The United States have developed a new weapon that destroys people but leaves buildings standing. It's called the stock market.   JAY LENO

I made a killing On Wall Street a few years ago . . . I shot my broker.
                                                                        GROUCHO MARX

A stockbroker urged me to buy a stock that would triple its value every year. I told him, 'At my age, I don't even buy green bananas!'   CLAUDE D. PEPPER

Iraq

(*on the Iraqi War*) The coalition. Yeah, right. 300,000 Americans, forty Brits and some guy from Australia to keep the beer cold.   WILL DURST

Well, we won that war, so you know what that means – in forty years, we'll all be driving Iraqi-made automobiles.   WILL DURST

President Bush spent the night calling world leaders to support the war with Iraq, and it is sad when the most powerful man on earth is yelling, 'I know you're there, pick up, pick up.'   CRAIG KILBORN

I think we should take Iraq and Iran and combine them into one country and call it Irate. All the pissed off people live in one place and get it over with.
                                                                        DENIS LEARY

In California fifty women protested against the war with Iraq by lying on the ground naked and spelling out the word 'peace'. Right idea, wrong president.
                                                                        JAY LENO

CNN said that after the war, there is a plan to divide Iraq into three parts – regular, premium and unleaded.   JAY LENO

After twenty-five years hookers are back on the streets of Baghdad. Do you really want a hooker who was working twenty-five years ago?
                                                                        DAVID LETTERMAN

I wonder why all the men in Iraq have black moustaches? They can't *all* think it suits them.   PAUL MERTON

The only way the French are going in is if we tell them we found truffles in Iraq.   DENNIS MILLER

That Saddam statue going down looked like a narcoleptic hailing a cab.
                                                                        DENNIS MILLER

Yesterday American and British troops handed out food to hundreds of Iraqis. Not surprisingly, the Iraqis handed the British food back.   CONAN O'BRIEN

Ireland and the Irish

Geographically, Ireland is a medium-sized rural island that is slowly but steadily being consumed by sheep.   DAVE BARRY

Dublin University contains the cream of Ireland — rich and thick.

SAMUEL BECKETT

Other people have a nationality. The Irish and the Jews have a psychosis.

BRENDAN BEHAN, *Richard's Cork Leg*

If there were only three Irishmen left in the world you'd find two of them in a corner talking about the other.

BRENDAN BEHAN

Demolishing a house in Dublin last year, workmen found a skeleton with a medal round its neck. The inscription read: Irish Hide and Seek Champion 1910.

FRANK CARSON

I know I've got Irish blood because I wake up every day with a hangover.

NOEL GALLAGHER

If you do somebody in Ireland a favour, you make an enemy for life.

HUGH LEONARD

The Irish are perceived as young, eloquent, romantic, tuneful, mystical, funny, and expert havers-of-a-good-time. And, as a bonus, in the same way that the English abroad are made doubly welcome once people realise they're not German, so the Irish are welcomed for not being English.

PETE McCARTHY, *McCarthy's Bar*

An Englishman thinks seated; a Frenchman, standing; an American, pacing; an Irishman afterward.

AUSTIN O'MALLEY

Put an Irishman on the spit, and you can always get another Irishman to turn him.

GEORGE BERNARD SHAW

Irritation

I don't have pet peeves, I have whole kennels of irritation.

WHOOPI GOLDBERG

Be master of your petty annoyances and conserve your energies for the big, worthwhile things. It isn't the mountain ahead that wears you out — it's the grain of sand in your shoe.

ROBERT SERVICE

Italy

Let's be frank, the Italians' technological contribution to humankind stopped with the pizza oven.

BILL BRYSON, *Neither Here Nor There*

Venice is like eating an entire box of chocolate liqueurs at one go.

TRUMAN CAPOTE

The trouble with eating Italian food is that five or six days later you're hungry again.

GEORGE MILLER

All right, but apart from the sanitation, medicine, education, wine, public order, irrigation, roads, the fresh water system and public health, what have the Romans ever done for us?

REG (JOHN CLEESE), *Monty Python's Life of Brian*

J

Michael Jackson

With his womanly voice, stark white skin and Medusa hair, his gash of red lipstick, heavy eyeliner, almost non-existent nose and lopsided face, Michael Jackson was making this appearance in order to scotch all rumours that he is not quite normal.

CRAIG BROWN

Michael Jackson looks great for forty-four but, between you and me, I think he's had some work done.

JIMMY FALLON

Michael Jackson was a poor black boy who grew up to be a rich white woman.

MOLLY IVINS

A lot of people think that I'm a Michael Jackson impersonator.

MICHAEL JACKSON

Michael Jackson is doing a record with his brothers to prove that white people and black people *can* work together.

CONAN O'BRIEN

He's a great singer — but he's not the most masculine guy, is he?

ALEXANDER O'NEAL

Michael Jackson's album was only called 'Bad' because there wasn't enough room on the sleeve for 'Pathetic'.

PRINCE

Honey, you gotta pick a race first. All of a sudden you're a black man, then you're Diana Ross, now you're Audrey Hepburn. Then he's got the little beard going on. He's like Lord of the Rings, the entire cast. Michael's about to jump species.   ROBIN WILLIAMS

Jazz

The jazz critics loved me as long as they thought I was black and dead.
                                                              STEVE ALLEN

The purpose of jazz is the destruction of music.   THOMAS BEECHAM

A jazz musician is a juggler who uses harmonies instead of oranges.
                                                              BENNY GREEN

When you've been blowing away for hours in smoky pubs and no one applauds because they're all watching football, it does cause some introspection.
                                                              SOWETO KINCH

Jazz is five guys playing different songs.   STEVE McGREW

Jazz will endure just as long as people hear it through their feet instead of their brains.   JOHN PHILIP SOUSA

Black people gave us jazz, and we turned it into Kenny G.   JON STEWART

Jazz is not dead, it just smells funny.   FRANK ZAPPA

Jewellery

My husband gave me a necklace. It's fake. Maybe I'm paranoid, but in this day and age I don't want something around my neck that's worth more than my head.   RITA RUDNER

Men who have a pierced ear are better prepared for marriage – they've experienced pain and bought jewellery.   RITA RUDNER

Jews

Jesus was a Jew, yes, but only on his mother's side.
                          ARCHIE BUNKER (CARROLL O'CONNOR), *All in the Family*

A Jewish nymphomaniac is a woman who will have sex on the same day she has her hair done.   MAUREEN LIPMAN

The Jews invented guilt and the Irish turned it into an art form.

WALTER MATTHAU

I'm not really a Jew; just Jew-ish, not the whole hog.

JONATHAN MILLER, *Beyond the Fringe*

I believe that the Jews have made a contribution to the human condition out of all proportion to their numbers: I believe them to be an immense people. Not only have they supplied the world with two leaders of the stature of Jesus Christ and Karl Marx, but they have even indulged in the luxury of following neither one nor the other.   PETER USTINOV, *Dear Me*

A Jewish grandmother was supposed to be looking after her grandson on Miami Beach. She turned her head for a moment and suddenly a wave came in and washed the kid way out to sea. They called a lifeguard, a helicopter and the police who eventually managed to grab the little kid. They brought him in and pumped him out for an hour. Finally the kid started to breathe again. The grandmother said, 'He had a hat . . .'   HENNY YOUNGMAN

Show me a Jewish boy who doesn't go to medical school and I'll show you a lawyer.

Jogging

If the poor overweight jogger only knew how far he had to run to work off the calories in a crust of bread, he might find it better in terms of pound per mile to go to a massage parlour.   DR CHRISTIAN BARNARD

My doctor told me that jogging would add years to my life. He was right — I feel ten years older already.   MILTON BERLE

The trouble with jogging is that the ice falls out of your glass.

MARTIN MULL

Jogging is for people who aren't intelligent enough to watch breakfast television.   VICTORIA WOOD

Lyndon B. Johnson

You can tell he used to be a rancher. He squeezes Republicans like he's milking a cow.   BOB HOPE

Hyperbole was to Lyndon Johnson what oxygen is to life.   BILL MOYERS

Journalism

Reporters are faced with the daily choice of painstakingly researching stories or writing whatever people tell them. Both approaches pay the same.

SCOTT ADAMS, *The Dilbert Principle*

Science is a good thing. News reporters are good things too. But it's never a good idea to put them in the same room.   SCOTT ADAMS

Journalism is literature in a hurry.   MATTHEW ARNOLD

Fleet Street can scent the possibilities of sex like a tile-tripping tomcat.

JULIAN BARNES, *Letters from London*

I figured out why I'm not getting seriously rich. I write newspaper columns. Nobody ever makes newspaper columns into major motion pictures starring Tom Cruise. The best you can hope for, with a newspaper column, is that people will like it enough to attach it to their refrigerators with magnets shaped like fruit.

DAVE BARRY

Journalists say a thing that they know isn't true, in the hope that if they keep on saying it long enough it *will* be true.   ARNOLD BENNETT, *The Title*

Journalism is the only thinkable alternative to working.

JEFFREY BERNARD

I was terrible at straight items. When I wrote obituaries, my mother said the only thing I ever got them to do was die in alphabetical order.

ERMA BOMBECK

Writs are the Oscars of my profession.   NIGEL DEMPSTER

(*as editor of satirical magazine* Private Eye) My own motto is publish and be sued.   RICHARD INGRAMS

Never trust a smiling reporter.   ED KOCH

Journalism is to politician as dog is to lamp-post.   H.L. MENCKEN

Interviewing Warren Beatty is like asking a haemophiliac for a pint of blood.

REX REED

All day long, Hollywood reporters lie in the sun, and when the sun goes down, they lie some more.   FRANK SINATRA

(*on foreign correspondents*) He's someone who flies around from hotel to hotel and thinks the most interesting thing about any story is the fact that he has arrived to cover it.   TOM STOPPARD, *Night and Day*

Rock journalism is people who can't write interviewing people who can't talk for people who can't read.   FRANK ZAPPA

Judgment

Before you judge a man, walk a mile in his shoes. After that, who cares? He's a mile away and you've got his shoes.   BILLY CONNOLLY

Juries

We operate under a jury system in this country, and as much as we complain about it, we have to admit that we know of no better system, except possibly flipping a coin.   DAVE BARRY

Look at the judge, a guy who spends half his life in school. He's a lawyer, then he's a lower judge, then an upper judge. He works his way up to some big important murder trial like this, and he doesn't even get to decide if the guy is guilty or not. No, that decision's made by five salesmen, three plumbers, two bank tellers and a dingbat.

ARCHIE BUNKER (CARROLL O'CONNOR), *All in the Family*

When you go into court you are putting your fate into the hands of twelve people who weren't smart enough to get out of jury duty.   NORM CROSBY

A jury consists of twelve persons chosen to decide who has the better lawyer.   ROBERT FROST

To escape jury duty in England, wear a bowler hat and carry a copy of the *Daily Telegraph*.   JOHN MORTIMER

Getting out of jury duty is easy. The trick is to say you're prejudiced against all races.   HOMER SIMPSON, *The Simpsons*

K

The Kennedys

I have always liked the Kennedys as politicians. They had such great hair.
PAMELA ANDERSON

Am I the only one to think that John F. Kennedy was killed by a peanut allergy? You may laugh but there was an empty packet of KP Dry Roasted found on the grassy knoll.
HARRY HILL

(*on John F. Kennedy's election success*) I must say the Senator's victory in Wisconsin was a triumph for democracy. It proves that a millionaire has just as good a chance as anybody else.
BOB HOPE

The main difference for the history of the world if I had been shot rather than Kennedy is that Onassis probably wouldn't have married Mrs Khrushchev.
NIKITA KHRUSHCHEV

People always ask me, 'Where were you when Kennedy was shot?' Well, I don't have an alibi.
EMO PHILIPS

John Kerry

If John Kerry had a dollar for every time he bragged about serving in Vietnam – oh wait, he does.
ANN COULTER

Today, John Kerry announced a foolproof plan to wipe out the 500 billion-dollar deficit: he's going to put it on his wife's Gold Card.
CRAIG KILBORN

John Kerry described his Republican critics as 'the most crooked, lying group I've ever seen.' Wow, that's saying something, because Kerry's both a lawyer and a politician.
JAY LENO

John Kerry has promised to take this country back from the wealthy. Who better than the guy worth $700 million to take the country back? See, he knows how the wealthy think. He can spy on them at his country club, at his place in Palm Beach, at his house in the Hamptons. He's like a mole for the working man.
JAY LENO

John Kerry speaks French fluently. Democrats are saying he's one in a million. A war hero who speaks French – isn't it more like one in a trillion?
JAY LENO

Ted Kennedy introduced Kerry as the 'comeback kid'. That used to be Bill Clinton's name — because every time he would come back to a city, he would find out if he had a kid or not.

JAY LENO

A new poll shows that Kerry's support in the South is strongest among blacks. Kerry's appeal to Southern blacks is obvious. He is a white man who lives far, far away.

DENNIS MILLER

Kindness

Remember there's no such thing as a small act of kindness. Every act creates a ripple with no logical end.

SCOTT ADAMS

Frasier Crane (Kelsey Grammer): No, Roz, it's really not necessary. You do not have to donate one of your boyfriends to Daphne.
Roz Doyle (Peri Gilpin): Gee, I'd be happy to.
Frasier: But still one hates to break up a collection.

Frasier

The most human thing we can do is comfort the afflicted and afflict the comfortable.

CLARENCE DARROW

If you can't be kind, at least be vague.

JUDITH MARTIN

Be kind to everybody. You never know who might show up on the jury at your trial.

Kissing

Never let a fool kiss you — or a kiss fool you.

JOEY ADAMS

French-kissing is a really sexy thing to do, according to French people, although you should bear in mind that they also like to eat snails.

DAVE BARRY

A kiss is a lovely trick designed by nature to stop speech when words become superfluous.

INGRID BERGMAN

(*on kissing Woody Allen*) It was like kissing the Berlin Wall.

HELENA BONHAM CARTER

I married the first man I ever kissed. When I tell my children that they just about throw up.

BARBARA BUSH

(*of Marilyn Monroe*) It's like kissing Hitler.

TONY CURTIS

I was hugging a woman and we were jumping up and down and embracing, and then I realised that it wasn't love but the Yankees had just won the World Series.
LARRY DAVID

Women still remember the first kiss after men have forgotten the last.
RÉMY DE GOURMONT

Kisses may not spread germs, but they certainly lower resistance.
LOUISE ERICKSON

If you don't kiss a girl on the first date, you are a gentleman. If you don't kiss her by the second, you are gay.
RICHARD FISH (GREG GERMANN), *Ally McBeal*

(*to Capucine*) Kissing you is like kissing the side of a beer bottle.
LAURENCE HARVEY

The sound of a kiss is not so loud as that of a cannon, but its echo lasts a great deal longer.
OLIVER WENDELL HOLMES, *The Professor at the Breakfast-Table*

Whoever named it necking was a poor judge of anatomy.
GROUCHO MARX

A kiss can be a comma, a question mark or an exclamation point. That's basic spelling that every woman ought to know.
MISTINGUETTE

I'd like to kiss ya, but I just washed ma hair.
MADGE NORWOOD (BETTE DAVIS), *Cabin in the Cotton*

We used to play spin the bottle when I was a kid. A girl would spin the bottle and if it pointed to you when it stopped, the girl could either kiss you or give you a dime. By the time I was 14, I owned my own home.
GENE PERRET

Why do you think people close their eyes when they kiss? Think about it. In the real world, if you see someone an inch and a half away, coming at you with their eyes open and their lips puckered, you'd scream. It's alarming.
PAUL REISER

(*on kissing Jennifer Aniston in* Friends) It's a job — someone's gotta do it. The reality is, Jennifer and I can do our job well because we truly are friends. But when the day's over, she goes home to her boyfriend and I go home to a magazine.
DAVID SCHWIMMER

(*on kissing Bruce Willis in* Moonlighting) His idea of a romantic kiss was to go 'blaaah' and gag me with his tongue. He only improved once he married Demi Moore.
CYBILL SHEPHERD

Everybody winds up kissing the wrong person goodnight.
ANDY WARHOL

Kissing is a means of getting two people so close together that they can't see anything wrong with each other.
GENE YASENAK

Kleptomania

I have kleptomania, but when it gets bad, I take something for it.
KEN DODD

Women like posh hotels; there's more for them to steal. Take them to a posh hotel and they all turn into the Artful Dodger.
JEFF GREEN

A kleptomaniac is a person who helps himself because he can't help himself.

Knighthood

Mother always told me my day was coming, but I never realised that I'd end up being the shortest knight of the year!
GORDON RICHARDS

Knowledge

Those people who think they know everything are a great annoyance to those of us who do.
ISAAC ASIMOV

A woman, especially if she have the misfortune of knowing anything, should conceal it as well as she can.
JANE AUSTEN, *Northanger Abbey*

I have tried to know absolutely nothing about a great many things, and I have succeeded fairly well.
ROBERT BENCHLEY

A head of lettuce knows something that you don't. It knows for sure if the light in the refrigerator really goes out when the door is closed.
SAM EWING

An investment in knowledge pays the best interest.
BENJAMIN FRANKLIN, *Poor Richard's Almanack*

In seventy years, the one surviving fragment of my knowledge, the only indisputable poor particle of certainty in my entire life is that in a public house lavatory incoming traffic has the right of way. HUGH LEONARD, *Da*

L

Language

A good metaphor can make any bad idea sound good. SCOTT ADAMS

Is there anything worse than speaking a foreign language to someone who turns out to be English? MICHAEL FRAYN, *Clouds*

If the Romans had been obliged to learn Latin they would never have found time to conquer the world. HEINRICH HEINE

Management speak has been infiltrated into our lives, a loathsome serpent crawling into our bed at night and choking the life out of our language. JOHN HUMPHRYS

I've done a bit of Latin in my time . . . but I can control it. EDDIE IZZARD

It's a strange world of language in which skating on thin ice can get you into hot water. FRANKLIN P. JONES

Writing in English is the most ingenious torture ever devised for sins committed in previous lives. JAMES JOYCE

We just used so many metaphors I forgot what the hell we were talking about. OSCAR MADISON (WALTER MATTHAU), *The Odd Couple II*

American is the language in which people say what they mean, as Italian is the language in which they say what they feel. English is the language in which what a character means or feels has to be deduced from what he or she says, which may be quite the opposite. JOHN MORTIMER

(*on a departing guest*) That girl speaks eighteen languages and she can't say 'no' in any of them. DOROTHY PARKER

There are known knowns. These are things we know that we know. There are known unknowns. That is to say, there are things we know we don't know. But, there are also unknown unknowns. These are things we don't know we don't know.

DONALD RUMSFELD

Osama Bin Laden is either alive and well, or alive and not too well, or not alive.

DONALD RUMSFELD

England and America are two countries separated by the same language.

GEORGE BERNARD SHAW

Man developed language to satisfy his deep need to complain.

LILY TOMLIN

We don't just borrow words; on occasion, English has pursued other languages down alleyways to beat them unconscious and rifle their pockets for new vocabulary.

BOOKER T. WASHINGTON

I speak two languages: English and Body.

MAE WEST

It's embarrassing when you land in Scandinavia and they speak better English than you do.

ALAN WHICKER

My English is a mixture between Arnold Schwarzenegger and Archbishop Tutu.

BILLY WILDER

Humour is the first of the gifts to perish in a foreign tongue.

VIRGINIA WOOLF, *The Common Reader*

Last words

(*asked if he would like to see the house doctor after being taken ill at a hotel*) No, get me a people doctor.

MAX BAER

I should never have switched from Scotch to Martinis.

HUMPHREY BOGART

(*executed in the electric chair*) How about this for a headline for tomorrow's paper? French fries.

JAMES FRENCH

(*asked if he thought dying was tough*) Yes, it's tough, but not as tough as doing comedy.

EDMUND GWENN

(*dismissing a priest*) Why should I talk to you? I've just been talking to your boss.   WILSON MIZNER

(*asked if he had any last requests before facing a firing squad*) Yes – a bullet-proof vest.   JAMES W. RODGERS

(*surveying the enemy lines at the Battle of Spotsylvania*) They couldn't hit an elephant at this dist . . .   JOHN SEDGWICK

(*having been told by his wife that he had inadvertently drunk some ink*) Bring me all the blotting paper there is in the house.   REV. SYDNEY SMITH

(*referring to his new bedroom wallpaper*) My wallpaper and I are fighting a duel to the death. One or the other of us has to go.   OSCAR WILDE

Laughter

When people are laughing, they're generally not killing one another.
   ALAN ALDA

I am thankful for laughter, except when milk comes out of my nose.
   WOODY ALLEN

Few women care to be laughed at and men not at all, except for large sums of money.   ALAN AYCKBOURN, *The Norman Conquests*

A joke on a printed page bears as much relation to laughter as a recipe does to a meal. It only comes to life when it gets through a human being.
   RABBI LIONEL BLUE

Laughter is the shortest distance between two people.   VICTOR BORGE

He who laughs last has not yet heard the bad news.   BERTOLT BRECHT

The person who knows how to laugh at himself will never cease to be amused.
   SHIRLEY MACLAINE

Law

The less people know about how sausages and laws are made, the better they'll sleep at night.   OTTO VON BISMARCK

The Scottish verdict 'not proven' means 'guilty, but don't do it again'.
   WINIFRED DUKE

I have come to regard the law courts not as a cathedral but rather as a casino.
RICHARD INGRAMS

Only one thing is impossible for God: to find any sense in any copyright law on the planet.
MARK TWAIN

Lawyers

I get paid for seeing that my clients have every break the law allows. But the guilty never escape unscathed. My fees are sufficient punishment for anyone.
F. LEE BAILEY

The vast majority of lawyers are responsible professionals as well as, in many ways, human beings.
DAVE BARRY

Lawyers are the only persons in whom ignorance of the law is not punished.
JEREMY BENTHAM

A lawyer is a learned gentleman who rescues your estate from your enemies and keeps it to himself.
HENRY BOUGHAM

It is better to have loved and lost, but only if you have a good lawyer.
HERB CAEN

On the whole barristers are more interested in their briefs than a girl's.
JILLY COOPER, *Men and Super Men*

Occasionally a lawyer sends you a legal document covered in kisses, and you really think you're getting somewhere until he tells you he only wants you to sign your name in three places.
JILLY COOPER

What do you call 500 lawyers lying on the bottom of the ocean? – A good start.
GAVIN D'AMATO (DANNY DEVITO), *The War of the Roses*

Always take a lawyer with you, and bring another lawyer to watch him.
BO DIDDLEY

A countryman between two lawyers is like a fish between two cats.
BENJAMIN FRANKLIN

A man may as well open an oyster without a knife, as a lawyer's mouth without a fee.
BARTON HOLYDAY

A lawyer is never entirely comfortable with a friendly divorce, any more than a good mortician wants to finish his job and then have the patient sit up on the table.   JEAN KERR

Terrorists hijacked an airplane full of lawyers. The terrorists threatened to release one every hour unless their demands were met.   DENIS LEARY

Lawyers are like rhinoceroses: thick-skinned, short-sighted, and always ready to charge.   DAVID MELLOR

No brilliance is needed in the law. Nothing but common sense, and relatively clean fingernails.   JOHN MORTIMER, *A Voyage Round My Father*

A disastrous probate case for a lawyer is when some of the heirs get nearly as much as he does.   JOHN MORTIMER

A lawyer will do anything to win a case. Sometimes he will even tell the truth.
                                                                    PATRICK MURRAY

The only difference between a dead skunk lying in the road and a dead lawyer lying in the road is that there are skid marks around the skunk.
                                                                    PATRICK MURRAY

A lawyer with a briefcase can steal more than a thousand men with guns.
                                                    MARIO PUZO, *The Godfather*

The only way you can beat the lawyers is to die with nothing.
                                                                     WILL ROGERS

The minute you read something you can't understand, you can almost be sure it was drawn up by a lawyer.   WILL ROGERS

Reduce the number of lawyers. They are like beavers – they get in the middle of the stream and dam it up.
                                                                DONALD RUMSFELD

If law school is so hard to get through, how come there are so many lawyers?
                                                                   CALVIN TRILLIN

And God said: 'Let there be Satan, so people don't blame everything on me. And let there be lawyers, so people don't blame everything on Satan.'
                                                                  JOHN WING Jr

An incompetent lawyer can delay a trial for months or years. A competent lawyer can delay one even longer.
EVELLE YOUNGER

It is better to be a mouse in a cat's mouth than a man in a lawyer's hands.
SPANISH PROVERB

Laziness

Of course I don't look busy, I did it right the first time.
SCOTT ADAMS, *The Dilbert Principle*

Given the choice between accomplishing something and just lying around, I'd rather just lie around. No contest.
ERIC CLAPTON

The laziest man I ever met put popcorn in his pancakes so they would turn over by themselves.
W.C. FIELDS

Well, we can't stand around here doing nothing. People will think we're workmen.
SPIKE MILLIGAN, *The Goon Show*

Laziness is nothing more than the habit of resting before you get tired.
JULES RENARD

It is better to have loafed and lost than never to have loafed at all.
JAMES THURBER, *Fables For Our Time*

Leadership

When trouble arises and things look bad, there is always one individual who perceives a solution and is willing to take command. Very often, that individual is crazy.
DAVE BARRY

(*on Conservative Party head Iain Duncan Smith*) He possesses fewer gifts of leadership than my Labrador.
MAX HASTINGS

You are more likely to find great leadership coming from a man who likes to have sex with a lot of women than one who doesn't.
ETHAN HAWKE

Only one man in a thousand is a leader of men – the other 999 follow women.
GROUCHO MARX

A truly great leader is one who never allows his followers to discover that he is as ignorant as they are.

Learning

You live and learn. At any rate, you live. DOUGLAS ADAMS

To you, Baldrick, the Renaissance was just something that happened to other people, wasn't it?
EDMUND BLACKADDER (ROWAN ATKINSON), *Blackadder*

I am always ready to learn although I did not always like being taught.
WINSTON CHURCHILL

There are three kinds of men: the one that learns by reading, the few who learn by observation, and the rest of them who have to pee on an electric fence for themselves. ROY ROGERS

Marge, don't discourage the boy! Weaseling out of things is important to learn. It's what separates us from the animals. Except the weasel.
HOMER SIMPSON, *The Simpsons*

Curiosity is the wick in the candle of learning. WILLIAM A. WARD

Legs

A girl's legs are her best friends, but even the best of friends must part.
REDD FOXX

There are two reasons why I'm in show business, and I'm standing on both of them. BETTY GRABLE

You have no idea what a long-legged gal can do without doing anything.
GERRY JEFFERS (CLAUDETTE COLBERT), *The Palm Beach Story*

In a recent survey ten per cent of men said they preferred women with fat legs, ten per cent preferred women with thin legs, and the other eighty per cent said they preferred something in-between. JAY LENO

Perhaps at fourteen every boy should be in love with some ideal woman to put on a pedestal and worship. As he grows up, of course, he will put her on a pedestal the better to view her legs. BARRY NORMAN

(*on his first meeting with the US national security advisor*) I have to confess, it was hard for me to concentrate in the conversation with Condoleezza Rice, because she has such nice legs. ARIEL SHARON

You can say what you like about long dresses, but they cover a multitude of shins.
MAE WEST

My wife is mad at me. I told her she had a run in her nylons, but she wasn't wearing any.
HENNY YOUNGMAN

If Mother Nature could have foreseen Bermuda shorts, she would surely have done a better job on the male knee.

Leisure

Leisure time is that five or six hours when you sleep at night.
GEORGE ALLEN

One of my friends went on a murder weekend. Now he's doing life for it.
JACK DEE

What's the point of going out? We're just going to wind up back here anyway.
HOMER SIMPSON, *The Simpsons*

Nothing gives a man more leisure time than being punctual for appointments.

Letters

At the end of a letter I like to write, 'P.S. – this is what part of the alphabet would look like if Q and R were eliminated.'
MITCH HEDBERG

Liars and lies

There's a reason that executives lie. The alternative is worse!
SCOTT ADAMS

The real trouble with liars . . . was there could never be any guarantee against their occasionally telling the truth.
KINGSLEY AMIS, *Girl*

(*of Lady Desborough*) She tells enough white lies to ice a wedding cake.
MARGOT ASQUITH

Anyone who lies about Gore Vidal is doing him a kindness.
WILLIAM F. BUCKLEY

A lie can be half-way round the world before the truth has got its boots on.
JAMES CALLAGHAN

Faces can lie, but not necks. Look at a horse's teeth and a woman's neck.
HENRY CECIL, *Portrait of a Judge*

Lying is like alcoholism. You are always recovering.
GRAHAM DALTON (JAMES SPADER), *Sex, Lies, and Videotape*

Old lie: the check is in the mail. New lie: I didn't check the e-mail.
BRIAN FINE

My father told me all about the birds and the bees. The liar — I went steady with a woodpecker till I was twenty-one.   BOB HOPE

In a controversy it is safest to assume that both sides are lying.
ROBERT LYND, *The Blue Lion*

Legend: a lie that has attained the dignity of age.   H.L. MENCKEN

You only lie to two people in your life: your girlfriend and the police.
JACK NICHOLSON

They think that whenever anyone in the White House now tells a lie, I get a royalty.   RICHARD NIXON

By the time you swear you're his,
Shivering and sighing,
And he vows his passion is
Infinite, undying —
Lady, make a note of this:
One of you is lying.   DOROTHY PARKER, *Unfortunate Coincidence*

Telling lies is a fault in a boy, an art in a lover, an accomplishment in a bachelor, and second nature in a married man.   HELEN ROWLAND

One man's chin is as rough as another's, and one man's lies are as smooth as another's.   HELEN ROWLAND

A little inaccuracy sometimes saves tons of explanation.
SAKI, *The Square Egg*

Marge, it takes two to lie — one to lie and one to listen.
HOMER SIMPSON, *The Simpsons*

(*during the 1952 Presidential campaign*) I offer my opponents a bargain: if they will stop telling falsehoods about us, I will stop telling the truth about them.

ADLAI STEVENSON

One of the most striking differences between a cat and a lie is that a cat has only nine lives.

MARK TWAIN, *Pudd'nhead Wilson*

Liberal Party

The Liberal-Democrats are not just empty. They are a void within a vacuum, surrounded by a vast inanition.

BORIS JOHNSON

As usual the Liberals offer a mixture of sound and original ideas. Unfortunately none of the sound ideas is original and none of the original ideas is sound.

HAROLD MACMILLAN

Liberals

If God had been a liberal there wouldn't have been Ten Commandments, there would have been ten suggestions.

MALCOLM BRADBURY, *After Dinner Game*

A liberal is a man who leaves a room before the fight begins.

HEYWOOD BROUN

Life

I don't want to get to the end of my life and find that I lived just the length of it. I want to have lived the width of it as well.

DIANE ACKERMAN

The world is a grindstone and life is your nose.

FRED ALLEN

Life is pleasant. Death is peaceful. It's the transition that's troublesome.

ISAAC ASIMOV

Life is like a cup of tea; the more heartily we drink, the sooner we reach the dregs.

J.M. BARRIE, *The Admirable Crichton*

The trouble with life is that there are so many beautiful women and so little time.

JOHN BARRYMORE

Brought up in the provinces in the Forties and Fifties one learned early the valuable lesson that life is generally something that happens elsewhere.

ALAN BENNETT, *Talking Heads*

Life, you know, is rather like opening a tin of sardines. We are all of us looking for the key.   ALAN BENNETT, *Beyond the Fringe*

I remember staying at a luxury hotel and the man from room service delivering vintage champagne to my suite. There was £20,000 in cash scattered on the bed while beneath the sheets was the current Miss Universe. The waiter shook his head sombrely. 'Tell me, Mr Best,' he sighed, 'where did it all go wrong?'
                                                                                GEORGE BEST

Life consists not in holding good cards but in playing those you hold well.
                                                                                JOSH BILLINGS

There is more to life than love, wine, bitterness and food – but not much.
                                                                                BOY GEORGE

Living on Earth may be expensive, but it includes an annual free trip around the sun.   ASHLEIGH BRILLIANT

In the book of life, the answers aren't in the back.   CHARLIE BROWN

Life is a moderately good play with a badly written third act.
                                                                                TRUMAN CAPOTE

The most unfair thing about life is the way it ends. I mean, life is tough. It takes up a lot of your time. What do you get at the end of it? Death. What's that, a bonus? I think the life cycle is all backwards. You should die first, get it out of the way. Then you live in an old age home. You get kicked out when you're too young, you get a gold watch, you go to work. You work forty years until you're young enough to enjoy your retirement. You do drugs, alcohol, you party, you get ready for high school. You go to grade school, you become a kid, you play, you have no responsibilities, you become a little baby, you go back into the womb, you spend your last nine months floating . . . you finish off as an orgasm.
                                                                                GEORGE CARLIN

Life is a tragedy when seen in close-up, but a comedy in long-shot.
                                                                                CHARLIE CHAPLIN

I wouldn't dream of taking life as it comes: it may not be colour-coordinated.
                                                                                JULIAN CLARY

Why do people say 'life is short'? Life is the longest damn thing anyone ever bloody does! What can you do that's longer?   BILLY CONNOLLY

Life is a maze in which we take the wrong turning before we have learnt to walk.
CYRIL CONNOLLY, *The Unquiet Grave*

Life was a funny thing that happened to me on the way to the grave.
QUENTIN CRISP, *The Naked Civil Servant*

If I had to live my life over again, I'd be a plumber.
ALBERT EINSTEIN

Life ain't easy. But then, if it was, everybody would be doing it.
HARLAN ELLISON

For most men life is a search for the proper manila envelope in which to get themselves filed.
CLIFTON FADIMAN

Life's tragedy is that we get old too soon and wise too late.
BENJAMIN FRANKLIN

Many people die at twenty-five and aren't buried until they are seventy-five.
MAX FRISCH

In three words I can sum up everything I've learned about life: it goes on.
ROBERT FROST

Life is a box of chocolates, Forrest. You never know what you're going to get.
MRS GUMP (SALLY FIELD), *Forrest Gump*

Life is a great big canvas, and you should throw all the paint on it you can.
DANNY KAYE

Life is a sexually transmitted disease and there is a 100 per cent mortality rate.
R.D. LAING

Life is something that happens when you can't get to sleep.
FRAN LEBOWITZ

Life is like a sewer. What you get out of it depends on what you put into it.
TOM LEHRER

Living is easy with your eyes closed.
JOHN LENNON

Life is a banquet and most poor suckers are starving to death.
AUNTIE MAME (ROSALIND RUSSELL), *Auntie Mame*

Life is a constant oscillation between the sharp horns of dilemmas.

H.L. MENCKEN

I want to walk through life instead of being dragged through it.

ALANIS MORISSETTE

Life is like a very short visit to a toyshop between birth and death.

DESMOND MORRIS

In spite of the cost of living, it's still popular.   KATHLEEN NORRIS

Coach (Nicholas Colasanto): How's the world treating you, Norm?
Norm Peterson (George Wendt): Like I just ran over its dog.   *Cheers*

If life is a soap opera, you shouldn't be in too much of hurry to get to the final credits.   MICHAEL PORTILLO

My life has been one long descent into respectability.

MANDY RICE-DAVIES

Half our life is spent trying to find something to do with the time we have rushed through life trying to save.   WILL ROGERS

My whole life is like a movie. It's just that there are no dissolves. I have to live every agonising moment of it. My life needs editing.   MORT SAHL

I think I've discovered the secret of life – you just hang around until you get used to it.   CHARLES SCHULZ

I like life. It's something to do.   RONNIE SHAKES

The whole of my life has been passed like a razor – in hot water or a scrape!
REV. SYDNEY SMITH

Life is like a train. You expect delays from time to time, but not a derailment.
WILLIE STARGELL

Life is a gamble, at terrible odds – if it was a bet, you wouldn't take it.
TOM STOPPARD, *Rosencrantz and Guildenstern are Dead*

I've been trying for some time to develop a lifestyle that doesn't require my presence.   GARY TRUDEAU

Let us so live that when we come to die even the undertaker will be sorry.
MARK TWAIN

Life is short but it would be awful if it were too long. I have the feeling the human body is like a rent-a-car. Your hope is to bring it back to the rent-a-car counter with dignity, not leave it in a country lane with an embarrassing red triangle indicating you have broken down.
PETER USTINOV

A well-developed sense of humour is the pole that adds balance to your steps as you walk the tightrope of life.
WILLIAM A. WARD

Abraham Lincoln

It's Lincoln's birthday, and they finally found the real reason he was shot. His cell phone kept ringing in the theatre.
JAY LENO

(*on Abraham Lincoln*) Nothing more than a well-meaning baboon.
GEORGE McCLELLAN

Lingerie

Little kids in a supermarket buy cereal the way men buy lingerie. They get stuff they have no interest in just to get the prize inside.
JEFF FOXWORTHY

There's a new bra that gives you a bigger cleavage by pushing your stomach up. Is that what you need, ladies, cleavage with a belly button?
JAY LENO

There's another new bra that uses bubble wrap for padding. You know how much fun it is to pop that stuff. Ladies, if you think guys can't keep their hands off your boobs now . . .
JAY LENO

I was the first woman to burn my bra – it took the fire department four days to put it out.
DOLLY PARTON

Diane Chambers (Shelley Long): Oh no! The thing I feared most has happened!
Carla Tortelli (Rhea Perlman): What? Your living bra died of boredom?
Cheers

Lisp

Lisp: to call a spade a thpade.
OLIVER HERFORD

Listening

If only we'd listened to that boy, instead of walling him up in the abandoned coke oven.   MONTGOMERY BURNS, *The Simpsons*

No man would listen to you talk if he didn't know it was his turn next.
                    EDGAR WATSON HOWE

A good listener is usually thinking about something else.   KIN HUBBARD

I'm a white male, age eighteen to forty-nine. Everyone listens to me – no matter how dumb my suggestions are.   HOMER SIMPSON, *The Simpsons*

A good listener is not someone who has nothing to say. A good listener is a good talker with a sore throat.   KATHARINE WHITEHORN

Literature

My father [Kingsley] always had doubts about the Booker Prize although they evaporated on the announcement that he had won it.   MARTIN AMIS

I'm not too keen on characters taking over; they do as they are damn well told.
                    IAIN BANKS

(*on Aldous Huxley*) The stupid person's idea of a clever person.
                    ELIZABETH BOWEN

The British have long had a taste for bad books, but they like them well written.
                    MALCOLM BRADBURY

I always wanted to write a book that ended with the word 'mayonnaise'.
                    RICHARD BRAUTIGAN

A good novel tells us the truth about its hero; but a bad novel tells us the truth about its author.   G.K. CHESTERTON

Coach (Nicholas Colasanto): I'm working on a novel. Going on six years now. I think I might finish it tonight.
Diane Chambers (Shelley Long): You're writing a novel?
Coach: No, reading it.   *Cheers*

The greatest masterpiece in literature is only a dictionary out of order.
                    JEAN COCTEAU

Robert Benchley has a style that is weak and lies down frequently to rest.
MAX EASTMAN

(*on Charlotte Brontë*) I wish her characters would talk a little less like the heroes and heroines of police reports.
GEORGE ELIOT

Henry James had a mind so fine that no idea could violate it.
T.S. ELIOT

Most new books are forgotten within a year, especially by those who borrow them.
EVAN ESAR

When you read a classic you do not see in the book more than you did before. You see more in you than there was before.
CLIFTON FADIMAN

(*on Gertrude Stein*) She was a master at making nothing happen very slowly.
CLIFTON FADIMAN

Best-selling suspense author Robert Ludlum died this week. Or did he?
JIMMY FALLON

(*on Ernest Hemingway*) He has never been known to use a word that might send the reader to a dictionary.
WILLIAM FAULKNER

(*on Mark Twain*) A hack writer who would have been considered fourth rate in Europe, who tried out a few of the old proven 'sure-fire' literary skeletons with sufficient local colour to intrigue the superficial and the lazy.
WILLIAM FAULKNER

(*on Henry James*) One of the nicest old ladies I ever met.
WILLIAM FAULKNER

[Joseph] Conrad spent a day finding the *mot juste*; then killed it.
FORD MADOX FORD

It's red hot, mate. I hate to think of this sort of book getting into the wrong hands. As soon as I've finished this, I shall recommend they ban it.
TONY HANCOCK, *Hancock's Half-Hour*

I always had my nose in a book. My parents couldn't afford Kleenex.
JOE HICKMAN

Literature is mostly about having sex, and not much about having children; life is the other way round.
DAVID LODGE, *The British Museum is Falling Down*

(*on J.D. Salinger*) The greatest mind ever to stay in prep school.

NORMAN MAILER

A sequel is an admission that you've been reduced to imitating yourself.

DON MARQUIS

Outside of a dog, a book is man's best friend. Inside of a dog, it's too dark to read.

GROUCHO MARX

(*on* Dawn Ginsbergh's Revenge *by S.J. Perelman*) From the moment I picked up your book until I laid it down I was convulsed with laughter. Someday I intend reading it.

GROUCHO MARX

(*on Henry James*) He did not live, he observed life from a window, and too often was inclined to content himself with no more than what his friends told him they saw when *they* looked out of a window.

W. SOMERSET MAUGHAM

A literary movement consists of five or six people who live in the same town and hate each other cordially.

GEORGE MOORE

(*of an unnamed writer*) Though he tortures the English language, he has never yet succeeded in forcing it to reveal its meaning.

J.B. MORTON

[Evelyn] Waugh, I always feel, is an antique in search of a period, a snob in search of a class.

MALCOLM MUGGERIDGE

Oxymoron is a literary device whereby two contradictory concepts are juxta-posed: as for example in 'the witty Jane Austen'.

PATRICK MURRAY

(*on P.G. Wodehouse*) English literature's performing flea.

SEAN O'CASEY

Dorothy Zbornak (Bea Arthur): I'd kill Gloria if she wrote a book about my sex life.
Sophia Petrillo (Estelle Getty): You'd kill your sister over a pamphlet?

The Golden Girls

To say Agatha [Christie]'s characters are cardboard cut-outs is an insult to card-board.

RUTH RENDELL

The biggest selling books are cookbooks and the second are diet books – how not to eat what you've just learned how to cook!

ANDY ROONEY

(*on Harry Potter*) I can do to him whatever I like. I'm allowed to torture him as much as I want. He's mine.

J.K. ROWLING

The big advantage of a book is it's very easy to rewind. Close it and you're right back at the beginning.

JERRY SEINFELD

(*of Virginia Woolf*) I enjoyed talking to her, but thought nothing of her writing. I considered her a 'beautiful little knitter'.

EDITH SITWELL

The Lord of the Rings: that is a book for engineering students called Dave.

LINDA SMITH

(*on Ben Jonson*) Reading him is like wading through glue.

ALFRED, LORD TENNYSON

With sixty staring me in the face, I have developed inflammation of the sentence structure and a definite hardening of the paragraphs.

JAMES THURBER

A classic is something that everyone wants to have read and nobody wants to read.

MARK TWAIN

It seems a great pity they allowed Jane Austen to die a natural death.

MARK TWAIN

(*on Henry James*) Once you've put one of his books down, you simply can't pick it up again.

MARK TWAIN

I don't think literature is ever finished in any country which has more prizes than it has writers.

GORE VIDAL

(*on fellow novelist Carson McCullers*) An hour with a dentist without Novocaine was like a minute with Carson McCullers.

GORE VIDAL

(*on Norman Mailer*) He is now what he wanted to be: the patron saint of bad journalism.

GORE VIDAL

(*on Gertrude Stein*) In her last days she resembled a spoiled pear.   GORE VIDAL

I think if you had ever written a book you were absolutely pleased with, you'd never write another. The same probably goes for having children.

FAY WELDON

(*on George Meredith*) As a writer he has mastered everything except language: as a novelist he can do everything except tell a story: as an artist he is everything except articulate.   OSCAR WILDE

One must have a heart of stone to read the death of Little Nell without laughing.   OSCAR WILDE

(*on Katherine Mansfield*) She stinks like a civet cat that had taken to street walking.   VIRGINIA WOOLF

(*on Katherine Mansfield*) Her mind is a very thin soil, laid an inch or two upon very barren rock.   VIRGINIA WOOLF

(*on E.M. Forster*) He is limp and damp and milder than the breath of a cow.   VIRGINIA WOOLF

(*on Osbert Sitwell*) I don't care for Osbert's prose; the rhododendrons grow to such a height in it.   VIRGINIA WOOLF

Liverpool

Liverpool is a kind of collision caused by the English trying to get out while the Irish are trying to get in.   NANCY BANKS-SMITH

I like to go to Liverpool, just to visit my hubcaps.   BERNARD MANNING

London

When it's three o'clock in New York, it's still 1938 in London.   BETTE MIDLER

The man who is tired of London is tired of looking for a parking space.   PAUL THEROUX

Losing

Every time you win, you're reborn; when you lose, you die a little.   GEORGE ALLEN

If you can accept defeat and open your pay envelope without feeling guilty, you're stealing.   GEORGE ALLEN

The minute you start talking about what you're going to do if you lose, you have lost.   GEORGE SHULTZ

In the game of life it's a good idea to have a few early losses, which relieves you of the pressure of trying to maintain an undefeated season.

BILL VAUGHAN

Love

I was nauseous and tingly all over. I was either in love or I had smallpox.

WOODY ALLEN

My wife and I thought we were in love, but it turned out to be benign.

WOODY ALLEN

Sex is a momentary itch; love never lets you go.

KINGSLEY AMIS

Once in his life, every man is entitled to fall madly in love with a gorgeous redhead.

LUCILLE BALL

Love is an exploding cigar we willingly smoke.

LYNDA BARRY

Love: two minds without a single thought.

PHILIP BARRY

Love . . . the delightful interval between meeting a beautiful girl and discovering that she looks like a haddock.

JOHN BARRYMORE

If you love a man, set him free. If he comes back, it means he's forgotten his sandwiches.

JASMINE BIRTLES

Love at first sight is easy to understand; it's when two people have been looking at each other for a lifetime that it becomes a miracle.

AMY BLOOM

Nothing takes the taste out of peanut butter quite like unrequited love.

CHARLIE BROWN

If grass can grow through cement, love can find you at every time in your life.

CHER

Many a man has fallen in love with a girl in a light so dim he would not have chosen a suit by it.

MAURICE CHEVALIER

You can't put a price tag on love, but you can on all its accessories.

MELANIE CLARK

What's the difference? Love stories, cop stories. Someone gets chased, someone gets caught, a woman screams at the end.

DAN CONNER (JOHN GOODMAN), *Roseanne*

Frasier Crane (Kelsey Grammer): You know that Maris loves you, right? But it's still nice to hear it.
Niles Crane (David Hyde Pierce): I imagine it would be, but let's stick to attainable goals.

Frasier

Love is a fire. But whether it is going to warm your heart or burn down your house, you can never tell.

JOAN CRAWFORD

We don't believe in rheumatism and true love until after the first attack.

MARIE EBNER VON ESCHENBACH

Love is an irresistible desire to be irresistibly desired.

ROBERT FROST

A man in love is incomplete until he has married. Then he's finished.

ZSA ZSA GABOR

Love is a perky elf dancing a merry little jig, and then suddenly he turns on you with a miniature machine gun.

MATT GROENING, *Life in Hell*

Ah, love – the walks over soft grass, the smiles over candlelight, the arguments over just about everything else.

MAX HEADROOM

Never judge someone by who he's in love with; judge him by his friends. People fall in love with the most appalling people. Take a cool, appraising glance at his pals.

CYNTHIA HEIMEL

Love is like measles – all the worse when it comes late in life.

DOUGLAS WILLIAM JERROLD

The surest way to hit a woman's heart is to take aim kneeling.

DOUGLAS WILLIAM JERROLD

Carrie Bradshaw (Sarah Jessica Parker): He fell asleep and I watched gay porn.
Samantha Jones (Kim Cattrall): That's what happens when people say 'I love you.'

Sex and the City

If you can stay in love for more than two years, you're on something.

FRAN LEBOWITZ

A poll showed that two out of five men would rather have love than money or health. Yeah, that's what a woman wants – a broke, sick guy!   JAY LENO

All love affairs end. Eventually the girl is gonna put curlers in her hair.
AL MCGUIRE

The head never rules the heart, but just becomes its partner in crime.
MIGNON MCLAUGHLIN

Love is like playing checkers. You have to know which man to move.
JACKIE MOMS MABLEY

Love is the delusion that one woman differs from another.   H.L. MENCKEN

Love is so confusing. You tell a girl she looks great and what's the first thing you do? Turn out the lights!   ROBERT ORBEN

Love is like quicksilver in the hand. Leave the fingers open and it stays. Clutch it and it darts away.   DOROTHY PARKER

Every love's the love before in a duller dress.   DOROTHY PARKER

Love is not the dying moan of a distant violin – it's the triumphant twang of a bedspring.   S.J. PERELMAN

Somehow, the moment a man has surrendered the key of his heart to a woman, he begins to think about changing the lock.   HELEN ROWLAND

Love does not consist in gazing at each other, but in looking outward together in the same direction.   ANTOINE DE SAINT-EXUPÉRY

The ideal love affair is one conducted by post.   GEORGE BERNARD SHAW

Fran Sinclair: Honey, you have to earn his love.
Earl Sinclair: That could take years. I want his love now. Genuine and unconditional. And I'm willing to pay for it.   *Dinosaurs*

If love is the answer, could you rephrase the question?   LILY TOMLIN

I believe in love and marriage, but not necessarily with the same person.
JOHN TRAVOLTA

Love conquers all things except poverty and toothache.   MAE WEST

A man falls in love through his eyes, a woman through her ears.
WOODROW WYATT

My two-year-old nephew says 'I love you' to everyone. My sister says he doesn't know what it means, he just says it to get something. I think he knows exactly what it means.
TIM YOUNG

I've been in love with the same woman for forty-nine years. If my wife ever finds out, she'll kill me!
HENNY YOUNGMAN

Lovers

(*greeting an ex-lover after several years*) I thought I told you to wait in the car.
TALLULAH BANKHEAD

My ex-boyfriend came round last night, which was a bit weird because I didn't even know he was in a coma.
JO BRAND

I asked my wife how she rated me as a lover on a scale of one to ten. She said, 'I'm no good at fractions'.
RODNEY DANGERFIELD

I'm a great lover, I'll bet.
EMO PHILIPS

It is easier to keep half a dozen lovers guessing than to keep one lover after he has stopped guessing.
HELEN ROWLAND, *A Guide to Men*

If I had as many love affairs as I've been given credit for, I'd be in a jar in the Harvard Medical School.
FRANK SINATRA

The most memorable is always the current one. The rest just merge into a sea of blondes.
ROD STEWART

(*on being told that ten men were waiting for her at her home*) I'm tired, send one of them home.
MAE WEST

Loyalty

Your idea of fidelity is not having more than one man in bed at the same time.
ROBERT GOLD (DIRK BOGARDE), *Darling*

My wife was in labour with our first child for thirty-two hours and I was faithful to her the whole time.
JONATHAN KATZ

Men are only as loyal as their options.   BILL MAHER

I'm very loyal in relationships. Even when I go out with my mom I don't look at other moms.   GARRY SHANDLING

I think I'm a fairly loyal person. Although there's probably a few girlfriends who would disagree with me.   ROD STEWART

Luck

We must believe in luck. For how else can we explain the success of those we don't like?   JEAN COCTEAU

Children need encouragement. So if a kid gets an answer right, tell him it was a lucky guess. That way, he develops a good, lucky feeling.
                    JACK HANDEY, *Deep Thoughts*

A black cat crossing your path signifies that the animal is going somewhere.
                    GROUCHO MARX

Luck is what happens when preparation meets opportunity.   DARRELL ROYAL

Success is simply a matter of luck. Ask any failure.   EARL WILSON

Lunch

I haven't trusted polls since I read that 62 per cent of women had affairs during their lunch hour. I've never met a woman in my life who would give up lunch for sex.   ERMA BOMBECK

Lunch is for wimps.   GORDON GEKKO (MICHAEL DOUGLAS), *Wall Street*

Ask not what you can do for your country, ask what's for lunch.
                    ORSON WELLES

Some weasel took the cork out of my lunch.
          LARSON WHIPSNADE (W.C. FIELDS), *You Can't Cheat an Honest Man*

Lust

Niles Crane (David Hyde Pierce): Are you quite finished undressing him with your eyes?
Roz Doyle (Peri Gilpin): Oh please, I'm already looking for my stockings and trying to remember where I parked my car.   *Frasier*

Luxury

Take care of the luxuries and the necessities will take care of themselves.
DOROTHY PARKER

Living in the lap of luxury isn't bad, except you never know when luxury is going to stand up.
ORSON WELLES

M

General Douglas MacArthur

God, whom you doubtless remember as that quaint old subordinate of General Douglas MacArthur . . .
S.J. PERELMAN

Never underestimate a man who overestimates himself.
FRANKLIN D. ROOSEVELT

I didn't fire him because he was a dumb son of a bitch, although he was, but that's not against the law for generals. If it was, half to three-quarters of them would be in jail.
HARRY S. TRUMAN

Macho

Everybody makes me out to be some kind of macho pig, humping women in the gutter. I do, but I put a pillow under them first.
JAMES CAAN

Macho does not mean mucho.
ZSA ZSA GABOR

Give me macho, or give me death.
MADONNA

Madonna

I look at my friendship with her as like having a gallstone. You deal with it, there is pain, and then you pass it.
SANDRA BERNHARD

She's a gay man trapped in a woman's body.
BOY GEORGE

I *acted* vulgar. Madonna *is* vulgar.
MARLENE DIETRICH

Madonna has just lost thirty pounds – she shaved her legs.
JOAN RIVERS

Madonna is like a McDonald's hamburger. When you ask for a Big Mac, you know exactly what you're getting. It's enjoyable, but it satisfies only for the moment.
SADE

I'm getting old. I watched Madonna writhe around on the hood of that car, and all I could think was, 'That's really going to drive up her insurance premiums.'
JON STEWART

She sings like Mickey Mouse on helium.
ANON

Magazines

I love *National Geographic*. Just when you think you've seen the last lost native tribe, *National Geographic* will find a new one.
SANDRA BERNHARD

Ya know what, I think I'm gonna go to my room and read *Cosmo*, maybe there's something helpful in there. Know what, at least maybe I can learn how to do an at-home bikini wax with leftover Christmas candles.
MONICA GELLER (COURTENEY COX), *Friends*

Playboy is coming out with a magazine for married men – every month the same centrefold.
CRAIG KILBORN

Magazines all too frequently lead to books and should be regarded as the heavy petting of literature.
FRAN LEBOWITZ

There's very little advice in men's magazines because men don't think there's a lot they don't know. Women do. Women want to learn. Men think, 'I know what I'm doing, just show me somebody naked.'
JERRY SEINFELD

Mail

The term 'fragile' is usually interpreted by postal workers as 'please throw underarm'.
MOREY AMSTERDAM

They did a study between postal workers and chimpanzees. They proved chimps were 32 per cent slower. Of course, they were better with public relations.
CLIFF CLAVIN (JOHN RATZENBERGER), *Cheers*

The English are obsessed with class. Even your letters travel first and second class. Do the first class letters get a little in-flight movie and paper-parasoled cocktail en route?
KATHY LETTE

The Post Office was so crowded today, a postal employee had to leave the building to go berserk. DAVID LETTERMAN

It's been so busy at the Post Office this Christmas, they've had to add three million 'This Window Closed' signs. DAVID LETTERMAN

You know why dogs hate mailmen? They just wanna be like everyone else. NORM PETERSON (GEORGE WENDT), *Cheers*

John Major

(*on Edwina Currie's revelation of an affair with the former Prime Minister*) I am a little surprised, not at Mrs Currie's indiscretion, but at a temporary lapse in John Major's taste. MARY ARCHER

It's quite a change to have a Prime Minister who hasn't got any political ideas at all. MICHAEL FOOT

He makes George Bush seem like a personality. JACKIE MASON

He delivers all his statements as though auditioning for the speaking clock. ANON

Manners

The hardest job kids face today is learning good manners without ever seeing any. FRED ASTAIRE

Manners are love in a cool climate. QUENTIN CRISP, *Manners from Heaven*

Courtesy is not dead – it has merely taken refuge in Great Britain. GEORGES DUHAMEL

To Americans, English manners are far more frightening than none at all. RANDALL JARRELL, *Pictures from an Institution*

I don't mind if you don't like my manners. I don't like them myself. They're pretty bad. I grieve over them long winter evenings. PHILIP MARLOWE (HUMPHREY BOGART), *The Big Sleep*

Men who listen to classical music tend not to spit. RITA RUDNER

Good breeding consists in concealing how much we think of ourselves and how little we think of other persons. MARK TWAIN

Manners are especially the need of the plain. The pretty can get away with anything.
EVELYN WAUGH

Maps

Men can read maps better than women – because only the male mind could conceive of one inch equalling a hundred miles.
ROSEANNE BARR

I have an existential map. It has 'you are here' written all over it.
STEVEN WRIGHT

Marriage

After a while marriage is a sibling relationship, marked by occasional, rather regrettable, episodes of incest.
MARTIN AMIS

I married beneath me – all women do.
NANCY ASTOR

You may marry the man of your dreams, ladies, but fourteen years later you're married to a couch that burps.
ROSEANNE BARR

Marriage always demands the greatest understanding of the art of insincerity between two human beings.
VICKI BAUM, *And Life Goes On*

People keep asking me if I'll marry again. It's as if after you've had one car crash you want another.
STEPHANIE BEACHAM

My notion of a wife at forty is that a man should be able to change her, like a bank note, for two twenties.
WARREN BEATTY

Never marry a man who hates his mother, because he'll end up hating you.
JILL BENNETT

Marriage – the state or condition of a community consisting of a master, a mistress and two slaves, making in all two.
AMBROSE BIERCE, *The Devil's Dictionary*

People shop for a bathing suit with more care than they do for a husband or wife. The rules are the same. Look for something you'll feel comfortable wearing. Allow for room to grow.
ERMA BOMBECK

Marriage is the most advanced form of warfare in the modern world.
MALCOLM BRADBURY, *The History Man*

Marriage is the deep, deep peace of the double bed after the hurly-burly of the *chaise longue*.   MRS PATRICK CAMPBELL

If variety is the spice of life, marriage is the big can of leftover Spam.
                                                                    JOHNNY CARSON

What is marriage but prostitution to one man instead of many?
                                          ANGELA CARTER, *Nights at the Circus*

So basically you're saying marriage is just a way of getting out of an embarrassing pause in conversation?
                              CHARLES (HUGH GRANT), *Four Weddings And A Funeral*

The trouble with some women is that they get all excited about nothing, and then marry him.   CHER

Marriage is an adventure, like going to war.   G.K. CHESTERTON

My wife and I were married in a toilet. It was a marriage of convenience.
                                                                    TOMMY COOPER

That married couples can live together day after day is a miracle the Vatican has overlooked.   BILL COSBY

I've sometimes thought of marrying, and then I've thought again.
                                                                    NOËL COWARD

Cliff Clavin (John Ratzenberger): How's married life treating ya? Quite a change, huh?
Frasier Crane (Kelsey Grammer): Well, Lilith and I did live together for a year before we wed, so other than the fact that I now see it stretching endlessly before me until I die rotting in the grave, there's no real difference.
                                                                    Cheers

The bonds of matrimony are like any other bonds – they mature slowly.
                                                                    PETER DE VRIES

Every woman should marry – and no man.   BENJAMIN DISRAELI, *Lothair*

They say marriages are made in heaven, but so are thunder and lightning.
                                                                    CLINT EASTWOOD

Men marry women with the hope they will never change. Women marry men with the hope they will change. Invariably they are both disappointed.

ALBERT EINSTEIN

(*on his ex-wife*) We were happily married for eight months. Unfortunately we were married for four and a half years.

NICK FALDO

I was married once — in San Francisco. I haven't seen her for many years. The great earthquake and fire in 1906 destroyed the marriage certificate. There's no legal proof . . . which proves that earthquakes aren't all bad.

W.C. FIELDS

Sex was for men and marriage, like lifeboats, was for women and children.

CARRIE FISHER

Women won't let me stay single, and I won't let myself stay married.

ERROL FLYNN

A girl must marry for love, and keep on marrying until she finds it.

ZSA ZSA GABOR

Ross Geller (David Schwimmer): I think my marriage might be kind of over.
Phoebe Buffay (Lisa Kudrow): Oh my god, why?
Ross: 'Cause Carol's a lesbian, and I'm not . . . and apparently it's not a mix and match situation.

Friends

If love means never having to say you're sorry, then marriage means always having to say everything twice.

ESTELLE GETTY

Marriage is like the witness protection programme: you get all new clothes, you live in the suburbs and you're not allowed to see your friends anymore.

JEREMY HARDY

In a few years, no doubt, marriage licences will be sold like dog licences, good for a period of twelve months.

ALDOUS HUXLEY, *Brave New World*

Since couples who are married for a long time begin to resemble one another, I think it would be wise if a little shrimpy guy married a very big and manly woman.

DAVE JAMES

Marriage is like wine. It is not properly judged until the second glass.

DOUGLAS WILLIAM JERROLD

Second marriage: the triumph of hope over experience. SAMUEL JOHNSON

Any woman who still thinks marriage is a fifty-fifty proposition is only proving that she doesn't understand either men or percentages.

FLORYNCE KENNEDY

Marrying a man is like buying something you've been admiring for a long time in a shop window. You may love it when you get it home, but it doesn't always go with everything else in the house. JEAN KERR

I'm against gay marriage. I think marriage is a sacred union between a man and a pregnant woman. CRAIG KILBORN

I love being married. I was single for a long time and I just got sick of finishing mu own sentences. BRIAN KILEY

An open marriage is nature's way of telling you that you need a divorce.

ANN LANDERS

The honeymoon is over when he phones to say he'll be late for supper and she's already left a note that it's in the refrigerator. BILL LAWRENCE

Sex when you're married is like going to a 7-Eleven. There's not as much variety, but at three in the morning, it's always there. CAROL LEIFER

My mother always said, 'Don't marry for money; divorce for money.'

WENDY LIEBMAN

Politics doesn't make strange bedfellows, marriage does. GROUCHO MARX

I was married by a judge. I should have asked for a jury. GROUCHO MARX

No married man's ever made up his mind till he's heard what his wife has got to say about it. W. SOMERSET MAUGHAM, *Sheppey*

The longest sentence you can form with two words is 'I do'.

H.L. MENCKEN

Every time I try to make my marriage more exciting, my wife finds out about it right away. BOB MONKHOUSE

It has been said that a bride's attitude towards her betrothed can be summed up in three words: Aisle, Altar, Hymn.   FRANK MUIR, *Upon My Word!*

One doesn't have to get anywhere in a marriage. It's not a public conveyance.   IRIS MURDOCH, *A Severed Head*

Marriage is the alliance of two people, one of whom never remembers birthdays and the other never forgets them.   OGDEN NASH

To keep your marriage brimming,
With love in the loving cup,
Whenever you're wrong, admit it;
Whenever you're right, shut up.   OGDEN NASH

Marriage is based on the theory that when a man discovers a brand of beer exactly to his taste he should at once throw up his job and go to work in the brewery.   GEORGE JEAN NATHAN

Staying married may have long-term benefits. You can elicit much more sympathy from friends over a bad marriage than you ever can from a good divorce.   P.J. O'ROURKE

Getting married's a lot like getting into a tub of hot water. After you get used to it, it ain't so hot.   MINNIE PEARL

B.J. Hunnicut (Mike Farrell): You married?
'Hawkeye' Pierce (Alan Alda): Someone's gonna have to get me pregnant first.   *M*A*S*H*

I am the only man who has a marriage licence made out 'to whom it may concern'.   MICKEY ROONEY

A married couple are well suited when both partners usually feel the need for a quarrel at the same time.   JEAN ROSTAND, *Le Mariage*

Marriage is like twirling a baton, turning handsprings or eating with chopsticks. It looks easy until you try it.   HELEN ROWLAND

When a girl marries she exchanges the attentions of many men for the inattention of one.   HELEN ROWLAND

Marriage is the only thing that affords a woman the pleasure of company and the perfect sensation of solitude at the same time.

HELEN ROWLAND, *Personally Speaking*

After marriage, a woman's sight becomes so keen that she can see right through her husband without looking at him, and a man's so dull that he can look right through his wife without seeing her.   HELEN ROWLAND, *A Guide to Men*

Marrying a divorced man is ecologically responsible. In a world where there are more women than men, it pays to recycle.   RITA RUDNER

I love being married. It's so great to find the one special person you want to annoy for the rest of your life.   RITA RUDNER

The main purpose of marriage is rearing children and when that's done you should be free to renew your option – about twenty years seems like a reasonable term to me.   WILLY RUSSELL

Marriage? It's like asparagus eaten with vinaigrette or hollandaise, a matter of taste but of no importance.   FRANÇOISE SAGAN

It takes two to make a marriage a success and only one a failure.

HERBERT SAMUEL

Marge Simpson: Homer, is this how you pictured marriage?
Homer Simpson: Yeah, pretty much, except we drove around in a van and solved mysteries.   *The Simpsons*

All men make mistakes, but married men find out about them sooner.

RED SKELTON

Marriage resembles a pair of shears, so joined that they cannot be separated, often moving in opposite directions, yet always punishing anyone who comes between them.   REV. SYDNEY SMITH

Why get married and make one man miserable when I can stay single and make thousands miserable?   CARRIE SNOW

I'd like to get married because I like the idea of a man being required by law to sleep with me every night.   CARRIE SNOW

(*on why she never married*) I can't mate in captivity.   GLORIA STEINEM

Instead of getting married again, I'm going to find a woman I don't like and just give her a house.
ROD STEWART

You can't bring logic into this. We're talking about marriage. Marriage is like the Middle East. There's no solution.
SHIRLEY VALENTINE-BRADSHAW (PAULINE COLLINS), *Shirley Valentine*

I've married a few people I shouldn't have, but haven't we all?
MAMIE VAN DOREN

For God's sakes, this is a woman I was married to for ten years. We made love. I'd hold her head over the toilet bowl when she threw up.
VAL WAXMAN (WOODY ALLEN), *Hollywood Ending*

Men marry because they are tired; women because they are curious; both are disappointed.
OSCAR WILDE, *The Picture of Dorian Gray*

Marriage is a bribe to make a housekeeper think she's a householder.
THOMTON WILDER, *The Matchmaker*

Every man should marry. After all, happiness isn't the only thing in life.

Marriage is a three ring circus: engagement ring, wedding ring, and suffering.

Marriage is the price men pay for sex; sex is the price women pay for marriage.

Marriage is the mourning after the knot before.

Just think, if it weren't for marriage, men would go through life thinking they had no faults at all.

Love: when a rainy day means more time to stay inside and talk.
Lust: when a rainy day means more time to stay inside and have sex.
Marriage: when a rainy day means it's time to clean the basement.

Often the difference between a successful marriage and a mediocre one consists of leaving about three or four things a day unsaid.

The formula for a happy marriage is the same as for living in California: when you find a fault, don't dwell on it.

Why do men get married? So they don't have to hold their stomachs in anymore.

You know your marriage is in trouble when new jars have appeared in the kitchen, labelled 'Anthrax' and 'Cyanide'.

You know your marriage is in trouble when your spouse has a picture of you hanging on the dartboard.

You know your marriage is in trouble when sex is scheduled for a Thursday evening in the boring bit between the news and the late night sports show.

Martial arts

Karate is a form of martial arts in which people who have had years and years of training can, using only their hands and feet, make some of the worst movies in the history of the world.   DAVE BARRY

The Marx Brothers

I never knew what bicarbonate of soda was until I wrote a Marx Brothers picture.
                                                            HERMAN J. MANKIEWICZ

There were three things that Chico was always on – a phone, a horse or a broad.   GROUCHO MARX

The only sure-fire way to test out a new gag was to try it out on Zeppo. If he liked it, we threw it out.   GROUCHO MARX

(*on Groucho Marx*) The man was a major comedian, which is to say that he had the compassion of an icicle, the effrontery of a carnival shrill, and the generosity of a pawnbroker.   S.J. PERELMAN

Working for the Marx brothers was not unlike being chained to a galley car and lashed at ten-minute intervals.   S.J. PERELMAN

Masochism

I had to give up masochism. I was enjoying it too much.   MEL CALMAN

Those S&M people are bossy.   MARGARET CHO

Masochists are people who have pain confused with pleasure. In a society which has television confused with entertainment, Doritos confused with food, and Dan Quayle confused with a national political leader, masochists are clearly less mixed up than the rest of us.   P.J. O'ROURKE

What do you call kinky sex with chocolate? S&M&M

Massage

I prefer a massage to sex, because you can't give yourself a massage.

WENDY LIEBMAN

Masturbation

I'm such a good lover because I practise a lot on my own.   WOODY ALLEN

The good thing about masturbation is that you don't have to dress up for it.

TRUMAN CAPOTE

Masturbation: shaking hands with the unemployed.   GEORGE CARLIN

If God had intended us not to masturbate, He would have made our arms shorter.

GEORGE CARLIN

If men have a hundred orgasms a year, it cuts down their chances of a heart attack by a third. So, guys, your life is pretty much in your own hands.

JAY LENO

Men peak sexually between eighteen and twenty-two, which is sad. I wasted the most passionate years of my life on me.   WILLIE MARSETTA

Masturbation is always very safe. You not only control the person you're with but you can leave when you want to.   DUDLEY MOORE

Hey, don't knock masturbation! It's sex with someone I love.

ALVY SINGER (WOODY ALLEN), *Annie Hall*

We got new advice as to what motivated man to walk upright – to free his hands for masturbation.   JANE WAGNER

Mums have mother's day, dads have father's day. What do single guys have? – Palm Sunday.

Maturity

Basically my wife was immature. I'd be at home in the bath and she'd come in and sink my boats.   WOODY ALLEN

The truth is, I was dying to sleep with him. But isn't delayed gratification the definition of maturity?

CARRIE BRADSHAW (SARAH JESSICA PARKER), Sex and the City

Meanness

Jack Benny's so cheap he wouldn't give you the parsley off his fish.

FRED ALLEN

(*in reply to a robber demanding, 'Your money or your life!'*) I'm thinking it over.

JACK BENNY

Cameron's so tight, if you stuck a piece of coal up his ass in two weeks you'd have a diamond.   FERRIS BUELLER (MATTHEW BRODERICK), *Ferris Bueller's Day Off*

(*on Jack Benny*) When he has a party, you not only bring your own scotch, you bring your own rocks.

GEORGE BURNS

(*on ex-husband Rod Stewart*) He was so mean it hurt him to go to the bathroom.

BRITT EKLAND

Every man serves a useful purpose: a miser, for example, makes a wonderful ancestor.

LAURENCE J. PETER

(*on her short-lived marriage to Nicolas Cage*) Look at the amounts Ben Affleck has lavished on J-Lo. When Nic opens his wallet, moths fly out.

LISA MARIE PRESLEY

(*on Rod Stewart*) He's tighter than two coats of paint.   RONNIE WOOD

Medicine

The best medicine I know for rheumatism is to thank the Lord it ain't the gout.

JOSH BILLINGS

I was stopped in the street by a woman with a clipboard. She said, 'Could you spare a few minutes for cancer research?' I said, 'All right, but we won't get much done.'

JIMMY CARR

The best medical speciality is dermatology. Your patients never call you out in the middle of the night, they never die of the disease, and they never get better.

MARTIN H. FISCHER

A snake bite emergency kit is a body bag.   MITCH HEDBERG

I just read that Prozac is no longer the number one selling anti-depressant drug. That makes me feel sad.

MITCH HEDBERG

A study found that the drug for male pattern baldness also lowers the risk of prostate cancer. The bad thing is that you grow hair on your prostate. Now there's a really had combover.

JAY LENO

Doctors are prescribing Prozac for women with severe PMS. Not in pill form. The husband shoots it into her from fifty feet away with a dart gun.

JAY LENO

The price of Prozac went up 50 per cent last year. When Prozac users were asked about it, they said, 'Whatever . . .'

CONAN O'BRIEN

Why does the pharmacist have to be two and a half feet above everybody else? Who the hell is he? He's a stockboy with pills as far as I can tell. The only hard part of his whole job that I can see is typing everything onto that tiny label. He has to get a lot of words on there plus keep that small paper in the roller of the typewriter. That impresses me. But putting pills in a bottle . . .

JERRY SEINFELD

Mediocrity

Some men are born mediocre, some men achieve mediocrity, and some men have mediocrity thrust upon them. With Major Major it had been all three.

JOSEPH HELLER, *Catch-22*

Some men are alive simply because it is against the law to kill them.

EDGAR WATSON HOWE

Only a mediocre person is always at his best.

W. SOMERSET MAUGHAM

Beware the lollipop of mediocrity; lick it once and you'll suck forever.

BRIAN WILSON

Meetings

If you had to identify, in one word, the reason why the human race has not achieved, and never will achieve, its full potential, that word would be 'meetings'.

DAVE BARRY

Meetings are indispensable when you don't want to do anything.

J.K. GALBRAITH

Whoever invented the meeting must have had Hollywood in mind. I think they should consider giving Oscars for meetings: Best Meeting of the Year, Best Supporting Meeting, Best Meeting Based on Material from Another Meeting.
WILLIAM GOLDMAN, *Adventures in the Screen Trade*

When the outcome of a meeting is to have another meeting, it has been a lousy meeting.
HERBERT HOOVER

I went to a meeting for premature ejaculators. I left early.
EMO PHILIPS

Never delay the end of a meeting or the beginning of a cocktail hour.

Memory

Nothing is more responsible for the good old days than a bad memory.
FRANKLIN P. ADAMS

God gave us our memories so that we might have roses in December.
J.M. BARRIE

Happiness is good health and a bad memory.
INGRID BERGMAN

Three things happen when you get to my age. First your memory starts to go . . . and I have forgotten the other two.
DENIS HEALEY

I'm a psychic amnesiac. I know in advance what I'll forget.
MIKE McSHANE

You never know how much a man can't remember until he is called as a witness.
WILL ROGERS

By the time you're eighty years old you've learned everything. You only have to remember it.
BILL VAUGHAN

Memories are like mulligatawny soup in a cheap restaurant. It is best not to stir them.
P.G. WODEHOUSE

Men

Man always assumed that he was more intelligent than dolphins because he had achieved so much – the wheel, New York, wars and so on – while all the dolphins had ever done was muck about in the water having a good time. But conversely, the dolphins had always believed that they were far more intelligent than man – for precisely the same reason.
DOUGLAS ADAMS

Men will take almost any kind of criticism except the observation that they have no sense of humour.   STEVE ALLEN

Guys would sleep with a bicycle if it had the right colour lip gloss on. They have no shame. They're like bull elks in a field. It's a scent to them, a smell.
                                                                    TORI AMOS

My mother's two categories: nice men did things for you, bad men did things to you.   MARGARET ATWOOD, *Lady Oracle*

A good man doesn't just happen, They have to be created by us women.
                                                              ROSEANNE BARR

He was like the flesh and blood equivalent of a DKNY dress — you know it's not your style, but it's right there, so you try it on anyway.
                        CARRIE BRADSHAW (SARAH JESSICA PARKER), *Sex and the City*

I don't hate men. I think men are absolutely fantastic . . . as a concept.
                                                                  JO BRAND

Hair is the first thing. And teeth the second. Hair and teeth. A man got those two things he's got it all.   JAMES BROWN

The only chance nice men have of going out with women is when they're between bastards.   GUY BROWNING

A single sentence will suffice for modern man: he fornicated and read the papers.   ALBERT CAMUS, *The Fall*

Men should be like Kleenex: soft, strong, and disposable.   CHER

The fastest way to a man's heart is through his chest.
                                ROSEANNE CONNER (ROSEANNE BARR), *Roseanne*

Crystal (Natalie West): How do you like your marshmallows, Roseanne?
Roseanne Conner (Roseanne Barr): Like my men, crispy on the outside and stuck to the end of a fork.   *Roseanne*

The male is a domestic animal which, if treated with firmness and kindness, can be trained to do most things.   JILLY COOPER, *Men and Super Men*

All modern men are descended from wormlike creatures, but it shows more on some people.   WILL CUPPY

The act of sex, gratifying as it may be, is God's joke on humanity. It is man's last desperate stand at superintendency.   BETTE DAVIS

If we men had periods, we wouldn't have discreet tampon boxes, would we? No. We'd have boxes with MY FUCKING TAMPONS printed on the outside.
                                                                         BEN ELTON

A beer and a bonk are available any time but a chap with his own blow dryer who's also a dab hand with a rag roller is well worth lusting over.
                                                                     VANESSA FELTZ

A man is as good as he has to be, and a woman is as bad as she dares.
                                                                   ELBERT HUBBARD

One hell of an outlay for a very small return.   GLENDA JACKSON

Why did God create men? Because vibrators can't mow the lawn.
                                        SARAH JENNINGS (MADONNA), *Dangerous Game*

They say that men, too, have a biological clock. It goes off when the little hand is on the zipper and the big hand is on the bra.   CRAIG KILBORN

Men are those creatures with two legs and eight hands.   JAYNE MANSFIELD

They're either married or gay. And if they're not gay, they've just broken up with the most wonderful woman in the world, or they've just broken up with a bitch who looks exactly like me.   MEG (MARY KAY PLACE), *The Big Chill*

I love men, even though they're lying, cheating scumbags.
                                                                 GWYNETH PALTROW

I require only three things of a man: he must be handsome, ruthless and stupid.
                                                                  DOROTHY PARKER

If humour was the foundation of my life, men were definitely the first floor.
                                                                    GILDA RADNER

There are only two kinds of men – the dead and the deadly.   HELEN ROWLAND

The tenderest spot in a man's make-up is sometimes the bald spot on top of his head.   HELEN ROWLAND, *Reflections of a Bachelor Girl*

Men have higher body temperatures than women. If your heating goes out in winter, I recommend sleeping next to a man. Men are like portable heaters that snore.   RITA RUDNER

All men think that they're nice guys. Some of them are not. Contact me for a list of names.   RITA RUDNER

I like men to behave like men – strong and childish.   FRANÇOISE SAGAN

The more things a man is ashamed of, the more respectable he is.
GEORGE BERNARD SHAW, *Man and Superman*

For millions of years, we men have been able to get away with being useless fathers, doing nothing around the house, and being terrible in bed. Now we're expected to be brilliant at all these things. It's so unfair.   ARTHUR SMITH

It's not the men in my life that count; it's the life in my men.
TIRA (MAE WEST), *I'm No Angel*

If you pick up a starving dog and make him prosperous, he will not bite you. This is the principal difference between a man and a dog.
MARK TWAIN, *Pudd'nhead Wilson*

Men love to be thought of as funny . . . except when they're in bed.
ELAINE VASSAL (JANE KRAKOWAKI), *Ally McBeal*

A hard man is good to find.   MAE WEST

I only like two kinds of men – domestic and imported.   MAE WEST

See, the problem is that God gives men a brain and a penis, and only enough blood to run one at a time.   ROBIN WILLIAMS

I wouldn't kidnap a man for sex, but I'm not saying I couldn't use someone to oil the mower.   VICTORIA WOOD

Men are like parking spaces: the good ones are already taken and the ones left are either too small or disabled.

Men are like photocopiers: you need them for reproduction, but that's about it.

Men are like textbooks: you have to spend a lot of time between the covers to gain a small amount of satisfaction.

Men are like lawnmowers: they're hard to get started, emit noxious odours and half the time they don't work.

Men are like chocolate bars: sweet, smooth, and heading straight for your hips.

Men are like placemats: they show up only when there's food on the table.

Metric system

The metric system did not really catch on in the United States, unless you count the increasing popularity of the nine-millimetre bullet.   DAVE BARRY

If God had intended for man to use the metric system, Jesus would have only had ten disciples.

Mexico

Mexico: where life is cheap, death is rich, and the buzzards are never unhappy.
                                                                EDWARD ABBEY

Poor Mexico, so far from God and so near to the United States!
                                                                PORFIRIO DÌAZ

You don't eat Mexican food – you just rent it.   ALEXEI SAYLE

Hell, everything's legal in Mexico. It's the American way.
                                                    UNCLE JIMBO, *South Park*

Middle age

Years ago we discovered the exact point, the dead centre of middle age. It occurs when you are too young to take up golf and too old to rush up to the net.   FRANKLIN P. ADAMS, *Nods and Becks*

Middle age is the time of life that a man first notices in his wife.
                                                            RICHARD ARMOUR

Middle age: when you begin to exchange your emotions for symptoms.
                                                        IRVIN SHREWSBURY COBB

The really frightening thing about middle age is that you know you'll grow out of it.   DORIS DAY

Middle age is when you're old enough to know better, but still young enough to keep on doing it.
SAM EWING

Setting a good example for our children takes all the fun out of middle age.
WILLIAM FEATHER, *The Business of Life*

Middle age is when your age starts to show around your middle.
BOB HOPE

Middle age is when you have the choice of two temptations and you choose the one that will get you home earlier.
EDGAR WATSON HOWE

I'm officially middle-aged. I don't need drugs anymore. I can get the same effect just by standing up real fast.
JONATHAN KATZ

Middle age is the time when a man is always thinking that in a week or two he will feel as good as ever.
DON MARQUIS

Middle age is when you've met so many people that every new person you meet reminds you of someone else.
OGDEN NASH

I hate middle age. Too young for the bowling green, too old for Ecstasy.
RAB C. NESBITT (GREGOR FISHER)

Male menopause is a lot more fun than female menopause. With female menopause you gain weight and get hot flushes. Male menopause – you get to date young girls and drive motorcycles.
RITA RUDNER

Middle age is when broadness of the mind and narrowness of the waist change places.

Middle age is the awkward period when Father Time starts catching up with Mother Nature.

Middle age is when your legs buckle – and your belt doesn't.

Middle East

(*on Israel*) Any country that can stand Milton Friedman as an adviser has nothing to fear from a few million Arabs.
J.K. GALBRAITH

The only thing chicken about Israel is their soup.
BOB HOPE

Let me tell you something that we Israelis have against Moses. He took us forty years through the desert in order to bring us to the one spot in the Middle East that has no oil!   GOLDA MEIR

(*of the Camp David Agreement, 1977*) I don't know whether Sadat and Begin deserve the Nobel Prize, but they both deserve Oscars.   GOLDA MEIR

The Middle Eastern states aren't nations, they're quarrels with borders.
                                                                    P.J. O'ROURKE

(*on Libya's Colonel Gaddafi*) The mad dog of the Middle East.

                                                                    RONALD REAGAN

Military

I think I've worked out how medieval armies broke through the defences of castles. They chose the weakest spot – the gift shop. All a determined enemy had to do was overpower the two old ladies who work there and the whole castle was taken.   BILL BAILEY

(*inspecting army uniforms*) Excuse me, sir. Is green the only colour these come in?   JUDY BENJAMIN (GOLDIE HAWN), *Private Benjamin*

We have women in the military, but they don't put us in the front lines. They don't know if we can fight, if we can kill. I think we can. All the general has to do is walk over to the women and say, 'You see the enemy over there? They say you look fat in those uniforms.'   ELAYNE BOOSLER

I am convinced that the best service a retired general can perform is to turn in his tongue along with his suit, and to mothball his opinions.   OMAR BRADLEY

(*on Field Marshal Montgomery*) In defeat unbeatable: in victory unbearable.
                                                                 WINSTON CHURCHILL

(*on Marshal Joseph Joffre*) The only time he ever put up a fight in his life was when we asked him for his resignation.   GEORGES CLEMENCEAU

I never joined the army because 'at ease' was never that easy to me. It seemed rather uptight still. I don't relax by parting my legs slightly and putting my hands behind my back. That does not equal ease. At ease was not being in the military.   MITCH HEDBERG

There's not much makeup in the army, is there? No. They only have that night-time look, and that's a bit slapdash isn't it?   Eddie Izzard

(*on Lord Kitchener*) One of those revolving lighthouses which radiate momentary gleams of light far out into the surrounding gloom, and then suddenly relapse into complete darkness. There were no intermediate stages.
   David Lloyd George

Military intelligence is a contradiction in terms.   Groucho Marx

(*on American troops in Britain during World War Two*) Overpaid, overfed, over-sexed and over here.   Tommy Trinder

Milk

I didn't mean to shoot the milkman last week . . . but no apricot yoghurt. I just lost my temper.   Jo Brand

My illness is due to my doctor's insistence that I drink milk, a whitish fluid they force down helpless babies.   W.C. Fields

He said, 'Do you want it pasteurised, cos pasteurised is best',
She said, 'Ernie, I'll be happy if it comes up to me chest.'
   Benny Hill, 'Ernie'

Who was the guy who first looked at a cow and said, 'I think I'll drink whatever comes out of these things when I squeeze 'em?'   Bill Watterson

Mime

Never get a mime talking. He won't stop.   Marcel Marceau

If you wanted to shoot a mime artist, would you use a silencer?

Minds

You have to open your mind to every new experience. This week I've been practising sneezing with my eyes open.   Billy Connolly

Minds are like parachutes; they only function when they are open.
   Thomas Robert Dewar

It's ten years since I went out of my mind – I'd never go back.   Ken Dodd (*on Woodrow Wilson*) Mr Wilson's mind, as has been the custom, will be closed all day Sunday.   GEORGE S. KAUFMAN

Men aren't attracted to me by my mind. They're attracted by what I don't mind.   GYPSY ROSE LEE

The trouble with having an open mind, of course, is that people will insist on coming along and trying to put things in it.   TERRY PRATCHETT

I didn't lose my mind, it was mine to give away.   ROBBIE WILLIAMS

(*on Warren Harding*) He has a bungalow mind – nothing upstairs.
                                                         WOODROW WILSON

The mind is like the stomach. It's not how much you put into it that counts, but how much it digests.

Miniskirts

Never in the history of fashion has so little material been raised so high to reveal so much that needs to be covered so badly.   CECIL BEATON

The miniskirt enables young ladies to run faster, and because of it, they may have to.   JOHN V. LINDSAY

Miracles

Jesus was well-known for his miracles and probably would have formed a band if Smokey Robinson hadn't done it.   JO BRAND

I see the Disciples saying, 'Jesus, stop turning water into wine. I'm trying to take a shower.'   STEVEN WRIGHT

Coincidence is when God works a miracle and chooses to remain anonymous.

Misfortune

Misfortunes and twins never come singly.   JOSH BILLINGS

I went to a discount massage parlour the other night – it was self-service.
                                                        RODNEY DANGERFIELD

Sometimes the giant hamster of misfortune doesn't seem to want to run on anybody's wheel but yours.   GEORGE OLSON

I'm so unlucky that if I was to fall into a barrel of nipples, I'd come out sucking my thumb.   FREDDIE STARR

I broke a mirror in my house, which is supposed to mean seven years' bad luck. My lawyer thinks he can get me five.   STEVEN WRIGHT

You know you're having a bad day when your mother approves of the person you're dating.

You know you're having a bad day when the fortune-teller offers you a refund.

You know you're having a bad day when your doctor says you're allergic to chocolate.

Mistakes

The greatest mistake I ever made was not to die in office.   DEAN ACHESON

To get maximum attention, it's hard to beat a good, big mistake.
                                                         JOSEPH R. ALSOP JR

The only thing I regret about my life is the length of it. If I had to live my life again, I'd make all the same mistakes only sooner.
                                                         TALLULAH BANKHEAD

Positive: being mistaken at the top of one's voice.
                                       AMBROSE BIERCE, *The Devil's Dictionary*

From a worldly point of view there is no mistake so great as that of being always right.   SAMUEL BUTLER, *Notebooks*

A Freudian slip is saying one thing and meaning a mother.
                                CLIFF CLAVIN (JOHN RATZENBERGER), *Cheers*

Now let me correct you on a couple of things, okay? Aristotle was not Belgian. The central message of Buddhism is not every man for himself . . . And the London Underground is not a political movement. Those are all mistakes, Otto. I looked them up.
                         WANDA GERSCHWITZ (JAMIE LEE CURTIS), *A Fish Called Wanda*

I am humble enough to recognise that I have made mistakes, but politically astute enough to know that I have forgotten what they are.
                                                         MICHAEL HESELTINE

I make mistakes; I'll be the second to admit it.   JEAN KERR

I never made a mistake in my life; at least, never one that I couldn't explain away afterwards.   RUDYARD KIPLING

You must learn from the mistakes of others. You can't possibly live long enough to make them all yourself.   SAM LEVENSON

Allowing an unimportant mistake to pass without comment is a wonderful social grace.   JUDITH MARTIN

Our old mistakes do come back to haunt us. Especially with video.
PETER O'TOOLE

By the time you reach my age, you've made plenty of mistakes if you've lived your life properly.   RONALD REAGAN, 1987

Men do not like to admit even momentary imperfection. My husband forgot the code to turn off the alarm. When the police came, he wouldn't admit he'd forgotten the code – he turned himself in.   RITA RUDNER

Smithers: Simpson, what are you doing here? Why aren't you at work?
Homer Simpson: I made a bad mistake and Lenny sent me home to think about what I did. I don't remember what it was, so I'm watching TV.
The Simpsons

I don't make mistakes. I make prophecies which are immediately proved wrong.
MURRAY WALKER

Mobile phones

I don't use Vodafone products. They say, 'Join the world's largest mobile community.' Now, correct me if I'm wrong, but that's the gypsies.   JIMMY CARR

The cell phone people say there's absolutely no danger from cell phone radiation. Boy, it didn't take those tobacco executives long to find new jobs, did it?
JAY LENO

Mobile phones are the only subject on which men boast who's got the smallest.

Models

The leading cause of death among fashion models is falling through street grates.   DAVE BARRY

I always like to compare models to supermodels in the way I compare Tampax to Super Tampax: supermodels cost a bit more and they are a lot thicker.

JO BRAND

I can do anything you want me to do so long as I don't have to speak.

LINDA EVANGELISTA

Supermodel Kate Moss has had a baby. Her friends congratulated her on losing six pounds two ounces.

CRAIG KILBORN

The reigning Miss Canada has been arrested for punching out another woman in a bar fight. Quite frankly, I think it's refreshing to finally find one beauty pageant winner who is against world peace.

JAY LENO

Model Kate Moss turned thirty-seven. To celebrate she threw up ice cream and cake.

JAY LENO

Moderation

An Iranian moderate is one who has run out of ammunition.

HENRY KISSINGER

I like restraint, if it doesn't go too far.

MAE WEST

Moderation is a fatal thing. Nothing succeeds like excess.

OSCAR WILDE, *A Woman of No Importance*

Modesty

Frasier Crane (Kelsey Grammer): I'm Dr Frasier Crane. This is my brother Dr Niles Crane, the eminent psychiatrist.
Niles Crane (David Hyde Pierce): My brother's too kind. He was already eminent when my eminence was merely imminent.   *Frasier*

(*of Joni Mitchell*) About as modest as Mussolini.

DAVID CROSBY

Modesty is the artifice of actors, similar to passion in call girls.

JACKIE GLEASON

Modesty: the gentle art of enhancing your charm by pretending not to be aware of it.

OLIVER HERFORD

It was the least I could do. I always do the least I can do.

'HAWKEYE' PIERCE (ALAN ALDA), *M*A*S*H*

Monarchy

A monarchy is a merchantman which sails well, but will sometimes strike on a rock and go to the bottom. A republic is a raft which will never sink, but then your feet are always in the water.   FISHER AMES

The monarchy is finished. It was finished a while ago, but they're still making the corpses dance.   SUE TOWNSEND

Money

Money is better than poverty, if only for financial reasons.
                    WOODY ALLEN, *Without Feathers*

My father's people were impressed only by money in the bank. Their only interest was interest.   RICHARD ARMOUR, *Pills, Potions – and Granny*

That money talks
I'll not deny.
I heard it once:
It said 'Goodbye'.   RICHARD ARMOUR

Money is something you have to make in case you don't die.   MAX ASNAS

It is a truth universally acknowledged, that a single man in possession of a good fortune must be in want of a wife.
                    JANE AUSTEN, *Pride and Prejudice*

Every crowd has a silver lining.   PHINEAS T. BARNUM

Live within your income, even if you have to borrow to do so.
                    JOSH BILLINGS

What good is money if it can't inspire terror in your fellow man?
                    MONTGOMERY BURNS, *The Simpsons*

The only thing money gives you is the freedom of not worrying about money.
                    JOHNNY CARSON

Money isn't everything, but it ranks right up there with oxygen.
                    RITA DAVENPORT

Recognition without finance is a nuisance.   BO DIDDLEY

It's a great mistake for any woman to have a heart bigger than her purse.
PRUDENCE DUVERNOY (LAURA HOPE CREWS), *Camille*

Money doesn't talk, it swears.
BOB DYLAN

I don't wake up for less than $10,000 a day.
LINDA EVANGELISTA

If there is anyone to whom I owe money, I am prepared to forget it if they are.
ERROL FLYNN

If you would like to know the value of money, go and try to borrow some.
BENJAMIN FRANKLIN

He's got a wonderful head for money. There's this long slit on the top.
DAVID FROST

If a thing is worth doing, it's worth doing for money.
DAVID GERROLD

Money isn't everything, but it sure keeps you in touch with your children.
J. PAUL GETTY

The safest way to double your money is to fold it over and put it in your pocket.
KIN HUBBARD, *Abe Martin's Broadcast*

It doesn't matter if you're rich or poor, as long as you've got money.
JOE E. LEWIS

Money is just the poor man's credit card.
MARSHALL McLUHAN, *Understanding Media*

I have enough money to last me the rest of my life – unless I have to buy something.
JACKIE MASON

Money is like a sixth sense, without which you cannot make a complete use of the other five.
W. SOMERSET MAUGHAM, *Of Human Bondage*

All I ask is the chance to prove that money can't make me happy.
SPIKE MILLIGAN

Money is like manure. If you spread it around it does a lot of good. But if you pile it up in one place it stinks like hell.
CLINT MURCHISON

Tests showed that almost all paper money in Europe has traces of cocaine. So not only is the euro stronger than the dollar, it's louder and more obnoxious as well.   CONAN O'BRIEN

Money cannot buy health, but I'd settle for a diamond-studded wheelchair.
                                                        DOROTHY PARKER

A guy told me, 'To a farmer manure smells like money.' I said, 'Maybe he should start keeping his wallet in his front pocket.'   TAMMY PATORELLI

Having money is rather like being a blonde. It is more fun but not vital.
                                                          MARY QUANT

Always try and rub up against money, for if you rub up against money long enough, some of it may rub off on you.   DAMON RUNYON

I'm living so far beyond my income that we may almost be said to be living apart.   SAKI, *The Unbearable Bassington*

Money doesn't make you happy. I now have $50 million but I was just as happy when I had $48 million.   ARNOLD SCHWARZENEGGER

A raise is like a martini: it elevates the spirit, but only temporarily.
                                                         DAN SELIGMAN

If you really need money, you can sell your kidney or even your car.
                                              HOMER SIMPSON, *The Simpsons*

The lack of money is the root of all evil.   MARK TWAIN

Money won't buy you happiness, but it will pay the salaries of a large research staff to study the problem.   BILL VAUGHAN

Let us all be happy, and live within our means, even if we have to borrow the money to do it.   ARTEMUS WARD

The easiest way for your children to learn about money is for you not to have any.   KATHARINE WHITEHORN, *How to Survive Children*

Anyone who lives within their means suffers from a lack of imagination.
                                                         OSCAR WILDE

Do you think that when they asked George Washington for ID that he just whipped out a quarter?   STEVEN WRIGHT

If you buy what you don't need, you steal from yourself.   SWEDISH PROVERB

Monogamy

If you're looking for monogamy, you'd better marry a swan.   NORA EPHRON

I don't think it's the nature of any man to be monogamous. Men are propelled by genetically ordained impulses over which they have no control to distribute their seed.   MARLON BRANDO

I have just learned that penguins are monogamous for life, which doesn't really surprise me that much because they all look exactly alike. It's not like they're going to meet a better-looking penguin someday.   ELLEN DeGENERES

Swans mate for life, and look how bad-tempered they are.   JEFF GREEN

Men would like monogamy better if it sounded less like monotony.
                                                        RITA RUDNER

Marilyn Monroe

A broad with a big future behind her.   CONSTANCE BENNETT

So minimally gifted as to be almost unemployable.   CLIVE JAMES

Copulation was, I'm sure, Marilyn's uncomplicated way of saying thank you.
                                                        NUNNALLY JOHNSON

An arrogant little tail-twitcher who learned to throw sex in your face.
                                                        NUNNALLY JOHNSON

Directing her was like directing Lassie. You needed fourteen takes to get each one of them right.   OTTO PREMINGER

A vacuum with nipples.   OTTO PREMINGER

Breasts like granite and a brain like Swiss cheese.   BILLY WILDER

I am the only director who ever made two pictures with Marilyn Monroe. Forget the Oscar, I deserve the Purple Heart.   BILLY WILDER

Moods

It is only our bad temper that we put down to being tired or worried or hungry; we put our good temper down to ourselves.   C.S. LEWIS

When I was a boy, my mother wore a mood ring. When she was in a good mood it turned blue. In a bad mood, it left a big red mark on my forehead.
JEFF SHAW

While not exactly disgruntled, he was far from feeling gruntled.
P.G. WODEHOUSE, *The Code of the Woosters*

Morality

What is moral is what you feel good after and what is immoral is what you feel bad after.   ERNEST HEMINGWAY, *Death in the Afternoon*

Turning the other cheek is a kind of moral jiu-jitsu.
GERALD STANLEY LEE, *Crowds*

Moral indignation is in most cases two per cent moral, forty-eight per cent indignation, and fifty per cent envy.   VITTORIO DE SICA

Moral indignation is jealousy with a halo.   H.G. WELLS

Morality is simply the attitude we adopt towards people whom we personally dislike.   OSCAR WILDE

Mothers

When Mel Brooks told his mother that he was marrying an Italian girl, she said, 'Bring her over, I'll be in the kitchen – with my head in the oven!'
ANNE BANCROFT

It is not until you become a mother that your judgement slowly turns to compassion and understanding.   ERMA BOMBECK

When your mother asks, 'Do you want a piece of advice?', it is a mere formality. It doesn't matter if you answer yes or no. You're going to get it anyway.
ERMA BOMBECK

It's great being a new mom. The only thing I worry about is that one day the FBI will break down my door and take the baby back to his real mother. But I guess it's normal for new moms to worry.   ANNA CHIN-WILLIAMS

Why do grandparents and grandchildren get along so well? They have the same enemy – the mother.
Claudette Colbert

My mother had morning sickness *after* I was born.
Rodney Dangerfield

A suburban mother's role is to deliver children obstetrically once, and by car forever after.
Peter De Vries

My mother hated me. Once she took me to an orphanage and told me to mingle.
Phyllis Diller

Take motherhood: nobody ever thought of putting it on a moral pedestal until some brash feminists pointed out, about a century ago, that the pay is lousy and the career ladder nonexistent.
Barbara Ehrenreich

My mother used to say that there are no strangers, only friends you haven't met yet. She's now in a maximum security twilight home in Australia.
Dame Edna Everage

My mother never saw the irony in calling me a son-of-a-bitch.
Richard Jeni

My mom was a ventriloquist and she was always throwing her voice. For ten years I thought the dog was telling me to kill my father.
Wendy Liebman

Her mother was a cultivated woman – she was born in a greenhouse.
Spike Milligan

My mother tried to kill me when I was a baby. She denied it. She said she thought the plastic bag would keep me fresh.
Bob Monkhouse

My mother wasn't the protective type. When my father left, she told us kids, 'Don't think this just had to do with me. Your father left all of us.'
Caroline Rhea

I was dating a transvestite. My mother said, 'Marry him. You'll double your wardrobe!'
Joan Rivers

All I heard when I was growing up was, 'Why can't you be more like your cousin Sheila? Why can't you be more like your cousin Sheila?' Sheila died at birth.
JOAN RIVERS

Neurotics build castles in the air, psychotics live in them. My mother cleans them.
RITA RUDNER

As a rule there is only one person an English girl hates more than she hates her eldest sister, and that's her mother.
GEORGE BERNARD SHAW, *Man and Superman*

Oh, honey, you're not the world's worst mother. What about that freezer lady in Georgia?
HOMER SIMPSON, *The Simpsons*

Do not join encounter groups. If you enjoy being made to feel inadequate, call your mother.
LIZ SMITH

All women become like their mothers. That is their tragedy. No man does. That's his.
OSCAR WILDE, *The Importance of Being Earnest*

Biology is the least of what makes someone a mother.
OPRAH WINFREY

God could not be everywhere, so he made mothers.
JEWISH PROVERB

The only place you're sure to find love is at the end of a letter from your mother.

Mountaineering

Did you hear about the Irish attempt on Mount Everest? – They ran out of scaffolding.
FRANK CARSON

Kilimanjaro is a pretty tricky climb, you know. Most of it's up, until you reach the very, very top, and then it tends to slope away rather sharply.
GEORGE (GRAHAM CHAPMAN), *Monty Python's Flying Circus*

You remember your first mountain in much the same way you remember your first sexual experience, except that climbing doesn't make as much mess and you don't cry for a week if Ben Nevis forgets to phone the next morning.
MURIEL GRAY

A blind man is attempting to climb Mount Everest. Why? 'Because somebody told me it was there.'
CRAIG KILBORN

Why do mountain climbers rope themselves together? To prevent the sensible ones from going home.

Mouths

His mouth had been used as a latrine by some small creature of the night, and then as its mausoleum.
KINGSLEY AMIS, *Lucky Jim*

Last time I saw a mouth like that it had a hook in it.
AL CZERVIK (RODNEY DANGERFIELD), *Caddyshack*

Movies

The badness of a movie is directly proportional to the number of helicopters in it.
DAVE BARRY

Men can sit through the most pointless, boring movie if there's even the slightest possibility that a woman will take her top off.
ELAINE BENES (JULIA LOUIS-DREYFUS), *Seinfeld*

What is a bad movie? Nobody sees it, that's a bad movie.
JACKIE CHAN

In Westerns you were permitted to kiss your horse but never your girl.
GARY COOPER

Whatever happened to the Elephant Man? He made that one cracker of a film and that was it.
JACK DEE

There's no thief like a bad movie.
SAM EWING

Gigli was so bad I had to see it twice to be sure Madonna wasn't in it.
MIKE GIBSON

Why should people go out and pay to see bad movies when they can stay at home and see bad television for nothing?
SAM GOLDWYN

A wide screen just makes a bad film twice as bad.
SAM GOLDWYN

(*on* Raise the Titanic) It would have been cheaper to lower the Atlantic.
LEW GRADE

The French are funny, sex is funny, and comedies are funny, yet no French sex comedies are funny.
MATT GROENING, *Life in Hell*

A movie is never any better than the stupidest man connected with it.

BEN HECHT

The length of a film should be directly related to the endurance of the human bladder.

ALFRED HITCHCOCK

A good film is when the price of the dinner, the theatre admission and the babysitter were worth it.

ALFRED HITCHCOCK

A James Cagney love scene is one where he lets the other guy live.

BOB HOPE

I thought *Deep Throat* was a movie about a giraffe.

BOB HOPE

If anyone thinks I look sexy stripped in *The Music Lovers*, they must think Minnie Mouse is sexy!

GLENDA JACKSON

The words 'Kiss Kiss Bang Bang', which I saw on an Italian movie poster, are perhaps the briefest statement imaginable on the basic appeal of movies.

PAULINE KAEL

Having your book turned into a movie is like seeing your oxen turned into bouillon cubes.

JOHN LE CARRÉ

Sequels can be disappointing. *Speed 2*, George W. Bush . . .

JAY LENO

Finding Nemo is number one at the box office. It's based on a game President Clinton used to play with the interns.

DAVID LETTERMAN

I've done my bit for motion pictures. I've stopped making them.

LIBERACE

(*on Victor Mature's appearance in* Samson and Delilah) I never go to movies where the hero's bust is bigger than the heroine's.

GROUCHO MARX

Religious experts who have seen Mel Gibson's movie on the life of Christ say the film is an accurate portrayal of the last hours of Jesus. When asked how he got the actor playing Jesus to convey so much suffering, Gibson said, 'I forced him to watch *Lethal Weapon 4*.'

CONAN O'BRIEN

You know the movie you're watching is a 'chick flick' if you wake up and your wife is crying.

RICK OIE

I've done an awful lot of stuff that's a monument to public patience.

TYRONE POWER

My movies were the kind they show in prisons and on aeroplanes, because no one can leave.

BURT REYNOLDS

I haven't had a film hit since Joan Collins was a virgin.

BURT REYNOLDS

Film is a wonderful medium and I love it, but I find that I cannot increase my talent by working in pictures, any more than a painter can do so by increasing the size of his brush.

RALPH RICHARDSON

Oh please don't kill me, Mr Ghostface, I wanna be in the sequel!

TATUM RILEY (ROSE McGOWAN), *Scream*

The movies are the only business where you can go out front and applaud yourself.

WILL ROGERS

I can't go to a bad movie by myself. What, am I gonna make sarcastic remarks to strangers?

JERRY SEINFELD

(*asked what he looked for in a script*) Days off.

SPENCER TRACY

People tell me that the movies should be more like real life. I disagree. It is real life that should be more like the movies.

WALTER WINCHELL

Murder

I do a lot of reading on serial killers – mostly *How To* books.

ROSEANNE BARR

Very stupid to kill the servants: now we don't even know where to find the marmalade.

EMILY BRENT (JUDITH ANDERSON), *And Then There Were None*

Being loved can never be a patch on being murdered. That's when someone really gives their all for you.

QUENTIN CRISP

I have never killed a man, but I have read many obituaries with a lot of pleasure.

CLARENCE DARROW

John Cage (Peter MacNicol): Let's not forget that Lizzie Borden was found innocent of killing her parents.

Richard Fish (Greg Germann): Oh, she did it; the jury just took pity on her for being an orphan.

Ally McBeal

There is nothing quite so good as burial at sea. It is simple, tidy, and not very incriminating.

ALFRED HITCHCOCK

If I made *Cinderella*, the audience would be looking out for a body in the coach.

ALFRED HITCHCOCK

I have a perfect cure for a sore throat – cut it.

ALFRED HITCHCOCK

Blondes are the best victims. They're like virgin snow which shows up the bloody footprints.

ALFRED HITCHCOCK

I had an interest in death from an early age. It fascinated me. When I heard 'Humpty Dumpty sat on a wall,' I thought, 'Did he fall or was he pushed?'

P.D. JAMES

A lady came up to me on the street and pointed at my suede jacket. 'You know a cow was murdered for that jacket?' she sneered. I replied in a psychotic tone: 'I didn't know there were any witnesses. Now I'll have to kill you too.'

JAKE JOHANSEN

Probably the toughest time in anyone's life is when you have to murder a loved one because they're the devil.

EMO PHILIPS

Murder is always a mistake. One should never do anything that one cannot talk about after dinner.

OSCAR WILDE, *The Picture of Dorian Gray*

Murphy's Laws of Computers

Experts agree that the best type of computer for your individual needs is one that comes on the market about two days after you actually purchase some other computer.

DAVE BARRY

No matter how many resources you have, it is never enough.

Any cool program always requires more memory than you have.

When you finally buy enough memory, you won't have enough disk space.

All components are obsolete.

The maintenance engineer will never have seen a model quite like yours before.

Any spares required will just have been discontinued and will no longer be in stock.

The hard drive on your computer will only crash when it contains vital information that has not been backed up.

Museums

There's a new Sex Museum in New York. Guys get through in five minutes. Women finish in a half hour — if they finish at all.   JAY LENO

I went to the museum where they had all the heads and arms from the statues that are in all the other museums.   STEVEN WRIGHT

Music

Even Bach comes down to the basic suck, blow, suck, suck, blow.
    LARRY ADLER

All music is folk music. I ain't ever heard no horse sing a song!
    LOUIS ARMSTRONG

You have delighted us long enough.   JANE AUSTEN, *Pride and Prejudice*

Great music is that which penetrates the ear with facility and leaves the memory with difficulty. Magical music never leaves the memory.   THOMAS BEECHAM

(*of Herbert von Karajan*) A kind of musical Malcolm Sargent.
    THOMAS BEECHAM

Music hath the charm to soothe a savage beast, but I'd try a revolver first.
    JOSH BILLINGS

I only know two pieces; one is 'Clair de Lune' and the other one isn't.
    VICTOR BORGE

If you can imagine a man having a vasectomy without anaesthetic to the sound of frantic sitar playing, you will have some idea of what popular Turkish music is like.   BILL BRYSON

Canned music is like audible wallpaper.   ALISTAIR COOKE

Writing about music is like dancing about architecture.   ELVIS COSTELLO

Extraordinary how potent cheap music is.   NOËL COWARD, *Private Lives*

Never clean your CDs with a blowtorch as it will void the warranty.
STEVEN DANILETTO

I opened the door for a lot of people, and they just ran through and left me holding the knob.   BO DIDDLEY

I hate music, especially when it's played.   JIMMY DURANTE

Music is the wine that fills the cup of silence.   ROBERT FRIPP

I bought an audio cleaning tape. I'm a big fan of theirs.   KEVIN GILDEA

The public doesn't want new music: the main thing it demands of a composer is that he be dead.   ARTHUR HONEGGER

Country music is three chords and the truth.   HARLAN HOWARD

Classical music is the kind we keep thinking will turn into a tune.
KIN HUBBARD

Music expresses that which cannot be put into words, yet cannot remain silent.
VICTOR HUGO

Music companies are going to start suing individual computer users who illegally download music, leading 16-year-olds to exclaim, 'You can buy music?'
CRAIG KILBORN

I always thought music was more important than sex. Then I thought, if I don't hear a concert for a year and a half it doesn't bother me.   JACKIE MASON

I went to watch Pavarotti once. He doesn't like it when you join in.
MICK MILLER

Learning music by reading about it is like making love by mail.
LUCIANO PAVAROTTI

Music is the brandy of the damned.
GEORGE BERNARD SHAW, *Man and Superman*

Too many pieces of music finish too long after the end. IGOR STRAVINSKY

[Andrew] Lloyd Webber's music is everywhere, but so is Aids.
MALCOLM WILLIAMSON

There's a basic rule which runs through all kinds of music, kind of an unwritten rule. I don't know what it is, but I've got it. RONNIE WOOD

All the good music has already been written by people with wigs and stuff.
FRANK ZAPPA

Music business

I decided not to pursue a career as a professional musician because there's one sentence that has never been uttered: 'Look! It's the banjo player's Porsche!'
STEVE MARTIN

Music is spiritual. The music business is not. VAN MORRISON

The music business was not safe, but it was fun. It was like falling in love with a woman you know is bad for you, but you love every minute with her, anyway.
LIONEL RICHIE

The music business is a cruel and shallow trench, a long plastic hallway where thieves and pimps run free, and good men lie like dogs. There is also a negative side. HUNTER S. THOMPSON

Musical instruments

When Jack Benny plays the violin it sounds as if the strings are still back in the cat. FRED ALLEN

The harpsichord sounds like two skeletons copulating on a corrugated tin roof.
THOMAS BEECHAM

The sound of the harpsichord resembles that of a bird-cage played with toasting forks. THOMAS BEECHAM

(*to an unnamed cellist*) Madam, you have between your legs an instrument capable of giving pleasure to thousands – and all you can do is scratch it.
THOMAS BEECHAM

The difference between a violin and a viola is that a viola burns longer.
VICTOR BORGE

I took accordion lessons once. My musical abilities were fine, but I flunked the 'making bizarre facial expressions' part.   *Crabby Road*

I'm a flute-player, not a flautist. I don't have a flaut, and I've never flauted.
JAMES GALWAY

Of all musicians, flautists are most obviously the ones who know something we don't know.   PAUL JENNINGS

What is a harp but an over-sized cheese-slicer with cultural pretensions?
DENIS NORDEN, *You Can't Have Your Kayak and Heat It*

Harpists spend ninety per cent of their lives tuning their harps and ten per cent playing out of tune.   IGOR STRAVINSKY

The cello is not one of my favourite instruments. It has such a lugubrious sound, like someone reading a will.   IRENE THOMAS

Musicals

Busby Berkeley production numbers look like colonies of bacteria staging a political rally under a microscope.   CLIVE JAMES

Cats closed today after eighteen years. Any cast members not adopted after four weeks will be put to sleep.   JAY LENO

A musical is a series of catastrophes ending with a floorshow.
OSCAR LEVANT

N

Nagging

Nagging is the repetition of unpalatable truths.   EDITH SUMMERSKILL

Men pretend they don't like to be nagged, but they love it really. It makes them feel wanted.   DENISE VAN OUTEN

Naivety

Maddie Hayes (Cybill Shepherd): I was *not* born yesterday.
David Addison (Bruce Willis): It's true. We had lunch yesterday. If she'd been born, I'd have noticed. *Moonlighting*

The people who fall for everything probably stand for nothing.

EVAN ESAR

Names

When I got married my feminist friends went mad. One sniffed, 'Are you going to take your husband's name?' I said, 'No, because I don't think "Dave" suits me very much.' JO BRAND

As I walk in the Valley of the Shadow of Death, I think to myself, 'This place obviously wasn't named by a real estate developer.' DOUG FINNEY

Colin is the sort of name you give your goldfish for a joke. COLIN FIRTH

Arantxa Sanchez-Vicario is the only sports person whose name is worth 175 in Scrabble. NICK HANCOCK

Never allow your child to call you by your first name. He hasn't known you long enough. FRAN LEBOWITZ

The name of a man is a numbing blow from which he never recovers.

MARSHALL McLUHAN

I cannot stand little notes on my pillow. 'We are all out of cornflakes, F.U.' It took me three hours to figure out 'F.U.' was Felix Ungar. It's not your fault, Felix; it's a rotten combination, that's all.

OSCAR MADISON (WALTER MATTHAU), *The Odd Couple*

No, Groucho is not my real name. I'm breaking it in for a friend.

GROUCHO MARX

The one thing I do not want to be called is First Lady. It sounds like a saddle horse. JACQUELINE KENNEDY ONASSIS

Yeah, that's easy for you to say, you're Mr White. You have a cool-sounding name. MR PINK (STEVE BUSCEMI), *Reservoir Dogs* (*on Ursula Andress*) The name has always seemed like a spoonerism to me.

JOHN SIMON

Just promise you'll name your first-born after me. If it's a girl, Maryann. If it's a boy . . . Maryann. I'll pay for therapy.

MARYANN THORPE (CHRISTINE BARANSKI), *Cybill*

Mike (Kenneth MacDonald): What name have they decided on?
Trigger (Roger Lloyd Pack): If it's a girl they're calling her Sigourney after an actress, and if it's a boy they're naming him Rodney after Dave.

Only Fools and Horses

(*on having a life-jacket named after her*) I've been in *Who's Who*, and I know what's what, but this is the first time I ever made the dictionary.

MAE WEST

Nations

Norwegian charisma is somewhere between a Presbyterian minister and a tree.

JOHNNY CARSON

The more underdeveloped the country, the more overdeveloped the women.

J.K. GALBRAITH

Official dignity tends to increase in inverse ratio to the importance of the country in which the office is held.   ALDOUS HUXLEY, *Beyond the Mexique Bay*

The great nations have always acted like gangsters, and the small nations like prostitutes.   STANLEY KUBRICK

If everyone could choose where he was going to be born, some countries would be left quite empty.   ERIC LINKLATER, *Love in Albania*

The Japanese have perfected good manners and made them indistinguishable from rudeness.   PAUL THEROUX

What has China ever given the world? Can you really respect a nation that has never taken to cutlery?   VICTORIA WOOD

You can't be a real country unless you have a beer and an airline. It helps if you have some kind of a football team or some nuclear weapons, but at the very least you need a beer.   FRANK ZAPPA

Nature

Of all the wonders of nature, a tree in summer is perhaps the most remarkable, with the possible exception of a moose singing 'Embraceable You' in spats.

WOODY ALLEN, *Without Feathers*

See those rocks sitting up there? Been standing there for 6,000 years. Still be there when you and I are gone. So arguing over who owns 'em is like a couple of fleas arguing over who owns the dog they're living on.

MICK DUNDEE (PAUL HOGAN), *Crocodile Dundee*

I hate the outdoors. To me the outdoors is where the car is. WILL DURST

I saw this nature show on TV about how the male elk douses himself with urine to smell sweeter to the opposite sex. What a coincidence! JACK HANDEY

To me the outdoors is what you must pass through in order to get from your apartment into a taxicab. FRAN LEBOWITZ

Gentlemen know that fresh air should be kept in its proper place – out of doors – and that, God having given us indoors and out-of-doors, we should not attempt to do away with this distinction. ROSE MACAULAY, *Crewe Train*

The country has charms only for those not obliged to stay there.

EDOUARD MANET

I think that I shall never see
A billboard lovely as a tree
Perhaps, unless the billboards fall,
I'll never see a tree at all. OGDEN NASH, *Song of the Open Road*

Need

Needing someone is like needing a parachute. If he isn't there the first time you need him, chances are you won't be needing him again.

SCOTT ADAMS, *The Dilbert Principle*

Sometimes I need what only you can provide – your absence.

ASHLEIGH BRILLIANT

Neighbours

Our neighbourhood was so rough, any cat with a tail was considered posh.

LES DAWSON

Sophisticated listening devices are nothing new. They're called 'neighbours'.
SAM EWING

On summer evenings a radio playing loudly can be a great source of annoyance to your neighbours. Another good way to annoy them is to set fire to their dust-bins.
MARTY FELDMAN

My next-door neighbour just had a pacemaker installed. They're still working the bugs out though. Every time he makes love, my garage door opens.
BOB HOPE

Nothing makes you more tolerant of a neighbour's noisy party than being there.
FRANKLIN P. JONES

My next-door neighbour is always bragging about the sex he and his wife have had. As if I hadn't been watching.
BRIAN KILEY

Nervousness

Many a man gets a reputation for being energetic when he's merely nervous.
EVAN ESAR

I know him. He's too nervous to kill himself. Wears his seat belt in a drive-in movie.
OSCAR MADISON (WALTER MATTHAU), *The Odd Couple*

Neuroses

In Los Angeles, there's a hotline for people in denial. So far no one has called.
GEORGE CARLIN

I'm pretty private about my neuroses. You're not neurotic if you talk to yourself – everyone does – you're only neurotic if you hear an answer.
RACHEL WEISZ

New Age

The New Age? It's just the old age stuck in a microwave oven for fifteen seconds.
JAMES RANDI

New England

The New England conscience does not stop you from doing what you shouldn't – it just stops you from enjoying it.
CLEVELAND AMORY

In New England there are three times of year. Either winter has just been, or winter is coming, or it's winter.   BILL BRYSON, *Notes from a Big Country*

If you don't like the weather in New England, just wait a few minutes.
RING LARDNER

New York

The last time anybody made a list of the top hundred character attributes of New Yorkers, common sense snuck in at number seventy-nine.
DOUGLAS ADAMS, *Mostly Harmless*

New York is the only city in the world where you can get deliberately run down on the sidewalk by a pedestrian.   RUSSELL BAKER

New York is the place where if you have talent, and you believe in yourself, and you show people what you can do, then some day, maybe – just maybe – you could get shoved in front of a moving subway train.   DAVE BARRY

You're never alone in New York, the city is your date.
CARRIE BRADSHAW (SARAH JESSICA PARKER), *Sex and the City*

(*in New York*) It would be absolutely magical if we could alleviate our hunger with something that tasted of food.   PATRICK CAMPBELL

Anytime four New Yorkers get into a cab together without arguing, a bank robbery has just taken place.   JOHNNY CARSON

Traffic signals in New York are just rough guidelines.
DAVID LETTERMAN

Someone did a study of the three most-often-heard phrases in New York City. One is, 'Hey, taxi.' Two is, 'What train do I take to get to Bloomingdale's?' And three is, 'Don't worry, it's just a flesh wound.'   DAVID LETTERMAN

It's the 150th anniversary of Central Park – or as Donald Trump calls it, 850 wasted acres.   DAVID LETTERMAN

Questions Asked By Tourists Visiting New York City:
'Does it always smell like this?'
'Do you think we'll ever see our luggage again?'
'Which way to the emergency room?'
'How do I get to Seinfeld's apartment?'

'Which way to the hookers?'
'Do what myself?'
DAVID LETTERMAN

I come from New York where, if you fall down, someone will pick you up by your wallet.
AL McGUIRE

A car is useless in New York, essential everywhere else. The same with good manners.
MIGNON McLAUGHLIN

When you go to New York you notice that you need two hands to open a letterbox while you fly a plane with one hand.
GEORGE MIKES

New York – the nation's thyroid gland.
CHRISTOPHER MORLEY, *Shore Leave*

Some call New York a jungle. It's not. It's a big jockstrap. It supports the men.
GAIL PARENT, *Sheila Levine is Dead and Living in New York*

In New York every rainbow has an empty pot of gold at the end with a chalk outline of a dead leprechaun.
BOB SARLATTE

I moved to New York City for my health. I'm paranoid, and New York was the only place where my fears were justified.
ANITA WEISS

Running for Senator in New York is like bobbing for piranhas.
ROBIN WILLIAMS

New Zealand

(*asked whether he enjoyed his trip to New Zealand*) I find it hard to say, because when I was there, it seemed to be shut.
CLEMENT FREUD

New Zealand is a country of 30,000 million sheep, three million of whom think they are human.
BARRY HUMPHRIES

New Zealanders are so laid back. A New Zealander in a frenzy is an American in a coma.
CAL WILSON

News

News is the first rough draft of history.
BEN BRADLEE

The one function that TV news performs very well is that, when there is no news, we give it to you with the same emphasis as if there were.
DAVID BRINKLEY

The Bureau of Indian Affairs has announced that they have located another Mohican. All the books are being recalled.　　　　　GEORGE CARLIN

What a beautiful day – the kind of day that starts with a hearty breakfast and ends with a newsreader saying, '. . . before turning the gun on himself.'
DAN CONNER (JOHN GOODMAN), *Roseanne*

And now, here are the headlines. Here they come right now. Pope actually found to be Jewish. Liberace is Anastasia and Ethel Merman jams Russian radar. The East Germans today claimed the Berlin Wall was a fraternity prank. Also, the Pope decided today to release Vatican-related bath products. An incredible thing, yes, it's the new Pope on a Rope. That's right. Pope on a Rope. Wash with it, go straight to heaven.
ADRIAN CRONAUER (ROBIN WILLIAMS), *Good Morning, Vietnam*

'Stunt skydiving' – every newsreader's nightmare.　　　ANGUS DEAYTON

We all want to get the news objectively, impartially and from our own point of view.　　　　　　BILL VAUGHAN

Good news rarely comes in a brown envelope.

Newspapers

Any foreigner visiting the United States can perform an easy magic trick: buy a newspaper and see your own country disappear.　　　JULIAN BARNES

A newspaper is lumber made malleable. It is ink made into words and pictures. It is conceived, born, grows up and dies of old age in a day.　　　JIM BISHOP

Countryside: the killing of [newspaper editor] Piers Morgan.　　STEPHEN FRY

Trying to determine what is going on in the world by reading newspapers is like trying to tell the time by watching the second hand of a clock.
BEN HECHT

I don't care what is written about me so long as it isn't true.
KATHARINE HEPBURN

An editor is a person employed on a newspaper, whose business it is to separate the wheat from the chaff, and to see that the chaff is printed.
ELBERT HUBBARD

Once a newspaper touches a story, the facts are lost forever, even to the protagonists.   NORMAN MAILER, *The Presidential Papers*

It's amazing that the amount of news that happens in the world every day always just exactly fits the newspaper.   JERRY SEINFELD

Accuracy to a newspaper is what virtue is to a lady, except that a newspaper can always print a retraction.   ADLAI STEVENSON

Never believe in mirrors or newspapers.   TOM STOPPARD

The *New York Times* is read by the people who run the country. The *Washington Post* is read by the people who think they run the country. The *National Enquirer* is read by the people who think Elvis is alive and running the country.
                                                ROBERT J. WOODHEAD

Nightmares

Nancy [Reagan] has this recurring nightmare – she's kidnapped, taken to A&S, and forced to buy dresses off the rack.   JOEY ADAMS

Have you noticed . . . there is never any third act in a nightmare? They bring you to a climax of terror and then leave you there. They are the work of poor dramatists.   MAX BEERBOHM

I had a nightmare last night. I dreamed Dolly Parton was my mother and I was a bottle-baby.   HENNY YOUNGMAN

Richard Nixon

He told us he was going to take crime off the streets. He did. He took it into the White House.   REV. RALPH ABERNATHY

Nixon is a purposeless man, but I have great faith in his cowardice.
                                                JIMMY BRESLIN

I worship the quicksand he walks on.   ART BUCHWALD

Nixon's motto was: 'If two wrongs don't make a right, try three'.
                                                NORMAN COUSINS

(*on a Nixon speech*) I may not know much, but I know chicken shit from chicken salad.   LYNDON B. JOHNSON

Nixon is the kind of guy who, if you were drowning twenty feet from shore, would throw you a fifteen-foot rope.
EUGENE MCCARTHY

Would you buy a second-hand car from this man?
MORT SAHL

Nixon is the kind of politician who would cut down a redwood tree, then mount its stump for a speech on conservation.
ADLAI STEVENSON

A monument to all the rancid genes and broken chromosomes that corrupt the possibilities of the American Dream.
HUNTER S. THOMPSON

(*on Vice-President Nixon's candidacy for the presidency, 1960*) You don't set a fox to watching the chickens just because he has a lot of experience in the hen house.
HARRY S. TRUMAN

He's one of the few in the history of the country to run for high office talking out of both sides of his mouth at the same time – and lying out of both sides.
HARRY S. TRUMAN

Normality

The only normal people are the ones you don't know very well.
JOE ANCIS

For years I worried because my penis hangs slightly to the left, and finally read in a book that this is within the realm of the normal, but then wondered, what sort of person would read books like that?
GARRISON KEILLOR

A 'normal' person is the sort of person that might be designed by a committee. You know, each person puts in a pretty colour and it comes out grey.
ALAN SHERMAN

Noses

What always staggers me is that when people blow their noses, they always look into their hankies to see what came out. What do they expect to find? A silver sixpence?
BILLY CONNOLLY

Jimmy Durante: Where are my glasses?
Friend: They're on your nose!
Jimmy Durante: Be more specific.

Whenever I go to a bar, I always go right up to the most beautiful woman in the room and say, 'You've got something hanging out of your nose.' Hey, since I've got no shot at her, I might as well humble her a little for the next guy!

MICHAEL HAYWARD

You can pick your nose and you can pick your friends — but you can't wipe your friends on a cinema seat.

Nostalgia

Someday we'll look back on this and plough into a parked car.

SCOTT ADAMS, The Dilbert Principle

He emerged from the hotel and walked up Eighth Avenue. Two men were mugging an elderly lady. My God, thought Weinstein, time was when one person could handle that job.

WOODY ALLEN, Without Feathers

The people who are always hankering loudest for some golden yesteryear usually drive new cars.

RUSSELL BAKER

I can remember when the air was clean and sex was dirty.

GEORGE BURNS

You know what nostalgia is, don't you? It's basically a matter of recalling the fun without reliving the pain.

BETTE DAVIS

Nostalgia is the realisation that things weren't as unbearable as they seemed at the time.

Nostalgia is the desire to possess what you never had.

Nudity

A naked woman out of doors is either a sun-worshipper or a rape victim; a man in the same state is either a sexual criminal or a plain lunatic.

KINGSLEY AMIS, The Green Man

I could go on stage, unzip my pants, and hang my dick out and people would think it was some statement or something.

BONO

In the theatre I'm playing, there's a hole in the wall between the ladies' dressing-room and mine. I've been meaning to plug it up, but what the hell . . . let 'em enjoy themselves.

GEORGE BURNS

(*after being found as an old man, sitting in the House of Commons smoking room with his fly-buttons undone*) Dead birds don't fall out of nests.

Winston Churchill

The trouble with nudist beaches is that everyone hides behind books trying to pretend they're not looking at everyone else.

Jilly Cooper, *Turn Right at the Spotted Dog*

When you've seen a nude infant doing a backward somersault you know why clothing exists.

Stephen Fry

I worked in strip joints, but I never got my clothes off. People were screaming: 'Don't do it!'

Whoopi Goldberg

About 250 naked men in Australia protested the war in Iraq. That's the most naked men ever assembled outside a Christina Aguilera video.

Jay Leno

Naked, I had a body that invited burial.

Spike Milligan, *Goodbye, Soldier*

(*asked whether she had really posed for a 1947 calendar with nothing on*) I had the radio on.

Marilyn Monroe

I only put clothes on so that I'm not naked when I go out shopping.

Julia Roberts

(*on Glenda Jackson*) In almost every play or film she inflicts her naked body on us which, considering its quality, is the supreme insult.

John Simon

I remember the first time I saw Mary getting undressed, thinking, 'God, I hope this skylight holds.'

Dick Solomon (John Lithgow), *3rd Rock From the Sun*

Anyone might become homosexual after seeing Glenda Jackson naked.

Auberon Waugh

I think on-stage nudity is disgusting, shameful and damaging to all things American. But if I were twenty-two with a great body, it would be artistic, tasteful, patriotic and a progressive religious experience.

Shelley Winters

Why is it that most nudists are people you don't want to see naked?

O

Obesity

All fat women look the same; they all look forty-two.   MARGARET ATWOOD

When I was a child, I was so fat I was the one chosen to play Bethlehem in the school Nativity.   JO BRAND

I burnt my bra and heated a small village in Cumbria.   JO BRAND

If someone calls me fat, I don't get angry. I just turn the other chin.   JO BRAND

Inside every fat person there's a thin person looking to get out. They've just eaten them.   JO BRAND

I must be anorexic because when anorexics look in a mirror they see a fat person, and so do I.   JO BRAND

I don't mind that I'm fat. You still get the same money.   MARLON BRANDO

I had an aunt who was so obese she had flesh-eating disease for twenty years and nobody noticed.   YVON DESCHAMPS

I'd love to slit my mother-in-law's corsets and watch her spread to death.   PHYLLIS DILLER

Did you ever notice they never take any fat hostages? You never see a guy coming out of Lebanon going, 'I was held hostage for seven months and I lost 175 pounds, I feel good and I look good, and I learned self-discipline. That's the important thing.'   DENIS LEARY

For the first time ever, overweight people outnumber average people in America. Doesn't that make overweight the average then? Last month you were fat, now you're average – hey, let's get a pizza.   JAY LENO

Those obese people who sued McDonald's for making them fat and lost, are suing again. Yes, they're going back for seconds.   CONAN O'BRIEN

Some people call me the Kitchen, some call me the Dining Room – and some call me the Cafeteria.　　　　　　　　　　　WILLIAM 'REFRIGERATOR' PERRY

I don't diet yet I never put on an ounce. I eat six meals a day – four steaks, ten pounds of potatoes, a dozen hamburgers, apple pie, ice cream and lots of beer. Yet I still weigh the same: 28 stone.　　　　　　　　　　CYRIL SMITH

We'd see Charles Laughton floating in his pool and it was just the reverse of an iceberg – ninety per cent of him was visible.　　　　PETER USTINOV

Why in America do we still have a meal called 'break fast'? Who is fasting in this country? We are the fattest people on the planet.　　　RUSTY WARD

Another sad thing about fat teenage girls is that people are always making them be bridesmaids. If you ever notice on a wedding photograph, there's always three normal ones – you know with the puffed sleeves and a sash – and a whopping great one on the end with the same material in a caftan.
　　　　　　　　　　　　　　　　　　　　　　　　VICTORIA WOOD

Why doesn't the fattest man in the world become a hockey goalie?
　　　　　　　　　　　　　　　　　　　　　　　　STEVEN WRIGHT

Objects

Inanimate objects are classified scientifically into three major categories – those that don't work, those that break down and those that get lost.
　　　　　　　　　　　　　　　　　　　　　　　　RUSSELL BAKER

The goal of all inanimate objects is to resist man and ultimately defeat him.
　　　　　　　　　　　　　　　　　　　　　　　　RUSSELL BAKER

If an article is attractive, or useful, or inexpensive, they'll stop making it tomorrow; if it's all three, they stopped making it yesterday.
　　　　　　　　　　　　MIGNON MCLAUGHLIN, *The Neurotic's Notebook*

Never fight an inanimate object.　　　　　　　　　　　P.J. O'ROURKE

No man who has wrestled with a self-adjusting card table can ever quite be the man he once was.　　　　　JAMES THURBER, *Let Your Mind Alone*

Obscenity

A Detroit couple is suing Campbell's soups, claiming a bowl of alphabet soup spelled out an obscene message to their children.　　　GEORGE CARLIN

Women should be obscene and not heard.   GROUCHO MARX

Obscenity is whatever gives a judge an erection.

Occupation

Crackpot is an excellent job because the expectations are so low. No one ever tells crackpots that they should be doing more.   SCOTT ADAMS

Sure, selling shoes is fun. But behind the glamour, it's like any other minimum wage slow death.   AL BUNDY (ED O'NEILL), *Married . . . With Children*

If you have to have a job in this world, a high-priced movie star is a pretty damned good gig.   TOM HANKS

There are very few jobs that actually require a penis or a vagina. All other jobs should be open to everybody.   FLORYNCE KENNEDY

I was into animal husbandry – until they caught me at it.   TOM LEHRER

The easiest job in the world has to be coroner. Surgery on dead people. What's the worst thing that could happen? If everything went wrong, may be you'd get a pulse.   DENNIS MILLER

A good rule of thumb is if you've made it to thirty-five and your job still requires you to wear a name tag, you've probably made a serious vocational error.
                          DENNIS MILLER

I used to work in a fire hydrant factory. You couldn't park anywhere near the place.   STEVEN WRIGHT

The Office

A memorandum is written not to inform the reader but to protect the writer.
                          DEAN ACHESON

His insomnia was so bad, he couldn't sleep during office hours.
                          ARTHUR BAER

To leave a message in a drawer marked private is the best way of spreading information round the office quickly.
                  MICHAEL GREEN, *The Art of Coarse Office Life*

I always arrive late at the office, but I make up for it by leaving early.

CHARLES LAMB

Fishnet stockings are now considered appropriate for office wear. So how are men going to be able to tell the professional women from the professional women?

JAY LENO

Never burn bridges. Today's junior prick, tomorrow's senior partner.

KATHARINE PARKER (SIGOURNEY WEAVER), *Working Girl*

Old age

I inhabit a weak, frail, decayed tenement; battered by the winds and broken in on by the storms, and, from all I can learn, the landlord does not intend to repair.

JOHN QUINCY ADAMS

The older one becomes the quicker the present fades into sepia and the past looms up in glorious technicolour.

BERYL BAINBRIDGE

To me, old age is always fifteen years older than I am.

BERNARD BARUCH

You're getting old when it takes you more time to recover than it did to tire you out.

MILTON BERLE

Old age, it's the only disease, Mr Thompson, that you don't look forward to being cured of.

BERNSTEIN (EVERETT SLOANE), *Citizen Kane*

I've never known a person to live to be one hundred and be remarkable for anything else.

JOSH BILLINGS

(*on his 100th birthday*) If I'd known I was gonna live this long, I'd have taken better care of myself.

EUBIE BLAKE

When I was a boy the Dead Sea was only sick.

GEORGE BURNS

I have my 87th birthday coming up and people ask me what I'd most appreciate getting. I'll tell you – a paternity suit.

GEORGE BURNS

You know you're getting old when you stoop to tie your shoelaces and wonder what else you could do while you're down there.

GEORGE BURNS

I was brought up to respect my elders so now I don't have to respect anybody.

GEORGE BURNS

If you live to the age of 100 you have it made because very few people die past the age of 100.
                                                                    GEORGE BURNS

Old is when your wife says, 'Let's go upstairs and make love,' and you answer, 'Honey, I can't do both.'
                                                                    RED BUTTONS

Everyone says I am terrified of getting old but the truth is, in my job becoming old and becoming extinct are one and the same thing.
                                                                    CHER

The joy of being older is that in one's life one can, towards the end of the run, over-act appallingly.
                                                                    QUENTIN CRISP

'Course I'm respectable. I'm old. Politicians, ugly buildings, and whores all get respectable if they last long enough.
                                    NOAH CROSS (JOHN HUSTON), *Chinatown*

I am in the departure lounge of life; my only hope is that my plane will be delayed.
                                                                    ROBIN DAY

I'm at the age where my back goes out more than I do.   PHYLLIS DILLER

When a man fell into his anecdotage it was a sign for him to retire from the world.
                                                    BENJAMIN DISRAELI, *Lothair*

It is only in going uphill that one realises how fast one is going downhill.
                                                            GEORGE DU MAURIER

Growing old is a bad habit which a busy man has no time to form.
                                                                    ANDRÉ GIDE

(*spotting a pretty girl at the age of eighty-six*) Oh, to be seventy again!
                                                    OLIVER WENDELL HOLMES, JR

You know you are getting old when the candles cost more than the cake.
                                                                    BOB HOPE

(*turning seventy*) You still chase women, but only downhill.   BOB HOPE

(*turning eighty*) That's the time of your life when even your birthday suit needs pressing.
                                                                    BOB HOPE

(*turning ninety*) I don't feel old. In fact, I don't generally feel anything until noon, then it's time for my nap.
                                                                    BOB HOPE

If they offered me a knighthood, it would have to be soon, while I can still get up from a kneeling position within an hour. ROY HUDD, 2003

Anna Nicole Smith says that she and her 90-year-old husband were very passionate in bed. Sometimes she'd bang her head against the headstone. JAY LENO

Old age is like a plane flying through a storm. Once you're aboard, there's nothing you can do. GOLDA MEIR

My 93-year-old neighbour calls his manhood Carpool Lane, because he knows it's there, but he can't use it. GEORGE MILLER

I can still enjoy sex at 74 — I live at 76 so it's no distance. BOB MONKHOUSE

Sex at age ninety is like trying to shoot pool with a rope. CAMILLE PAGLIA

Growing old is like being increasingly penalised for a crime you haven't committed. ANTHONY POWELL, *Temporary Kings*

As we grow older, our bodies get shorter and our anecdotes get longer. ROBERT QUILLEN

You know you're getting old when work is a lot less fun — and fun is a lot more work. JOAN RIVERS

Aw, Dad, you've done a lot of great things, but you're a very old man now, and old people are useless. HOMER SIMPSON, *The Simpsons*

I discovered George Burns's secret for staying young. He never overextends himself. He wouldn't even whistle for a cab. He figures when he finally gets up a pucker, why waste it on a taxi . . . ? CONNIE STEVENS

The greatest problem about old age is the fear that it may go on too long. A.J.P. TAYLOR

My grandmother is over eighty and still doesn't need glasses. Drinks right out of the bottle. HENNY YOUNGMAN

There's one great advantage to living to 105 — no peer pressure.

You know you're getting old when almost everything hurts, and what doesn't hurt, doesn't work.

You know you're getting old when you feel like the morning after and you haven't been anywhere.

You know you're getting old when every time you suck in your gut, your ankles swell.

You know you're getting old when you have too much room in the house and not enough in the medicine cabinet.

Opera

The opera is like a husband with a foreign title — expensive to support, hard to understand and therefore a supreme social challenge.

CLEVELAND AMORY

I do not mind what language an opera is sung in so long as it is a language I don't understand.
EDWARD APPLETON

No good opera can be sensible — for people do not sing when they are feeling sensible.
W.H. AUDEN

No operatic tenor has yet died soon enough for me.   THOMAS BEECHAM

Opera is where a guy gets stabbed in the back, and instead of dying, he sings.
ROBERT BENCHLEY

And now for my next trick. I'm going to make my boyfriend disappear. I say the magic word: opera.

CAROLINE DUFFY (LEA THOMPSON), *Caroline in the City*

The higher the voice the smaller the intellect.   ERNEST NEWMAN

I sometimes wonder which would be nicer — an opera without an interval, or an interval without an opera.
ERNEST NEWMAN

Oh how wonderful, really wonderful, opera would be if there were no singers!
GIOACCHINO ROSSINI

I like this opera crowd. I feel tough.

JERRY SEINFELD, *Seinfeld*

Opera is a sham art. Large, plain, middle-aged women galumph around posing as pretty young girls singing to portly, plain, middle-aged men posing as handsome young heroes.
WOODROW WYATT

Opinion

When a man gives his opinion he's a man. When a woman gives her opinion she's a bitch.
BETTE DAVIS

A point of view can be a dangerous luxury when substituted for insight and understanding.
MARSHALL MCLUHAN

Everyone's entitled to my opinion.
MADONNA

When I want your opinion, I'll give it to you.
LAURENCE J. PETER

Opportunity

If opportunity doesn't knock, build a door.
MILTON BERLE

Opportunities are usually disguised as hard work, so most people don't recognise them.
ANN LANDERS

Sometimes opportunity knocks, but most of the time it sneaks up and then quietly steals away.
DOUG LARSON

Equal opportunity means everyone will have a fair chance at being incompetent.
LAURENCE J. PETER

The follies which a man regrets most in his life are those which he didn't commit when he had the opportunity.
HELEN ROWLAND, *Guide To Men*

Opportunities are like sunrises. If you wait too long, you miss them.
WILLIAM A. WARD

Optimism

An optimist is simply a pessimist with no job experience.
SCOTT ADAMS

(*on his Manchester United manager Sir Matt Busby*) Matt was the eternal optimist. In 1968 he still hoped that Glenn Miller was just missing.
PAT CRERAND

An optimist is a person who starts a new diet on Thanksgiving Day.

IRV KUPCINET

I am neither an optimist nor pessimist, but a possibilist.   MAX LERNER

An optimist is a driver who thinks that empty space at the kerb won't have a hydrant beside it.   JULES RENARD

I'm an optimist. But I'm an optimist who takes his raincoat.

HAROLD WILSON

Oral sex

Clinton lied. A man might forget where he parks or where he lives, but he never forgets oral sex, no matter how bad it is.   LENNY CLARKE

I don't give blow jobs because I find it really off-putting seeing a grown man look so pathetically grateful.   JENNY ECLAIR

Even if you have only two seconds, drop everything and give him a blow job. That way, he won't really want sex with anyone else.   JERRY HALL

Oral sex is a great way to tone up your cheekbones.   CYNTHIA HEIMEL

Maybe you're on your knees, but you've got him by the balls.

SAMANTHA JONES (KIM CATTRALL), *Sex and the City*

Could you shave or something? Every time I blow you I feel like I'm flossing.

SAMANTHA JONES (KIM CATTRALL), *Sex and the City*

According to President Clinton oral sex is not really sex. If that's true, there's a hooker who owes me fifty bucks.   DAVID LETTERMAN

You know the worst thing about oral sex? The view.   MAUREEN LIPMAN

[Bill] Clinton put a face on oral sex.   BILL MAHER

There's a type of food that makes women give up oral sex: wedding cake.

BILL MAHER

A Jewish girl is not interested in oral sex – in an oral *surgeon*, maybe.

JACKIE MASON

A poll showed 14 per cent of men have received oral sex while driving. They must be the same 14 per cent who are deathly afraid of speed bumps.

CONAN O'BRIEN

Orchestras

There are two golden rules for an orchestra: start together and finish together. The public doesn't give a damn what goes on in between.

THOMAS BEECHAM

At a rehearsal I let the orchestra play as they like. At the concert I make them play as *I* like.

THOMAS BEECHAM

If anyone has conducted a Beethoven performance, and then doesn't have to go to an osteopath, then there's something wrong.

SIMON RATTLE

(*advice to conductors*) Never look at the trombones, it only encourages them.

RICHARD STRAUSS

(*berating an orchestra*) After I die, I shall return to earth as a gatekeeper of a bordello and I won't let any of you – not one of you – enter!

ARTURO TOSCANINI

(*to an Austrian orchestra*) Can't you read? The score demands *con amore* and what are you doing? You are playing it like married men!

ARTURO TOSCANINI

Orgasm

The only time my wife and I had a simultaneous orgasm was when the judge signed the divorce papers.

WOODY ALLEN

I have to be physically attracted to someone. But I can't just be with someone just because it's great sex. Because orgasms don't last long enough.

COURTENEY COX ARQUETTE

I may not be a great actress but I've become the greatest at screen orgasms. Ten seconds of heavy breathing, roll your head from side to side, simulate a slight asthma attack and die a little.

CANDICE BERGEN

You women shouldn't fake orgasms, because we don't care if you have them.

KENNETH BRENNAN

(*on having an orgasm every time she has sex*) Well I'll admit that I've had to polish myself off once or twice but yes! When I R.S.V.P. to a party I make it my business to come.   SAMANTHA JONES (KIM CATTRALL), *Sex and the City*

The only reason my wife has an orgasm is so she'll have something else to moan about.   BOB MONKHOUSE

The orgasm has replaced the Cross as the focus of longing and the image of fulfilment.   MALCOLM MUGGERIDGE

I finally had an orgasm and my doctor told me it was the wrong kind.   POLLY (TISA FARROW), *Manhattan*

Everybody talks about multiple orgasm. Multiple orgasm – I'm lucky if both sides of my toaster pop!   JOAN RIVERS

I'm a terrible lover. I gave my girlfriend an anti-climax.   SCOTT ROEBEN

Women might be able to fake orgasms, but men can fake whole relationships.   SHARON STONE

An orgasm a day keeps the doctor away.   MAE WEST

Originality

About the most originality that any writer can hope to achieve honestly is to steal with good judgement.   JOSH BILLINGS

What is originality? Undetected plagiarism.   WILLIAM RALPH INGE, *Assessments and Anticipations*

Originality is the art of concealing your source.   FRANKLIN P. JONES

Originality is the fine art of remembering what you hear, but forgetting where you heard it.   LAURENCE J. PETER

It is better to be good than to be original.   MIES VAN DER ROHE

P

Pacifism

An appeaser is one who feeds a crocodile hoping it will eat him last.

WINSTON CHURCHILL

War hath no fury like a non-combatant.

C.E. MONTAGUE

Pain

A guy could have one major limb lying on the ground a full ten feet from the rest of his body, and he'd claim it was 'just a sprain'.

DAVE BARRY

(*after having both arms hacked off*) It's just a flesh wound.

THE BLACK KNIGHT (JOHN CLEESE), *Monty Python and the Holy Grail*

I've been dumped before. This isn't pain I'm feeling, it's nostalgia.

ALLY MCBEAL (CALISTA FLOCKHART), *Ally McBeal*

I tell you this, and I tell you plain:
What you have done, you will do again;
You will bite your tongue, careful or not,
Upon the already-bitten spot.

MIGNON MCLAUGHLIN, *The Neurotic's Notebook*

I once heard two ladies going on and on about the pains of childbirth and how men don't seem to know what real pain is. I asked if either of them ever got themselves caught in a zipper.

EMO PHILIPS

Men know nothing of pain. They have never experienced labour, cramps or a bikini wax.

JOAN RIVERS

Pampering

Spoon feeding in the long run teaches us nothing but the shape of the spoon.

E.M. FORSTER

Paranoia

Sometimes I get the feeling the whole world is against me, but deep down I know that's not true. Some smaller countries are neutral.

ROBERT ORBEN

I am a kind of paranoiac in reverse. I suspect people of plotting to make me happy.
                                                              J.D. SALINGER

My first psychiatrist said I was paranoid, but I want a second opinion because I think he's out to get me.
                                                              TOM WILSON

Parents

When I was kidnapped, my parents snapped into action. They rented out my room.
                                                              WOODY ALLEN

Children always assume the sexual lives of their parents come to a grinding halt at their conception.
                                                              ALAN BENNETT

Parents are the last people on earth who ought to have children.
                                                      SAMUEL BUTLER, *Notebooks*

No matter how calmly you try to referee, parenting will eventually produce bizarre behaviour, and I'm not talking about the kids. Their behaviour is always normal.
                                                              BILL COSBY

Parents are not interested in justice, they're interested in peace and quiet.
                                                              BILL COSBY

If one is not going to take the necessary precautions to avoid having parents, one must undertake to bring them up.
                                                QUENTIN CRISP, *The Naked Civil Servant*

If you have never been hated by your child, you have never been a parent.
                                                              BETTE DAVIS

There are times when parenthood seems nothing but feeding the mouth that bites you.
                                                PETER DE VRIES, *The Tunnel of Love*

I grew up to have my father's looks, my father's speech patterns, my father's posture, my father's walk, my father's opinions, and my mother's contempt for my father.
                                                              JULES FEIFFER

Most of us become parents long before we have stopped being children.
                                                              MIGNON MCLAUGHLIN

Parents should conduct their arguments in quiet, respectful tones, but in a foreign language. You'd be surprised what an inducement that is to the education of children. JUDITH MARTIN

Children aren't happy without something to ignore
And that's what parents were created for. OGDEN NASH, *The Parents*

My parents brought me up with the three magic words: total sensory deprivation. EMO PHILIPS

If you must hold yourself up to your children as an object lesson, hold yourself up as a warning and not as an example. GEORGE BERNARD SHAW

I don't visit my parents because Delta Airlines won't wait in the yard while I run in. MARGARET SMITH

Parents are the bones on which children sharpen their teeth.
PETER USTINOV, *Dear Me*

To lose one parent, Mr Worthing, may be regarded as a misfortune; to lose both looks like carelessness. OSCAR WILDE, *The Importance of Being Earnest*

Parking

Once again, we find ourselves enmeshed in the holiday season, that very special time of year when we join with our loved ones in sharing centuries-old traditions such as trying to find a parking space at the mall. DAVE BARRY

To my wife, double parking means on top of another car. DAVE BARRY

Parking is such sweet sorrow. HERB CAEN

My father didn't pay for parking, my mother, my brother, nobody. It's like going to a prostitute. Why should I pay for it? If I apply myself, maybe I can get it for free. GEORGE COSTANZA (JASON ALEXANDER), *Seinfeld*

When Solomon said that there was a time and a place for everything, he had not encountered the problem of parking an automobile. BOB EDWARDS

To park your car in London's Soho costs 20p for three minutes, that's £4 an hour, which is more than the minimum wage. There are people working in McDonald's in Soho who can look out the window and see parking meters earning more than they are. SIMON EVANS

I used to complain that I had no shoes until I met a man who had no feet. Then I complained because he got the good parking spot.
JIM EVARTS

(*as Annie parks the car*) Don't worry, we can walk to the kerb from here.
ALVY SINGER (WOODY ALLEN), *Annie Hall*

Parliament

Sir Humphrey Appleby (Nigel Hawthorne): Make sure he [the Minister] spends more time where he can't get under our feet and can't do any damage.
Bernard Woolley (Derek Fowlds): But where?
Sir Humphrey: Well, the House of Commons for instance.
Yes, Minister

The House of Lords is like a glass of champagne that has stood for five days.
CLEMENT ATTLEE

Mr Speaker, I withdraw my statement that half the cabinet are asses. Half the cabinet are not asses.
BENJAMIN DISRAELI

The House of Lords is a model of how to care for the elderly.
FRANK FIELD

(*on the House of Commons*) There are eleven bars, no crèche and no shop. It would be an ideal place for a small Waitrose. It could replace the rifle range.
BARBARA FOLLETT

The House of Lords must be the only institution in the world which is kept efficient by the persistent absenteeism of most of its members.
HERBERT SAMUEL

Parliament is the longest running farce in the West End.
CYRIL SMITH

You know you have to get out of Westminster when you start wanting to punch people.
TEDDY TAYLOR

Parties

I think everyone would like to have a surprise party thrown for them, but not if it's a 'surprise, I want a divorce' party or a 'surprise, I have a new lover' party.
KEN ALWINE

I've got a thingy shaped like a turnip. I'm a big hit at parties: I hide in the vegetable rack and frighten the children.
BALDRICK (TONY ROBINSON), *Blackadder*

The mark of a good party is that you wake up the next morning wanting to change your name and start a new life in a different city.

VANCE BOURJAILY

Tall girls stand about at parties looking gentle and apologetic, like Great Danes.

JILLY COOPER, *Women and Super Women*

Beware of the man who goes to cocktail parties, not to drink but to listen.

PIERRE DANINOS

I was at Elton John's for his birthday party. It was slightly bigger than the whole estate I grew up on.

CRAIG DAVID

You moon the wrong person at an office party, and suddenly you're not 'professional' any more!

JEFF FOXWORTHY

I have just returned from a children's party. I am one of the survivors. There are not many of us.

PERCY FRENCH

I don't believe in the Republican Party or the Democrat Party. I just believe in parties.

SAMANTHA JONES (KIM CATTRALL), *Sex and the City*

Things You Don't Want To Hear After Your Office Christmas Party:
'Man, you are one hairy son-of-a-bitch.'
'I've never seen anyone drink so much Xerox toner.'
'Hey, dude, thanks for the kidney.'
'You should sue the hell out of whoever posted those photos on the web.'
'Until you, no one had the guts to call Steinbrenner a bastard to his face.'
'Hey, dude, thanks for your other kidney.'
'What time this morning did the paramedics dislodge the stapler?'
'Security! He's back!'

DAVID LETTERMAN

Look, if you don't like my parties, you can leave in a huff. If that's too soon, leave in a minute and a huff.

GROUCHO MARX

The cocktail party is easily the worst invention since castor oil.

ELSA MAXWELL

I was at a gay nineties party the other night. All the men were gay and all the women were ninety.

ERIC MORECAMBE

When giving children's parties, never serve eight jugs of orangeade in a house which has only one bathroom.

DENIS NORDEN, *You Can't Have Your Kayak and Heat It*

What is your hosts' purpose in having a party? Surely not for you to enjoy yourself; if that were their sole purpose, they'd have simply sent champagne and women over to your place by taxi.

P.J. O'ROURKE

One more drink and I would have been under the host.

DOROTHY PARKER

Don't you hate it when you go to a party and someone else is wearing the same dress you are? And it's your date!

JOAN RIVERS

You know in fact, Hank, what I was thinking was next year when we have the going away party, let me and Artie take care of the stripper because we can probably find one that doesn't know you.

LARRY SANDERS (GARRY SHANDLING), *The Larry Sanders Show*

In America you can always find a party. In Russia the party always finds you.

YAKOV SMIRNOFF

Passion

I said to my wife, 'Do you feel that the excitement has gone out of our marriage?' She said, 'I'll discuss it with you during the next commercial break.'

MILTON BERLE

(*to Sean as he goes to put his arm around her*): Any part of you that touches me, you're not getting back.

DARLENE CONNER (SARA GILBERT), *Roseanne*

Martin Crane (John Mahoney): When your mother got mad at me, I'd just grab her, bend her backwards and give her a kiss that made her glad she was a woman.

Niles Crane (David Hyde Pierce): I can't do that with Maris. She has abnormally rigid vertebrae — she'd snap like a twig.

Frasier

Passion makes the world go round. Love just makes it a safer place.

ICE-T

I wish you'd keep my hands to yourself.

GROUCHO MARX

Patience

Good things come to those who wait, but shit pretty much shows up right away.

RICH HALL

Patience is what parents have when there are witnesses.

FRANKLIN P. JONES

Patience is the ability to let your light shine after your fuse has blown.

BOB LEVEY

I am extraordinarily patient provided I get my own way in the end.

MARGARET THATCHER

If I'm not back in five minutes, just wait longer.

ACE VENTURA (JIM CARREY), *Ace Ventura: Pet Detective*

Never chase girls or streetcars, there will always be another one coming along soon.

AMERICAN PROVERB

The things that come to those who wait may be the things left by those who got there first.

Patriotism

Patriotism is often an arbitrary veneration of real estate above principles.

GEORGE JEAN NATHAN

Patriotism is your conviction that this country is superior to all others because you were born in it.

GEORGE BERNARD SHAW

A real patriot is the fellow who gets a parking ticket and rejoices that the system works.

BILL VAUGHAN

Peerage

When I want a peerage, I shall buy one like an honest man.

LORD NORTHCLIFFE

I've been offered titles but I think they get one into disreputable company.

GEORGE BERNARD SHAW

An English peer of the right sort can be bored nearer to the point where mortification sets in, without showing it, than anyone else in the world.

P.G. WODEHOUSE, *Something Fresh*

People

There are two types of people in this world, good and bad. The good sleep better, but the bad seem to enjoy the waking hours much more.

WOODY ALLEN

The world is made up of people who never quite get into the first team, and who just miss the prizes at the flower show.

JACOB BRONOWSKI, *The Face of Violence*

People who say they don't care what people think are usually desperate to have people think they don't care what people think.

GEORGE CARLIN

There are some people who leave impressions not so lasting as the imprint of an oar upon the water.

KATE CHOPIN, *The Awakening*

I hate it when people say, 'It's always the last place you look.' Of course it is. Why the hell would you keep looking after you've found it?

BILLY CONNOLLY

(*assessing the British*) Sheep with a nasty side.

CYRIL CONNOLLY

The only reason some people get lost in thought is because it's unfamiliar territory.

PAUL FIX

People who have no weaknesses are terrible; there is no way of taking advantage of them.

ANATOLE FRANCE, *The Crime of Sylvestre Bonnard*

It's odd how people waiting for you stand out far less clearly than people you are waiting for.

JEAN GIRAUDOUX, *Tiger at the Gates*

Dogs never bite me – just humans.

MARILYN MONROE

People are more violently opposed to fur than leather because it's safer to harass rich women than motorcycle gangs.

ALEXEI SAYLE

I love mankind; it's people I can't stand.

CHARLES SCHULZ

People who count their chickens before they are hatched act very wisely; because chickens run about so absurdly that it is impossible to count them accurately.

OSCAR WILDE

Perversion

I'm really into bondage. When I'm in the mood I'll tie my wife up and gag her and go into the living room and watch a football game. TOM ARNOLD

Kinky sex involves the use of duck feathers. Perverted sex involves the whole duck. LEWIS GRIZZARD

In Germany a guy got his manhood caught in his vacuum cleaner. He told the doctors the relationship was purely sexual. He didn't want any attachments. JAY LENO

'Trapper' John McIntyre (Wayne Rogers): Klinger's not a pervert.
'Hotlips' Houlihan (Loretta Swit): How do you know?
'Trapper' John: Because I'm a pervert. We have meetings. He's never there. *M*A*S*H*

Pessimism

Things are never so bad they can't be made worse. HUMPHREY BOGART

The optimist proclaims that we live in the best of all possible worlds; the pessimist fears this is true. JAMES BRANCH CABELL, *The Silver Stallion*

I don't consider myself a pessimist at all. I think of a pessimist as someone who is waiting for it to rain. And I feel completely soaked to the skin. LEONARD COHEN

Optimists in this country are now outnumbered by pessimists. But you were probably expecting that. ANGUS DEAYTON, *Have I Got News For You*

I guess I just prefer to see the dark side of things. The glass is half empty. And cracked. And I just cut my lip on it. And chipped a tooth. JANEANE GAROFALO

If we see light at the end of a tunnel it is the light of an oncoming train. ROBERT LOWELL, *Day by Day*

A pessimist is a man who looks both ways before crossing a one-way street. LAURENCE J. PETER

An optimist stays up until midnight to see the New Year in. A pessimist stays up to make sure the old year leaves. BILL VAUGHAN

A pessimist is one who builds dungeons in the air.   WALTER WINCHELL

Pets

To my mind, the only possible pet is a cow . . . They will listen to your problems and never ask a thing in return. They will be your friends forever. And when you get tired of them, you can kill and eat them. Perfect.
BILL BRYSON, *Neither Here Nor There*

Maris is unable to have pets. She distrusts anything that loves her unconditionally.   NILES CRANE (DAVID HYDE PIERCE), *Frasier*

I used to work in a pet store. People kept asking how big I'd get.
RODNEY DANGERFIELD

You enter into a certain amount of madness when you marry a person with pets.
NORA EPHRON

No animal should ever jump on the dining-room furniture unless absolutely certain that he can hold his own in the conversation.
FRAN LEBOWITZ, *Social Studies*

It's not pining, it's passed on. This parrot is no more. It has ceased to be. It's expired and gone to meet its maker. This is a late parrot. It's a stiff. Bereft of life, it rests in peace. If you hadn't nailed it to the perch, it would be pushing up the daisies. It's rung down the curtain and joined the choir invisible. This is an ex-parrot.   MR PRALINE (JOHN CLEESE), *Monty Python's Flying Circus*

Philosophy

[I recall] the philosophical attitude of a flamingo I once saw standing in a crocodile pool on one leg. Because it only had one leg. One more bite and it would be a duck.   NANCY BANKS-SMITH

Philosophy is a route of many roads leading from nowhere to nothing.
— AMBROSE BIERCE, *The Devil's Dictionary*

All are lunatics, but he who can analyse his delusions is called a philosopher.
AMBROSE BIERCE

Philosophy is common sense in a dress suit.   OLIVER S. BRASTON

Frisbeetarianism is the philosophy that when you die, your soul goes up on a roof and gets stuck.   GEORGE CARLIN

'What would Jesus do?' may be a good philosophy of life for some, but I find that it rarely helps me decide how much to tip a hooker.

CHARLES GULLEDGE

There is only one thing a philosopher can be relied upon to do, and that is to contradict other philosophers.
WILLIAM JAMES

Photography

Even as you read these words, white-coated laboratory geeks are working on a revolutionary new camera that will not only focus automatically, set the exposure automatically, flash automatically, and advance the film automatically, but will also automatically refuse to take stupid pictures, such as the wing out the airplane window.
DAVE BARRY

There is nothing more miserable in the world than to arrive in paradise and look like your passport photo.
ERMA BOMBECK

My photographs do me an injustice. They look just like me.

PHYLLIS DILLER

If you find yourself in a situation where you could either save a drowning man, or you could take a Pulitzer prize winning photograph of him drowning, what shutter speed and setting would you use?
PAUL HARVEY

One time a guy handed me a picture of himself and said, 'Here's a picture of me when I was younger.' Every picture of you is of when you were younger. 'Here's a picture of me when I am older. Hey, how'd you pull that off . . . ?'
MITCH HEDBERG

I don't have a photograph, but you can have my footprints. They're upstairs in my socks.
GROUCHO MARX

Physique

I have the body of an 18-year-old. I keep it in the fridge.
SPIKE MILLIGAN

In three movies I was overweight. And they all made 100 million, so I knew people weren't coming to see my body.
JOHN TRAVOLTA

Piano

The music teacher came twice each week to bridge the awful gap between Dorothy and Chopin.
GEORGE ADE

The neighbours love it when I play the piano. They break my window to hear me better.

LES DAWSON

I used to be a great classical player but I let that slip. Sometimes I play the piano live but then I can't sing. It's like rubbing your stomach and head at the same time.

DIDO

(*of Phyllis Diller*) When she started to play, Steinway himself came down personally and rubbed his name off the piano.

BOB HOPE

Do you know that the piano is America's most popular instrument? That is, of course, if you don't count the vibrator.

JOAN RIVERS

The notes I handle no better than many pianists. But the pauses between the notes – ah, that is where the art resides.

ARTUR SCHNABEL

(*advice to a fellow pianist*) When a piece gets difficult, make faces.

ARTUR SCHNABEL

I was playing the piano when an elephant walked past with a tear in his eye. I said, 'Do you recognise the tune?' He said, 'No, I recognise the ivory.'

TIM VINE

Pigs

I am fond of pigs. Dogs look up to us. Cats look down on us. Pigs treat us as equals.

WINSTON CHURCHILL

The pig, if I am not mistaken,
Supplies us sausage, ham, and bacon.
Let others say his heart is big.
I think it stupid of the pig.

OGDEN NASH

Thou shalt not kill. Thou shalt not commit adultery. Don't eat pork. I'm sorry, what was that last one? Don't eat pork. God has spoken. Is that the word of God or is that pigs trying to outsmart everybody?

JON STEWART

Plagiarism

Composers shouldn't think too much – it interferes with their plagiarism.

HOWARD DIETZ

Plagiarists, at least, have the merit of preservation.

BENJAMIN DISRAELI

Immature poets imitate; mature poets steal. T.S. ELIOT

(*on David Frost*) The bubonic plagiarist. JONATHAN MILLER

If you steal from one author, it's plagiarism; if you steal from many, it's research.
WILSON MIZNER

(*of an unnamed author*) The only 'ism' she believes in is plagiarism.
DOROTHY PARKER

Pleasure

You gotta have a swine to show you where the truffles are.
EDWARD ALBEE, *Who's Afraid of Virginia Woolf?*

People seem to enjoy things more when they know a lot of other people have
been left out of the pleasure. RUSSELL BAKER

The only safe pleasure for a parliamentarian is a bag of boiled sweets.
JULIAN CRITCHLEY

Pleasure is the carrot dangled to lead the ass to market – or the precipice.
ROBINSON JEFFERS

Do not bite at the bait of pleasure till you know there is no hook beneath it.
THOMAS JEFFERSON

The way I see it, if you want the rainbow, you gotta put up with the rain.
DOLLY PARTON

I'll tell you what I love doing more than anything: trying to pack myself into a
small suitcase. I can hardly contain myself. TIM VINE

All the things I really like to do are either illegal, immoral or fattening.
ALEXANDER WOOLLCOTT

Poetry

Anticipating that most poetry will be worse than carrying heavy luggage through
O'Hare Airport, the public, to its loss, reads very little of it.
RUSSELL BAKER

I gave up on new poetry myself thirty years ago when most of it began to read like coded messages passing between lonely aliens in a hostile world.

RUSSELL BAKER

Baldrick, I'd rather French-kiss a skunk than listen to your poetry.

EDMUND BLACKADDER (ROWAN ATKINSON), *Blackadder*

I recently bought a book of free verse — for twelve dollars.

GEORGE CARLIN

Roses are red,
Violets are blue.
I'm schizophrenic
And so am I.

BILLY CONNOLLY

Writing free verse is like playing tennis with the net down.

ROBERT FROST

Poetry is what gets lost in translation.

ROBERT FROST

If there's no money in poetry, neither is there poetry in money.

ROBERT GRAVES

Ordering a man to write a poem is like commanding a pregnant woman to give birth to a red-headed child.

CARL SANDBURG

Poetry is like fish: if it's fresh, it's good; if it's stale, it's bad; and if you're not certain, try it on the cat.

OSBERT SITWELL

Poetry is to prose as dancing is to walking.

JOHN WAIN

Poets

Never trust a poet who can drive. Never trust a poet at the wheel. If he *can* drive, distrust the poems.

MARTIN AMIS, *The Information*

(*on Russian poet Yevgeny Yevtushenko*) An ego that can crack crystal at a distance of twenty feet.

JOHN CHEEVER

If it were thought that anything I wrote was influenced by Robert Frost I would take that particular work of mine, shred it and flush it down the toilet, hoping not to clog the pipes.

JAMES DICKEY

(*on Sylvia Plath*) I see her as a kind of Hammer Films poet. PHILIP LARKIN

Walt Whitman laid end to end words never seen in each other's company before outside of a dictionary. DAVID LODGE

(*on William Wordsworth*) An old, half-witted sheep which bleats articulate monotony. JAMES KENNETH STEPHEN

Nobody knows a poet is alive until he's dead.

Police

It says Scotland Yard are looking for a very small man with one eye. If he's that small, you'd think they'd use both eyes.
ARKWRIGHT (RONNIE BARKER), *Open All Hours*

I never came across a situation so dismal that a policeman couldn't make it worse. BRENDAN BEHAN

A Beverly Hills cop pulled me over because my left speaker was out.
RICHARD BELZER

Paddy was put in a line-up at the police station on an assault charge. When the woman who had been attacked was led in, he shouted: 'That's her!'
FRANK CARSON

Wilma, I promise you; whatever scum did this, not one man on this force will rest one minute until he's behind bars. Now, let's grab a bite to eat.
LT. FRANK DREBIN (LESLIE NIELSEN), *The Naked Gun*

After spending last night in jail, I came to the conclusion that the guy who coined the phrase 'cop a feel' never tried it on a real cop.
CHARLES GULLEDGE

Detectives are only policemen with smaller feet.
CHARLOTTE INWOOD (MARLENE DIETRICH), *Stage Fright*

A recent police study found that you're much more likely to get shot by a fat cop if you run. DENNIS MILLER

Policemen are numbered in case they get lost.
SPIKE MILLIGAN, *The Last Goon Show Of All*

Are you going to come quietly or do I have to use ear-plugs?
SPIKE MILLIGAN, *The Goon Show*

Thieves broke into a local police station and stole all of the toilets. The police say they have nothing to go on.
The Two Ronnies

Meanwhile the search for the man who terrorises nudist camps with a bacon slicer goes on. Inspector Jones had a tip-off this morning, but hopes to be back on duty tomorrow.
The Two Ronnies

Perhaps the crime situation would be improved if we could get more cops off television and onto the streets.
BILL VAUGHAN

Political insults

[Charles] Sumner's mind had reached the calm of water which receives and reflects images without absorbing them; it contained nothing but itself.
HENRY ADAMS

(*on Sir Stafford Cripps*) He has a brilliant mind until it is made up.
LADY ASQUITH

(*of David Lloyd George*) He can't see a belt without hitting below it.
MARGOT ASQUITH

(*of Michael Dukakis*) He's the only man I know who could look at the swimsuit issue of *Sports Illustrated* and complain because the bathing suits weren't flame retardant.
JAMES BAKER

(*on SDP leader Dr David Owen*) He has conferred on the practice of vacillation the aura of statesmanship.
KENNETH BAKER

(*on David Lloyd George*) He did not care in which direction the car was travelling, so long as he remained in the driver's seat.
LORD BEAVERBROOK

(*to German MEP Martin Schulz*) Mr Schulz, in Italy they're producing a film on Nazi concentration camps. I would like to suggest you for the role of commandant. You would be perfect.
SILVIO BERLUSCONI

(*of Neville Chamberlain*) The worst thing I can say about democracy is that it has tolerated the right honourable gentleman for four and a half years.
ANEURIN BEVAN

(*of Harold Macmillan*) The Prime Minister has an absolute genius for putting flamboyant labels on empty luggage. ANEURIN BEVAN

(*of Clement Attlee*) He brings to the fierce struggle of politics the tepid enthusiasm of a lazy summer afternoon at a cricket match. ANEURIN BEVAN

(*on Michael Dukakis*) He's the stealth candidate. His campaign jets from place to place, but no issues show up on the radar screen. GEORGE BUSH

As with mosquitoes, horseflies, and most bloodsucking parasites, Kenneth Starr was spawned in stagnant water. JAMES CARVILLE

(*on Ramsay Macdonald*) I remember, when I was a child, being taken to the celebrated Barnum's circus, which contained an exhibition of freaks and monstrosities, but the exhibit on the programme which I most desired to see was the one described as 'The Boneless Wonder'. My parents judged that that spectacle would be too revolting and demoralising for my youthful eyes, and I have waited fifty years to see the boneless wonder sitting on the Treasury Bench. WINSTON CHURCHILL

(*on Woodrow Wilson*) The spacious philanthropy which he exhaled upon Europe stopped quite sharply at the coasts of his own country. WINSTON CHURCHILL

(*on Stanley Baldwin*) He occasionally stumbles over the truth, but he always hastily picks himself up and hurries on as if nothing had happened. WINSTON CHURCHILL

(*on Sir Stafford Cripps*) He has all of the virtues I dislike and none of the vices I admire. WINSTON CHURCHILL

(*on Clement Attlee*) He is a sheep in sheep's clothing. WINSTON CHURCHILL

(*on Clement Attlee*) A modest little man with much to be modest about. WINSTON CHURCHILL

(*on Charles de Gaulle*) The greatest cross I have to bear is the cross of Lorraine. WINSTON CHURCHILL

(*on Michael Heseltine*) He could not see a parapet without ducking beneath it. JULIAN CRITCHLEY (*on Sir Robert Peel*) The right honourable gentleman is reminiscent of a poker. The only difference is that a poker gives off the occasional signs of warmth.

BENJAMIN DISRAELI

(*on Sir Robert Peel*) The right honourable gentleman's smile is like the silver fittings on a coffin.   BENJAMIN DISRAELI

(*on Lord John Russell*) If a traveller were informed that such a man was Leader of the House of Commons, he might begin to comprehend how the Egyptians worshipped an insect.   BENJAMIN DISRAELI

Disraeli is a self-made man who worships his creator.   JOHN BRIGHT

(*on Edwina Currie*) When she goes to the dentist, he's the one who needs the anaesthetic.   FRANK DOBSON

Walter Mondale has all the charisma of a speed bump.   WILL DURST

(*on Norman Tebbit*) It is not necessary that every time he rises he should give his famous imitation of a semi-house-trained polecat.   MICHAEL FOOT

(*on Senator William Scott of Virginia*) If he were any dumber, he'd be a tree.

BARRY GOLDWATER

(*on Robin Cook*) The Foreign Office is being run like a *Dad's Army* outfit by a Foreign Secretary who combines the pompousness of Captain Mainwaring and the incompetence of Private Pike and the calm of Corporal Jones.

WILLIAM HAGUE

(*on Irish politician Edmund Burke*)
Oft I have wondered that on Irish ground
No poisonous reptiles ever yet were found;
Reveals the secret strands of nature's work,
She'd saved her venom to create a Burke.   WARREN HASTINGS

(*on Malcolm Fraser*) He is the cutlery man of Australian politics. He was born with a silver spoon in his mouth, speaks with a forked tongue, and knifes his colleagues in the back.   BOB HAWKE

(*on Sir Geoffrey Howe*) Being attacked in the House by him is like being savaged by a dead sheep.   DENIS HEALEY

(*on Sir Keith Joseph*) A mixture of Rasputin and Tommy Cooper.

DENIS HEALEY

(*on Neil Kinnock*) The self-appointed king of the gutter.   MICHAEL HESELTINE

(*on fellow legislator Thomas Jefferson Green*) He has all the characteristics of a dog except loyalty.   SAM HOUSTON

(*to Malcolm Fraser*) You look like an Easter Island statue with an arse full of razor blades.   PAUL KEATING

(*on John Howard*) What we have got is a dead carcass, swinging in the breeze, but nobody will cut it down to replace him.   PAUL KEATING

(*on John Howard*) He is the greatest job and investment destroyer since the bubonic plague.   PAUL KEATING

(*on John Dean*) I wouldn't waste the 25 cents to buy the cartridge that would propel the bullet.   G. GORDON LIDDY

(*on David Lloyd George*) This goat-footed bard, this half-human visitor to our age from the hag-ridden magic and enchanted woods of Celtic antiquity.

JOHN MAYNARD KEYNES

(*on President William Taft*) He looked at me as if I was a side dish he hadn't ordered.   RING LARDNER

(*on Lord Birkenhead*) He would sooner keep hot coals in his mouth than a witticism.   ANDREW BONAR

(*on an unnamed politician*) He'll doublecross that bridge when he comes to it.   OSCAR LEVANT

(*on Harold Macmillan*) It was almost impossible to believe he was anything but a down-at-heel actor resting between engagements at the decrepit theatres of minor provincial towns.   BERNARD LEVIN

When they circumcised Herbert Samuel, they threw away the wrong bit.

DAVID LLOYD GEORGE

(*on the contribution to history of Arthur Balfour*) No more than the whiff of scent on a lady's pocket handkerchief.   DAVID LLOYD GEORGE (*on Irish politician Eamon de Valera*) Negotiating with de Valera is like trying to pick up mercury with a fork.   DAVID LLOYD GEORGE

(*on Ramsay Macdonald*) Sufficient conscience to bother him, but not sufficient to keep him straight.   DAVID LLOYD GEORGE

(*on Anthony Eden*) He is forever poised between a cliché and an indiscretion.   HAROLD MACMILLAN

Dick Cheney. If he were any duller he'd be on *Big Brother*. He can explain to George W. the tricky stuff – like how a bill becomes a law. Cheney adds one thing to the Republican ticket: adult supervision.   BILL MAHER

(*of Neil Kinnock*) The chameleon of politics, consistent only in his inconsistency.   JOHN MAJOR

When I arrived at the Environment Ministry in 1997, John Prescott thought that biodiversity was a kind of washing powder.   MICHAEL MEACHER

(*on Grover Cleveland*) He sailed through American history like a steel ship loaded with monoliths of granite.   H.L. MENCKEN

(*on Theodore Roosevelt*) A glorified bouncer engaged eternally in cleaning out bar-rooms.   H.L. MENCKEN

[Harold] Macmillan seemed, in his very person, to embody the national decay he supposed himself to be confuting. He exuded a flavour of moth-balls.   MALCOLM MUGGERIDGE

(*on Clement Attlee*) He reminds me of nothing so much as a dead fish before it has had time to stiffen.   GEORGE ORWELL

(*on Woodrow Wilson*) The air currents of the world never ventilated his mind.   WALTER H. PAGE

(*on Michael Foot*) A kind of walking obituary for the Labour Party.   CHRIS PATTEN

(*on Herbert Hoover*) He wouldn't commit himself to the time from a hatful of watches.   WESTBROOK PEGLER

(*on Labour Party pollster Philip Gould*) All that glitters isn't Gould.   JOHN PRESCOTT

[William] McKinley has no more backbone than a chocolate éclair.

THEODORE ROOSEVELT

(*on John Tyler*) He has been called a mediocre man, but this is unwarranted flattery.

THEODORE ROOSEVELT

When Bob Dole does smile, he looks as if he's just evicted a widow.

MIKE ROYKO

(*on being asked to apologise for calling a fellow MP a liar*) Mr Speaker, I said the honourable member was a liar it is true and I am sorry for it. The honourable member may place the punctuation where he pleases.

RICHARD BRINSLEY SHERIDAN

(*on Woodrow Wilson*) I feel certain that he would not recognise a generous impulse if he met it in the street.

WILLIAM TAFT

(*on Neil Kinnock*) You don't reach Downing Street by pretending you've travelled the road to Damascus when you haven't even left home.

MARGARET THATCHER

(*after Harold Macmillan's Cabinet purge, 1962*) Greater love hath no man than this, that he lay down his friends for his life.

JEREMY THORPE

The real trouble with [Adlai] Stevenson is that he's no better than a regular sissy.

HARRY S. TRUMAN

(*on William F. Buckley*) The Marie Antoinette of American politics.

GORE VIDAL

(*on Michael Howard*) He has something of the night in him.

ANN WIDDECOMBE

(*on Tony Benn*) He immatures with age.

HAROLD WILSON

(*on Harold Macmillan*) The right honourable gentleman has inherited the streak of charlatanry in Disraeli without his vision, and the self-righteousness of Gladstone without his dedication to principle.

HAROLD WILSON

(*on Chester Arthur*) A non-entity with sidewhiskers.

WOODROW WILSON

(*on Governor Hughes's election campaign*) Never murder a man who is committing suicide.

WOODROW WILSON

(*of Irish leader Charles Haughey*) Give him enough rope and he'll hang you.

New Zealand Prime Minister David Lange is the only 16-stone world leader that can be considered a lightweight.

(*on Robert Muldoon*) He is a bull who carries his own china shop with him.

Politicians

Being an MP is the sort of job all working-class parents want for their children – clean, indoors, and no heavy lifting.   DIANE ABBOTT

Jim Hacker (Paul Eddington): Humphrey, do you see it as part of your job to help ministers make fools of themselves?
Sir Humphrey Appleby (Nigel Hawthorne): Well, I never met one that needed any help.   *Yes, Minister*

The politician is an acrobat; he keeps his balance by doing the opposite of what he says.   MAURICE BARRES

If Californians hated Gray Davis so much, why did they elect him governor TWICE? Did Gray have photos of the entire California electorate naked? Can we see them?   DAVE BARRY

Vote for the man who promises least; he'll be the least disappointing.   BERNARD BARUCH

My opponent has a problem. He won't get elected unless things get worse – and things won't get worse unless he's elected.   GEORGE BUSH

An honest politician is one who, when he is bought, will stay bought.   SIMON CAMERON

Everybody said I was the worst Chancellor of the Exchequer that ever was. And I am inclined to agree with them.   WINSTON CHURCHILL

There are no true friends in politics. We are all sharks circling, and waiting, for traces of blood to appear in the water.   ALAN CLARK

Don't vote for politicians. It just encourages them.   BILLY CONNOLLY

A politician is an arse upon which everyone has sat except a man.

E.E. CUMMINGS

You campaign in poetry. You govern in prose.   MARIO CUOMO

Since a politician never believes what he says, he is quite surprised to be taken at his word.   CHARLES DE GAULLE

A politician is a man who can be verbose in fewer words than anybody else.

PETER DE VRIES

(*of Aneurin Bevan*) He was the only man I knew who could make a curse sound like a caress.   MICHAEL FOOT

Politicians are the same the world over: they promise to build a bridge even where there is no river.   NIKITA KHRUSHCHEV

The problem is that many MPs never see the London that exists beyond the wine bars and brothels of Westminster.   KEN LIVINGSTONE

It's useless to hold a person to anything he says while he's in love, drunk, or running for office.   SHIRLEY MacLAINE

Nothing is so abject and so pathetic as a politician who has lost his job, save only a retired stud horse.   H. L. MENCKEN, *Chrestomathy*

The reason there are so few female politicians is that it's too much trouble putting make-up on two faces.   MAUREEN MURPHY

Politicians are wonderful people as long as they stay away from things they don't understand, such as working for a living.   P.J. O'ROURKE

Listen, I'm a politician, which means I'm a cheat and a liar, and when I'm not kissing babies I'm stealing their lollipops. But it also means I keep my options open.   JEFFREY PELT (RICHARD JORDAN), *The Hunt for Red October*

The mistake a lot of politicians make is forgetting they've been appointed and thinking they've been anointed.   CLAUDE D. PEPPER

Politicians who complain about the media are like ships' captains who complain about the sea.   ENOCH POWELL

(*on Clint Eastwood's bid to be elected mayor of Carmel*) What makes him think a middle-aged actor, who's played with a chimp, could have a future in politics?
RONALD REAGAN

(*of Mikhail Gorbachev*) I don't resent his popularity or anything else. Good Lord, I co-starred with Errol Flynn once!
RONALD REAGAN

Politicians are wedded to the truth, but like many other married couples they sometimes live apart.
SAKI, *The Unbearable Bassington*

(*on running for Governor of California*) It was the most difficult decision of my life – except the one in 1978 when I decided to get a bikini wax.
ARNOLD SCHWARZENEGGER

Marge, the reason we have elected officials is so we don't have to think!
HOMER SIMPSON, *The Simpsons*

All politicians have vanity. Some wear it more gently than others.
DAVID STEEL

A politician is a person who approaches every subject with an open mouth.
ADLAI STEVENSON

Ninety-nine per cent of the adults in this country are decent, hard-working, honest Americans. It's the other lousy one per cent that gets all the publicity and gives us a bad name. But then . . . we elected them.
LILY TOMLIN

A statesman is any politician it's considered safe to name a school after.
BILL VAUGHAN

The main essentials of a successful prime minister are sleep and a sense of history.
HAROLD WILSON

Politicians are like nappies. They should be changed regularly and for the same reason.

Politics

(*on leaving his post as Secretary of State*) I will undoubtedly have to seek what is happily known as gainful employment, which I am glad to say does not describe holding public office.
DEAN ACHESON

Politics – the gentle art of getting votes from the poor and campaign funds from the rich, by promising to protect each from the other.

OSCAR AMERINGER

Politics is like boxing – you try to knock out your opponent.   IDI AMIN

The dirty work at political conventions is almost always done in the grim hours between midnight and dawn. Hangmen and politicians work best when the human spirit is at its lowest ebb.   RUSSELL BAKER

We know what happens to people who stay in the middle of the road. They get run over.   ANEURIN BEVAN

I got fed up with all the sex and sleaze and backhanders of rock 'n' roll so I went into politics.   TONY BLAIR

My wife [Cherie] is smarter than me, which is one reason why she chose to go into the law and not politics.   TONY BLAIR

I didn't ride in here on a water-melon cart. I know how it works.

GEORGE BUSH

It would be a great reform in politics if wisdom could be made to spread as easily and as rapidly as folly.   WINSTON CHURCHILL

Politics is not the art of the possible. It consists in choosing between the disastrous and the unpalatable.   J.K. GALBRAITH

The cardinal rule of politics: never get caught in bed with a live man or a dead woman.   LARRY HAGMAN

Politics is show business for ugly people. The women aren't as attractive. The men aren't as handsome. The money is not as good. Being in politics is basically like being in B movies.   JAY LENO

Being in politics is like being a football coach; you have to be smart enough to understand the game, and dumb enough to think it's important.

EUGENE MCCARTHY

I have never found, in a long experience of politics, that criticism is ever inhibited by ignorance.   HAROLD MACMILLAN

Politics is the art of looking for trouble, finding it everywhere, diagnosing it incorrectly and applying the wrong remedy.   GROUCHO MARX

Any party which takes credit for the rain must not be surprised if its opponents blame it for the drought.   DWIGHT D. MORROW

Finishing second in the Olympics gets you silver. Finishing second in politics gets you oblivion.   RICHARD NIXON

Political language is designed to make lies sound truthful and murder respectable, and to give an appearance of solidity to pure wind.   GEORGE ORWELL

Assuming that either the left wing or the right wing gained control of the country, it would probably fly around in circles.   PAT PAULSEN

Politics is the skilled use of blunt objects.   LESTER PEARSON

Politics is just like show business. You have a hell of an opening, coast for a while and then have a hell of a close.   RONALD REAGAN

Politics is supposed to be the second oldest profession. I have come to realise that it bears a very close resemblance to the first.   RONALD REAGAN

If you've got half a mind to go into politics, that's all you'll need.

WILL ROGERS

There is but one way for a newspaperman to look at a politician, and that is down.   FRANK H. SIMONDS

In politics if you want anything said, ask a man. If you want anything done, ask a woman.   MARGARET THATCHER

If you want a friend in Washington, get a dog.   HARRY S. TRUMAN

A week is a long time in politics.   HAROLD WILSON

Pollution

There's so much pollution in the air now that if it weren't for our lungs there'd be no place to put it all.   ROBERT ORBEN

Trees that grow in smoggy cities are needed to make carbon paper.

STEVEN WRIGHT

Polygamy

It is not wrong for a man to marry more than one wife provided he can share out his love equally among his wives.   IDI AMIN

Pop music

I wish I was a pop star,
Colourful and brash,
With me earoles full of crotchets
And me wallet full of cash.   PAM AYRES

Pop music tells you that everything is OK and rock music tells you that it's not, but that you can change it.   BONO

I think popular music in this country is one of the few things in the twentieth century that have made giant strides in reverse.   BING CROSBY

I'm writing Kylie Minogue's biography. It's called Superstar – Jesus Christ!
                                                    BARRY CRYER

The only good thing about the Spice Girls is that you can look at them with the sound turned down.   GEORGE HARRISON

Hear'say are the ugliest band I've ever seen. A boy band or a girl band have got to be good looking. Danny looks like Shrek!   ELTON JOHN

I am the only man who can say he's been in Take That and at least two members of the Spice Girls.   ROBBIE WILLIAMS

(*on Geri Halliwell*) She can't sing, she can't dance, and by the looks of things she can't hold down a meal.   GINA YASHERE

Pope

I admire the Pope. I have a lot of respect for anyone who can tour without an album.   RITA RUDNER

The Pope is single too. You don't hear people saying he has commitment problems.   GARRY SHANDLING.

Popularity

An actor's popularity is fleeting. His success has the life expectancy of a small boy who is about to look into a gas tank with a lighted match.   FRED ALLEN

Frank Burns (Larry Linville): I didn't come here to be liked.
'Radar' O'Reilly (Gary Burghoff): You certainly came to the right place.

M*A*S*H

I am very popular in Eastern Europe. I'm proud to say I was the first Brit to get a Lithuanian Visa. What a bloody useless credit card that was.

ALEXEI SAYLE

Marge, I can't wear a pink shirt to work. Everybody wears white shirts. I'm not popular enough to be different. HOMER SIMPSON, *The Simpsons*

You can spend your whole life trying to be popular but, at the end of the day, the size of the crowd at your funeral will be largely dictated by the weather.

FRANK SKINNER

Pornography

(*on working with actresses he finds unattractive*) You have to work extra hard. This is what makes you a professional porn actor. You have to leave her, go to the bathroom, close your eyes, fantasise and use your right hand. Get a raging boner going and then run back on to the set and yell, 'Roll, shoot! Shoot! Quick while it lasts!' RON JEREMY

My reaction to porno films is as follows: after the first ten minutes, I want to go home and screw. After the first twenty minutes, I never want to screw again as long as I live. ERICA JONG

The difference between pornography and erotica is lighting.

GLORIA LEONARD

I saw my first porno film recently. It was a Jewish porno film – one minute of sex and nine minutes of guilt. JOAN RIVERS

In adolescence, pornography is a substitute for sex whereas in adulthood sex is a substitute for pornography. EDMUND WHITE

Pornography is in the groin of the beholder.

Poverty

Anyone who has ever struggled with poverty knows how extremely expensive it is to be poor. JAMES BALDWIN

Money, as it turned out, was exactly like sex. You thought of nothing else if you didn't have it. JAMES BALDWIN, *Nobody Knows My Name*

I'm as poor as a church mouse that's just had an enormous tax bill on the very day his wife ran off with another mouse, taking all the cheese. EDMUND BLACKADDER (ROWAN ATKINSON), *Blackadder*

We were so poor my mother couldn't afford to have me. The lady next door gave birth to me. MEL BROOKS

Poverty is hereditary – you get it from your children. PHYLLIS DILLER

I used to think I was poor. Then they told me I wasn't poor. I was needy. Then they told me it was self-defeating to think of myself as needy. I was underprivileged. Then they told me that underprivileged was overused. I was disadvantaged. I still don't have a dime. But I have a great vocabulary. JULES FEIFFER

My parents were so poor, they got married for the rice. BOB HOPE

I realise it's a penny here and a penny there, but look at me: I've worked myself up from nothing to a state of extreme poverty. GROUCHO MARX, *Monkey Business*

We were so poor my daddy unplugged the clocks when we went to bed. CHRIS ROCK

Poverty is no disgrace to a man, but it is confoundedly inconvenient. REV. SYDNEY SMITH

There were times when my pants were so thin, I could sit on a dime and know if it was heads or tails. SPENCER TRACY

Power

Anyone who is capable of getting themselves into a position of power should on no account be allowed to do the job. DOUGLAS ADAMS

We still think of a powerful man as a born leader and a powerful woman as an anomaly. MARGARET ATWOOD

Lipstick isn't sexy. Lipstick is power. BARBARA FOLLETT

Being powerful is like being a lady. If you have to tell people you are, you aren't.
MARGARET THATCHER

Women are always attracted to power. I do not think there could ever be a conqueror so bloody that most women would not willingly lie with him in the hope of bearing a son who would be every bit as ferocious as the father.
GORE VIDAL, *Creation*

Prayer

Most of us spend the first six days of each week sowing wild oats, then we go to church on Sunday and pray for a crop failure.   FRED ALLEN

I know I am God because when I pray to him I find I'm talking to myself.
PETER BARNES, *The Ruling Class*

I don't like being interrupted, if I'm praying for something. There's something about putting God on hold . . .   JOAN RIVERS

Dear God, this is Marge Simpson. If you stop this hurricane and save our family, we will be forever grateful and recommend you to all our friends.
MARGE SIMPSON, *The Simpsons*

When we talk to God, we're praying. When God talks to us, we're schizophrenic.
LILY TOMLIN

(*on co-star William Frawley*) Please God, I won't have to climb into bed this week with that square-headed little Irishman!   VIVIAN VANCE

Prayer must never be answered: if it is, it ceases to be prayer and becomes correspondence.   OSCAR WILDE

Pregnancy

You should never say anything to a woman that even remotely suggests you think she's pregnant unless you can see an actual baby emerging from her at that moment.   DAVE BARRY

When I was pregnant, my friends sneered: 'Eating for two, are we?' I said, 'Get lost, I'm not cutting down.'   JO BRAND

Phoebe Buffay (Lisa Kudrow): Being pregnant is tough on your tummy.
Joey Tribbiani (Matt LeBlanc): Hey, but at least you got that cool, pregnant lady glow.
Phoebe: That's sweat. You throw up all morning, you'll have that glow too.

Friends

One advantage of being pregnant, you don't have to worry about getting pregnant.   PETER NICHOLS

If pregnancy were a book they would cut the last two chapters.
RACHEL SAMSTAT (MERYL STREEP), *Heartburn*

Presidency

Over the years the quality of our presidential timber has declined; today we are pretty much satisfied if our president stays out of jail and occasionally emits a complete sentence.   DAVE BARRY

I do not like broccoli and I haven't liked it since I was a little kid. I am President of the United States and I am not going to eat it any more.
GEORGE BUSH

(*accepting an honorary doctorate from Yale University*) To those of you who received honours, awards and distinctions, I say, 'Well done.' And to the 'C' students, I say: 'You too can be President!'   GEORGE W. BUSH

(*on life in the White House*) I don't know whether it's the finest public housing in America or the crown jewel of the federal prison system.   BILL CLINTON

I always figured the American public wanted a solemn ass for President, so I went along with them.   CALVIN COOLIDGE

There is one thing about being President — nobody can tell you when to sit down.   DWIGHT D. EISENHOWER

(*on being elected to the White House*) I guess it proves that in America anyone can be President.   GERALD FORD

(*addressing an audience*) I am Al Gore, and I used to be the next President of the United States of America.   AL GORE

I have performed for twelve Presidents . . . and entertained only six.
BOB HOPE

No man will ever bring out of the Presidency the reputation which carries him into it.
THOMAS JEFFERSON

Mothers all want their sons to grow up to be President, but they don't want them to become politicians in the process.
JOHN F. KENNEDY

(*on the virtues of being President*) The pay is good and I can walk to work.
JOHN F. KENNEDY

Al Gore's new running mate, Joe Lieberman, would be the first Jewish person to serve directly under a President since . . . Monica Lewinsky.
DAVID LETTERMAN

In America any boy may become President, and I suppose it's just one of the risks he takes.
ADLAI STEVENSON

Being a president is like riding a tiger. A man has to keep riding it or be swallowed.
HARRY S. TRUMAN

The vice-presidency is like the last cookie on the plate. Everybody insists he won't take it, but somebody always does.
BILL VAUGHAN

Elvis Presley

Presley sounded like Jayne Mansfield looked – blousy and loud and low.
JULIE BURCHILL

If life was fair, Elvis would be alive and all the impersonators would be dead.
JOHNNY CARSON

In the 1950s Elvis was rebelling against the establishment. In the 1960s he was embraced by the establishment. In the 1970s he *was* the establishment.
JERRY HOPKINS

Elvis was already pretty far gone by the first time I saw him. It made sense when women threw their bras at him. Obviously, he needed them.
TOM KENNY

His kind of music is deplorable, a rancid smelling aphrodisiac.
FRANK SINATRA

Press

If I rescued a child from drowning, the Press would no doubt headline the story: 'Benn Grabs Child'. TONY BENN

I read the newspaper avidly. It is my one form of continuous fiction. ANEURIN BEVAN

(*on newspaper proprietors*) Never pick a fight with people who buy ink by the barrel. BILL CLINTON

(*on the role of the media in soccer*) I've always said there's a place for the Press but they haven't dug it yet. TOMMY DOCHERTY

If I blow my nose, it gets written all over the world. AUDREY HEPBURN

The freedom of the Press works in such a way that there is not much freedom from it. GRACE KELLY

The first thing I saw at the opening of *The Vagina Monologues* was a table with a sign saying, 'Vagina opening. Press.' That's what men need: easy-to-follow instructions. ROB MORSE

If I were to walk on water, the Press would say I'm only doing it because I can't swim. BOB STANFIELD

I'm all for a free Press. It's the newspapers I can't stand. TOM STOPPARD

Pride

One of the best temporary cures for pride and affectation is sea-sickness; a man who wants to vomit never puts on airs. JOSH BILLINGS

Always hold your head up, but be careful to keep your nose at a friendly level. MAX L. FORMAN

Bart Simpson: I am through with working. Working is for chumps.
Homer Simpson: Son, I'm proud of you. I was twice your age before I figured that out. *The Simpsons*

Priests

Dougal, how did you get into the church in the first place? Was it, like, 'collect twelve crisp packets to become a priest?'

FATHER TED CRILLY (DERMOT MORGAN), *Father Ted*

I'm not a fascist. I'm a priest. Fascists dress up in black and tell people what to do, whereas priests . . . more drink!

FATHER TED CRILLY (DERMOT MORGAN), *Father Ted*

My idea of a good Christian is a priest who can speed-read the Mass, not a semi-demented American with a permanent grin.   HARRY ENFIELD

In the Middle East they have armed guards in kindergarten classes to protect the kids. So I guess they have problems with priests there, too.   JAY LENO

A priest in New York City was arrested on gun possession. These days, you better be happy that the bulge in his pocket is a .38.   DAVID LETTERMAN

I finally found out how priests get holy water. They boil the hell out of it.

JOAN RIVERS

Principles

It is easier to fight for one's principles than to live up to them.

ALFRED ADLER

I would rather be an opportunist and float than go to the bottom with my principles around my neck.   STANLEY BALDWIN

Those are my principles. If you don't like them, I have others.

GROUCHO MARX

Oscar [Levant] was a man of principle. He never sponged off anybody he didn't admire.   HARPO MARX

I'm a parent. I haven't got the luxury of principles.

BENJAMIN MARTIN (MEL GIBSON), *The Patriot*

You can't learn too soon that the most useful thing about a principle is that it can always be sacrificed to expediency.   SOMERSET MAUGHAM, *The Circle*

Prison

Mr Barrowclough (Brian Wilde): No, I never get used to bolting these doors, you know. I think of all of you locked in these little cells and I . . . I think of me going out of here and going home to my little house and my wife who's waiting for me . . .

Norman Stanley Fletcher (Ronnie Barker): What's the matter, Mr Barrowclough?

Mr Barrowclough: I sometimes wish I was in here with you lot!

Porridge

If it weren't for my lawyer, I'd still be in prison. It went a lot faster with two people digging. MISTER BOFFO

A jail is just like a nut with a worm in it. The worm can always get out. JOHN DILLINGER

Lennie Godber (Richard Beckinsale): Desire, greed, lust. We're all here for different reasons, aren't we?

Norman Stanley Fletcher (Ronnie Barker): With respect, Godber, we're all here for the same reason — we got caught. *Porridge*

Probably the only place where a man can feel really secure is in a maximum security prison, except for the imminent threat of release.

GERMAINE GREER, *The Female Eunuch*

(*facing the prospect of jail, 1976*) The only thing I really mind about going to prison is the thought of Lord Longford coming to visit me.

RICHARD INGRAMS

Don't threaten me with jail, Blanche, because it's not a threat. With my expenses and my alimony, a prisoner takes home more pay than I do.

OSCAR MADISON (WALTER MATTHAU), *The Odd Couple*

The only difference between me and my fellow actors is that I've spent more time in jail. ROBERT MITCHUM

(*on life in jail*) If this is the way Queen Victoria treats her prisoners, she doesn't deserve to have any. OSCAR WILDE

Problems

I don't have any solution but I certainly admire the problem.

ASHLEIGH BRILLIANT

It's so much easier to suggest solutions when you don't know too much about the problem.
MALCOLM FORBES

No problem is so formidable that you can't walk away from it.
CHARLES SCHULZ

When will I learn? The answer to life's problems aren't at the bottom of a bottle – they're on TV!
HOMER SIMPSON, *The Simpsons*

There are very few problems that cannot be solved by orders ending with 'or die'.
ALASTAIR YOUNG

Procrastination

There's no time like the present for postponing what you don't want to do.
ARTHUR BLOCH, *Murphy's Law*

Procrastination is the art of keeping up with yesterday.
DON MARQUIS

My friend is a procrastinator. He didn't get his birthmark until he was eight years old.
STEVEN WRIGHT

Prodigy

Prodigy: a child who plays the piano when he ought to be in bed.
J.B. MORTON

Professionalism

A professional is a man who can do his job when he doesn't feel like it. An amateur is a man who can't do his job when he does feel like it.
JAMES AGATE

One time a guy pulled a knife on me. I could tell it wasn't a professional job, it had butter on it.
RODNEY DANGERFIELD

Professionals built the *Titanic*; amateurs built the Ark.

Professors

A professor is one who talks in someone else's sleep.
W.H. AUDEN

I have known two professors of Greek who ceased speaking to one another because of divergent views on the pluperfect subjunctive.
STEPHEN LEACOCK

Progress

What we call progress is the exchange of one nuisance for another nuisance.
HAVELOCK ELLIS

Is it progress if a cannibal uses a knife and fork? STANISLAW LEC

Progress in the Foreign Service is either vaginal or rectal. You marry the boss's daughter or you crawl up his bottom.
NICHOLAS MONSARRAT, *Smith and Jones*

Do not confuse motion and progress. A rocking horse keeps moving but does not make any progress. ALFRED A. MONTAPERT

Progress might have been all right once, but it's gone on too long.
OGDEN NASH

You can't say that civilisation doesn't advance, for in every war they kill you a new way. WILL ROGERS

Promiscuity

She bangs like a privy door when the plague's in town.
EDMUND BLACKADDER (ROWAN ATKINSON), *Blackadder*

I think my girlfriend has had sixty-one boyfriends before me, because she calls me her sixty-second lover. RODNEY DANGERFIELD

By the time my friend was eighteen she had sown enough wild oats to make a grain deal with Russia. PHYLLIS DILLER

A nymphomaniac is a woman as obsessed with sex as the average man.
MIGNON MCLAUGHLIN

Everyone probably thinks that I'm a raving nymphomaniac, that I have an insatiable sexual appetite, when the truth is I'd rather read a book.
MADONNA

There are double standards even today. A man can sleep around and nobody asks any questions; a woman, you make nineteen, twenty, mistakes and right away you're a tramp! JOAN RIVERS

I'm not saying she's easy, but she's been in so many motel rooms her nickname is 'Gideon'. JOAN RIVERS

Propaganda

Propaganda is the art of persuading others of what one does not believe oneself.
ABBA EBAN

Propaganda is that branch of lying which often deceives your friends without ever deceiving your enemies.
WALTER LIPPMANN

In Russia we only had two TV channels. Channel One was propaganda. Channel Two consisted of a KGB officer telling you: 'Turn back at once to Channel One.'
YAKOV SMIRNOFF

Proposal

I haven't found men unduly loath to say, 'I love you'; the real trick is to get them to say, 'Will you marry me?'
ILKA CHASE

He proposed on a Valentine's Day, although he didn't do it face to face, he did it in one of the little Valentine bits in the paper. I think he had to pay for it by the word because it just said 'Lee love Dawn, marriage?', which you know I like, because it's not often you get something that's both romantic and thrifty.
DAWN (LUCY DAVIS), *The Office*

I'm afraid I was very much the traditionalist. I went down on one knee and dictated a proposal, which my secretary faxed over straight away.
STEPHEN FRY

Harrison Ford proposed to Calista Flockhart and then slipped the ring around her waist.
DAVID LETTERMAN

Prostitution

You wanna hear my personal opinion on prostitution? If men knew how to do it, they wouldn't have to pay for it.
ROSEANNE BARR

'The best things in life are free': try explaining that to an angry prostitute.
DANIEL BOKOR

What do hookers do on their nights off – type?
ELAYNE BOOSLER

Next time a prostitute solicits your business, ask for the clergymen's rate.
GEORGE CARLIN

Prostitution gives her an opportunity to meet people. It provides fresh air and wholesome exercise, and it keeps her out of trouble.

JOSEPH HELLER, *Catch-22*

(*quoting her doctor*) A few days on your feet and we'll soon have you back in bed.
CHRISTINE KEELER

A new study shows that the more sex you have, the younger you look. Yeah, don't hookers always have that fresh rosy glow?
JAY LENO

On Long Island the vice squad picked up an 81-year-old man for soliciting a prostitute. The undercover lady said, 'Buddy, you've had it,' and he said, 'Fine. How much do I owe you?'
DAVID LETTERMAN

I've made so many movies playing a hooker that they don't pay me in the regular way any more. They leave it on the dresser.
SHIRLEY MACLAINE

A hooker told me she'd do anything for $50. I told her, 'Paint my house.'
HENNY YOUNGMAN

Protest

I've had death threats before . . . well okay, a petition.
JACK DEE

I'm against picketing, but I don't know how to show it.
MITCH HEDBERG

I went down to campaign against the bypass scheme, but I got stuck in traffic.
HARRY HILL

Lisa, if you don't like your job you don't go on strike. You just go in every day and do it really half-assed. That's the American way.
HOMER SIMPSON, *The Simpsons*

The only possible way there'd be an uprising in this country would be if they banned car boot sales and caravanning.
VICTORIA WOOD

Proverbs and sayings

When all is said and done . . . it'll be pretty boring.
LARRY BAUM

Where there's a will there's a won't.
AMBROSE BIERCE

If you can't beat them, arrange to have them beaten.
GEORGE CARLIN

A bird in the hand invariably shits on your wrist.   BILLY CONNOLLY

Beauty is in the eye of the beholder. Get it out with Optrex.

SPIKE MILLIGAN

Brevity is the soul of lingerie.   DOROTHY PARKER

Early to rise and early to bed makes a male healthy and wealthy and dead.
JAMES THURBER, *Fables For Our Time*

Familiarity breeds contempt – and children.   MARK TWAIN

An apple a day keeps the doctor away: an onion a day should take care of everyone else.

Early to bed and early to rise probably indicates unskilled labour.

Birds of a feather flock together . . . then crap on your car.

What goes around . . . usually gets dizzy and falls over.

One good turn gets most of the blanket.

A fool and his money can throw one hell of a party.

The early bird gets the worm, but the second mouse gets the cheese.

Where there's smoke, there's toast.

A proverb is a short sentence based on long experience.

Psychiatry

A drink a day keeps the shrink away.   EDWARD ABBEY

A psychiatrist asks you lots of questions that your wife asks for nothing.
JOEY ADAMS

A psychiatrist is the next man you start talking to after you start talking to yourself.   FRED ALLEN

In Hollywood, everyone goes to a therapist, is a therapist, or is a therapist going to a therapist.   TRUMAN CAPOTE

Woody Allen didn't even buy sheets without talking to his psychiatrist. I know that several sessions went into his switch from polyester-satin to cotton.

MIA FARROW

A psychiatrist is suing Mike Tyson for $45,000 in unpaid bills. I'm with Mike on this one. If ever a guy deserved a refund on psychiatry bills, it's Mike Tyson.

JAY LENO

Psychiatry enables us to correct our faults by confessing our parents' shortcomings.

LAURENCE J. PETER

Other people have analysis. I have Utah.

ROBERT REDFORD

A psychiatrist is a man who goes to the Folies Bergères and looks at the audience.

MERVYN STOCKWOOD

Prosecuting Attorney (John Larch): Doctor, can you give the court your impression of Mr Striker?
Dr Stone (John Vernon): I'm sorry, I don't do impressions, my training is in psychiatry.

Airplane II: The Sequel

Psychology

Experiments with laboratory rats have shown that, if one psychologist in the room laughs at something a rat does, all of the other psychologists in the room will laugh equally.

GARRISON KEILLOR

Publicity

A telescope will magnify a star a thousand times, but a good press agent can do even better.

FRED ALLEN

Live by publicity, you'll probably die by publicity.

RUSSELL BAKER

All publicity is good, except an obituary notice.

BRENDAN BEHAN

Some are born great, some achieve greatness, and some hire public relations officers.

DANIEL J. BOORSTIN

A dozen press agents working overtime can do terrible things to the human spirit.

CECIL B. DE MILLE

(after Dwight Eisenhower's death prevented her from appearing on the front cover of Newsweek*)* Fourteen heart attacks and he had to die in my week.

JANIS JOPLIN

Don't pay any attention to what they write about you. Just measure it in inches.

ANDY WARHOL

Publishing

As repressed sadists are supposed to become policemen or butchers, so those with an irrational fear of life become publishers. CYRIL CONNOLLY

Seventeen publishers rejected the manuscript, at which time we knew we had something pretty hot. KINKY FRIEDMAN

Punishment

Tired mothers find that spanking takes less time than reasoning and penetrates sooner to the seat of the memory. WILL DURANT

If a child shows himself incorrigible, he should be decently and quietly beheaded at the age of twelve. DON MARQUIS

(on corporal punishment) I'm all for bringing back the birch, but only between consenting adults. GORE VIDAL

I told my father I was punished in school because I didn't know where the Azores where. He told me to remember where I put things in future.

HENNY YOUNGMAN

Puns

Hanging is too good for a man who makes puns; he should be drawn and quoted.

FRED ALLEN

A pun is a pistol let off in the ear; not a feather to tickle the intellect.

CHARLES LAMB, *Last Essays of Elia*

A pun is the lowest form of humour . . . when you don't think of it first.

OSCAR LEVANT

Puritanism

Puritanism is the haunting fear that someone, somewhere, may be happy.

H.L. MENCKEN, *Chrestomathy*

Put-downs

(*on columnist Joyce Haber*) She needs open-heart surgery, and they should go in through her feet. JULIE ANDREWS

Roseanne [Barr] went on *Saturday Night Live* and said I had a three-inch penis. Well, even a 747 looks small if it's landing in the Grand Canyon.

TOM ARNOLD

(*to Tennessee Williams after seeing the film of* Orpheus Descending) Darling, they've absolutely ruined your perfectly dreadful play. TALLULAH BANKHEAD

(*to a young actress*) If you really want to help the American theatre darling, be an audience. TALLULAH BANKHEAD

Of course we all know that [William] Morris was a wonderful all-round man, but the act of walking round him has always tired me. MAX BEERBOHM

(*on Arianna Stassinopoulos*) So boring you fall asleep halfway through her name.

ALAN BENNETT

(*on Vanilla Ice*) He was the Pat Boone of rap. JELLO BIAFRA

(*to Anne Robinson*) You're really quite attractive, Anne – in a Mr Burns from *The Simpsons* kind of way. MATT BLAIZE

(*on Camille Paglia*) The 'g' is silent – the only thing about her that is.

JULIE BURCHILL

She doesn't need a steak knife. Rona [Barrett] cuts her food with her tongue.

JOHNNY CARSON

(*on Liberace*) A deadly, winking, sniggering, snuggling, chromium-plated, scent-impregnated, luminous, quivering, giggling, mincing heap of mother love.

CASSANDRA

(*on George Orwell*) He would not blow his nose without moralizing on conditions in the handkerchief industry. CYRIL CONNOLLY

(*to Claudette Colbert*) I'd wring your neck – if you had one. NOËL COWARD

(*on Jeanette MacDonald and Nelson Eddy*) An affair between a mad rocking-horse and a rawhide suitcase. NOËL COWARD

Alexander Woollcott, in a rage, has all the tenderness and restraint of a newly caged cobra. NOËL COWARD

(*on playwright Alfred Lunt*) He has his head in the clouds and his feet in the box office. NOËL COWARD

(*on Randolph Churchill*) He's utterly unspoiled by failure. NOËL COWARD

(*on Clare Boothe Luce*) No woman of her time has gone further with less mental equipment. CLIFTON FADIMAN

(*on Desi Amaz*) The Cuban heel. WILLIAM FRAWLEY

(*on an unnamed victim*) He has left his body to science, – and science is contesting the will. DAVID FROST

Why don't you do the world a favour? Pull your lip over your head and swallow. MAX GOLDMAN (WALTER MATTHAU), *Grumpier Old Men*

(*on the Association of American States*) They couldn't pour piss out of a shoe if the instructions were written on the heel. LYNDON B. JOHNSON

(*on Herman Mankiewicz*) To know him was to like him; not to know him was to love him. BERT KALMAR

(*on an unnamed adversary*) He uses statistics as a drunkard uses a lamppost – for support rather than illumination. ANDREW LANG

The trouble with Ian [Fleming] is that he gets off with women because he can't get on with them. ROSAMOND LEHMANN

(*on Phyllis Diller*) I treasure every moment that I do not see her. OSCAR LEVANT

When I can't sleep, I read a book by Steve Allen. OSCAR LEVANT

(*to George Gershwin*) Play us a medley of your hit. OSCAR LEVANT

(*on Lillian Hellman*) Every word she writes is a lie, including 'and' and 'the'. MARY McCARTHY

(*on Eleanor Roosevelt*) She's upstairs filing her teeth. GROUCHO MARX (*to an unnamed acquaintance*) I never forget a face, but in your case I'll be glad to make an exception. GROUCHO MARX

(*to an unnamed host*) I've had a wonderful evening, but this wasn't it. GROUCHO MARX

Mark Thatcher got lost in the desert and his mum cried. Then everyone cried when they found him. PAUL MERTON

(*to Angus Deayton*) You must have some talent locked up in that body of yours. It can't be reading out loud and that's it, surely! PAUL MERTON, *Have I Got News For You*

Quite frankly, I've never understood what Mick Jagger saw in that bucktoothed Texas nag. There are a thousand home-grown Texas drag queens who could do Jerry Hall better than she does herself. CAMILLE PAGLIA

(*of Drew Barrymore*) She's like an apple turnover that got crushed in a grocery bag on a hot day. CAMILLE PAGLIA

(*on hearing that Clare Boothe Luce was kind to her inferiors*) Wherever does she find them? DOROTHY PARKER

(*on a rival*) I know she's outspoken, but by whom? DOROTHY PARKER

If a swamp alligator could talk, it would sound like Tennessee Williams. REX REED

Olivia Newton-John is Australia's gifts to insomniacs. It's nothing but the blonde singing the bland. MINNIE RIPERTON

Boy George is all England needs – another queen who can't dress. JOAN RIVERS

Joan Collins has had so many men, she is known in the States as the British Open. JOAN RIVERS

(*on Marie Osmond*) She is so pure even Moses couldn't part her knees. JOAN RIVERS

(*on Yoko Ono*) If I found her floating in my pool, I'd punish my dog. JOAN RIVERS (*on Johnny Carson*) He's an anaesthetist – Prince Valium.   MORT SAHL

[George] Bernard Shaw has discovered himself, and gave ungrudgingly of his discovery to the world.   · SAKI

(*on Ralph Waldo Emerson*) Waldo is one of those people who would be enormously improved by death.   SAKI

(*on David Blaine's 2003 London stunt*) I am 100 per cent behind David Blaine in his 44-day exercise in shameless exhibitionism, pointless fasting and all-round freakish showmanship.   WILL SELF

(*on Will Rogers*) This bosom friend of senators and congressmen was about as daring as an early Shirley Temple movie.   JAMES THURBER

(*on empire-builder Cecil Rhodes*) I admire him, I freely confess it. And when his time comes I shall buy a piece of the rope for a keepsake.

MARK TWAIN

(*on Malcolm Muggeridge*) A garden gnome expelled from Eden.

KENNETH TYNAN

(*on Truman Capote*) A Republican housewife from Kansas with all the prejudices.   GORE VIDAL

(*on an unnamed adversary*) His mother should have thrown him away and kept the stork.   MAE WEST

The gods bestowed on Max [Beerbohm] the gift of perpetual old age.

OSCAR WILDE

Frank Harris is invited to all of the great houses in England – once.

OSCAR WILDE

I always said little Truman [Capote] had a voice so high it could only be detected by a bat.   TENNESSEE WILLIAMS

(*on Oscar Levant*) A tortured man who sprayed his loathing on anyone within range.   SHELLEY WINTERS

(*on artist Dorothy Todd*) She is like a slug with a bleeding gash for a mouth.

VIRGINIA WOOLF

There is absolutely nothing wrong with Oscar Levant that a miracle cannot fix.
ALEXANDER WOOLLCOTT

(*on Mrs Patrick Campbell in Hollywood*) What enchanted me was her unwavering and ingenious rudeness to everyone there who could possibly have been of assistance to her . . . Her failure to be politic took on the proportions of a magnificent gesture. She was like a sinking ship firing on the rescuers.
ALEXANDER WOOLLCOTT

(*on Dorothy Parker*) A combination of Little Nell and Lady Macbeth.
ALEXANDER WOOLLCOTT

(*on Barbara Walters*) A hyena in syrup.
YEVGENY YEVTUSHENKO

Before they made S.J. Perelman they broke the mould.

Puzzles

If crime fighters fight crime and fire fighters fight fire, what do freedom fighters fight?
GEORGE CARLIN

If someone with multiple personalities threatens to kill himself, is it considered a hostage situation?
GEORGE CARLIN

If the cops arrest a mime, do they tell him he has the right to remain silent?
GEORGE CARLIN

Why don't sheep shrink when it rains?
GEORGE CARLIN

When you're sick, why does it always contain bits of tomato and diced carrot? I don't even eat diced carrot!
BILLY CONNOLLY

I'm desperately trying to figure out why kamikaze pilots wear helmets.
DAVE EDISON

Occasional tables. What are they the rest of the time?
HARRY HILL

If toast always lands butter-side down and cats always land on their feet, what happens if you strap toast on the back of a cat and drop it?
STEVEN WRIGHT

Why do people pay to go up tall buildings and then put money in binoculars to look at things on the ground?

If time heals all wounds, how come the belly button stays the same?

Why do people say they slept like a baby when babies wake up every two hours?

Why is it that night falls but day breaks?

If quizzes are quizzical, what are tests?

Why do they have the back pain medicine on the bottom shelf at the pharmacy?

If carrots are so good for the eyes, how come I see so many dead rabbits on the highway?

If corn oil is made from corn, and vegetable oil is made from vegetables, then what is baby oil made from?

Why do they call it a one-night stand when you're horizontal most of the time?

Why do they sterilise needles for lethal injections?

Why is there an expiry date on sour cream containers?

Why isn't the word 'phonetically' spelled with an 'f'?

Why is there only one Monopolies Commission?

Why is it considered necessary to nail down the lid of a coffin?

Why do you have to put your two cents in, but it's only a penny for your thoughts? Where's that extra penny going to?

Q

Dan Quayle

If life were fair, Dan Quayle would be making a living asking, 'Do you want fries with that?'
                                                        JOHN CLEESE

Dan Quayle is more stupid than Ronald Reagan put together.
                                                        MATT GROENING

He looks like Robert Redford's retarded brother that they kept in the attic, and he got out somehow.

Questions

If there are no stupid questions, then what kind of questions do stupid people ask? Do they get smart just in time to ask questions?   Scott Adams

I hate people who say: 'Can I ask you a question?' They don't really give you a choice.   Billy Connolly

There's nothing quite as exciting as a first date. You're both so full of questions. What's your favourite food? Do you have brothers or sisters? If you came back as an animal, what sort of animal would you be?
Daphne Moon (Jane Leeves), *Frasier*

Rose Nylund (Betty White): Can I ask a dumb question?
Dorothy Zbomak (Bea Arthur): Like no one else.   *The Golden Girls*

There aren't any embarrassing questions – only embarrassing answers.
Carl Rowan

Do I know what rhetorical means?   Homer Simpson, *The Simpsons*

Archie Bunker (Carroll O'Connor): Can't you ask me an intelligent question?
Mike Stivic (Rob Reiner): I didn't want to confuse you.   *All in the Family*

It is better to know some of the questions than all of the answers.
James Thurber

The man who sees both sides of a question is a man who sees absolutely nothing at all.   Oscar Wilde

Quotation

The surest way to make a monkey out of a man is to quote him.
Robert Benchley

I improve on misquotation.   Cary Grant

I often quote myself. It adds spice to my conversation.
George Bernard Shaw

R

Race

Very few blacks will take up golf until the requirement for plaid pants is dropped.
FRANKLIN AJAYE

It is a great shock at the age of five or six to find that in a world of Gary Coopers you are the Indian.
JAMES BALDWIN

If I weren't earning $3 million a year to dunk a basketball, most people in the street would run in the other direction if they saw me coming.
CHARLES BARKLEY

You know it's going to hell when the best rapper out there is white and the best golfer is black.
CHARLES BARKLEY

Bernard Manning says things like, 'These black guys, they come over here and shag our women.' And I have to say we're really grateful if you're the alternative, Bernard.
JO BRAND

I wasn't always black . . . There was this freckle, and it got bigger and bigger.
BILL COSBY

Being a star has made it possible for me to get insulted in places where the average Negro could never hope to go and get insulted.
SAMMY DAVIS JR

(before a round of golf, asked what his handicap was) I'm a coloured, one-eyed Jew – do I need anything else?
SAMMY DAVIS JR

Racism is so stupid. There's more than enough reasons to dislike people on an individual basis.
WILL DURST

We should be thankful to lynch mobs. I've got a brother who can run a half-mile faster than any white boy in the world.
DICK GREGORY

When we're unemployed, we're called lazy; when the whites are unemployed, it's called a depression.
JESSE JACKSON

Fifty years ago, forty white men chasing a black man was the Ku Klux Klan. Now it's the U.S. Open golf championship.
BERNARD MANNING

It's better to be black than gay because when you're black you don't have to tell your mother.

CHARLES PIERCE

The key to eating a black and white cookie is you want to get some black and white in each bite. Nothing mixes better than vanilla and chocolate. And yet, still, somehow racial harmony eludes us. If people would only look to the cookie. All our problems would be solved.

JERRY SEINFELD

Reading

I can read a book twice as fast as anybody else. First I read the beginning, and then I read the ending, and then I start in the middle and read toward whichever end I like best.

GRACIE ALLEN

I took a speedy reading course and read *War and Peace* in twenty minutes. It involves Russia.

WOODY ALLEN

As a result of the *Lord of the Rings* movies, more and more children are picking up the original Tolkien books and saying, 'Blimey, a thousand pages, you're having a laugh, I'm not reading that!'

JIMMY CARR

I honestly believe there is absolutely nothing like going to bed with a good book – or a friend who's read one.

PHYLLIS DILLER

I always read the last page of a book first so that if I die before I finish, I will know how it turned out.

NORA EPHRON

Reading is an escape, an education, a delving into the brain of another human being on such an intimate level that every nuance of thought, every snapping of synapse, every slippery desire of the author is laid open before you like, well, a book.

CYNTHIA HEIMEL

I'm trying to read a book on how to relax, but I keep falling asleep.

JIM LOY

Always read something that will make you look good if you die in the middle of it.

P.J. O'ROURKE

There are two motives for reading a book: one, that you enjoy it, the other that you can boast about it.

BERTRAND RUSSELL, *The Conquest of Happiness*

It's a waste of time, like exercise or reading to your kids.

KAREN WALKER (MEGAN MULLALLY), *Will and Grace*

Ronald Reagan

When Ronald Reagan got Alzheimer's disease, how could they tell?

GEORGE CARLIN

Someday our grandchildren will look up at us and say: 'Where were you, Grandma, and what were you doing when you first realised that President Reagan was not playing with a full deck?'

BARBARA EHRENREICH

Ronald Reagan must love poor people because he's creating so many more of them.

EDWARD KENNEDY

I believe that Ronald Reagan can make this country what it once was – an Arctic region covered with ice.

STEVE MARTIN

The battle for the mind of Ronald Reagan was like the trench warfare of World War One: never have so many fought so hard for such barren terrain.

PEGGY NOONAN

Reagan won because he stood against Jimmy Carter. If he'd run unopposed, he would have lost.

MORT SAHL

Washington could not tell a lie; Nixon could not tell the truth; Reagon cannot tell the difference.

MORT SAHL

We've got the kind of president who thinks arms control means some kind of deodorant.

PATRICIA SCHROEDER

Satire is alive and well and living in the White House.

ROBIN WILLIAMS

You'll notice that Nancy Reagan never drinks water when Ronnie speaks.

ROBIN WILLIAMS

Realism

You may be sure that when a man begins to call himself a realist he is preparing to do something that he is secretly ashamed of doing.

SYDNEY HARRIS

The pessimist complains about the wind; the optimist expects it to change and the realist adjusts the sails.

WILLIAM A. WARD

Reality

What I'm above all primarily concerned with is the substance of life, the pith of reality. If I had to sum up my work, I suppose that's it really: I'm taking the pith out of reality.   ALAN BENNETT

I wrestled with reality for thirty-five years, doctor, and I'm happy I finally won out over it.   ELWOOD P. DOWD (JAMES STEWART), *Harvey*

I believe in looking reality straight in the eye and denying it.
                                              GARRISON KEILLOR

Reality is nothing but a collective hunch.   LILY TOMLIN

Reality is just a crutch for people who can't cope with drugs.
                                              ROBIN WILLIAMS

Rednecks

I was born in Alabama, I was raised in Georgia. I'm so Southern I'm related to myself. I have a twelve-year-old daughter. She takes after my daddy. She ought to – she's his.   BRETT BUTLER

A redneck died and left his entire fortune to his beloved wife. She couldn't touch it until she was fourteen.   JEFF FOXWORTHY

You know you're a redneck if you've ever had hot flushes at a cattle auction.
                                              JEFF FOXWORTHY

You know you're a redneck if you think possum is 'the other white meat'.
                                              JEFF FOXWORTHY

You know you're a redneck if you carried a fishing pole into Sea World.
                                              JEFF FOXWORTHY

You know you're a redneck if you had to remove a toothpick for your wedding pictures.   JEFF FOXWORTHY

You know you're a redneck if you use a weedeater in your living room.
                                              JEFF FOXWORTHY

You know you're a redneck if your family tree has no forks.
                                              JEFF FOXWORTHY

If you own a home with wheels on it and several cars without, you just might be a redneck.
JEFF FOXWORTHY

Referees

I never comment on referees and I'm not going to break the habit of a lifetime for that prat.
RON ATKINSON

We don't need referees in basketball, but it gives the white guys something to do.
CHARLES BARKLEY

My wife, who was in the stand, told me that at one stage the entire row in front of her stood up and gave me the V-sign. I asked her what she did and she said she didn't want them to know who she was so she stood up and joined in.
NEIL MIDGLEY

Regrets

A man is not old until regrets take the place of dreams.
JOHN BARRYMORE

Marge, I'm going to miss you so much. And it's not just the sex. It's also the food preparation.
HOMER SIMPSON, *The Simpsons*

My biggest regret is not having married another twelve women before I found my current wife. I would have liked a little more practice.
ANTONY WORRALL THOMPSON

If you do something you'll regret in the morning, sleep till noon.

Reincarnation

If there is reincarnation, I'd like to come back as Warren Beatty's fingertips.
WOODY ALLEN

I think if I had a choice I'd like to come back as a slug because not many people would choose a slug and so I could have the pick of them – maybe even king slug. Also, if I didn't like my new slug life, slugs don't live long so in a couple of weeks I could choose again.
HARRY HILL

(*to Ed Sullivan*) There's absolutely nothing wrong with you that reincarnation won't cure.
JACK E. LEONARD

I don't believe in reincarnation, and I didn't believe in it when I was a hamster.
SHANE RICHIE

I spend money with reckless abandon. Last month I blew $5,000 at a reincarnation. I thought, what the hell, you only live once!   RONNIE SHAKES

Relationships

I'm single by choice. Not my choice.   ORNY ADAMS

The easiest kind of relationship for me is with 10,000 people. The hardest is with one.   JOAN BAEZ

If someone had told me years ago that sharing a sense of humour was so vital to partnerships, I could have avoided a lot of sex!   KATE BECKINSALE

Well, what kind of a relationship do you see us having considering you have your foot so far up my leg that you can count the change in my pocket?
                              CHANDLER BING (MATTHEW PERRY), *Friends*

Maybe men and women aren't from different planets as pop culture would have us believe. Maybe we live a lot closer to each other. Perhaps, dare I even say it, in the same zip code.
            CARRIE BRADSHAW (SARAH JESSICA PARKER), *Sex and the City*

The best way to get rid of cockroaches is to tell them you want a long-term relationship.   JO BRAND

A girl can wait for the right man to come along but in the meantime that still doesn't mean she can't have a wonderful time with all the wrong ones.
                                                                          CHER

I really quite like being single. Except for the bit about not having a man.
                              JANE CHRISTIE (GINA BELLMAN), *Coupling*

If you can't say something bad about a relationship, you shouldn't say anything at all.   GEORGE COSTANZA (JASON ALEXANDER), *Seinfeld*

The war between the sexes is the only one in which both sides regularly sleep with the enemy.   QUENTIN CRISP

There are two dilemmas that rattle the human skull: how do you hang on to someone who won't stay? And how do you get rid of someone who won't go?
                      GAVIN D'AMATO (DANNY DEVITO), *The War of the Roses*

Most women set out to try to change a man, and when they have changed him they do not like him.　MARLENE DIETRICH

The trouble is, you can't live with men, but then you can't chop them into little pieces and boil the flesh off their bones because that would be cooking.　JENNY ECLAIR

Relationships are hard. It's like a full-time job, and we should treat it like one. If your boyfriend or girlfriend wants to leave you, they should give you two weeks' notice. There should be severance pay, and before they leave you, they should have to find you a temp.　BOB ETTINGER

Maybe the most you can expect from a relationship that goes bad is to come out of it with a few good songs.　MARIANNE FAITHFULL

Exes should never, never go out with, or marry, other people but should remain celibate to the end of their days in order to provide you with a mental fallback position.　HELEN FIELDING, *Bridget Jones's Diary*

A woman must choose: with a man liked by women, she is not sure; with a man disliked by women, she is not happy.　ANATOLE FRANCE

The only place men want depth in a woman is in her *décolletage*.　ZSA ZSA GABOR

I want a man who's kind and understanding. Is that too much to ask of a millionaire?　ZSA ZSA GABOR

It is a royal pain to read a note from a woman. Even when she's dumping you, she'll put a smiley face at the end of the note.　MATT GROENING

A woman will dress up to: go shopping, water the plants, empty the garbage, answer the phone, read a book, get the mail. A man will dress up for: weddings, funerals.　MATT GROENING

My mother said it was simple to keep a man: you must be a maid in the living room, a cook in the kitchen and a whore in the bedroom. I said I'd hire the other two and take care of the bedroom bit.　JERRY HALL

I don't have a girlfriend. I just have a girl who'd get very mad if she heard me say that.　MITCH HEDBERG

A woman needs a man like a fish needs a net.　CYNTHIA HEIMEL

It's no good pretending that any relationship has a future if your record collections disagree violently or if your favourite films wouldn't even speak to each other if they met at a party.

NICK HORNBY, *High Fidelity*

I know we've only known each other four weeks and three days, but to me it seems like nine weeks and five days.

NAVIN JOHNSON (STEVE MARTIN), *The Jerk*

Maria: You call this a relationship?
Samantha Jones (Kim Cattrall): Well it's tedious and the sex is dwindling so from what I've heard, yes.

Sex and the City

You see a lot of smart guys with dumb women, but you hardly ever see a smart woman with a dumb guy.

ERICA JONG

Personally, I think that if a woman hasn't met the right man by the time she's twenty-four, she may be lucky.

DEBORAH KERR

A misogynist is a man who hates women as much as women hate each other.

H.L. MENCKEN

I just broke up with someone and the last thing she said to me was, 'You'll never find anyone like me again!'I'm thinking, 'I should hope not! If I don't want you, why would I want someone like you?'

DENNIS MILLER

I am always looking for meaningful one-night stands.

DUDLEY MOORE

(*on Lindsey Buckingham*) He and I were about as compatible as a rat and a boa constrictor.

STEVIE NICKS

For three years everything was going great, and then she just upped and left me to find a guy who wouldn't hit her.

JIM NORTON

(*asked to describe the ideal woman for ex-fiancé Ben Affleck*) A stripper with a Budweiser in each hand.

GWYNETH PALTROW

My fiancé and I are having a little disagreement. What I want is a big church wedding with bridesmaids and flowers and a no expense spared reception; and what he wants is to break off our engagement.

SALLY POPLIN

A man leaves a woman for another woman, but a woman leaves a man for herself.

STEFANIE POWERS

A good woman inspires a man; a brilliant woman interests him; a beautiful woman fascinates him; and a sympathetic woman gets him.

HELEN ROWLAND

A man always mistakes a woman's clinging devotion for weakness, until he discovers that it requires the strength of Samson, the patience of Job, and the finesse of Solomon to untwine it.   HELEN ROWLAND

I was always meeting men who didn't want to get involved. I dated my last boyfriend for about two years and finally I just gave him an ultimatum. I said, 'Listen, either you tell me your name or it's over.'   RITA RUDNER

If you've had a relationship with someone and you try to become friends afterwards, it's very difficult. Because you know each other so well it's like two magicians trying to entertain each other. The one goes, 'Look, a rabbit.' The other goes, 'So? . . . I believe this is your card.' 'Look, why don't we just saw each other in half and call it a night?'   JERRY SEINFELD

I broke up with my girlfriend. She moved in with another guy and I draw the line at that.   GARRY SHANDLING

A relationship I think is . . . is like a shark. You know it has to constantly move forward or it dies.   ALVY SINGER (WOODY ALLEN), *Annie Hall*

I can't get a relationship to last longer than it takes to make copies of their tapes.   MARGARET SMITH

A woman without a man is like a fish without a bicycle.   GLORIA STEINEM

When you're in a relationship, it's better to be with somebody who has an affair than with somebody who doesn't flush the toilet.   UMA THURMAN

Why do you have to break up with her? Be a man. Just stop calling.

JOEY TRIBBIANI (MATT LEBLANC), *Friends*

This relationship business is one big waste of time. It is just Mother Nature urging you to breed, breed, breed. Learn from nature. Learn from our friend the spider. Just mate once and then kill him.   RUBY WAX

I miss not having someone to curl up with at night and say hello to in the morning. And having someone to hold your hand while you're being sick. That's always useful!   ROBBIE WILLIAMS

Assumptions are the termites of relationships.   HENRY WINKLER

The only time a woman really succeeds in changing a man is when he's a baby.
                                                        NATALIE WOOD

A man is designed to walk three miles in the rain to phone for help when the car breaks down – and a woman is designed to say, 'You took your time' when he comes back dripping wet.   VICTORIA WOOD

Relativity

When you are courting a nice girl an hour seems like a second. When you sit on a red-hot cinder a second seems like an hour. That's relativity.
                                                        ALBERT EINSTEIN

I heard that in relativity theory, space and time are the same thing. Einstein discovered this when he kept showing up three miles late for his meetings.
                                                        STEVEN WRIGHT

Religion

When a woman gets too old to be attractive to Man, she turns to God.
                                                        HONORÉ DE BALZAC

If there really is a God who created the entire universe with all of its glories, and He decides to deliver a message to humanity, He will not use, as His messenger, a person on cable TV with a bad hairstyle.   DAVE BARRY

People who want to share their religious views with you almost never want you to share yours with them.   DAVE BARRY

The problem with writing about religion is that you run the risk of offending sincerely religious people, and then they come after you with machetes.
                                                        DAVE BARRY

Pound notes are the best religion in the world.   BRENDAN BEHAN

Because I'm Jewish, a lot of people ask why I killed Christ. What can I say? It was an accident. It was one of those parties that got out of hand.
                                                        LENNY BRUCE

The trouble with born-again Christians is that they are an even bigger pain the second time around.   HERB CAEN

I would never want to be a member of a group whose symbol was a guy nailed to two pieces of wood.
GEORGE CARLIN

I was thinking about how people seem to read the Bible a whole lot more as they get older. Then it dawned on me – they're cramming for their final exam.
GEORGE CARLIN

The one story from Sunday School that sticks in my head is the story of the baby Jesus having no crib for a bed. How sad is that? Correct me if I'm wrong but this Joseph guy – he was a carpenter, wasn't he?
BRUCE CLARK

He's not the Messiah, he's a very naughty boy.
MANDY COHEN (TERRY JONES), *Monty Python's Life of Brian*

Faith, to my mind, is a stiffening process, a sort of mental starch, which should be applied as sparingly as possible.
E.M. FORSTER

A lot of Christians wear crosses around their necks. Do you think when Jesus comes back he ever wants to see a cross? It's like going up to Jackie Onassis with a rifle pendant on.
BILL HICKS

What's the point of going to war over religion? You're basically killing each other to see who's got the better imaginary friend.
RICHARD JENI

Give a man a fish, and you'll feed him for a day. Give him a religion, and he'll starve to death while praying for a fish.
TIMOTHY JONES

All religions are the same – basically guilt, with different holidays.
CATHY LADMAN

I'm Catholic, my wife's Jewish, so we had a Quaker marry us. They're the Switzerland of religions.
JOHN LEGUIZAMO

Becoming a Jehovah's Witness is the only known way of stopping Jehovah's Witnesses from knocking on your front door and disturbing you week after week.
VICTOR LEWIS-SMITH

Theology: an effort to explain the unknowable by putting it into the terms of the not worth knowing.
H.L. MENCKEN

We must respect the other fellow's religion, but only in the sense and to the extent that we respect his theory that his wife is beautiful and his children smart.
H.L. MENCKEN, *Notebooks*

Born again? No, I'm not. Excuse me for getting it right the first time.

DENNIS MILLER

Moses was brave, coming down from that mountain and saying to the Israelites, 'I've got him down to ten!'

TOM O'CONNOR

Making fun of born-again Christians is like hunting dairy cows with a high-powered rifle and scope.

P.J. O'ROURKE

I am never molested when travelling alone on trains. There are just a few words I have to say to ensure that I am left alone: 'Are you a born-again Christian?'

RITA RUDNER

Lisa, if the Bible has taught us nothing else, and it hasn't, it's that girls should stick to girls sports, such as hot oil wrestling and foxy boxing and such and such.

HOMER SIMPSON, *The Simpsons*

I thank God I was raised Catholic, so sex will always be dirty.

JOHN WATERS

Why do born-again people so often make you wish they'd never been born the first time?

KATHARINE WHITEHORN

Republicans

I like Republicans, and I would trust them with anything in the world except public office.

ADLAI STEVENSON

You might be a Republican if you came of age in the Sixties and don't remember Bob Dylan.

You might be a Republican if you've ever uttered the phrase, 'Why don't we just bomb the sons of bitches!'

Reputation

Glass, china and reputation are easily cracked and never well mended.

BENJAMIN FRANKLIN

Nothing succeeds like reputation.

JOHN HUSTON

You can't build a reputation on what you intend to do.

LIZ SMITH

I'm the girl who lost her reputation, but never missed it.

MAE WEST

Reputation is character minus what you've been caught doing.

Resignation

Galbraith's law states that anyone who says he won't resign four times, will.

J.K. GALBRAITH

Respect

Maybe, just once, someone will call me 'sir' without adding, 'you're making a scene.'
HOMER SIMPSON, *The Simpsons*

Ally McBeal (Calista Flockhart): I mean, with all due respect, you sort of walk around with uppity breasts, and the hair flips aren't the most subtle. And your perfume – you could be flammable. Now what if somebody shut you down as a safety hazard, how would you feel then?
Elaine Vassal (Jane Krakowaki): That was with all due respect?

ALLY MCBEAL

Restaurants

They say life's what happens when you're busy making other plans. But sometimes in New York, life is what happens when you're waiting for a table.
CARRIE BRADSHAW (SARAH JESSICA PARKER), *Sex and the City*

I never really mind bad service in a restaurant. It makes me feel better about not leaving a tip.
BILL BRYSON

The other night I ate at a real nice family restaurant. Every table had an argument going.
GEORGE CARLIN

In this country we've got 'eat as much as you like' restaurants, whereas in America they've got 'eat as much as you can.' They've added an element of competition. You can be enjoying a delicious meal and also be going for a personal best.
JIMMY CARR

I'd like a petite filet mignon, very lean, not so lean that it lacks flavour, but not so fat that it leaves drippings on the plate, and I don't want it cooked, just lightly seared on either side, pink in the middle, not a true pink but not a mauve either, something in between, bearing in mind the slightest error either way and it's ruined.
NILES CRANE (DAVID HYDE PIERCE), *Frasier*

Tell the cook this is low grade dogfood . . . This steak still has marks from where the jockey was hitting it. AL CZERVIK (RODNEY DANGERFIELD), *Caddyshack*

Nouvelle Cuisine, roughly translated, means: I can't believe I paid $96 and I'm still hungry. MIKE KALIN

If I'm in a restaurant and I'm eating, and someone says, 'Hey, mind if I smoke?' I say, 'Uh, no. Do you mind if I fart?' STEVE MARTIN

Great restaurants are, of course, nothing but mouth-brothels. There is no point going to them if one intends to keep one's belt buckled. FREDERIC RAPHAEL

Is my lamb too pink? A good vet could have this back on its feet again.
STICK (SAMMY JOHNSON), *Spender*

I never eat in a restaurant that's over a hundred feet off the ground and won't stand still. CALVIN TRILLIN

Tell the cook of this restaurant with my compliments that these are the very worst sandwiches in the whole world, and that, when I ask for a watercress sandwich, I do not mean a loaf with a field in the middle of it.
OSCAR WILDE

I went to this restaurant last night that was set up like a big buffet in the shape of an Ouija board. You'd think about what kind of food you want, and the table would move across the floor to it. STEVEN WRIGHT

Retirement

You can only milk a cow so long, then you're left holding the pail.
HANK AARON

(*asked if he was thinking of retiring*) Retire to what? I'm a golfer and a fisherman. There's nothing to retire to. JULIUS BOROS

Retire? I'm going to stay in show business until I'm the only one left.
GEORGE BURNS

Retirement is twice as much husband on half as much money. BETTE MIDLER

Actors don't retire, they just get offered fewer roles. DAVID NIVEN

When men reach their sixties and retire they go to pieces. Women just go on cooking.
GAIL SHEEHY

Revenge

An eye for an eye only leads to more blindness.
MARGARET ATWOOD, (*Cat's Eye*)

What's the matter with revenge? It's the perfect way to get even!
ARCHIE BUNKER (CARROLL O'CONNOR), *All in the Family*

I could crush him like an ant. But it would be too easy. No, revenge is a dish best served cold. I'll bide my time until . . . Oh, what the hell. I'll just crush him like an ant.
MONTGOMERY BURNS, *The Simpsons*

When a man steals your wife there is no better revenge than to let him keep her.
SACHA GUITRY

Nobody ever forgets where he buried the hatchet.
KIN HUBBARD, *Abe Martin's Broadcast*

A woman scorned is a woman who quickly learns her way around a courtroom.
COLETTE MANN

Reviews

Literary
The covers of this book are too far apart.
AMBROSE BIERCE

I regard Danielle Steel's *Message from Nam* as a work without any redeeming social value, unless it can be recycled as a cardboard box.
ELLEN GOODMAN

All the expert help from Earl Mountbatten has not managed to correct Barbara Cartland's apparent belief that Trafalgar came very shortly before Waterloo. Perhaps she has confused English history with the London Underground system.
BERNARD LEVIN

(*on an unnamed book*) This is not a novel to be tossed aside lightly. It should be thrown with great force.
DOROTHY PARKER

(*Ulysses*) The work of a queasy undergraduate scratching his pimples.
VIRGINIA WOOLF

Movie (listed by reviewer)

James Agee

(*Random Harvest*) I would like to recommend this film to those who can stay interested in Ronald Colman's amnesia for two hours and who could with pleasure eat a bowl of Yardley's shaving soap for breakfast.

(*Star Spangled Rhythm*) A variety show including everyone at Paramount who was not overseas, in hiding or out to lunch.

(*Tycoon*) Several tons of dynamite are set off in this picture – none of it under the right people.

(*You Were Meant For Me*) That's what you think.

Nigel Andrews

(*Bonfire of the Vanities*, adapted from Tom Wolfe's novel) Warner Brothers spent $50 million dressing Wolfe in sheep's clothing.

Anon.

In the film version of *Kiss the Boys Goodbye*, the producers have kept the boys and kissed the script goodbye.

(*Bonnie Prince Charlie*) David Niven rallying his hardy Highlanders to his standard in a voice hardly large enough to summon a waiter.

(*Cleopatra*) Elizabeth Taylor is the first Cleopatra to sail down the Nile to Las Vegas.

(*Divorce His, Divorce Hers*) All the joy of standing by at an autopsy.

(*A Bridge Too Far*) A film too long.

(*Stepping Out*, starring Liza Minnelli) Putting on a sad show, courtesy of Liza with a zzzzz.

(*The Devil's Advocate*) Putting Reeves up against Pacino is like throwing wood on a fire to see if it burns.

Lew Ayres

(*Fingers at the Window*) The kind of picture actors do when they need work.

John Barbour

(*At Long Last Love*) If this film were any more of a dog, it would shed.

Rona Barrett

(*Meteor*) How could director Ronald Neame spend almost $17 million and then the best special effect is Sean Connery's toupee?

Laura Baum

(*Heaven's Gate*) A film so dire it deserves to be reviewed in the obituary column.

Leonard Bernstein

(*West Side Story*) Natalie Wood played Maria, the Puerto Rican damsel in *West Side Story*. Natalie lost.

Michael Billington

(*Murder by Death*) Plenty of scene-stealing actors but not many scenes worth stealing.

Alan Brien

(*The Stud*) Watching it is rather like being buried alive in a coffin stuffed with back copies of *Men Only*.

Geoff Brown

(*Watership Down*) All one can say about this animated feature is thank God for myxomatosis.

(*Clash of the Titans*) There's a real possibility some audiences will be turned to stone before Medusa even appears.

Vincent Canby

(Michael Cimino's *Heaven's Gate*) It fails so completely that you might suspect Michael Cimino sold his soul to the devil to obtain the success of *The Deer Hunter*, and the devil has just come around to collect.

Charles Champlin

(*Raise the Titanic*) The mistake was keeping the *Titanic* afloat long after the picture had begun to sink.

Jay Cocks

(*What's Up, Doc?*) Ryan O' Neal is so stiff and clumsy that he can't even manage a part requiring him to be stiff and clumsy.

Richard Combs

(*The Eiger Sanction*) All the villains have been constructed from prefabricated Bond models.

Richard Corliss

(*Titanic*) The regretful verdict here: Dead in the water.

Peter Cox

(*Hook*) Sitting through two hours and twenty minutes is at times like running through treacle wearing flippers.

Judith Crist

(*The Agony and the Ecstasy*) All agony, no ecstasy.

(*The Return of a Man Called Horse*) Maintains a tidy balance between nausea and boredom.

Giovanni Dadomo

(*Let's Get Laid*) Like a George Formby movie with tits.

Frank DeCaro

(*What Women Want*) Who cares?

Jack De Manio

(on Glenda Jackson in *Women in Love*) She has a face to launch a thousand dredgers.

Nigel Floyd

(*Creepshow 2*) The only thing terrifying about *Creepshow 2* is the thought of *Creepshow 3*.

(*Mannequin*, starring Kim Cattrall) A film about, by, and for dummies.

Alan Frank

(*anon horror film*) Only a terror of possible coma kept audiences awake.

Libby Gelman-Waxner (aka Paul Rudnick)

(*Titanic*) James Cameron had to invent a Romeo-and-Juliet-style fictional couple to heat up what was a real-life catastrophe. This seems a tiny bit like giving Anne Frank a wacky best friend, to perk up the attic.

John Gill

(*Silkwood*) Ultimately it's rather akin to making a film about Joan of Arc and concentrating on her period pains.

Benny Green

(*The Return of the Pink Panther*) The first film to be upstaged by its own credit titles.

(*The Incredible Sarah*) A job lot of obligatory Hollywood platitudes strung together with all the skill of Captain Hook trying to thread a needle.

Graham Greene

(*The Tenth Man*) Mr John Lodge continues to suffer from a kind of lockjaw, an inability to move the tight muscles of his mouth, to do anything but glare with the dumbness and glossiness of an injured seal.

(*Nurse Edith Cavell*) Anna Neagle moves rigidly on the set, as if wheels were concealed under the stately skirt: she says her piece with flat dignity and trolleys out again, rather like a mechanical marvel from the World's Fair.

A.P. Herbert

(*The Terror*) The characters speak as if they were dictating important letters.

Clive Hirschorn

(*Footsteps in the Dark*) The footsteps were those of restless patrons on their way to buy popcorn.

Tom Hutchinson

(*Naked Lunch*) This is the movie of the book they said could never be filmed. They were right.

Iain Johnstone

(*The Last Boy Scout*) As interesting as watching stubble grow on Bruce Willis's chin.

Pauline Kael

(*The Sound of Music*) The Sound of Mucus.

Stanley Kauffmann

(*Isadora*) This long but tiny film.

David Lardner

(*Panama Hattie*) This film needs a certain something. Possibly burial.

Caroline A. Lejeune

(*on Charlton Heston's performance as a doctor*) It makes me want to call out, 'Is there an apple in the house?'

(*No Leave No Love*) No Comment.

(*I am a Camera*) Me no leica.

Dwight MacDonald

(*Ben Hur*) Charlton Heston throws all his punches in the first ten minutes (three grimaces and two intonations) so that he has nothing left long before he stumbles to the end, four hours later, and has to react to the crucifixion. (He does make it clear, I must admit, that he disapproves of it.)

Pauline McLeod

(*Hook*) Peter down the pan.

Rod McShane

(*Endless Love*) Endless? It's interminable.

Tom Milne

(*When Time Ran Out*) Disaster movies don't come any more disastrous than this.

(*Blade Runner*) A narrative so lame that it seems in need of a wheelchair.

Mike Nelson

(*The Postman*) According to *The Postman*'s recommendations, if you liked *The Postman*, you'll also like *Demolition Man* and *Sphere*. I don't doubt it. However, if you liked *The Postman*, you might also enjoy a nine-hour flight to Fargo, North Dakota, with a small child kicking your seat the entire way.

Frank Nugent

(*The Buccaneer*) [Fredric] March came in like a lion and went out like a ham.

Rex Reed

(*The Bible*) At a time when religion needs all the help it can get, John Huston may have set its cause back a couple of thousand years.

(*The Chase*) The worst thing that has happened to movies since Lassie played a war veteran with amnesia.

Frank Rich

(*The Hindenberg*) Manages to make one of the century's most sensational real-life catastrophes seem roughly as terrifying as a stubbed toe.

Will Rogers

(*The Ten Commandments*) A fine film up to the point where God finishes and the script writer takes over.

Mort Sahl

(*Ben Hur*) Loved Ben, hated Hur.

Wilfrid Sheed

(*Hurry Sundown*) To criticise it would be like tripping a dwarf.

Joel Siegel

(*Monkeybone*) This is the worst movie I've seen in a year that didn't star John Travolta or Sylvester Stallone.

John Simon

(*Camelot*) This film is the Platonic idea of boredom, roughly comparable to reading a three-volume novel in a language of which one knows only the alphabet.

(*Jonathan Livingstone Seagull*) Seagulls, as the film stresses, subsist on garbage, and, I guess, you are what you eat.

Mark Steyn

(*Parting Shots*) Essentially the equivalent of vanity publishing: a film directed by Michael Winner, produced by Michael Winner, written by Michael Winner, edited by Michael Winner, and made for Michael Winner to watch, perhaps in company with Michael Winner's current girlfriend.

Paul Taylor

(Pink Floyd's *The Wall*) All in all, it's just another flick to appal.

Christopher Tookey

(*The Rookie*) Charlie Sheen shows his usual acting ability and might do well to check which department stores need Santas next year.

(*Desperate Hours*) This film should never have been released, not even on parole.

(*Suburban Commando*) Paul Hogan's timing makes Arnold Schwarzenegger look like Cary Grant.

(*The Mummy Returns*) Depth! Seriousness! Great acting! Plausible plotting! All this and more are utterly absent.

(*Charlie's Angels: Full Throttle*) At last – a movie that makes *Dumb and Dumber* look threateningly intellectual.

(*Gigli*) Now we can see why the Jennifer Lopez–Ben Affleck marriage was called off. It was on grounds of unreasonable cruelty to audiences.

(*Steal*) [Steven] Berkoff once again proves triumphantly that the last three letters of his name are superfluous.

Richard Winnington

(*Pandora and the Flying Dutchman*) This is an Anglo-American production and one of the occasions, I think, when we might be generous and let Hollywood have all the credit.

Stage (listed by reviewer)

Franklin P. Adams

(*on Helen Hayes in Caesar and Cleopatra*) Fallen archness.

Anon.

(*on an unnamed play*) Guido Natzo was natzo guido.

Brooks Atkinson

(*Halfway to Hell*) When Mr Wilbur calls his play *Halfway to Hell* he underestimates the distance.

Tallulah Bankhead

(*Aglavaine and Selsyette*) There is less in this than meets the eye.

Felix Barker

(*on Anthony Hopkins as Macbeth, 1973*) Frequently he gives the impression that he is a Rotarian pork butcher about to tell the stalls a dirty story.

Clive Barnes

(*Oh! Calcutta!*) The sort of show that gives pornography a bad name.

Brendan Behan

(*anon. play*) The play's impact was like the banging together of two damp dish-cloths.

Robert Benchley

(*Perfectly Scandalous*) One of those plays in which all the actors unfortunately enunciated very clearly.

Michael Billington

(Peter O'Toole's *Macbeth*) He delivers every line with a monotonous bark as if addressing an audience of Eskimos who have never heard of Shakespeare.

(revival of *Godspell*) For those who missed it the first time, this is your golden opportunity: you can miss it again.

Heywood Broun

(on Tallulah Bankhead's performance in *The Exciters*) Don't look now, Tallulah, but your show is slipping.

(*anon. play*) It opened at 8.40 sharp and closed at 10.40 dull.

James Mason Brown

(*Antony and Cleopatra*) Tallulah Bankhead barged down the Nile last night as Cleopatra and sank.

Mrs Patrick Campbell

(*on Lillian Gish*) She comes on stage as if she'd been sent for to sew rings on the new curtains.

Michael Coveney

(*anon. play*) The only thing moving about Charlton Heston's performance was his wig.

(*Mr Nobody*) A play about amnesia that is totally forgettable.

Noël Coward

(*anon. play featuring a child actor*) Two things should be cut: the second act and the child's throat.

(*when a horse defecated on stage during a play featuring child actress Bonnie Langford*) If they'd stuffed the child's head up the horse's arse, they would have solved two problems at once.

(on the male nude scenes in *The Changing Room*) I didn't pay £3.50 just to see half a dozen acorns and a chipolata.

(*on Dame Edith Evans*) She took her curtain call as though she had just been unnailed from the cross.

A.E. Matthews ambled his way through the play like a charming retriever who had buried a bone and couldn't quite remember where.

Kyle Crichton

(*Tom Jones*) Good Fielding. No Hit.

Robert Cushman

(Peter O'Toole's *Macbeth*) His performance suggests that he is taking some kind of personal revenge on the play.

W.A. Darlington

(*Rosencrantz and Guildenstern are Dead*) It is the kind of play . . . that one might enjoy more at a second hearing, if only the first time through hadn't left such a strong feeling that once is enough.

Robert Garland

(*Uncle Vanya*) If you were to ask me what *Uncle Vanya* is about, I would say about as much as I can take.

(*Victory Belles*) Must be seen to be depreciated.

Roger Gellert

(*Naked*) Diane Cilento, an attractive but unreal blend of Nefertiti and Sheila Hancock, wages a losing battle to convince us that we ought to care.

William S. Gilbert

(*to an actor who had given a poor performance*) My dear chap! Good isn't the word!

Hubert Griffith

(*Dr Faustus*) Cedric Hardwicke conducted the soul-selling transaction with the thoughtful dignity of a grocer selling a pound of cheese.

Percy Hammond

(*anon. musical*) I have knocked everything in this play except the chorus girls' knees, and there God anticipated me.

Harold Hobson

(*Hamlet*) The best thing about Ian McKellen's Hamlet is his curtain-call.

George S. Kaufman

(*anon. play*) I don't like the play, but then I saw it under adverse conditions – the curtain was up.

(to Howard Dietz on his play *Between the Sheets*) I understand your new play is full of single entendre.

Stewart Klein

(*Break a Leg*) I have seen stronger plots in a cemetery.

Bernard Levin

(*The World of Suzie Wong*) A lot of Chinese junk.

(*Sons of Light*) This play is certainly obscure enough to satisfy the most tenacious holder of the belief that being bored in the theatre is good for you.

Johnny Mercer

(*anon. musical*) I could eat alphabet soup and SHIT better lyrics!

Sheridan Morley

(*Jesus Christ Superstar*) *Jesus Christ Superstar* is by *Godspell* out of *Hair*. In terms of taste it is an unimpeachable as vanilla ice-cream and every bit as bland.

George Jean Nathan

(*Tonight or Never*) Very well then: I say Never.

(on Vincent Price in *Yours, A. Lincoln*) The Price Lincoln, had Booth not taken the job himself, would have been shot on the spot by every dramatic critic present in Ford's theatre on the fateful night.

(*Richard III*) Shakespeare's tragedy was for the most part transformed into something vaguely resembling *Dr Jekyll and Mr Hyde*, without Mr Hyde.

Dorothy Parker

(*Redemption*) It isn't what you might call sunny. I went into the Plymouth Theatre a comparatively young woman and I staggered out of it three hours later, twenty years older, haggard and broken with suffering.

(*anon. play*) If you don't knit, bring a good book.

(*anon. musical*) I know who wrote those lyrics and I know the names of the people in the cast, but I'm not going to tell on them.

The House Beautiful is play lousy.

Frank Rich

(*La Cage aux Folles*) As synthetic and padded as the transvestite's cleavage.

(*Starlight Express*) A confusing jamboree of piercing noise, routine roller-skating, misogyny and Orwellian special effects, *Starlight Express* is the perfect gift for the kid who has everything except parents.

George Bernard Shaw

(*Fedora*) It is greatly to Mrs Patrick Campbell's credit that, bad as the play was, her acting was worse.

John Simon

(*Singing in the Rain*) Like springs, adaptations can only go downhill.

James Thurber

(*anon. play*) It had only one fault. It was kind of lousy.

Kenneth Tynan

(*The Glorious Days*) There was a heated diversion of opinion in the lobbies during the interval but a small conservative majority took the view that it might be as well to remain in the theatre.

(*anon. play*) It contains a number of tunes one goes into the theatre humming.

Irving Wardle

(*What's Got Into You?*) I left the show feeling very keen to get home to the washing up.

Earl Wilson

(*anon. play*) I've seen more excitement at the opening of an umbrella.

Walter Winchell

(*anon. show*) I saw it at a disadvantage – the curtain was up.

Alexander Woollcott

(*anon. play*) The scenery was beautiful, but the actors got in front of it.

Right

Lisa Simpson: Dad, is it all right to take things from people you don't like?
Homer Simpson: Sure it is, honey. You do mean stealing, don't you?
The Simpsons

Always do the right thing. This will gratify some people and astonish the rest.
MARK TWAIN

To be good is noble, but to teach others to be good is nobler – and less trouble.
MARK TWAIN

Risk

Living at risk is jumping off the cliff and building your wings on the way down.
RAY BRADBURY

I believe in getting into hot water. I think it keeps you clean.

G.K. CHESTERTON

Stupid risks make life worth living. HOMER SIMPSON, *The Simpsons*

Rock 'n' roll

After a few boring years, socially meaningful rock 'n' roll died out. It was replaced by disco, which offers no guidance to any form of life more advanced than the lichen family. DAVE BARRY

The hippies wanted peace and love. We wanted Ferraris, blondes and switch-blades. ALICE COOPER

(*on Marilyn Manson*) He has a woman's name and wears make-up. How original! ALICE COOPER

Rock music should be gross, that's the fun of it. It gets up and drops its trousers.

BRUCE DICKINSON

I'm only interested in heavy metal when it's me who's playing it. I suppose it's a bit like smelling your own farts. JOHN ENTWISTLE

(*on Robbie Williams*) A fat dancer from Take That. NOEL GALLAGHER

(*on his band the Grateful Dead*) We're like bad architecture or an old whore. If you stick around long enough, eventually you get respectable.

JERRY GARCIA

Most people get into bands for three very simple rock and roll reasons: to get rich, get famous and get laid. BOB GELDOF

(*on the mid 1950s*) Rock 'n' roll was two pegs below being a prisoner-of-war back then. RONNIE HAWKINS

The whole rock 'n' roll thing is pretty over-rated. Take away the drugs and the drink, and what's left? CHRISSIE HYNDE

A typical day in the life of a heavy metal musician consists of a round of golf and an AA meeting. BILLY JOEL

(*on the relationship between Gwyneth Paltrow and Coldplay's Chris Martin*) Chris Martin was a virgin ten minutes ago. Now he's banging Hollywood superstars.
KELLY JONES

Aerosmith were inducted into the Rock and Roll Hall of Fame for their uncanny ability to do the same song seven times with no one noticing.
CRAIG KILBORN

I believe my music is the healing music. I believe my music can make the blind see, the lame walk, the deaf and dumb hear and talk, because it inspires and uplifts people. It regenerates the ears, makes the liver quiver, the bladder splatter, and the knees freeze.
LITTLE RICHARD

(*on Grace Slick*) She's like somebody's mum who'd a few too many drinks at a cocktail party.
NICK LOWE

Groups like Genesis and Yes are about as exciting as used Kleenex.
NICK LOWE

(*on Billy Idol*) The Perry Como of punk.
JOHN LYDON

(*attending a Ramones concert*) For me it was like I was an old car and I was being taken out for a ride at 100mph; and I kind of liked it because I was really getting rid of a lot of rust.
NORMAN MAILER

(*on Billy Idol*) Is he just doing a bad Elvis pout, or was he born that way?
FREDDIE MERCURY

I heard guys say they got into rock and roll to pick up women. I didn't get into rock to pick up women, but I sure adapted!
TED NUGENT

I don't really follow what's going on in music. It's like if you work in a garage – you don't go home and fix your car.
OZZY OSBOURNE

While we [Led Zeppelin] had a reputation as rampaging sexual vandals, the truth is that most of the time we were looking for nothing at bedtime other than a good paperback.
ROBERT PLANT

I like writing songs. I like the camaraderie of the band. I like touring. I love playing bass. And then there's free beer.
KEANU REEVES

Duran Duran is as good an example as anybody of what the early Eighties were. Excessive, bright, and full of hope. And not realising that you were gonna get the bill at the end of the decade.   NICK RHODES

To me the most important thing about any musician is, can you walk in a bar and get a free drink with a song?   KEITH RICHARDS

(*on Elton John*) His writing is limited to songs for dead blondes.
                                                KEITH RICHARDS

(*on Chuck Berry*) I love his work but I couldn't warm to him even if I was cremated next to him.   KEITH RICHARDS

Rock and roll is not so much a question of electric guitars as it is striped pants.
                                                DAVID LEE ROTH

We [Bon Jovi] are modern-day cowboys. We ride into town, put on a show, take the money, hit the bar, take the ladies, and we're gone. And we do the same thing the next night in another place.   RICHIE SAMBORA

(*on the challenges of being in an all-girl band, the Go-Go's*) Well, after we've been out on tour together, we all get our periods at the same time, absolutely.
                                                GINA SCHOCK

Real rock 'n' roll is a man's job. I want to see a man up there. I want to see a man's muscles, a man's veins. I don't want to see no chick's tit banging against a bass.   PATTI SMITH

The life of a rock and roll band will last as long as you can look down into the audience and see yourself.   BRUCE SPRINGSTEEN

It's not easy being in a group. It's like marriage without sex. The only lubricant we have is our music.   STING

(*on The Sex Pistols*) They wouldn't recognise the Antichrist even if he hit them in the face with a kipper.   JOE STRUMMER

Remember when you used to watch TV in the Sixties and you'd see Perry Como in a cashmere sweater? That's what rock 'n' roll is becoming. It's your parents' music.   NEIL YOUNG

No change in musical style will survive unless it's accompanied by a change in clothing style. Rock is to dress up to.   FRANK ZAPPA

Jon Bon Jovi sounds like he's got a brick dangling from his willy and a food-mixer making purée of his tonsils.   ANON

The Rolling Stones

They were there at the start and I think they'll be the ones to turn the lights out. 'Ladies and gentlemen, this has been rock 'n' roll. Goodnight.'

MARC ALMOND

I met Mick Jagger when I was playing for Oxford United and the Rolling Stones played a concert there. Little did I know that one day he'd be almost as famous as me.   RON ATKINSON

(*on Mick Jagger*) He moves like a parody between a majorette girl and Fred Astaire.   TRUMAN CAPOTE

Mick Jagger is about as sexy as a pissing toad.   TRUMAN CAPOTE

(*on Keith Richards*) He's pathetic. It's like a monkey with arthritis, trying to go on stage and look young.   ELTON JOHN

Them touring at their age is like Evita going on tour stuffed in that glass case of hers.   LEMMY

At the Grammy Awards, Keith Richards became the first performer ever to accept a posthumous award in person.   JAY LENO

The Rolling Stones are at Madison Square Garden. I knew they were a little older when they played, 'Hey, You, Get Off Of My Lawn.'   DAVID LETTERMAN

(*on Mick Jagger*) This man has got childbearing lips.   JOAN RIVERS

The last Rolling Stones tour grossed more than the national product of Guyana, and had a worse human rights record.   ALEXEI SAYLE

(*on the death of Brian Jones*) It's an ordinary day for Brian. Like, he died every day, you know.   PETE TOWNSHEND

Romance

The only truly romantic drug is alcohol. There's nothing like rolling your lady over so she won't choke on her own vomit.   DAVE ATTELL

Your idea of romance is popping the can away from my face.

ROSEANNE CONNER (ROSEANNE BARR), *Roseanne*

The romance is dead if he drinks champagne from your slipper and chokes on a Dr Scholl's foot pad.

PHYLLIS DILLER

So I step out of the shower, and I look out the window, and I notice the garbage man looking right in at me. So I say, 'Did you get a good look?' And he says, 'Not completely, turn around.' Then he smiled and he was missing a tooth, and that's when the romance went right out of it.

ROZ DOYLE (PERI GILPIN), *Frasier*

Fifty per cent of America's population spends less than ten dollars a month on romance. You know what we call these people? Men.

JAY LENO

When guys are persistent, it's romantic, they make movies about that. If it's a woman, they cast Glenn Close.

ALLY MCBEAL (CALISTA FLOCKHART), *Ally McBeal*

Some people claim that marriage interferes with romance. There's no doubt about it. Anytime you have a romance, your wife is bound to interfere.

GROUCHO MARX

Mom, romance is dead. It was acquired in a hostile takeover by Hallmark and Disney, homogenized, and sold off piece by piece.

LISA SIMPSON, *The Simpsons*

Romance should never begin with sentiment. It should begin with science and end with a settlement.

OSCAR WILDE

Roots

I was raised in the country, where touching meant you're standing on the same carpet. Any closer and you're engaged.

SCOTT ADAMS

I come from a small town whose population never changed. Each time a woman got pregnant, someone left town.

MICHAEL PRICHARD

Diana Ross

Her desire for fame is like her hair. It keeps getting bigger.   JOHNNY MATHIS

She is a piece of liquorice in shoes. She walks into a pool hall and they chalk her head.

JOAN RIVERS

Diana Ross doesn't think of herself as a Supreme: she thinks she *is* supreme. On the census where it said place of birth, she wrote 'manger'.

JOAN RIVERS

Rowing

The only Oxford and Cambridge Boat Races ever remembered are those in which one side has gratifyingly sunk.   MILES KINGTON, *Miles and Miles*

Rowing seemed to me a monotonous pursuit, and somehow wasteful to be making all that effort to be going in the wrong direction.

PETER USTINOV, Dear Me

Royalty

When I appear in public, people expect me to neigh, grind my teeth, paw the ground and swish my tail – none of which is easy.

ANNE, THE PRINCESS ROYAL

(*of Princess Anne*) A bossy, unattractive, galumphing girl.   CECIL BEATON

George the Third
Ought never to have occurred.
One can only wonder
At so grotesque a blunder.   EDMUND CLERIHEW BENTLEY

The Duke of Edinburgh has perfected the art of saying hello and goodbye in the same handshake.   JENNIE BOND

(*of Diana, Princess of Wales*) She looked on me as an emotional washing machine.

PAUL BURRELL

(*on Prince William*) He has spectacularly lost his looks. He's turned into Princess Anne.   GERMAINE GREER

(*on Prince Philip*) It's like being an ambassador to a country and going, 'Hello! Fuck you all! You're all bastards! I hate you personally. Byeee!'

EDDIE IZZARD

(*on King Edward VIII*) He had hidden shallows.   CLIVE JAMES

I'm prepared to take advice on leisure from Prince Philip. He's a world expert on leisure. He's been practising for most of his adult life.   NEIL KINNOCK

(*on Diana, Princess of Wales*) During her anorexic period, she and Karen Carpenter were the only two famous people whose pictures could fit on to the spine of a CD cover.
VICTOR LEWIS-SMITH

Prince William just turned twenty-one, so he sat Prince Charles down for that talk: 'Why did you cheat on my Mom with a woman who looks like a saddle?'
BILL MAHER

I have as much privacy as a goldfish in a bowl.
PRINCESS MARGARET

(*on Anne, the Princess Royal*) Such an active lass. So outdoorsy. She loves nature in spite of what it did to her.
BETTE MIDLER

(*on Princess Margaret*) She looked like a huge ball of fur on two well-developed legs.
NANCY MITFORD

(*on George V*) For seventeen years he did nothing at all but kill animals and stick in stamps.
HAROLD NICOLSON

(*of Prince Edward*) One of the chief flag-bearers for the Republican cause.
WILL SELF

(*in Norway*) Your Royals look so good. Ours look like bulldogs.
ROBBIE WILLIAMS

Of course, I do have a slight advantage over the rest of you. It helps in a pinch to be able to remind your bride that you gave up a throne for her.
DUKE OF WINDSOR

Rugby

We've lost seven of our last eight matches. The only team that we have beaten is Western Samoa. It's a good job we didn't play the whole of Samoa!
GARETH DAVIES

I once dated a famous Aussie rugby player who treated me just like a football; made a pass, played footsie, then dropped me as soon as he'd scored.
KATHY LETTE

I enjoy the violence in rugby, except when they start biting each other's ears off.
ELIZABETH TAYLOR

Ruin

There are three roads to ruin: women, gambling and technology. The most pleasant is with women, the quickest is with gambling, but the surest is with technology.
GEORGES POMPIDOU

Rules

As a rule, anything in a binder has very little value, except as building material.
SCOTT ADAMS, *Seven Years of Highly Defective People*

Sacred cows make the best hamburgers.
ABBIE HOFFMAN

The code of the schoolyard, Marge! The rules that teach a boy to be a man. Let's see. Don't tattle. Always make fun of those different from you. Never say anything, unless you're sure everyone feels exactly the same way you do. What else . . .
HOMER SIMPSON, *The Simpsons*

Rumour

Trying to squash a rumour is like trying to unring a bell.
SHANA ALEXANDER

A rumour is one thing that gets thicker instead of thinner as it is spread.
RICHARD ARMOUR

I hate to spread rumours, but what else can one do with them?
AMANDA LEAR

The public will believe anything, so long as it is not founded on truth.
EDITH SITWELL

Russia

I went to Moscow once. It was so cold at night one guy fell out of bed and broke his pyjamas.
BOB HOPE

Everything Reagan does, Gorbachev does one better. Reagan wears the flag of his country on his lapel, Gorby wears the map of his country on his forehead.
BOB HOPE

Before I went to Moscow I knew two things about Lenin. One, it wasn't his real name. Two, he couldn't possibly be forty feet high, as his pictures and statues tended to suggest.
MILES KINGTON

We don't have American Express in Russia, we have Russian Express. Their slogan is 'Don't Leave Home'.   YAKOV SMIRNOFF

The Soviet Union is the only country where the artist is held in such esteem that he is frequently put in prison to prevent him leaving.   PETER USTINOV

The Russians love Brooke Shields because her eyebrows remind them of Leonid Brezhnev.   ROBIN WILLIAMS

S

Safety

The safest place to be during an earthquake would be in a stationery store.
                                                                   GEORGE CARLIN

Sailing

(*on his yachting success*) I have no interest in sailing round the world. Not that there is any lack of requests for me to do so.   EDWARD HEATH

Ocean racing is like standing under a cold shower in a howling gale tearing up ten-pound notes.   EDWARD HEATH

Any man who has to ask about the annual upkeep of a yacht can't afford one.
                                                                J. PIERPONT MORGAN

Salespeople

I went to a bookstore and asked the saleswoman, 'Where's the self-help section?' She said if she told me it would defeat the purpose.   GEORGE CARLIN

I used to impale the heads of door-to-door salespeople on pikes in the garden as a warning to others — until I learned that it's bad Feng Shui.
                                                                     GREG GLYNN

Conan O'Brien: Did you really sell ties at Bloomingdale's?
David Hyde Pierce: No, so they fired me.

God has mercifully withheld from humanity a foreknowledge of what will sell.
                                                                   BERNARD MILES

Santa Claus

Let me see if I've got this Santa business straight. You say he wears a beard, has no discernible source of income and flies to cities all over the world under cover of darkness? You sure this guy isn't laundering illegal drug money?

TOM ARMSTRONG, *Marvin*

I stopped believing in Santa Claus when I was six. Mother took me to see him in a department store and he asked for my autograph.

SHIRLEY TEMPLE BLACK

I never believed in Santa Claus because I knew no white dude would come into my neighbourhood after dark.

DICK GREGORY

Things a Department Store Santa Doesn't Want To Hear From Kids:
Remember me? I'm the kid with the weak bladder.
You smell like supermarket gin.
I want a 2004 Pontiac Aztek.
I'm Jewish.

DAVID LETTERMAN

Scandal

(*reacting to a survey that ranked the Monica Lewinsky scandal as the 53rd most significant story of the century*) What's a man got to do to get in the top fifty?

BILL CLINTON

(*trying to re-establish himself on TV*) When one door closes, another one falls on top of you.

ANGUS DEAYTON

(*on Watergate*) Once the toothpaste is out of the tube, it is awfully hard to get it back in.

H.R. HALDEMAN

School

When I first moved to this country, I was in third grade. And all the other kids in my school were white Americanos. And I noticed that when I went to the urinal to take a leak, my pene was bigger than all the other kids. So I went home to my grandmother and said, 'Abuelita, why is my pene bigger than other kids'? Because I'm Latino?' She said, 'No. Because you're twenty-three.'

FRED ARMISEN

I won't say ours was a tough school, but we had our own coroner.

LENNY BRUCE

I can't understand why I flunked American history. When I was a kid there was so little of it.
GEORGE BURNS

On my first day at school, my parents dropped me off at the wrong nursery. There I was, surrounded by trees and bushes.
KEN DODD

My father wanted me to have all the educational opportunities he never had. So he sent me to a girls' school.
KEN DODD

I quit school in the sixth grade because of pneumonia. Not because I had it, but because I couldn't spell it.
ROCKY GRAZIANO

I was bullied at school, called all kinds of different names. But one day I turned to my bullies and said, 'Sticks and stones may break my bones but names will never hurt me.' And it worked. From then on it was sticks and stones all the way.
HARRY HILL

Show me a man who has enjoyed his schooldays and I'll show you a bully and a bore.
ROBERT MORLEY

In school we had a name for guys trying to get in touch with themselves.
P.J. O'ROURKE

In our school you were searched for guns and knives on the way in and if you didn't have any, they gave you some.
EMO PHILIPS

You can't expect a boy to be depraved until he has been to a good school.
SAKI, *A Baker's Dozen*

The more expensive a school is, the more crooks it has.
J.D. SALINGER, *The Catcher in the Rye*

That's two independent thought alarms in one day. Willie, the children are over-stimulated. Remove all the coloured chalk from the classrooms.
PRINCIPAL SKINNER, *The Simpsons*

I have never let my schooling interfere with my education.
MARK TWAIN

Anyone who has been to an English public school will always feel comparatively at home in prison.
EVELYN WAUGH, *Decline and Fall*

He pursued his studies but never overtook them.
H.G. WELLS

Arnold Schwarzenegger

In his bodybuilding days Arnold Schwarzenegger was known as the Austrian Oak. Then he started acting and was known as . . . the Austrian Oak.

JACK DEE

He has so many muscles he has to make an appointment to move his fingers.

PHYLLIS DILLER

(*on his election as Governor of California*) It's a triumph of grope over experience.

BORIS JOHNSON

A human special effect.

BARRY NORMAN

Apparently Arnold was inspired by President Bush, who proved you can be a successful politician in this country even if English is your second language.

CONAN O'BRIEN

Arnold Schwarzenegger's acted in plenty of movies but spoken less dialogue than any actor except maybe Lassie.

ROBIN WILLIAMS

Science

It's a scientific fact that your body will not absorb cholesterol if you take it from another person's plate.

DAVE BARRY

As an adolescent I aspired to lasting fame, I craved factual certainty, and I thirsted for a meaningful vision of human life – so I became a scientist. This is like becoming an archbishop so you can meet girls.

MATT CARTMILL

I was saying to someone the other day that technically the weight of an object largely relies on its position in the Earth's gravitational tear, to which they replied: 'Look, you haven't won the cake. Please move away from the stall.'

HARRY HILL

Scientists have completed the first human genome map. It's the greatest scientific discovery in history, if you don't count silicone breast implants.

CRAIG KILBORN

Great moments in science: Einstein discovers that time is actually money.

GARY LARSON

Animal testing is a terrible idea; they get all nervous and give the wrong answers.

HUGH LAURIE, *A Bit of Fry and Laurie*

Scientists say the only way to control killer bees is to mate them with milder bees. So if we have a mass murderer, we don't execute him? We fix him up with Marie Osmond?
DAVID LETTERMAN

Enzymes are things invented by biologists that explain things which otherwise require harder thinking.
JEROME LETTVIN

Scientists announced that they have located the gene for alcoholism. They found it at a party, talking way too loud.
CONAN O'BRIEN

Dentopedalogy is the science of opening your mouth and putting your foot in it. I've been practising it for years.
PRINCE PHILIP

If it squirms, it's biology; if it stinks, it's chemistry; if it doesn't work, it's physics; and if you can't understand it, it's mathematics.
MAGNUS PYKE

The scientific theory I like best is that the rings of Saturn are composed entirely of lost airline luggage.
MARK RUSSELL

Science is always wrong. It never solves a problem without creating ten more.
GEORGE BERNARD SHAW

Isn't there any way I can change my DNA, like sitting on the microwave?
LISA SIMPSON, *The Simpsons*

It's a good thing we have gravity, or else when birds died they'd just stay right up there.
STEVEN WRIGHT

Science fiction

Science fiction is no more written for scientists than ghost stories are written for ghosts.
BRIAN ALDISS

If I can't blow up the world in the first ten seconds, then the show is a flop.
IRWIN ALLEN

Scotland and the Scots

There are few more impressive sights in the world than a Scotsman on the make.
J.M. BARRIE, *What Every Woman Knows*

There are two seasons in Scotland. June and winter.
BILLY CONNOLLY

The great thing about Glasgow is that if there's a nuclear attack, it'll look exactly the same afterwards.

BILLY CONNOLLY

Scottish-Americans tell you that if you want to identify tartans, it's easy – you simply look under the kilt. If it's a quarter-pounder, you know it's a McDonald's.

BILLY CONNOLLY

A Scot is a man who keeps the Sabbath, and everything else he can lay his hands on.

CHIC MURRAY

It is never difficult to distinguish between a Scotsman with a grievance and a ray of sunshine.

P.G. WODEHOUSE, *Blandings Castle*

Scouts

A scout troop consists of twelve little kids dressed like schmucks following a big schmuck dressed like a kid.

JACK BENNY

Sealife

Whatever they tell you, the best aphrodisiac for women is eating oysters because if you can swallow oysters, you can swallow anything.

HATTIE HAYRIDGE

A winkle is just a bogey with a crash helmet on.

MICK MILLER

Oysters are horrible – it's like licking phlegm off a tortoise.

FRANK SKINNER

Seasickness

A sure cure for seasickness is to sit under a tree.

SPIKE MILLIGAN

The transatlantic crossing was so rough the only thing I could keep on my stomach was the first mate.

DOROTHY PARKER

Secrecy

Three may keep a secret, if two of them are dead.

BENJAMIN FRANKLIN, *Poor Richard's Almanack*

When it was revealed that magician David Copperfield never had sex with super-model Claudia Schiffer, he said it was because he didn't want to reveal how it's done.

JAY LENO

Jim Hacker (Paul Eddington): Shred it! No one must ever be able to find it again!

Bernard Woolley (Derek Fowlds): In that case Minister, I think it's best that I file it. *Yes, Minister*

Give your love to your wife, but tell your secrets to your mother.

IRISH PROVERB

Seduction

Trying to seduce an audience is the basis of rock and roll. JON BON JOVI

I'm looking for a perfume to overpower men. I'm sick of karate.

PHYLLIS DILLER

I love the lines men use to get us into a bed. 'Please, I'll only put it in for a minute.' What am I, a microwave? BEVERLY MICKENS

Listen, I appreciate this whole seduction scene you got going, but let me give you a tip: I'm a sure thing. VIVIAN WARD (JULIA ROBERTS), *Pretty Woman*

Self-image

It's too bad I'm not as wonderful a person as people say I am, because the world could use a few people like that. ALAN ALDA

I am the astronaut of boxing. Joe Louis and Dempsey were just jet pilots. I'm in a world of my own. MUHAMMAD ALI

I have been described as having a face like a wedding cake left out in the rain.
W. H. AUDEN

I'm as pure as the driven slush. TALLULAH BANKHEAD

You got to believe in yourself. Hell, I believe I'm the best-looking guy in the world and I might be right. CHARLES BARKLEY

I really did look like a baked bean until I was thirteen. BONO

I look like Ann Widdecombe's younger, not so attractive, sister. JO BRAND

I have the eyes of a dead pig. MARLON BRANDO

My face looks like a rock quarry that somebody has dynamited.

CHARLES BRONSON

A spoiled genius from the Welsh gutter, a drinker, a womaniser. It's rather an attractive image.　　　　　　　　　　　　　RICHARD BURTON

I always get the feeling that when lesbians are looking at me, they're thinking, 'That's why I'm not a heterosexual.'

GEORGE COSTANZA (JASON ALEXANDER), *Seinfeld*

I don't mind being a bastard, as long as I'm an interesting bastard.

ROBERT DE NIRO

I've got a brain the size of a pea.　　　　DIANA, PRINCESS OF WALES

I'm equal part genius, equal part buffoon.　　　　NOEL GALLAGHER

I know who I am. No one else knows who I am. If I was a giraffe, and someone said I was a snake, I'd think, no, actually I'm a giraffe.　　RICHARD GERE

My face is like five miles of bad country road.　　　RICHARD HARRIS

My voice is a cross between Donald Duck and a Stradivarius.

KATHARINE HEPBURN

I have the face of an ageing choirboy and the build of an undernourished featherweight. If you can figure out my success on the screen, you're a better man than I.　　　　　　　　　　　　　　ALAN LADD

Most people seem to think I'm the kind of guy who shaves with a blowtorch. Actually I'm bookish and worrisome.　　　　BURT LANCASTER

I have a face like an elephant's behind.　　　CHARLES LAUGHTON

I'm so in touch with my feminine side, I'm practically going out with it.

LAURENCE LLEWELYN-BOWEN

I am the Nureyev of rock 'n' roll.　　　　　　MEAT LOAF

I'm just a little, insignificant bald guy.　　　　　MOBY

I seem to be a whole superstructure with no foundation.　MARILYN MONROE

I am the lizard king. I can do anything.   JIM MORRISON

Despite massive discouragement, I remain myself. Somebody has to be me so it might as well be me.   MORRISSEY

I have a face that is a cross between two pounds of halibut and an explosion in an old clothes closet.   DAVID NIVEN

I look like a duck. It's the way my mouth curls up.   MICHELLE PFEIFFER

I'm meant to be the bloke who walks around looking like he's going to club a baby seal.   JOHN PRESCOTT

I look like a lampshade on legs.   JULIA ROBERTS

I feel like the oldest ovary-producing person in America.   SUSAN SARANDON

There used to be a me but I had it surgically removed.   PETER SELLERS

I'm not handsome in the classical sense. The eyes droop, the mouth is crooked, the teeth aren't straight, the voice sounds like a Mafioso pallbearer, but somehow it all works.   SYLVESTER STALLONE

I rather think of myself as ethnically filthy – and proud of it.   PETER USTINOV

The only thing I really like about myself is my huge willy!

                                ROBBIE WILLIAMS

We're all worms, but I do believe I'm a glow-worm.   ROBIN WILLIAMS

I'm the intelligent, independent-type woman. In other words, a girl who can't get a man.   SHELLEY WINTERS

Selfishness

If you always do what interests you, at least one person is pleased.

                                KATHARINE HEPBURN

I met a new girl at a barbecue, very pretty, a blonde I think. I don't know, her hair was on fire, and all she talked about was herself. You know these kind of girls: 'I'm hot, I'm on fire. Me, me, me.' You know, 'Help me, put me out!' Come on, could we talk about me just a little bit?   GARRY SHANDLING

Senility

Don't worry about senility – when it hits you, you won't know it.

BILL COSBY

My nan, she gets things mixed up, bless her. She gets the telephone mixed up with the hairdryer. You might have seen her around – wet hair, chapped lips.

HARRY HILL

Sentimentality

Sentimentality – that's what we call the sentiment we don't share.

GRAHAM GREENE

Sentimentality is the emotional promiscuity of those who have no sentiment.

NORMAN MAILER, *Cannibals and Christians*

Sentimentality is only sentiment that rubs you up the wrong way.

W. SOMERSET MAUGHAM, *A Writer's Notebook*

A sentimentalist is simply one who desires to have the luxury of an emotion without paying for it.

OSCAR WILDE

Servants

Tell your secret to your servant, and you make him your master.

NATHANIEL BAILEY

Baldrick (Tony Robinson): But my lord, I've been in your family since 1532.
Edmund Blackadder (Rowan Atkinson): So has syphilis. Now get out!

Blackadder

Ah, the patter of little feet around the house. There's nothing like having a midget for a butler.

W.C. FIELDS

Jeeves coughed one soft, low, gentle cough like a sheep with a blade of grass stuck in its throat.

P.G. WODEHOUSE, *The Inimitable Jeeves*

Sex

The last time I was inside a woman was when I visited the Statue of Liberty.

WOODY ALLEN

Sex without love is an empty experience, but as empty experiences go it's one of the best.

WOODY ALLEN

I've tried several varieties of sex. The conventional position makes me claustrophobic and the others give me a stiff neck or lockjaw.

TALLULAH BANKHEAD

My husband complained to me. He said, 'I can't remember when we last had sex.' And I said, 'Well I can and that's why we ain't doin' it.'

ROSEANNE BARR

Sex: the thing that takes up the least amount of time and causes the most amount of trouble.

JOHN BARRYMORE

The big difference between sex for money and sex for free is that sex for money usually costs a lot less.

BRENDAN BEHAN

Sex has never been an obsession with me. It's just like eating a bag of crisps. Quite nice, but nothing marvellous.

BOY GEORGE

Fat people are brilliant in bed. If I'm sitting on top of you, who's going to argue?

JO BRAND

Come on baby. We've got things to do; eyes to blindfold and babies to make.

AL BUNDY (ED O'NEILL), *Married . . . With Children*

Sex, on the whole, was meant to be short, nasty and brutish. If what you want is cuddling, you should buy a puppy.

JULIE BURCHILL, *Sex and Sensibility*

There is nothing wrong with making love with the light on – just make sure the car door is closed.

GEORGE BURNS

It doesn't matter what you do in the bedroom as long as you don't do it in the street and frighten the horses.

MRS PATRICK CAMPBELL

Sam Malone (Ted Danson): You know . . . you know I always wanted to pop you one? Maybe this is my lucky day, huh?
Diane Chambers (Shelley Long): You disgust me. I hate you.
Sam: Are you as turned on as I am?
Diane: More.

Cheers

Fasten your seat-belts, it's going to be a bumpy night.

MARGO CHANNING (BETTE DAVIS), *All About Eve*

The pleasure is momentary, the position ridiculous, and the expense damnable.

LORD CHESTERFIELD

He makes love like a footballer: he dribbles before he shoots.

JOHN COOPER CLARKE

An erection at will is the moral equivalent of a valid credit card.

ALEX COMFORT

If it wasn't for pickpockets I'd have no sex life at all.   RODNEY DANGERFIELD

I asked her if she enjoys a cigarette after sex. She said, 'No. One drag is enough.'

RODNEY DANGERFIELD

My wife wants Olympic sex – once every four years.   RODNEY DANGERFIELD

At my age I like threesomes – in case one of us dies.   RODNEY DANGERFIELD

My wife is a sex object. Every time I ask for sex, she objects.

LES DAWSON

Sex in marriage is like medicine. Three times a day for the first week. Then once a day for another week. Then once every three or four days until the condition clears up.   PETER DE VRIES

I admit I have a tremendous sex drive. My boyfriend lives forty miles away.

PHYLLIS DILLER

Of course I believe in safe sex – I've got a handrail around the bed.

KEN DODD

It wasn't that Gary was bad in bed. He knew where all the parts were. Unfortunately, most of them were his.   ROZ DOYLE (PERI GILPIN), *Frasier*

At the request of the Catholic Church, a three-day sex orgy to be held near Rio de Janeiro was cancelled. So instead I spent the weekend cleaning my apartment.   TINA FEY

Older women are best because they always think they may be doing it for the last time.   IAN FLEMING

Conventional sexual intercourse is like squirting jam into a doughnut.

GERMAINE GREER

Don't you think it's better for a girl to be preoccupied with sex than occupied with it?   DONALD GRESHAM (WILLIAM HOLDEN), *The Moon is Blue*

When authorities warn you of the sinfulness of sex, there is an important lesson to be learned. Do not have sex with the authorities.   MATT GROENING

Some men are heterosexual, and some men are homosexual, and some men don't think about sex at all. They become lawyers.
                    BORIS GRUSHENKO (WOODY ALLEN), *Love and Death*

The major civilising force in the world is not religion, it is sex.
                                        HUGH HEFNER

'Slut' used to mean a slovenly woman. Now it means a woman who will go to bed with everyone. This is considered a bad thing in a woman, although perfectly fabulous in a man. 'Bitch' means a woman who will go to bed with everyone but you.
  CYNTHIA HEIMEL, *Get Your Tongue Out of My Mouth, I'm Kissing You Good-bye*

Sex without love is merely healthy exercise.   ROBERT A. HEINLEIN

I know I must be really good in bed, because women always ask me if there's any possible way I could make it last longer.   BILL HEWINS

Great sex is great, but bad sex is like a peanut butter and jelly sandwich.
                                        BILLY IDOL

My girlfriend always laughs during sex, no matter what she's reading.
                                        STEVE JOBS

A study shows that ninety per cent of men inflate the number of their sex partners, while the other ten per cent inflate their sex partners.
                                        CRAIG KILBORN

Making love to a woman is like buying real estate: location, location, location.
                                        CAROL LEIFER

Women are removing sperm from the bodies of their dead husbands. Kind of ironic. When they're alive, most men can't give it away.   JAY LENO

To please a woman in bed, all a man has to do is a poetry course. They also have to learn that the *Kama Sutra* is not an Indian takeaway and that the mutual orgasm is not an insurance company.   KATHY LETTE

I'm glad I'm not bisexual. I couldn't stand being rejected by men as well as women.   BERNARD MANNING

Nothing risqué, nothing gained.   JAYNE MANSFIELD

I believe that sex is one of the most beautiful, natural, wholesome things that money can buy.   STEVE MARTIN

I feel like a million tonight – but one at a time.   BETTE MIDLER

If sex is such a natural phenomenon, how come there are so many books on how to do it?   BETTE MIDLER

Sex is one of the nine reasons for reincarnation. The other eight are unimportant.   HENRY MILLER, *Sexus*

We were making love in the back of a truck and we got carried away.
                              SPIKE MILLIGAN

My wife says me lovemaking is like a news bulletin: brief, unexpected, and usually a disaster.   BOB MONKHOUSE

(*on Tantric sex*) It's very slow. My favourite position is called the plumber. You stay in all day, but nobody comes.   JOHN MORTIMER

An orgy looks particularly alluring seen through the mists of righteous indignation.   MALCOLM MUGGERIDGE

I haven't had sex since 1959. Of course it's only 21:00 now.
                              TOM O'CONNOR

My sex life has gone from bad to pathetic. My G Spot stands for godforsaken.
                              JOAN RIVERS

I'm a double bagger. Not only does my husband put a bag over my head when we're making love, but he also puts a bag over his own head in case mine falls off.   JOAN RIVERS

Last night I asked my husband, 'What's your favourite sexual position?' He said, 'Next door.'   JOAN RIVERS

After lovemaking do you a) go to sleep? b) light a cigarette? c) return to the front of the bus?   JOAN RIVERS

Women need a reason to have sex. Men just need a place.
                              MITCH ROBBINS (BILLY CRYSTAL), *City Slickers*

Sex is like art. Most of it is pretty bad, and the good stuff is out of your price range.

SCOTT ROEBEN

Men wake up aroused in the morning. We can't help it. We just wake up and we want you. And the women are thinking, 'How can he want me the way I look in the morning?' It's because we can't see you. We have no blood anywhere near our optic nerve.

ANDY ROONEY

Men reach their sexual peak at eighteen. Women reach theirs at thirty-five. Do you get the feeling that God is playing a practical joke?

RITA RUDNER

However carefully you phrase the history of your sex life, you're bound to emerge as a boaster, a braggart, a liar, or a laughing stock.

WILLIAM RUSHTON

Seems to me the basic conflict between men and women, sexually, is that men are like firemen. To men, sex is an emergency, and no matter what we're doing we can be ready in two minutes. Women, on the other hand, are like fire. They're very excited, but the conditions have to be exactly right for it to occur.

JERRY SEINFELD

I practise safe sex: I use an airbag.

GARRY SHANDLING

I once made love for an hour and 15 minutes, but it was the night the clocks are set ahead.

GARRY SHANDLING

Most men approach sex a lot like shooting a game of pinball. We don't have any idea about the internal workings or what we should do to win, we're just gonna try to keep the ball in play as long as possible.

TIM STEEVES

(*setting the record straight about Tantric sex*) I think I mentioned I could make love for eight hours. What I didn't say was that this included four hours of begging and then dinner and a movie.

STING

Sex is like supermarkets — very overrated. Just a lot of pushing and shoving and you still come out with very little at the end of it.

SHIRLEY VALENTINE-BRADSHAW (PAULINE COLLINS), *Shirley Valentine*

Sex is emotion in motion.

MAE WEST

(*on Jayne Mansfield*) When it comes to men, I heard she never turns anything down except the bedcovers.

MAE WEST

Real mothers think sex is like full-time employment: it's a nice idea, but it'll never happen again in their lifetime.   VICTORIA WOOD

(*on first having sex with Michael Hutchence*) Michael did six things I was firmly convinced were illegal.   PAULA YATES

Sex aids

Due to a court ruling, sex toys are now legal in Alabama. The whole state is buzzing.   JAY LENO

There are a number of mechanical devices which increase sexual arousal, particularly in women. Chief among these is the Mercedes-Benz 380SL convertible.
                                    P.J. O'ROURKE

Sex appeal

I have never considered myself to be a sex symbol. Nobody asked me to do sex scenes – it would only have depressed people.   LAUREN BACALL

(*on his sex appeal*) When the hall empties out after one of my concerts, those girls leave behind them thousands of sticky seats.   DAVID CASSIDY

For lack of a better term, they've labelled me a sex symbol. It's flattering and it should happen to every bald, overweight guy.   DENNIS FRANZ

Sex appeal is fifty per cent what you've got and fifty per cent what people think you've got.   SOPHIA LOREN

I have no sex appeal. A peeping Tom saw me and pulled down the shade.
                                    JOAN RIVERS

Being a sex symbol has to do with attitude, not looks. Most men think it's looks, most women know otherwise.   KATHLEEN TURNER

Shadow

The only reason I exist is so my shadow would have something to do.
                                    STEVEN WRIGHT

I got a new shadow. I had to get rid of the old one, it wasn't doing what I was doing.   STEVEN WRIGHT

William Shakespeare

I read once that Shakespeare had a vocabulary of 17,000 words. That's pretty impressive, but I bet he used some of them twice.   JEFF ALEXANDER

(on *Hamlet*) I mean, it's a great story. It's got some great things in it. I mean, there's something like eight violent deaths.   MEL GIBSON

Playing Shakespeare is very tiring. You never get to sit down unless you're a King.   JOSEPHINE HULL

George Bernard Shaw

Shaw's plays are the price we pay for Shaw's prefaces.   JAMES AGATE

I remember coming across him at the Grand Canyon and finding him peevish, refusing to admire it or even look at it properly. He was jealous of it.
J.B. PRIESTLEY, *Thoughts in the Wilderness*

The spinster aunt of English literature.   KENNETH TYNAN

Sheep

Sheep are evil. They've got no eyebrows. You never know if what you're saying to them is having any effect.   TOMMY TIERNAN

Shoes

If everybody were a guy, the human race could easily get by on less than one twentieth the current number of shoes.   DAVE BARRY

Show me a woman wearing red patent-leather stiletto-heeled shoes, and I'll show you a racing certainty.   JEFFREY BERNARD

I have spent $40,000 on shoes and I have no place to live. I will literally be the old woman who lived in her shoes.
CARRIE BRADSHAW (SARAH JESSICA PARKER), *Sex and the City*

I have a teenaged son who is a runner. He has, at a conservative estimate, 6,100 pairs of running shoes, and every one of them represents a greater investment of cumulative design effort than, say, Milton Keynes.
BILL BRYSON, *Notes from a Big Country*

Judiciously worn stilettos are remarkably effective in commanding extra help with household chores.   VANESSA FELTZ

If high heels were so wonderful, men would be wearing them.

SUE GRAFTON

What is it about people who repair shoes that makes them so good at cutting keys?

HARRY HILL

Put kitty litter in your shoes, and it'll take away the odour. Unless, of course, you own a cat.

JAY LENO

My first wife divorced me because I didn't match her shoes. I was a lazy white loafer.

KELLY MONTEITH

High heels were invented by a woman who had been kissed on the forehead.

CHRISTOPHER MORLEY

Sometimes you have to sacrifice your performance for high heels.

GWEN STEFANI

Shopping

It's amazing how fast later comes when you buy now!

MILTON BERLE

Shopping is a woman thing. It's a contact sport like football. Women enjoy the scrimmage, the noisy crowds, the danger of being trampled to death, and the ecstasy of the purchase.

ERMA BOMBECK

A safety check would reveal that there isn't a shopping cart that does not have all four wheels working. Unfortunately, all four are locked in stable directions. Three wheels want to shop and the fourth wants to go to the parking lot.

ERMA BOMBECK

Why would anyone steal a shopping cart? It's like stealing a two-year-old.

ERMA BOMBECK

We used to build civilisations. Now we build shopping malls.

BILL BRYSON, *Neither Here Nor There*

I bought some HP sauce the other day. It's costing me 6p a month for the next two years.

TOMMY COOPER

Whoever said money can't buy happiness simply didn't know where to go shopping.

BO DEREK

Lots of people can't count to ten. They are usually the ones in front of you in the supermarket express lane.
SAM EWING

If men liked shopping, they'd call it research.
CYNTHIA NELMS

The only time a woman has a true orgasm is when she is shopping.
JOAN RIVERS

Most men hate to shop. That's why the men's department is usually on the ground floor of a department store — two inches from the door.
RITA RUDNER

A man who goes into a supermarket for a few items would rather walk around balancing them than put them in one of those little baskets.
RITA RUDNER

I was in a supermarket and I saw Paul Newman's face on salad dressing and spaghetti sauce. I thought he was missing . . .
BOB SAGET

I've been watching women in department stores. Women don't try on the clothes, they get behind the clothes. They take a dress off the rack, and they hold it up against themselves. They can tell something from this. They stick one leg way out 'cause they need to know: 'If some day I'm one-legged, and at a forty-five-degree angle, what am I gonna wear?'
JERRY SEINFELD

I went down the street to the 24-hour grocer. When I got there, the guy was locking the front. I said, 'Hey, the sign says you're open 24 hours.' He said, 'Yes, but not in a row.'
STEVEN WRIGHT

My wife is a compulsive shopper. She would buy anything marked down. Once she came home with an escalator.
HENNY YOUNGMAN

Once you've seen one shopping centre, you've seen a mall.

Show business

In show business there are more chorus girls kept than promises.
FRED ALLEN, *Treadmill to Oblivion*

You're the worst entertainer since St Paul the Evangelist toured Palestine with his trampoline act.
EDMUND BLACKADDER (ROWAN ATKINSON), *Blackadder*

I'm on a little tour of the United States. I call it a 'tourette', but I don't use bad language.
DAME EDNA EVERAGE

The trouble with this business is that the stars keep ninety per cent of my money.
LEW GRADE

When the light goes on in the refrigerator, I do twenty minutes.
JERRY LEWIS

To be successful in show business, all you need are fifty good breaks.
WALTER MATTHAU

A trick I learned in this business is that if you sweat a lot in your clothes, they don't want them back.
BILL MURRAY

Shyness

I'm an intensely shy and vulnerable woman. My husband has never seen me naked. Nor has he expressed the least desire to do so.
DAME EDNA EVERAGE (BARRY HUMPHRIES)

They've just found a gene for shyness. They would have found it earlier but it was hiding behind a couple of other genes.
JONATHAN KATZ

Shyness is just egotism out of its depth.
PENELOPE KEITH

I'm too shy to express my sexual needs — except over the phone to people I don't know.
GARRY SHANDLING

Signature

A signature always reveals a man's character — and sometimes even his name.
EVAN ESAR

The only thing some men can do better than anyone else is to read their own signature.
EVAN ESAR

Silence

Silence: the unbearable repartee.
G.K. CHESTERTON

If you don't say anything, you won't be called on to repeat it.
CALVIN COOLIDGE

One of the lessons of history is that nothing is often a good thing to do and always a clever thing to say.
WILL DURANT

Blessed is the man who, having nothing to say, abstains from giving us worthy evidence of the fact.
GEORGE ELIOT

Better to be silent and be thought a fool than to speak and remove all doubt.
ABRAHAM LINCOLN

Silence is not only golden, it is seldom misquoted.
BOB MONKHOUSE

Silence is sometimes the answer.
ESTONIAN PROVERB

Silence is having nothing to say and saying it.

Sin

Not all the sins of my past life passed in front of me but as many as could find room in the queue.
BRENDAN BEHAN

It is much easier to repent of sins that we have committed than to repent of those we intend to commit.
JOSH BILLINGS

Christ died for our sins. Dare we make his martyrdom meaningless by not committing them?
JULES FEIFFER

Sin has many tools, but a lie is the handle that fits them all.
OLIVER WENDELL HOLMES

I have a head for business and a bod for sin. Is there anything wrong with that?
TESS McGILL (MELANIE GRIFFITH), *Working Girl*

Many are saved from sin by being so inept at it.
MIGNON McLAUGHLIN, *The Neurotic's Notebook*

Everything that used to be a sin is now a disease.
BILL MAHER

Blanche Devereaux (Rue McClanahan): Is it okay to sleep with a man on the first date?
Sophia Petrillo (Estelle Getty): It's a sin. I don't care what anyone says, it's a sin. But I'd go back to eating fish on Fridays if his holiness gave that one the green light.
The Golden Girls

The wages of sin are death, but by the time taxes are taken out, it's just sort of a tired feeling. PAULA POUNDSTONE

Frank Sinatra

(*explaining why he gave 'My Way' to Frank Sinatra*) I didn't want to find a horse's head in my bed. PAUL ANKA

He's the kind of guy that when he dies, he's going to heaven and give God a bad time for making him bald. MARLON BRANDO

My mother was against me being an actress – until I introduced her to Frank Sinatra.
ANGIE DICKINSON

When Sinatra dies, they're giving his zipper to the Smithsonian.
DEAN MARTIN

Make yourself at home, Frank. Hit somebody. DON RICKLES

When you enter a room, you have to kiss his ring. I don't mind, but he has it in his back pocket. DON RICKLES

The Sixties

The 1960s were when hallucinogenic drugs were really big. And I don't think it's a coincidence that we had shows then like *The Flying Nun*.
ELLEN DEGENERES

If you remember the Sixties, you weren't there. GEORGE HARRISON

The Fifties was the most sexually frustrated decade ever: ten years of foreplay. And the Sixties, well, the Sixties was like coitus interruptus. The only thing we didn't pull out of was Vietnam. LILY TOMLIN

Skiing

Skiing combines outdoor fun with knocking down trees with your face.
DAVE BARRY

I say, why pay outrageous prices for ski trips when I can just stick my face in the freezer and fall down on the kitchen floor. *CRABBY ROAD*

I unpacked and changed into a day-glo orange, yellow and lilac windcheater, which is the sort of thing you have to wear in a ski resort if you don't want to be conspicuous.   HUGH LAURIE, *The Gun Seller*

There are really only three things to learn in skiing: how to put on your skis, how to slide downhill, and how to walk along the hospital corridor.
                                    LORD MANCROFT, *A Chinaman in My Bath*

The sport of skiing consists of wearing $300 worth of clothes and equipment and driving 200 miles in the snow in order to stand around at a bar and get drunk.   P.J. O'ROURKE, *Modern Manners*

Sky-diving

A fellow told me he was going to sky-diving school. He said, 'I've been going for three months.' I said, 'How many successful jumps do you need to make before you graduate?' He said, 'All of them.'   RED SKELTON

For sale, parachute. Never opened. Used only once, small stain.
                                    STEVEN WRIGHT

Sleep

I sleep better at night knowing that scientists can clone sheep.   JEFF AYERS

No woman is worth the loss of a night's sleep.   THOMAS BEECHAM

[My wife] Cherie has many excellent qualities, but once she goes to sleep, it takes a minor nuclear explosion to wake her up.   TONY BLAIR

I think I'll have a lie down. No I won't, I'll go and hit some guests.
                                    BASIL FAWLTY (JOHN CLEESE), *Fawlty Towers*

Sometimes I fall asleep at night with my clothes on. I'm going to have all my clothes made out of blankets.   MITCH HEDBERG

Sleep is death without the responsibility.   FRAN LEBOWITZ, *Metropolitan Life*

Taking a nap in the afternoon can really refresh you — so much that you'll be able to go out and find a new job after your boss fires you.   JAY LENO

I tend to sleep in the nude, which isn't a bad thing, except for maybe on those long flights.   BOB MONKHOUSE

I have orders to be awakened at any time in case of a national emergency – even if I'm in a cabinet meeting.   RONALD REAGAN

If your husband has difficulty getting to sleep, the words 'we need to talk about our relationship' may help.   RITA RUDNER

Don't go to sleep; so many people die there.
                                    MARK TWAIN, *The Sayings of Mark Twain*

Sometimes, when I'm sure people can only see the back of my head, I enjoy sneaking in a quick catnap at work. They never last too long though, because invariably someone rings the bell telling me they want to get off my bus.
                                    BRAD WILKERSON

Smell

I think the reason guys like women in leather outfits so much is because they have that 'new car' smell.   GEORGE FARA

If men have a smell, it's usually an accident.   JEFF FOXWORTHY

Smells are far more evocative of the past than noises can ever be. Sounds are the clichés of memory.   ROY HATTERSLEY

Perfume: any smell that is used to drown a worse one.   ELBERT HUBBARD

I can't smell mothballs because it's so difficult to get their little legs apart.
                                    STEVE MARTIN

Smile

Maddie Hayes (Cybill Shepherd): Wipe that stupid grin off your face.
David Addison (Bruce Willis): This happens to be the smartest grin I own.
                                    Moonlighting

She gave me a smile I could feel in my hip pocket.
                                    RAYMOND CHANDLER, *Farewell My Lovely*

A smile is a curve that sets everything straight.   PHYLLIS DILLER

Start every day off with a smile and get it over with.   W.C. FIELDS

My best feature's my smile. And smiles – praise heaven – don't get fat.
                                    JACK NICHOLSON

If you smile when no one else is around, you really mean it.   Andy Rooney

When I look at the smiles on all the children's faces, I just know they're about to jab me with something.   Homer Simpson, *The Simpsons*

Smoking

The spokespeople for tobacco companies always look half dead. The Surgeon General should make them put their pictures on every pack.
Scott Adams

Asthma doesn't seem to bother me any more unless I'm around cigars or dogs. The thing that would bother me most would be a dog smoking a cigar.
Steve Allen

Remember, if you smoke after sex you're doing it too fast.
Woody Allen

Cigarette sales would drop to zero if the warning said: 'Cigarettes Contain Fat'.
Dave Barry

(*to a smoker*) No, I don't mind if you smoke – not if you don't mind my being sick all over you.   Thomas Beecham

To quit smoking, my dad tried that thing with the needles. What do you call it? Heroin. He loves it!   Bill Braudis

I'm not really a heavy smoker any more. I only get through two lighters a day now.   Bill Hicks

Smoking is one of the leading causes of statistics.   Fletcher Knebel

Smoking is the great romance of a lifetime. If I could find someone I wanted forty-five times a day, perhaps I could stop.   Fran Lebowitz

The World Health Organisation now says that smoking is worse for you than was first thought. We used to think it could kill you – now what? Does it stomp on your head when you die?   Jay Leno

It was sort of a fair trade. We gave the Native Americans deadly diseases, and they gave us tobacco.   Jay Leno

A woman is an occasional pleasure but a cigar is always a smoke.
GROUCHO MARX

People today are healthier and drinking less. You know, if it wasn't for the junior high school next door, no one would even use the cigarette machine.
BARTENDER MOE, *The Simpsons*

These days smoking really does shorten your life because if you light up, some non-smoker will kill you.   GENE PERRETT

Giving up smoking is easy. I've done it hundreds of times.   MARK TWAIN

Snobbery

My aunt was a bit of a social climber although very much on the lower slopes. I was once on a tram with her going past the gas works in Wellington Road and she said, 'Alan, this is the biggest gas works in England. And I know the manager.'   ALAN BENNETT

The one thing I can't stand is snobbery – people who try to pretend they're superior. It makes it so much harder for those of us who really are.
HYACINTH BUCKET (PATRICIA ROUTLEDGE), *Keeping Up Appearances*

I worry about my daughter getting into the best gang.   MIKE GIBBONS

Snow

Don't you just hate it when you're shovelling snow and uncover a Jehovah's Witness?   DAVID LETTERMAN

Snowmen fall from Heaven unassembled.

One good thing about a snowfall is that it makes your lawn look as good as your neighbour's.

Snowboarding

I now realise that the small hills you see on ski slopes are formed around the bodies of 47-year-olds who tried to learn snowboarding.   DAVE BARRY

Soccer

The three toughest jobs are football management, lion taming and mountain rescue – in that order.   JIMMY ARMFIELD

If that was a penalty, I'll plait sawdust.   RON ATKINSON

(*on the goal famine of his Aston Villa team*) Devon Loch was a better finisher.
RON ATKINSON

I used to go missing a lot: Miss Canada, Miss United Kingdom, Miss World . . .
GEORGE BEST

If you'd given me the choice of beating four men and smashing in a goal from
30 yards against Liverpool or going to bed with Miss World, it would have been
a difficult choice. Luckily I had both. It's just that you do one of those things in
front of 50,000 people.   GEORGE BEST

Football is a fertility festival: eleven sperm trying to get into the egg. I feel sorry
for the goalkeeper.   BJÖRK

Footballers are only interested in drinking, clothes and the size of their willies.
KARREN BRADY

(*expressing an interest in becoming manager of the Republic of Ireland*) It's easy
enough to get to Ireland. It's just a straight walk across the Irish Sea as far as
I'm concerned.   BRIAN CLOUGH

Trevor Brooking floats like a butterfly and stings like one.   BRIAN CLOUGH

(*on Gary Megson*) He couldn't trap a landmine.   BRIAN CLOUGH

David Beckham's had his eyebrows plucked, so now he's got nothing in front of
his eyes either.   JACK DEE

(*on Aston Villa chairman Doug Ellis*) He said he was right behind me. I told him
I'd sooner have him in front of me where I could see him.
TOMMY DOCHERTY

(*after leaving Preston North End*) They offered me a handshake to settle amicably.
I told them they would have to be more amicable than that.
TOMMY DOCHERTY

(*on his goal-shy Wolverhampton Wanderers team*) Our strikers couldn't score in
a brothel. We don't use a stopwatch to judge our golden goal competition now,
we use a calendar.   TOMMY DOCHERTY

(*on Ray Wilkins*) He can't run, he can't tackle and he can't head the ball. The only time he goes forward is to toss the coin.   TOMMY DOCHERTY

(*on Alan Shearer*) A man so dull he once made the papers for having a one-in-the-bed romp.   NICK HANCOCK

Radio football is football reduced to its lowest common denominator. Shorn of the game's aesthetic pleasures, or the comfort of a crowd that feels the same way as you, or the sense of security that you get when you see that your defenders and goalkeeper are more or less where they should be, all that is left is naked fear.   NICK HORNBY, *Fever Pitch*

(*as manager of cash-strapped Halifax Town*) I'm going to have to listen to offers for all my players — and the club cat Benny, who's pissed off because all the mice have died of starvation.   JOHN MCGRATH

Things were so bad I received a letter from *Reader's Digest* saying I hadn't been included in their prize draw.   JOHN MCGRATH

Premier League football is a multi-million pound industry with the aroma of a blocked toilet and the principles of a knocking shop.
                    MICHAEL PARKINSON

Being a manager is like parachuting — sometimes the chute doesn't open and you splatter on the ground.   CLAUDIO RANIERI

I'm sure sex wouldn't be as rewarding as winning the World Cup. It's not that sex isn't good, but the World Cup is every four years and sex is not. RONALDO

Football's not a matter of life and death. It's much more important than that.
                    BILL SHANKLY

Tommy Smith could start a riot in a graveyard.   BILL SHANKLY

Did you hear about the guy who was prevented from taking his father's ashes to a game in Spain? It comes to something when you can't take a bottle of pop to a match.   FRANK SKINNER

There's only two types of manager. Those who've been sacked and those who will be sacked in the future.   HOWARD WILKINSON

The rules of soccer are very simple. Basically it is this: if it moves, kick it. If it doesn't move, kick it until it does. PHIL WOOSNAM

(*asked who his Zambia team feared at the 1998 World Cup*) No one. I fear nobody in the world, except my wife. BURKHARD ZIESE

Socialism

There is nothing in socialism that a little age or a little money will not cure. WILL DURANT

The function of socialism is to raise suffering to a higher level. NORMAN MAILER

(*on leading the Labour Party*) This party is a bit like an old stagecoach. If you drive along at a rapid rate, everyone aboard is either so exhilarated or so seasick that you don't have a lot of difficulty. HAROLD WILSON

Society

Every society honours its live conformists and its dead troublemakers. MIGNON MCLAUGHLIN

I don't think you want too much sincerity in society. It would be like an iron girder in a house of cards. W. SOMERSET MAUGHAM, *The Circle*

Sociology: the study of people who don't need to be studied by people who do. E.S. TURNER

If one could only teach the English how to talk and the Irish how to listen, society would be quite civilized. OSCAR WILDE, *An Ideal Husband*

Socks

I have always dressed according to certain Basic Guy Fashion Rules, including: both of your socks should always be the same color, or they should at least both be fairly dark. DAVE BARRY

One of the few lessons I have learned in life is that there is invariably something odd about women who wear ankle socks. ALAN BENNETT, *Old Country*

Sex and socks are not compatible. ANGELA CARTER

If it weren't for women, men would still be wearing last week's socks.

CYNTHIA NELMS

(*on staying single*) I can think of nothing worse than coming home having to remember where some man had put his socks. ANN WIDDECOMBE

Sodomy

It is impossible to obtain a conviction for sodomy from an English jury. Half of them don't believe that it can physically be done, and the other half are doing it. WINSTON CHURCHILL

Solitude

Solitude: a good place to visit, but a poor place to stay. JOSH BILLINGS

Everybody's alone. It's just easier to take in a relationship.

RICHARD FISH (GREG GERMANN), *Ally McBeal*

Songs and singers

Drew Barrymore sings so badly, deaf people refuse to watch her lips move.

WOODY ALLEN

Never hate a song that's sold half a million copies. IRVING BERLIN

Celine Dion's in a 4,000-seat auditorium built specially to handle her voice. But it doesn't work. I could still hear her. LEWIS BLACK

I love to sing, and I love to drink scotch. Most people would rather hear me drink scotch. GEORGE BURNS

The closest thing to Roseanne Barr's singing the national anthem was my cat being neutered. JOHNNY CARSON

(*on Bryan Adams*) As far as his love numbers go, I'm afraid someone who sings like he's got a throat infection is not going to get me smooching.

LAURA LEE DAVIES

Song is the licensed medium for bawling in public things too silly or sacred to be uttered in ordinary speech. OLIVER HERFORD

It's ill-becoming for an old broad to sing about how bad she wants it. But occasionally we do. LENA HORNE

I can hold a note longer than the Chase National Bank.   ETHEL MERMAN

(*on Cole Porter*) He sang like a hinge.   ETHEL MERMAN

(*on Shirley Temple*) A lovely person, but I can't hear 'On the Good Ship Lollipop' without tasting vomit at the back of my throat.   PAUL MERTON

(*on Helen Reddy*) She ought to be arrested for loitering in front of an orchestra.   BETTE MIDLER

Cilla Black's voice is like labour pains set to music.   BOB MONKHOUSE

(on his singing role in the film *Love Actually*) That was the beginning and end of my singing career. The British public has suffered enough.   BILL NIGHY

Yoko Ono: her voice sounded like an eagle being goosed.   RALPH NOVAK

(*on Bryan Ferry*) He sings like he's throwing up.   ANDREW O'CONNOR

Leonard Cohen gives you the feeling that your dog just died.   *Q Magazine*

My money says that the guy who wrote 'I Believe I Can Fly' has never actually tried it.   DOUG RENDALL

(*on Bob Dylan*) I always thought he sounded just like Yogi Bear.   MICK RONSON

(*on Barry Manilow*) Like a bluebottle caught in the curtains.   JEAN ROOK

Bing Crosby sings like all people think they sing in the shower.   DINAH SHORE

(*on Frankie Laine*) His approach to the microphone is that of an accused man pleading with a hostile jury.   KENNETH TYNAN

(*to actor Cliff Osmond*) You have Van Gogh's ear for music.   BILLY WILDER

You've got to have smelled a lot of mule manure before you can sing like a hillbilly.   HANK WILLIAMS

There are more love songs than anything else. If songs could make you do some-thing, we'd all love one another . . . I wrote a song about dental floss but did anyone's teeth get cleaner? FRANK ZAPPA

Kate Bush sounds like the consequences of mating Patti Smith with a Hoover.

Gary Numan has a voice like David Bowie holding his nose very hard.

Sorrow

It is a sad woman who buys her own perfume. LENA JEGER

Sorrow is tranquillity remembered in emotion. DOROTHY PARKER

There are few sorrows, however poignant, in which a good income is of no avail. LOGAN PEARSALL SMITH, *Afterthoughts*

Crying is the refuge of plain women, but the ruin of pretty ones.
OSCAR WILDE, *Lady Windermere's Fan*

Space

The ships hung in the sky in much the same way that bricks don't.
DOUGLAS ADAMS, *The Hitch-Hiker's Guide to the Galaxy*

Space is big. Really big. You just won't believe how vastly hugely mind-bogglingly big it is. I mean, you may think it's a long way down the road to the chemist, but that's just peanuts to space.
DOUGLAS ADAMS, *The Hitch-Hiker's Guide to the Galaxy*

Interestingly, according to modern astronomers, space is finite. This is a very comforting thought – particularly for people who can never remember where they have left things. WOODY ALLEN

What happens if a big asteroid hits the Earth? Judging from realistic simula-tions involving a sledgehammer and a common laboratory frog, we can assume it will be pretty bad. DAVE BARRY

If you stacked all the US currency together, you could probably reach the moon, but I bet the Apollo programme was still more economical. LARRY BAUM

Astronomers have discovered two giant new solar systems, and with George W. Bush taking over the Presidency, it's good to know we have options.

LEWIS BLACK

Thanks to the invention of the telescope, planets that are 100 billion miles away look to be only 50 billion miles away.   *Crabby Road*

I'm absolutely sure there is no life on Mars — it's not listed on my teenage daughter's phone bills.   LARRY MATHEWS

It's a very sobering feeling to be up in space and realise that one's safety factor was determined by the lowest bidder on a government contract.

ALAN SHEPARD

Oh my God! Space aliens! Don't eat me, I have a wife and kids! Eat them!

HOMER SIMPSON, *The Simpsons*

Dorothy Zbornak (Bea Arthur): Now look, all this nonsense has to stop, Rose. What we saw was not a UFO.
Rose Nylund (Betty White): Well, it wasn't a plane. Planes aren't that thin, or that bright.
Dorothy: Neither is Oprah Winfrey, but that doesn't make her a flying saucer.

The Golden Girls

Spectacles

I put my spectacles on for the first time and the insults started, you know 'four eyes', 'goggle box', 'Joe 90'. To which I replied, 'Look, you're not the only opticians around here!'   HARRY HILL

Speeches

The human brain starts working the moment you are born and never stops until you stand up to speak in public.   GEORGE JESSEL

(*advice to speech-makers*) If you haven't struck oil in the first three minutes, stop boring!   GEORGE JESSEL

A speech is like a love affair. Any fool can start it, but to end it requires considerable skill.   LORD MANCROFT

(*comparing Clement Attlee as a public speaker with Winston Churchill*) Like a village fiddler after Paganini.   HAROLD NICOLSON

A recent survey stated that the average person's greatest fear is having to give a speech in public. Somehow this ranked even higher than death, which was third on the list. So you're telling me that at a funeral, most people would rather be the guy in the coffin than have to stand up and give a eulogy.

JERRY SEINFELD

You know that old public speaking trick of picturing your audience naked? I like to pretend they're on fire. That way, it makes a lot more sense when I run screaming from the stage.   CRAIG STACEY

It usually takes me more than three weeks to prepare a good impromptu speech.

MARK TWAIN

If I am to speak for ten minutes, I need a week for preparation; if fifteen minutes, three days; if half an hour, two days; if an hour, I am ready now.

WOODROW T. WILSON

Sport

Squash is boxing with racquets.   JONAH BARRINGTON

I held the record for the 100 metres at school. I was having a fag behind the bike shed when the dinner bell went.   JO BRAND

Swimming isn't a sport. It's just a way to keep from drowning.

GEORGE CARLIN

Torvill and Dean, oh they're very good on ice. But you get them out on the street . . . all over the place.   HARRY HILL

When it comes to sports I am not particularly interested. Generally speaking, I look upon them as dangerous and tiring activities performed by people with whom I share nothing except the right to trial by jury.

FRAN LEBOWITZ

Can you believe Lance Armstrong? Just 48 hours after winning the Tour de France he won another race in Austria. I take the garbage out, and I'm pooped for a week.

JAY LENO

Nothing is ever so bad it can't be made worse by firing the coach.

JIM MURRAY

I don't think the discus will ever attract any interest until we start throwing them at each other. AL OERTER

Men forget everything. That's why they need instant replays in sports. They've already forgotten what happened. RITA RUDNER

In Russia, if a male athlete loses, he becomes a female athlete. YAKOV SMIRNOFF

Playing polo is like trying to play golf during an earthquake. SYLVESTER STALLONE

An astonishing number of international games were invented by the British, who, whenever they are surpassed by other nations, coolly invent another one. PETER USTINOV, *Dear Me*

Of course I have played outdoor games. I once played dominoes in an open air café in Paris. OSCAR WILDE

The original Olympics were all held in the nude. That sure changed men's hurdles. The white guys won a lot more races. TIM YOUNG

If one synchronised swimmer drowns, do the rest have to drown too?

Standards

Elaine Benes (Julia Louis-Dreyfus): Your standards are too high.
Jerry Seinfeld: I went out with you.
Elaine: That's because my standards are too low. *Seinfeld*

Cliff Clavin (John Ratzenberger): I have impossibly high standards for a woman.
Norm Peterson (George Wendt): Yeah, she has to like you. *Cheers*

I believe in the theory that anyone can get laid, it's just a matter of lowering your standards enough. MICHAEL STIPE

Stardom

You're not a star until they can spell your name in Karachi.

HUMPHERY BOGART

I'm an instant star. Just add water and stir. DAVID BOWIE

Stars are not the people who are best at what they do; they are merely the people who want it most. JULIE BURCHILL

Give me two years, and I'll make her an overnight star. HARRY COHN

I never go out unless I look like Joan Crawford the movie star. If you want to see the girl next door, go next door. JOAN CRAWFORD

After *The Graduate* I was walking down Fifth Avenue in broad daylight when a beautiful girl lifted up her dress to reveal these beautiful breasts. She asked me to sign them. That's when I knew I'd become a star.

DUSTIN HOFFMAN

I could go on stage and make a pizza and still they'd come to see me.

FRANK SINATRA

Statistics

There are three kinds of lies: lies, damned lies, and statistics.

BENJAMIN DISRAELI

Definition of statistics: the science of producing unreliable facts from reliable figures. EVAN ESAR

Statistician: a man who believes figures don't lie, but admits that under analysis some of them won't stand up either. EVAN ESAR

I could prove God statistically. GEORGE GALLUP

Statistics are like a bikini. What they reveal is suggestive, but what they conceal is vital. AARON LEVENSTEIN

Statistics are like loose women. Once you get your hands on them you can do anything you like with them. WALT MICHAELS

Storytelling

The trouble with telling a good story is that it invariably reminds the other fellow of a dull one. SID CAESAR

Strangers

Sometimes I wave to people I don't know. It is very dangerous to wave to people you don't know, because what if they don't have a hand? They'll think you're cocky.   MITCH HEDBERG

I wish I were less awkward around strangers. I never know what to say when someone asks me who I am and what the hell I'm doing in their house.
                                                                    ANDY IHNATKO

Barbra Streisand

She takes every ballad and turns it into a three-act opera. She simply cannot leave a song alone!   TRUMAN CAPOTE

My toughest job? Being married to Barbra Streisand.   ELLIOTT GOULD

Working with Barbra Streisand is pretty stressful. It's like sitting down to a picnic in the middle of a freeway.   KRIS KRISTOFFERSON

Filming with Streisand is an experience which may have cured me of movies.
                                                            KRIS KRISTOFFERSON

I don't mean to be a diva, but some days you wake up and you're Barbra Streisand.   COURTNEY LOVE

(to Streisand on the set of *Hello Dolly*) I have more talent in my smallest fart than you have in your entire body.   WALTER MATTHAU

I'd love to work with Barbra Streisand again. In something appropriate. Perhaps *Macbeth*.   WALTER MATTHAU

She's a ball-buster. Protect me from her.   NICK NOLTE

The sensitivity of a starving elephant.   FRANK PIERSON

To know her is not necessarily to love her.   REX REED

I think her biggest problem is that she wants to be a woman and she wants to be beautiful, and she is neither.   OMAR SHARIF

A cross between an aardvark and an albino rat.   JOHN SIMON

Strength

A thick skin is a gift from God.   KONRAD ADENAUER

(*of Lady Desborough*) She's as strong as an ox. She'll be turned into Bovril when she dies.   MARGOT ASQUITH

Youngsters of the age of two and three are endowed with extraordinary strength. They can lift a dog twice their own weight and dump him into the bathtub.
                          ERMA BOMBECK

Atlas had a great reputation, but I'd like to have seen him carry a mattress upstairs.   KIN HUBBARD

Girls have got balls. They're just a little higher up, that's all.   JOAN JETT

If you can keep your head when all about are losing theirs, it's just possible you haven't grasped the situation.
                          JEAN KERR, *Please Don't Eat the Daisies*

He had the kind of handshake that ought never to be used except as a tourniquet.   DENIS NORDEN, *You Can't Have Your Kayak and Heat It*

Where there is no struggle, there is no strength.   OPRAH WINFREY

Stress

Stress is your body's way of saying you haven't worked enough unpaid overtime.   SCOTT ADAMS, *Dilbert*

For the first time in my life I'm in a relationship where absolutely nothing is wrong – my anxiety-free relationship is driving me mad.
                          CARRIE BRADSHAW (SARAH JESSICA PARKER), *Sex and the City*

Stress is when you wake up screaming and realise you haven't fallen asleep yet.

Stress wouldn't be so hard to take if it were chocolate-covered.

Stupidity

No matter how smart you are, you spend much of your day being an idiot.
                          SCOTT ADAMS

His head is as empty as a hermit's address book.
EDMUND BLACKADDER (ROWAN ATKINSON), *Blackadder*

Everything goes over your head, doesn't it, George? You should go to Jamaica and become a limbo dancer.
EDMUND BLACKADDER (ROWAN ATKINSON), *Blackadder*

Man has made use of his intelligence – he invented stupidity.
RÉMY DE GOURMONT

You know, Lloyd, just when I think you couldn't possibly get any dumber, you go and do something like this . . . and totally redeem yourself!
HARRY DUNN (JEFF DANIELS), *Dumb and Dumber*

Only two things are infinite – the universe and human stupidity – and I'm not sure about the former.
ALBERT EINSTEIN

To call you stupid would be an insult to stupid people! I've known sheep that could outwit you! I've worn dresses with higher IQs.
WANDA GERSCHWITZ
(JAMIE LEE CURTIS), *A Fish Called Wanda*

John Carter (Noah Wyle): Can't believe I was that stupid, sneaking off and drinking while I was on call.
Mark Greene (Anthony Edwards): I can, you're a medical student.   *ER*

Genius may have its limitations, but stupidity is not thus handicapped.
ELBERT HUBBARD

You cannot fashion a wit out of two half-wits.   NEIL KINNOCK

Rose Nylund (Betty White): Ned was the sort of town idiot.
Sophia Petrillo (Estelle Getty): When, on your days off?
The Golden Girls

(*on Bo Derek*) She is so stupid she returns bowling balls because they've got holes in them.   JOAN RIVERS

Melanie Griffith is very sweet but dumb – the lights are on but the dogs aren't barking.   JOAN RIVERS

There is only one quality worse than hardness of heart and that is softness of head.
THEODORE ROOSEVELT

When a stupid man is doing something he is ashamed of, he always declares that it is his duty.
GEORGE BERNARD SHAW, *Caesar and Cleopatra*

The great advantage of having a reputation for being stupid: people are less suspicious of you.
TOM (JAMES FLEET), *Four Weddings And A Funeral*

Stupidity is the basic building block of the universe.
FRANK ZAPPA

Style

I like my whisky old and my women young.
ERROL FLYNN

The public has always expected me to be a playboy, and a decent chap never lets his public down.
ERROL FLYNN

My mother was a very elegant woman. When a flying saucer landed on the lawn, she turned it over to see if it was Wedgwood.
JOAN RIVERS

Fashions fade, style is eternal.
YVES ST LAURENT

Style is knowing who you are, what you want to say, and not giving a damn.
GORE VIDAL

Suburbia

I grew up in the suburbs in a neighbourhood that was not very tough at all. Even our school bully was only passively aggressive. He wouldn't take your lunch, he'd just say, 'You're gonna eat all that?'
BRIAN KILEY

Suburbia is where the developer bulldozes out the trees, then names the streets after them.
BILL VAUGHAN

Success

Eighty per cent of success is showing up.
WOODY ALLEN

The penalty for success is to be bored by the people who used to snub you.
NANCY ASTOR

Many a man owes his success to his first wife and his second wife to his success.
JIM BACKUS

Behind almost every woman you ever heard of stands a man who let her down.
NAOMI BLIVEN

Too much success can ruin you as surely as too much failure.
MARLON BRANDO

A successful man is one who can lay a firm foundation with the bricks others have thrown at him.
DAVID BRINKLEY

Behind every successful man there's a lot of unsuccessful years.
BOB BROWN

If at first you don't succeed, failure may be your thing.
GEORGE BURNS

Success is having to worry about every damn thing in the world except money.
JOHNNY CASH

I don't know the key to success, but the key to failure is trying to please everybody.
BILL COSBY

If at first you don't succeed, try, try again. Then quit. No use being a damn fool about it.
W.C. FIELDS

My formula for success is rise early, work late, and strike oil.
J. PAUL GETTY

Success is more dangerous than failure, the ripples break over a wider coastline.
GRAHAM GREENE

Behind every successful man stands a proud wife and a surprised mother-in-law.
BROOKS HAYS

Success is like a shot of heroin. It's up to you to decide whether you want to continue to put the needle in your arm.
DON MCLEAN

The road to success is always under construction.
ARNOLD PALMER

I don't measure a man's success by how high he climbs but how high he bounces when he hits bottom.
GEORGE S. PATTON

Behind every successful man you'll find a woman – who has absolutely nothing to wear.
JAMES STEWART

Success to me is having ten honeydew melons and eating only the top half of each one.
                                                              BARBRA STREISAND

Success is a great deodorant. It takes away all your past smells.
                                                              ELIZABETH TAYLOR

Success is a poison that should only be taken late in life and then only in small doses.
                                                              ANTHONY TROLLOPE

A successful man is one who makes more money than his wife can spend. A successful woman is one who can find such a man.
                                                              LANA TURNER

Nothing recedes like success.
                                                              WALTER WINCHELL

Success has gone to my stomach.
                                                              MICHAEL WINNER

I couldn't wait for success, so I went ahead without it.
                                                              JONATHAN WINTERS

Suicide

Dr Klein, his analyst, got him to see that jumping in front of a moving train was more hostile than self-destructive but in either case would ruin the crease in his pants.
                                                              WOODY ALLEN, *Without Feathers*

There have been times when I've thought about suicide, but with my luck it would probably turn out to be only a temporary solution.
                                                              WOODY ALLEN

Suicide is cheating the doctors out of a job.
                                                              JOSH BILLINGS

There are many who dare not kill themselves for fear of what the neighbours will say.
                                                              CYRIL CONNOLLY, *The Unquiet Grave*

I survived an overdose in Australia in the 1960s. I feel it is really bad manners to commit suicide in someone else's country.
                                                              MARIANNE FAITHFULL

Suicide is man's way of telling God: 'You can't fire me – I quit!'
                                                              BILL MAHER

Suicide is belated acquiescence in the opinion of one's wife's relatives.
                                                              H.L. MENCKEN

For years I've thought about killing myself. It's the only thing that kept me going.
                                                              DALE PUTLEY (ROBIN WILLIAMS), *Fathers' Day*

Sun

When the sun comes up, I have morals again. ELAYNE BOOSLER

Sunburn is very becoming – but only when it is even – one must be careful not to look like a mixed grill. NOËL COWARD, *The Lido Beach*

Pontoon boats are for people who can't get sunburned enough on land. *Crabby Road*

I like her from a distance. You know, the way you like the sun. Maris is like the sun . . . except without the warmth. FRASIER CRANE (KELSEY GRAMMER), *Frasier*

Superstition

You don't have to be superstitious to think it's unlucky to have thirteen children. EVAN ESAR

Oh come on, Ma, that's superstitious nonsense. You know, step on a crack, break your mother's back, it doesn't work – I know. DOROTHY ZBOMAK (BEA ARTHUR), *The Golden Girls*

Surgery

All them surgeons are highway robbers. Why do you think they wear masks when they operate? ARCHIE BUNKER (CARROLL O'CONNOR), *All in the Family*

My girlfriend has got to have a kidney transplant but I'm not worried. She hasn't rejected an organ for over fifteen years. TOM COTTER

Sybil Fawlty (Prunella Scales): I'm actually about to undergo an operation, Basil.
Basil Fawlty (John Cleese): Oh yes, how is the old toe-nail? Still growing in, hmmm? Still burrowing its way down into the bone? Still macheting its way through the nerve, eh? Nasty old nail. *Fawlty Towers*

The only weapon with which the unconscious patient can immediately retaliate upon the incompetent surgeon is the haemorrhage. WILLIAM STEWART HALSTED

Doctors are getting ready to do the first full face transplant. How bad must you feel when you get turned down as a donor? Uh, maybe we'll take your kidney.
JAY LENO

Surgeons replaced a man's penis with one of his fingers. Now his pants fit him like a glove, but his manicurist has filed a sexual harassment suit.
JAY LENO

They had me on the operating table all day. They looked into my stomach, my gall bladder, they examined everything inside of me. Know what they decided? I need glasses.
JOE E. LEWIS

I think we can save your husband's arm. Where would you like it sent?
NURSE (DORIS HESS), *Naked Gun*

(*hearing that Randolph Churchill had a non-cancerous lung removed*) A typical triumph of modern science to find the only part of Randolph that was not malignant and remove it.
EVELYN WAUGH

Suspicion

I suspect everyone, and I suspect no one.
INSPECTOR CLOUSEAU (PETER SELLERS), *The Pink Panther Strikes Again*

That guy looks suspicious. He's in a gay bar eating a hot dog without any irony.
WILL TRUMAN (ERIC MCCORMACK), *Will and Grace*

Switzerland

Everyone in the Swiss Army owns a Swiss Army knife. That's why no one messes with Switzerland.
CLIFF CLAVIN (JOHN RATZENBERGER), *Cheers*

The Swiss are not a people so much as a neat clean quite solvent business.
WILLIAM FAULKNER, *Intruder in the Dust*

In Italy for thirty-eight years under the Borgias they had warfare, terror, murder, bloodshed, but they produced Michelangelo, Leonardo da Vinci and the Renaissance. In Switzerland they had brotherly love, they had 500 years of democracy and peace. And what did they produce? The cuckoo-clock.
HARRY LIME (ORSON WELLES), *The Third Man*

(*of the Alps*) They say that if the Swiss had designed these mountains they'd be rather flatter.
PAUL THEROUX, *The Great Railway Bazaar*

Sympathy

Sympathy is such a wonderful thing, it's a crime to waste it on others.

EVAN ESAR

I have little compassion for people in trailer parks who refuse to move after getting tornado warnings. How hard is it for them to relocate? Their houses have wheels.

CARLOS MENCIA

I can sympathise with everything, except suffering.

OSCAR WILDE

T

Tact

Tact is the art of making guests feel at home when that's really where you wish they were.

GEORGE E. BERGMAN

Tact is simply a delicate form of lying.

GEORGE A. BIRMINGHAM, *General John Regan*

Tact is the ability to describe others as they see themselves.

ABRAHAM LINCOLN

Step aside everyone! Sensitive love letters are my speciality: 'Dear Baby, Welcome to Dumpsville. Population: you.'

HOMER SIMPSON, *The Simpsons*

Talent

Ed Sullivan will be around as long as someone else has talent.

FRED ALLEN

It took me fifteen years to discover that I had no talent for writing, but I couldn't give it up because by that time I was too famous.

ROBERT BENCHLEY

I've stretched a talent which is so thin it's almost transparent.

BING CROSBY

You could put all the talent I had in your left eye and still not suffer from impaired vision.

VERONICA LAKE

Genius does what it must, and Talent does what it can.   EARL OF LYTTON

I still believe that at any time the no-talent police will come and arrest me.
MIKE MYERS

Taste

Bad taste is simply saying the truth before it should be said.   MEL BROOKS

My tastes are simple. I am easily satisfied by the best.   WINSTON CHURCHILL

Taste is the feminine of genius.   EDWARD FITZGERALD

Good taste and humour are a contradiction in terms, like a chaste whore.
MALCOLM MUGGERIDGE

My granddad used to say, 'If everybody liked the same thing, they'd all be after
your grandma.'   GARY MULE DEER

While redecorating, I realised my wife and I have drastically different tastes in
furniture. She wanted to keep only the pieces that reflected the French provincial theme she was creating; I wanted to keep all the stuff we'd had sex on.
BRAD OSBERG

Good taste is the enemy of creativity.   PABLO PICASSO

Do not do unto others as you would have them do unto you. Their tastes may
not be the same.   GEORGE BERNARD SHAW, *Maxims for Revolutionists*

Tattoos

Grandmother used to take my mother to the circus to see the fat lady and the
tattooed man – now they're everywhere.   JOAN COLLINS

Women, don't get a tattoo. That butterfly looks great on your breast when you're
twenty or thirty, but when you get to seventy, it stretches into a condor.
BILLY ELMER

I have a tattoo on my most private part of Mickey and Minnie Mouse in a sexual
act. That's just my sense of humour.   JANET JACKSON

Pamela Lee said her name is tattooed on her husband's penis, which explains
why she changed her name from Anderson to Lee.   CONAN O'BRIEN

My boyfriend had a 'W' tattooed on each cheek. So when he bends over it says 'WOW'.

MARGARET SMITH

Taxation

He's spending a year dead for tax reasons.

DOUGLAS ADAMS, *The Restaurant at the End of the Universe*

(*objecting to the Bureau of Internal Revenue claiming unpaid tax back from him*)
They can't collect legal taxes from illegal money.

AL CAPONE

The hardest thing in the world to understand is income tax.

ALBERT EINSTEIN

In this world nothing can be said to be certain, except death and taxes.

BENJAMIN FRANKLIN

The creed of the Inland Revenue is simple: if we can bring one little smile to one little face today – then somebody's slipped up somewhere.

DAVID FROST

The way taxes are, you might as well marry for love.

JOE E. LEWIS

Death and taxes and childbirth! There's never a convenient time for any of them.

MARGARET MITCHELL, *Gone with the Wind*

Why, oh, why do we have taxes, huh? Just so we can have bloody parking restrictions, and bloody ugly traffic wardens, and bollocky pedestrian bloody crossings! Why not just have a Stupidity Tax? Just tax stupid people!

EDINA MONSOON (JENNIFER SAUNDERS), *Absolutely Fabulous*

Income tax has made more liars out of the American people than golf.

WILL ROGERS

What it comes down to is, when you come into the world you have nothing . . . when you leave you have nothing . . . and in between there's the IRS.

BOB THAVES

What is the difference between a taxidermist and a tax collector? The taxidermist takes only your skin.

MARK TWAIN

Taxis

I have done almost every human activity inside a taxi which does not require main drainage.   ALAN BRIEN

Too bad that all the people who know how to run the country are busy driving taxicabs and cutting hair.   GEORGE BURNS

Gas prices are so high in Chicago that cab drivers are taking the real way to the airport.   JAY LENO

New York has 200 new portable toilets. They're yellow, have four wheels, and a driver with a weird name.   DAVID LETTERMAN

People say New Yorkers can't get along. Not true. The other night I saw two New Yorkers, complete strangers, sharing a cab. One guy took the tyres and the radio, the other guy took the engine.   DAVID LETTERMAN

Tourists, have some fun with New York's hard-boiled cabbies. When you get to your destination, say to your driver: 'Pay? I was hitchhiking.'
                                                             DAVID LETTERMAN

Things You Don't Want To Hear From a Cab Driver:
You don't mind if I swing by my apartment to reload my gun, do you?
Does the back seat smell like a dead guy?
You can help yourself to the loose potato chips under the seat.
I'm letting you know up front, any touching is fifty bucks extra.
You know it's four o'clock and three couples already had sex back there.
My passengers have a nearly 80 per cent survival rate.
                                                             DAVID LETTERMAN

I'm not really a cab driver. I'm just waiting for something better to come along. You know, like death.   ALEX RIEGER (JUDD HIRSCH), *Taxi*

London cabbies spend years learning the street layout. In New York, cabbies learn which thermos is for coffee and which is for urine, and which they should drink in front of the passengers.   JON STEWART

No nice men are good at getting taxis.   KATHARINE WHITEHORN

Elizabeth Taylor

I knew Elizabeth Taylor when she didn't know where her next husband was coming from.   ANNE BAXTER

Her breasts, hanging and huge, like those of a peasant woman suckling her young in Peru.   CECIL BEATON

A spoiled, indulgent child, a blemish on public decency.   JOAN CRAWFORD

I remember my brother once saying, 'I'd like to marry Elizabeth Taylor,' and my father said, 'Don't worry, your turn will come.'   SPIKE MILLIGAN

Is Elizabeth Taylor fat? Her favourite food is seconds.   JOAN RIVERS

Every minute this broad spends outside of bed is a waste of time.
MIKE TODD

It would be very glamorous to be reincarnated as a great big ring on Liz Taylor's finger.   ANDY WARHOL

Teaching

Authorities say a severely disturbed geography teacher has shot and killed six people who did not know the capital of Scotland. He is still at large, and they remind everyone that the capital of Scotland is Edinburgh.
GEORGE CARLIN

Teaching is the last refuge of feeble minds with classical education.
ALDOUS HUXLEY

There's always one teacher you had a crush on. For me, it's my wife's aerobics instructor.   BRIAN KILEY

Things You Don't Want To Hear From Your Teacher On The First Day At School:
If my methods seem unconventional, it's because I forged my teaching credentials.
Is it just me, or is chalk delicious?
Study, don't study – honestly, I only care about tonight's Lotto numbers.
I was George W. Bush's English teacher.   DAVID LETTERMAN

You don't have to think too hard when you talk to a teacher.
J.D. SALINGER, *The Catcher in the Rye*

For every person wishing to teach there are thirty not wanting to be taught.
W.C. SELLAR, *And Now All This*

He who can, does. He who cannot, teaches.
GEORGE BERNARD SHAW, *Maxims for Revolutionists*

Technology

We don't know where the digital revolution is taking us, only that when we get there we will not have enough RAM.   DAVE BARRY

An escalator can never break; it can only become stairs.   MITCH HEDBERG

The thing with high-tech is that you always end up using scissors.
DAVID HOCKNEY

It is only when they go wrong that machines remind you how powerful they are.   CLIVE JAMES

For a list of all the ways technology has failed to improve the quality of life, please press three.   ALICE KAHN

Never send a human to do a machine's job.
AGENT SMITH (HUGO WEAVING), *The Matrix*

Teenagers

To the adolescent, there is nothing in the world more embarrassing than a parent.   DAVE BARRY

Nobody understands anyone eighteen, including those who are eighteen.
JIM BISHOP

Adolescence is just one big walking pimple.   CAROL BURNETT

I was a veteran before I was a teenager.   MICHAEL JACKSON

There's nothing wrong with teenagers that reasoning with them won't aggravate.   JEAN KERR

Remember that as a teenager you are at the last stage in your life when you will be happy to hear that the phone is for you.
FRAN LEBOWITZ, *Social Studies*

The invention of the teenager was a mistake. Once you identify a period of life in which people get to stay out late but don't have to pay taxes – naturally, nobody wants to live any other way.   JUDITH MARTIN

I was going through puberty at the same time my mother went through the change. The menfolk kept away.   JULIE WALTERS

Adolescence: a stage between infancy and adultery.

Adolescence begins when children stop asking questions – because they know all the answers.

Teenagers are well informed about anything they don't have to study.

Mother Nature is wonderful. She gives us twelve years to develop a love for our children before turning them into teenagers.

Telling a teenager the facts of life is like giving a fish a bath.

Teeth

There is probably no moment more appalling than that in which the tongue comes suddenly upon the ragged edge of a space from which the old familiar filling has disappeared.   ROBERT BENCHLEY, *One Minute Please*

Mr Craven's always been on the side of progress: he had false teeth when he was twenty-seven.   ALAN BENNETT, *Enjoy*

I hate flossing; I wish I just had one long curvy tooth.   MITCH HEDBERG

(*on Chelsea Clinton*) She's got more teeth than a Ferrari gearbox.
PATRICK KIELTY

(*on buck-toothed footballer Ronaldo*) He must be the only man alive who can eat an apple through a tennis racket.   GARY LINEKER

I didn't know my uncle had an upper plate until it came out in conversation.
BOB MONKHOUSE

Toothache: the pain that drives you to extraction.

Telegrams

A man never feels more important than when he receives a telegram containing more than ten words.   GEORGE ADE

(*on arriving in Venice*) Streets flooded. Please advise.   ROBERT BENCHLEY

(*first night telegram of congratulations to Gertrude Lawrence*) A warm hand on your opening.   NOËL COWARD

(*to Harry Secombe*) I hope you go before me because I don't want you singing at my funeral.
SPIKE MILLIGAN

Audience with me all the way. Managed to shake them off at the station.
HARRY SECOMBE

Telephone

I rang up British Telecom. I said, 'I want to report a nuisance caller.' They said, 'Not you again.'
FRANK CARSON

People who say, 'Anything is possible' have never tried to complain to a recorded announcement.
SAM EWING

(*answering the phone*) Bridget Jones, wanton sex goddess, with a very bad man between her thighs . . . Mum!
BRIDGET JONES (RENE ZELLWEGER), *Bridget Jones's Diary*

Ask not for whom the bell tolls – let the answering machine get it.
JEAN KERR

Utility is when you have one telephone, luxury is when you have two, and paradise is when you have none.
DOUG LARSON

The telephone is a good way to talk to people without having to offer them a drink.
FRAN LEBOWITZ

I tried phone sex. I got an ear infection.
RICHARD LEWIS

I despise automated answering services. After you've been hanging on the phone, listening to synthetic Vivaldi for twenty minutes, you're in such a bad mood that when you finally get through to an operator, you swear at them, and they hang up on you.
RORY McGRATH

Men like phones with lots of buttons. It makes them feel important.
RITA RUDNER

Have you ever called someone up and been disappointed when they answered the phone? You wanted the machine, and you're kind of thrown. You go, 'Oh, I, uh, didn't know you were there. I just wanted to leave a message saying "Sorry I missed you."'
JERRY SEINFELD

Operator! Give me the number for 911!
HOMER SIMPSON, *The Simpsons*

Well, if I called the wrong *number, why did you* answer the phone?
JAMES THURBER

I got home and the phone was ringing. I picked it up and said, 'Who's speaking please?' And a voice said, 'You are.'
TIM VINE

When a man talks dirty to a woman, it's sexual harassment. When a woman talks dirty to a man, it's $3.95 a minute.
STEVEN WRIGHT

I phoned the incontinence hotline. They put me on hold.
STEVEN WRIGHT

Television

(on the television adaptation of *The Hitch-Hiker's Guide to the Galaxy*) I had a great deal of say . . . but the producer didn't have a great deal of listen.
DOUGLAS ADAMS

The first thing a television viewer realises when watching a golf tournament is how the sport tends to make one inclined to whisper and avoid sudden movements, such as walking to the refrigerator during a possible birdie putt.
PETER ALFANO

Television is a device that permits people who haven't anything to do watch people who can't do anything.
FRED ALLEN

Sex on television can't hurt you – unless you fall off.
WOODY ALLEN

In Beverly Hills they don't throw their garbage away. They make it into television shows.
WOODY ALLEN

There's three kinds of death in this world. There's heart death, there's brain death, and there's being off the network.
GUY ALMES

Violence and smut are of course everywhere on the airwaves. You cannot turn on your television without seeing them, although sometimes you have to hunt around.
DAVE BARRY

They caught the first female serial killer, but she didn't kill the men herself. She gained access to their apartments, hid their remote controls and they killed themselves.
ELAYNE BOOSLER

Some television programmes are so much chewing-gum for the eyes.
JOHN MASON BROWN

Art is a moral passion married to entertainment. Moral passion without entertainment is propaganda, and entertainment without moral passion is television.
RITA MAE BROWN

Every time you think television has hit its lowest ebb, a new programme comes along to make you wonder where you thought the ebb was.
ART BUCHWALD

In TV today, you can say I pricked my finger, but you can't say it the other way around.
GEORGE CARLIN

They say violence on TV leads to violence in society. Well, there's a lot of comedy on TV. Does that cause comedy in the streets?
DICK CAVETT

You can always tell a detective on TV. He never takes his hat off.
RAYMOND CHANDLER

Television is more interesting than people. If it were not, we would have people standing in the corners of our rooms.
ALAN COREN

My father hated radio and could not wait for television to be invented so he could hate that too.
PETER DE VRIES

Television is an invention that permits you to be entertained in your living room by people you wouldn't have in your home.
DAVID FROST

I don't watch television. I think it destroys the art of talking about oneself.
STEPHEN FRY, *Paperweight*

Today, watching television often means fighting, violence, and foul language – and that's just deciding who gets to hold the remote control.
DONNA GEPHART

With all the advances in television technology, why is there still no 'Everyone Gets Naked' button?
JOHN GEPHART

All of my shows are great. Some of them are bad. But they are all great.
LEW GRADE

(on *Moses the Lawgiver*) It looks good in the rushes.
LEW GRADE

To waste one second of one's life is a betrayal of one's self . . . I wonder what's on television.
TONY HANCOCK, *Hancock's Half-Hour*

I'm getting tired of cable. Day after day it's the same ninety-seven channels.

JOE HICKMAN

Television has done much for psychiatry, by spreading information about it as well as contributing to the need for it.

ALFRED HITCHCOCK

Television is like a toaster, you push the button and the same thing pops up every time.

ALFRED HITCHCOCK

It's television, you see. If you are not on the thing every week, the public think you are either dead or deported.

FRANKIE HOWERD

You know the really great thing about television? If something important happens, anywhere in the world, night or day, you can always change the channel.

'REVEREND' JIM IGNATOWSKI (CHRISTOPHER LLOYD), *Taxi*

Even in moments of tranquillity Murray Walker sounds like a man whose trousers are on fire.

CLIVE JAMES

I'm glad cave people didn't invent television, because they would have just sat around and watched talk shows all day instead of creating tools.

DAVE JAMES

Working in television is like making love to a gorilla. You don't stop when you want to stop; you stop when the gorilla wants to stop.

DAVID JANSSEN

We've been on the air two years, but we're calling it our seventh anniversary because the camera adds five years.

CRAIG KILBORN

Television has proved that people will look at anything rather than each other.

ANN LANDERS

Former vice-president Dan Quayle said that if you take out the profanity, the TV show *The Osbournes* is a show about good family values. If you take out the profanity, *The Osbournes* is about thirty seconds long!

JAY LENO

(about *Big Brother*) They have cameras everywhere. If I want to see a guy urinate, I'll go to the subway.

DAVID LETTERMAN

CBS has a new show about a rapper who's also a cop. It's called *NYPDiddy*.

DAVID LETTERMAN

Al Gore is on the show tonight, and security is tighter than Joan Rivers' face.

DAVID LETTERMAN

I never watch the Dinah Shore show — I'm a diabetic.   OSCAR LEVANT

I am always delighted to see Ms [Vanessa] Feltz on my television because the sight always convinces me that I was wise to invest in a widescreen set.

VICTOR LEWIS-SMITH

The cable TV sex channels don't expand our horizons, don't make us better people and don't come in clearly enough.   BILL MAHER

I must say I find television very educational. The minute somebody turns it on, I go to the library and read a good book.   GROUCHO MARX

(*to talk show host Michael Parkinson*) I've always wanted to get on your show. To think that I had to expose myself to an LA cop to do it.

GEORGE MICHAEL

When politicians complain that TV turns the proceedings into a circus, it should be made clear that the circus was already there, and that TV has merely demonstrated that not all the performers are well trained.   ED MURROW

Just because your voice reaches halfway around the world doesn't mean you are wiser than when it reached only to the end of the bar.   ED MURROW

Al Gore turned down a chance to be on *The Simpsons*. He explained, 'I've never been animated and I'm not going to start now.'   CONAN O'BRIEN

A new study reveals that guests on daytime talk shows are predominantly female. Of course, most of them weren't born that way.   CONAN O'BRIEN

The Jerry Springer Show just celebrated its tenth anniversary. So the teenagers on the first show are probably grandparents by now.   CONAN O'BRIEN

A talk show is an unnatural act between consenting adults in public.

MICHAEL PARKINSON

If TV had covered the crucifixion, the cameras would have packed it in just before the third day.   OLIVER PRITCHETT

Never eat spinach just before going on the air.   DAN RATHER (*to Conan O'Brien*) Being on your show is like sex, because even when it isn't going well, I'm just glad I'm being paid.   CAROLINE RHEA

Why would anyone play *Jeopardy* now? Hard questions for $500. On the other shows you can say how many people are in the Jackson 5 for a million.

CHRIS ROCK

You know those shows where people call in and vote on different issues? Did you ever notice there's always like 18 per cent that say, 'I don't know.' It costs 90 cents to call up and vote. They're voting 'I don't know.' Imagine it: 'Honey, I feel very strongly about this. Give me the phone. Sometimes you have to stand up for what you believe you're not sure about.' This guy probably calls up phone sex girls for $2.95 to say, 'I'm not in the mood.'   ANDY ROONEY

Men don't care what's on TV. They only care what else is on TV.

JERRY SEINFELD

Jerry Seinfeld: Anyway, Larry, we're going to enjoy watching you in syndication after this.
Larry Sanders (Garry Shandling): This show isn't going to be syndicated.
Seinfeld: Oh that's right, that's me.   *The Larry Sanders Show*

TV respects me. It laughs with me, not at me.

HOMER SIMPSON, *The Simpsons*

Dear God, just give me one channel!   HOMER SIMPSON, *The Simpsons*

You have to work years in hit shows to make people sick and tired of you, but you can accomplish this in a few weeks on television.

WALTER SLEZAK

You'd have to be pretty special to be able to cheapen TV any further. It's like finding a way of making the sun hotter.   JERRY SPRINGER

The weirdest thing on the show was the guy that married his horse – and the horse wasn't even that attractive.   JERRY SPRINGER

What's with the warning, 'May contain some nudity'? Well, I have to know for sure.   TIM STEEVES

Acting on television is like being asked by the captain to entertain the passengers while the ship goes down.   PETER USTINOV

I hate television. I hate it as much as peanuts. But I can't stop eating peanuts.
ORSON WELLES

(*on the advent of television*) I'm delighted with it, because it used to be that films were the lowest form of art. Now we've got something to look down on.
BILLY WILDER

Television is the device that has changed a generation of youngsters from an irresistible force into immovable objects.

Temptation

Don't worry about temptation. As you grow older, it starts avoiding you.
ELBERT HUBBARD

Lead us not into temptation. Just tell us where it is, we'll find it.
SAM LEVENSON

Most people would like to be delivered from temptation but would like it to keep in touch.
ROBERT ORBEN

I can resist everything except temptation.
OSCAR WILDE, *Lady Windermere's Fan*

Tennis

You don't play people. You play a ball. You don't ever hit a guy in the butt and knock him over the net – unless you're really upset.
VIC BRADEN

Martina [Navratilova] was so far in the closet she was in danger of being a garment bag.
RITA MAE BROWN

Pete Sampras does have a weakness. He cannot cook for a start.
MICHAEL CHANG

New Yorkers love it when you spill your guts out there. Spill your guts at Wimbledon and they make you stop and clean it up.
JIMMY CONNORS

(*on John McEnroe*) I don't know that my behaviour has improved that much with age. They just found someone worse.
JIMMY CONNORS

The serve was invented so that the net could play.
BILL COSBY

The depressing thing about tennis is that no matter how good I get, I'll never be as good as a wall. They're so relentless.   Mitch Hedberg

If you don't do something special against Chris Evert you find yourself losing concentration after thirty-five shots.   Julie Heldman

Tennis is a perfect combination of violent action taking place in an atmosphere of total tranquillity.   Billie Jean King

If you're up against a girl with big boobs, bring her to the net and make her hit backhand volleys.   Billie Jean King

Michael Chang has all the fire and passion of a public service announcement, so much so that he makes Pete Sampras appear fascinating.   Alex Ramsey

Don't marry a tennis player – love means nothing to them.   Joan Rivers

Tim Henman is so anonymous. He's like a human form of beige.

Linda Smith

(*on growing up in a Los Angeles ghetto*) If you can keep playing tennis when somebody is shooting a gun down the street that's concentration.

Serena Williams

Texas

Most Texans think Hanukkah is some sort of duck call.   Richard Lewis

Look, you shoot off a guy's head with his pants down, believe me, Texas is not the place you want to get caught.

Louise Sawyer (Susan Sarandon), *Thelma and Louise*

If I owned Texas and Hell, I would rent out Texas and live in Hell.

Phil Sheridan

Thanksgiving

Here's a Thanksgiving tip. Generally, your turkey is not cooked enough if it passes you the cranberry sauce.   Joan Rivers

I love Thanksgiving turkey – it's the only time in Los Angeles that you see natural breasts.   Arnold Schwarzenegger

Margaret Thatcher

I am not prepared to accept the economics of a housewife.

JACQUES CHIRAC

She cannot see an institution without hitting it with her handbag.

JULIAN CRITCHLEY

She is happier getting in and out of tanks than in and out of museums or theatre seats. She seems to derive more pleasure from admiring new missiles than great works of art. What else can we expect from an ex-Spam hoarder from Grantham presiding over the social and economic decline of the country?

JULIAN CRITCHLEY

Attila the Hen.

CLEMENT FREUD

The great she-elephant, she who-must-be-obeyed.

DENIS HEALEY

A bargain-basement Boadicea.

DENIS HEALEY

Mrs Thatcher is doing for monetarism what the Boston Strangler did for door-to-door salesmen.

DENIS HEALEY

The nanny appeared to be extinct until 1975 when, like the coelacanth, she suddenly and unexpectedly reappeared in the shape of Margaret Thatcher.

SIMON HOGGART

She sounded like the Book of Revelations read out over a railway station public address system by a headmistress of a certain age wearing calico knickers.

CLIVE JAMES

She has the mouth of Marilyn Monroe and the eyes of Caligula.

FRANÇOIS MITTERAND

I cannot bring myself to vote for a woman who has been voice-trained to speak to me as though my dog has just died.   KEITH WATERHOUSE

She's just the sort of woman who wouldn't give you your ball back.   ANON

Theatre

Theatre director: a person engaged by the management to conceal the fact that the players cannot act.   JAMES AGATE

An evening of pantomime – one of the only spectator events outside of a fire that he could hope to understand. WOODY ALLEN, *Getting Even*

It is one of the tragic ironies of the theatre that only one man in it can count on steady work – the night watchman. TALLULAH BANKHEAD

I'm in bed with Burt Reynolds most of the time in the play. Oh, I know it's dirty work, but somebody has to do it. CAROL BURNETT

Watching Tallulah Bankhead on the stage is like watching somebody skating on thin ice – everyone wants to be there when it breaks.
MRS PATRICK CAMPBELL

I go to the theatre to be entertained. I don't want to see plays about rape, sodomy and drug addiction, I can get all that at home.
PETER COOK

Theatre is dead, but sometimes I like to go and watch the corpse decompose.
STEPHEN FRY

Apart from that, Mrs Lincoln, how did you enjoy the play? TOM LEHRER

Opening night: the night before the play is ready to open.
GEORGE JEAN NATHAN

I think first nights should come towards the end of a play's run – as indeed they often do. PETER USTINOV

Theme parks

Disneyland celebrated its 40th anniversary by buying a time capsule. They say it will be dug up in fifty years – or when the last person in line at Space Mountain gets to the front, whichever comes first. JAY LENO

With the Epcot Center the Disney corporation has accomplished something I didn't think possible in today's world. They have created a land of make-believe that's worse than regular life. P.J. O'ROURKE

Thought

If I'd wanted you to know what I'm thinking, I'd be talking.
AL BUNDY (ED O'NEILL), *Married . . . With Children*

Some people think of the glass as half full. Some people think of the glass as half empty. I think of the glass as too big.
GEORGE CARLIN

It is a far, far better thing to have a firm anchor in nonsense than to put out on the troubled seas of thought.
J.K. GALBRAITH, *The Affluent Society*

A great many people think they are thinking when they are merely rearranging their prejudices.
WILLIAM JAMES

The trouble with talking too fast is you may say something you haven't thought of yet.
ANN LANDERS

Thoughts, like fleas, jump from man to man. But they don't bite everybody.
STANISLAW LEC

I think, therefore I'm single.
LIZZ WINSTEAD

Tidiness

A clean desk is a sign of an empty mind.
JUSTICE FELIX FRANKFURTER

By the time the youngest children have learned to keep the house tidy, the oldest grandchildren are on hand to tear it to pieces.
CHRISTOPHER MORLEY

Time

Time is an illusion. Lunchtime doubly so.
DOUGLAS ADAMS

We spend our lives on the run. We get up by the clock, eat and sleep by the clock, get up again, go to work. And then we retire. And what do they give us? A bloody clock!
DAVE ALLEN

Time is nature's way of keeping everything from happening at once.
WOODY ALLEN

Time is a dressmaker specialising in alterations.
FAITH BALDWIN

One good thing about punctuality is that it's a sure way to help you enjoy a few minutes of privacy.
ORLANDO A. BATTISTA

Time is a great teacher, but unfortunately it kills all its pupils.
HECTOR BERLIOZ

The smallest interval of time known to man is that which occurs in Manhattan between the traffic signal turning green and the taxi driver behind you blowing his horn. JOHNNY CARSON

There is never enough time, unless you're serving it. MALCOLM FORBES

Either he's dead or my watch has stopped.
DR HACKENBUSH (GROUCHO MARX), *A Day at the Races*

If you go flying back through time and you see somebody else flying forward into the future, it's probably best to avoid eye contact. JACK HANDEY

The trouble with being punctual is that nobody's there to appreciate it.
FRANKLIN P. JONES

(*on Daylight Saving Time*) Spring forward; fall back. It sounds like Robert Downey Jr getting out of bed. DAVID LETTERMAN

If time were a colour, I bet it would be a tasteful off-white. GREG PARRISH

Only time can heal your broken heart, just as only time can heal his broken arms and legs. MISS PIGGY

Punctuality is the virtue of the bored. EVELYN WAUGH

The days of the digital watch are numbered.

How long a minute is, depends on what side of the bathroom door you're on.

Time may be a great healer, but it's also a lousy beautician.

Torture

If you wanted to torture me, you'd tie me down and force me to watch our first five videos. JON BON JOVI

Tourism

The worst thing about being a tourist is having other tourists recognise you as a tourist. RUSSELL BAKER

A tourist is someone who goes three thousand miles to get a picture of himself in front of his car. ROBERT BENCHLEY

To be a Frenchman abroad is to be miserable; to be an American abroad is to make other people miserable.   AMBROSE BIERCE

I suppose some people like to know that you could get sixteen and a half London buses into the dome of St Paul's Cathedral, but it isn't really what Sir Christopher Wren had in mind.   BASIL BOOTHROYD, *Boothroyd at Bay*

The main hazard for the holidaymaker abroad is other holidaymakers abroad.
                                                OLIVER PRITCHETT

Towels

Those press-on towels are a real rip-off, aren't they? I used six of them and couldn't even get my arms dry.   JACK DEE

A towel is the only thing that gets wet as it dries.

Toys

When I was a kid, all I knew was rejection. My yo-yo, it never came back.
                                                RODNEY DANGERFIELD

I went to the park and saw this kid flying a kite. The kid was really excited. I don't know why, that's what they're supposed to do. Now if he'd had a chair on the other end of that string, I would have been impressed.
                                                MITCH HEDBERG

Signs That There's Trouble in the Barbie and Ken Marriage:
Ken overheard at bar saying he'd like to find a woman with bendable elbows.
Years-old feud about who can go longer without blinking.
While Ken's asleep, Barbie covers him with bacon grease so neighbour's dog will chew him to shreds and bury him.
She wants the kids raised as dolls, and he wants them raised as action figures.
He's been coming home late at night reeking of Silly Putty.
Personal ad reads, 'Curvy blonde seeks anatomically-correct guy.'
                                                DAVID LETTERMAN

Apparently the new high-tech Star Wars toys will be in stores any day now. The toys can talk and are interactive, so they can be easily distinguished from Star Wars fans.   CONAN O'BRIEN

My mother gave all my toys away while I was in the war. She said, 'Well, I'm sorry, but how was I to know you were going to live?'
                                                JONATHAN WINTERS

I didn't get a train like the other kids, I got a toy subway instead. You couldn't see anything but every now and then you'd hear this rumbling noise go by.

STEVEN WRIGHT

Tragedy

Hush, Hush,
Nobody cares!
Christopher Robin
Has
   Fallen
     Down
       Stairs

J.B. MORTON

The worst thing that ever happened to me was that I offered a fellow a crisp from my bag and he took two.

VIC REEVES

Trains

The only way to be sure of catching a train is to miss the one before it.

G.K. CHESTERTON

Next train's gone!   HARBOTTLE (MOORE MARRIOTT), *Oh, Mr Porter!*

On a train, why do I always end up sitting next to the woman who's eating the individual fruit pie by sucking the filling out through the hole in the middle?

VICTORIA WOOD

Transsexuals

I know a transsexual guy whose only ambition is to eat, drink, and be Mary.

GEORGE CARLIN

Travel

It is impossible to travel faster than the speed of light, and certainly not desirable, as one's hat keeps blowing off.

WOODY ALLEN

Americans travelling abroad are so disorientated by foreign currency that every now and then one of them will buy a single croissant and leave a tip large enough for the waiter to retire for life.

DAVE BARRY

The only way to buy a railway ticket in advance is to go online and spend three hours entering approximately 900 details of your proposed journey, including preferred width of track and whether you have a nut allergy.

BILL BRYSON

It is easier to find a travelling companion than to get rid of one.

ART BUCHWALD

When you travel, remember that a foreign country is not designed to make you comfortable. It is designed to make its own people comfortable.

CLIFTON FADIMAN

Writing and travel broaden your ass if not your mind.   ERNEST HEMINGWAY

(*asked whether he had visited the Parthenon during his trip to Greece*) I can't really remember the names of the clubs that we went to.

SHAQUILLE O'NEAL

In an underdeveloped country don't drink the water. In a developed country don't breathe the air.   JONATHAN RABAN

We've sent a man to the moon, and that's 290,000 miles away. The centre of the Earth is only 4,000 miles away. You could drive that in a week, but for some reason nobody's ever done it.   ANDY ROONEY

Travel is only glamorous in retrospect.   PAUL THEROUX

So tell us all about Europe. What movie did they show on the plane?

MARYANN THORPE (CHRISTINE BARANSKI), *Cybill*

The vast majority of passengers on a cruise liner are there against their will.

PETER TINNISWOOD

There ain't no surer way to find out whether you like people or hate them than to travel with them.   MARK TWAIN

Look at all the buses now that want exact change. I figure if I give them exact change, they should take me exactly where I want to go.

GEORGE WALLACE

When you're safe at home you wish you were having an adventure; when you're having an adventure you wish you were safe at home.

THORNTON WILDER

Why do they call it rush hour when nothing moves?   ROBIN WILLIAMS

Treaties

Treaties are like roses and young girls – they last while they last.

CHARLES DE GAULLE

Trends

Never forget that only dead fish swim with the stream.

MALCOLM MUGGERIDGE

Trends, like horses, are easier to ride in the direction they are already going.

JOHN NAISBITT

Fashions are induced epidemics.

GEORGE BERNARD SHAW

Trouble

Trouble is only opportunity in work clothes.

HENRY JOHN KAISER

When you're in deep water it's a good idea to keep your mouth shut.
The best way to keep your kids out of hot water is to put some dishes in it.

Harry S. Truman

He rules the country with an iron fist, the same way he plays the piano.

BOB HOPE

(*on Truman's 1948 campaign promises*) If there had been any formidable body of cannibals in the country he would have promised to provide them with free missionaries, fattened at the taxpayer's expense.   H.L. MENCKEN

To err is Truman.

WALTER WINCHELL

Among his many weaknesses was his utter inability to discriminate between history and histrionics.

ANON

Trust

Never trust a man with testicles.

JO BRAND

Never trust a man who, when he's alone in a room with a tea cozy, doesn't try it on.

BILLY CONNOLLY

Never trust a man who says, 'Don't struggle.'

JENNY ECLAIR

I distrust a man who says when. If he's got to be careful not to drink too much, it's because he's not to be trusted when he does.
KASPER GUTMAN (SIDNEY GREENSTREET), The Maltese Falcon

Once the trust goes out of a relationship, it's really no fun lying to 'em any more.
NORM PETERSON (GEORGE WENDT), Cheers

Tell a man there are 500 billion stars in the universe and he will believe you; tell him a fence has just been painted and he has to touch it first.

Never trust a man who says he's the boss at home — he probably lies about other things, too.

Truth

Some men love truth so much that they seem to be in continual fear lest she should catch a cold on overexposure.
SAMUEL BUTLER, Notebooks

In war, truth is so precious it must always be accompanied by a bodyguard of lies.
WINSTON CHURCHILL

I told my wife the truth. I told her I was seeing a psychiatrist. Then she told me the truth: that she was seeing a psychiatrist, two plumbers and a bartender.
RODNEY DANGERFIELD

Half the truth is often a whole lie.
BENJAMIN FRANKLIN

I don't want the truth. I want something I can tell Parliament.
JIM HACKER (PAUL EDDINGTON), Yes, Minister

It is always the best policy to speak the truth, unless of course you are an exceptionally good liar.
JEROME K. JEROME

A gaffe is when a politician tells the truth.
MICHAEL KINSLEY

A man generally has two reasons for doing a thing. One that sounds good, and a real one.
J. PIERPONT MORGAN

Truth is like the sun. You can shut it out for a time, but it ain't goin' away.
ELVIS PRESLEY

If truth is beauty, how come no one has their hair done in the library?
LILY TOMLIN

Truth is the most valuable thing we have. Let us economize it.

MARK TWAIN, *Following the Equator*

Truth is like iced water; it shocks you when it hits you, but no one's ever died from it.

Tina Turner

All legs and hair with a mouth that could swallow the whole stadium and the hot-dog stand. LAURA LEE DAVIES

Typing

I was regarded as a good typist; at my high school typing was regarded as a female secondary sex characteristic, like breasts.

MARGARET ATWOOD, *Lady Oracle*

I type 101 words a minute. But it's in my own language. MITCH HEDBERG

U

Ugliness

I know a woman who has a husband so ugly she met him when a friend sent him over to her house to cure her hiccups. PHYLLIS DILLER

Beauty may be skin deep, but ugly goes clear to the bone. REDD FOXX

Ugliness is in a way superior to beauty because it lasts.

SERGE GAINSBOURG

God must have loved plain people; he made so many of them.

ABRAHAM LINCOLN

I was so plain as a child, I was petting with a boy and his hand went to sleep.

JOAN RIVERS

There are no ugly women, only lazy ones.

HELENA RUBINSTEIN, *My Life for Beauty*

Last week I stated that this woman was the ugliest woman I had ever seen. I have since been visited by her sister and now wish to withdraw that statement.

MARK TWAIN

Understanding

I have suffered from being misunderstood, but I would have suffered a hell of a lot more if I had been understood.　　　　CLARENCE DARROW

Why, a four-year-old child could understand this report. Run out and find me a four-year-old child. I can't make head or tail of it.

RUFUS T. FIREFLY (GROUCHO MARX), *Duck Soup*

Underwear

I like men's underwear with slogans on, like 'my knob is in here.'

JO BRAND

Instead of doing a wash, I just keep buying underwear. My goal is to have over 360 pair. That way I only have to wash once a year.

GEORGE COSTANZA (JASON ALEXANDER), *Seinfeld*

I got some new underwear the other day. Well . . . new to me.　　EMO PHILIPS

Denise Royle (Caroline Aherne): Dad, stop fiddling with yeself!
Jim Royle (Ricky Tomlinson): I'm not fiddling with meself. I paid a quid for these underpants and I've got 50 pence worth stuck up me arse!

The Royle Family

Marge, you being a cop makes you the man . . . which makes me the woman. I have no interest in that, besides occasionally wearing the underwear, which, as we discussed, is strictly a comfort thing.

HOMER SIMPSON, *The Simpsons*

Unemployment

Well, there's good news and bad news. The bad news is that Neil will be taking over both branches, and some of you will lose your jobs. Those of you who are kept on will have to relocate to Swindon if you wanna stay. I know, gutting. On a more positive note, the good news is, I've been promoted, so . . . every cloud. You're still thinking about the bad news, aren't you?

DAVID BRENT (RICKY GERVAIS), *The Office*

Well, that's odd. I've just robbed a man of his livelihood, and yet I feel strangely empty. Tell you what, Smithers – have him beaten to a pulp.

MONTGOMERY BURNS, The Simpsons

Sesame Street Workshop announced that they are laying off sixty workers. News of the firings was brought to the employees by the letters F and U.

JIMMY FALLON

One thing about being a cabbie is that you don't have to worry about being fired from a good job.

ALEX RIEGER (JUDD HIRSCH), Taxi

The trouble with unemployment is that the minute you wake up in the morning, you're on the job.

SLAPPY WHITE

Universe

The creator of the universe works in mysterious ways. But he uses a base ten counting system and likes round numbers.

SCOTT ADAMS

The universe is merely a fleeting idea in God's mind – a pretty uncomfortable thought, particularly if you've just made a down payment on a house.

WOODY ALLEN

I'm astounded by people who want to 'know' the universe when it's hard enough to find your way around Chinatown.

WOODY ALLEN, Getting Even

According to my son, I understand the universe about as well as a barnacle understands a nuclear aircraft carrier.

DAVE BARRY

The two most abundant things in the universe are hydrogen and stupidity.

HARLAN ELLISON

I don't think I'm alone when I say I'd like to see more and more planets fall under the ruthless domination of our solar system.

JACK HANDEY

My theology, briefly, is that the universe was dictated but not signed.

CHRISTOPHER MORLEY

Nine-tenths of the universe, in fact, is the paperwork.

TERRY PRATCHETT, Thief of Time

The surest sign that intelligent life exists elsewhere in the universe is that it has never tried to contact us.

BILL WATTERSON, Calvin and Hobbes

University

I have a daughter who goes to SMU. She could've gone to UCLA here in California, but it's one more letter she'd have to remember. SHECKY GREENE

Everyone has a right to a university degree in America, even if it's in Hamburger Technology. CLIVE JAMES

I find the three major administrative problems on a campus are sex for the students, athletics for the alumni and parking for the faculty. CLARK KERR

(*on the Yale prom*) If all the girls attending it were laid end to end, I wouldn't be at all surprised. DOROTHY PARKER

When bad ideas have nowhere else to go, they emigrate to America and become university courses. FREDERIC RAPHAEL

I was thrown out of NYU my freshman year for cheating on my metaphysics final; I looked within the soul of the boy sitting next to me. ALVY SINGER (WOODY ALLEN), *Annie Hall*

Personally, I liked the University. They gave us money and facilities, we didn't have to produce anything. You've never been out of college. You don't know what it's like out there. I've worked in the private sector – they expect results. DR RAY STANTZ (DAN AYKROYD), *Ghostbusters*

A university is a collection of mutually repellent individuals held together only by a common interest in parking. GEORGE F. WILL

Unwritten laws

Newton's first law of furniture buying: The amount you will hate a given piece of furniture is equal to its cost multiplied by the length of time, in months, it takes to arrive. DAVE BARRY

Anything you buy will go on sale next week. ERMA BOMBECK

Anything you lose automatically doubles in value. MIGNON MCLAUGHLIN, *The Second Neurotic's Notebook*

The 50-50-90 rule: anytime you have a 50–50 chance of getting something right, there's a 90 per cent probability you'll get it wrong. ANDY ROONEY

At bank, post office or supermarket, there is one universal law which you ignore at your own peril: the shortest line moves the slowest. BILL VAUGHAN

Paper is strongest at the perforations.

Bills travel through the mail at twice the speed of cheques.

If a nail is hit with exactly the right amount of force from exactly the right angle, it will bend over.

If something's old and you're trying to sell it, it's obsolete. But if you're trying to buy it, it's a collector's item.

The easiest way to find something lost around the house is to buy a replacement.

The one who snores will fall asleep first.

You will always find what you are looking for in the last place you look.

The severity of the itch is proportional to the reach.

Use

You're about as useful as a one-legged man at an arse-kicking contest.
EDMUND BLACKADDER (ROWAN ATKINSON), *Blackadder*

Men are useful. I think their testicles are a great area for testing anti-wrinkle cream. JO BRAND

Look, Rose, God doesn't make mistakes. We were all put on this planet for a purpose. Blanche, you're here to work in a museum, so that art can be appreciated by humanity. Dorothy, you're here as a substitute teacher to educate our youth. And Rose, you're here because the rhythm method was very popular in the Twenties. SOPHIA PETRILLO (ESTELLE GETTY), *The Golden Girls*

Even a clock that is not going is right twice a day. Polish proverb

V

Vacation

No self-respecting mother would run out of intimidations on the eve of a major holiday.
                                                                                    ERMA BOMBECK

If the Norfolk Broads are so broad, then why do we need a narrow-boat to go on holiday there?
                                                                                    JASPER CARROTT

Vacation: two weeks on the sunny sands, the rest of the year on the financial rocks.
                                                                                    SAM EWING

For a successful vacation, tourists need to take along half the clothes they planned and twice the money.
                                                                                    SAM EWING

Did anybody get the concept behind summer vacations with your folks? We did not get along together in a five-bedroomed house. Dad's idea was to put all of us in a car and drive through the desert at the hottest time of the year. Good call, Dad.
                                                                                    BILL HICKS

No one needs a vacation so much as the person who has just had one.
                                                                                    ELBERT HUBBARD

(*declining Alexander Woollcott's invitation to share a holiday on the French Riviera*): I can think of forty better places to spend the summer, all of them on Long Island in a hammock.
                                                                                    HARPO MARX

Valentine

For Valentine's Day a German company has made chocolate in shapes of couples making love. I don't like them . . . I don't want my chocolate to have more fun than me.
                                                                                    JAY LENO

I feel bad for people who die on Valentine's Day. How much would flowers cost then? Ten grand?
                                                                                    JAY LENO

I wanted to make it really special on Valentine's Day, so I tied my boyfriend up. And for three solid hours I watched whatever I wanted on TV.
                                                                                    TRACY SMITH

Vanity

Conceit. God's gift to little men.
BRUCE BARTON

To say that a man is vain means merely that he is pleased with the effect he produces on other people.
MAX BEERBOHM

Most of the shadows of this life are caused by standing in one's own sunshine.
RALPH WALDO EMERSON

He that falls in love with himself will have no rivals.
BENJAMIN FRANKLIN

(*on the alleged vanity of his team-mate*) If Graeme Souness was a chocolate drop, he'd eat himself.
ARCHIE GEMMILL

Conceit is the finest armour a man can wear.
JEROME K. JEROME, *Idle Thoughts of an Idle Fellow*

Some of the greatest love affairs I've known involved one actor, unassisted.
WILSON MIZNER

The affair between Margot Asquith and Margot Asquith will live as one of the prettiest love stories in all literature.
DOROTHY PARKER

When a man is wrapped up in himself he makes a pretty small package.
JOHN RUSKIN

(*on her then husband*) Richard Burton is so discriminating that he won't go to see a play with anybody in it but himself.
ELIZABETH TAYLOR

(*on Warren Beatty*) He's the type of man who will end up dying in his own arms.
MAMIE VAN DOREN

A narcissist is someone better looking than you are.
GORE VIDAL

To love oneself is the beginning of a lifelong romance.
OSCAR WILDE

The surest cure for vanity is loneliness.
TOM WOLFE

Vegetarians

You're thinking I'm one of those wise-ass Californian vegetarians who is going to tell you that eating a few strips of bacon is bad for your health. I'm not. I say it's a free country and you should be able to kill yourself at any rate you choose, as long as your cold, dead body is not blocking my driveway.

SCOTT ADAMS

Nothing wrong with vegetarians. Some of my best friends are vegetarians. Admittedly, they're also quadrupeds.   PETER ANDERTON

I tell vegetarians, 'Hey, vegetables are living things too. They're just easier to catch.'   KEVIN BRENNAN

Most vegetarians look so much like the food they eat that they can be classified as cannibals.   FINLEY PETER DUNNE

I won't eat anything that has intelligent life, but I'd gladly eat a network executive or a politician.   MARTY FELDMAN

I'm not a vegetarian, but I eat animals who are.   GROUCHO MARX

I was a vegetarian until I started leaning toward the sunlight.

RITA RUDNER

Animals are my friends . . . and I don't eat my friends.

GEORGE BERNARD SHAW

Lisa Simpson: Dad! Can't you have some other type of party, one where you don't serve meat?
Homer Simpson: All normal people love meat. If I went to a barbecue and there was no meat, I'd say, 'Yo Goober! Where's the meat?' I'm trying to impress people here, Lisa. You don't win friends with salad.   *The Simpsons*

Venom

The first thing I do in the morning is brush my teeth and sharpen my tongue.

OSCAR LEVANT

If you haven't got anything nice to say about anyone, come and sit by me.

ALICE ROOSEVELT LONGWORTH

When one woman strikes at the heart of another she seldom misses – and the wound is invariably fatal.

MARQUISE DE MERTEUIL (GLENN CLOSE), *Dangerous Liaisons*

Versatility

(*on Natalie Imbruglia*) She's the kind of girl you could either rob a bank with or take to church.

BONO

Viagra

Old men don't use Viagra because they're impotent. Old men use Viagra because old women are so ugly.

JIMMY CARR

They're testing a new Viagra nasal spray on dogs. Pity the poor mailman now!

JAY LENO

There's now a better Viagra pill that works in a minute instead of an hour. You know a man invented this. It cuts out foreplay completely.

JAY LENO

Bob Dole revealed he is one of the test subjects for Viagra. He said on Larry King: 'I wish I had bought stock in it.' Only a Republican would think the best part of Viagra is the fact that you could make money out of it.

JAY LENO

I only take Viagra when I am with more than one woman.

JACK NICHOLSON

There's a new Viagra virus going around the Internet. It doesn't affect your hard drive, but you can't minimise anything for hours.

JOAN RIVERS

My girlfriend was complaining about my stamina in the sack, so I popped six Viagras and drank a case of Red Bull. Her funeral is Tuesday.

HARLAN WILLIAMS

Vice

A small town is a place where there's no place to go where you shouldn't.

BURT BACHARACH

It is good to be without vices, but it is not good to be without temptations.

WALTER BAGEHOT

Cheating is the gift man gives himself.

MONTGOMERY BURNS, *The Simpsons*

(*on his debut in the* Harry Potter *films*) I know I'm going to become a role model so I suppose I'll have to stop being pictured being thrown out of nightclubs at two in the morning.   ROBBIE COLTRANE

If you resolve to give up smoking, drinking and loving, you don't actually live longer; it just seems longer.   CLEMENT FREUD

It's all right letting yourself go, as long as you can let yourself back.
                                                            MICK JAGGER

She's the kind of girl who climbed the ladder of success, wrong by wrong.
                                    TIRA (MAE WEST), *I'm No Angel*

I've been in more laps than a napkin.   MAE WEST

Never support two weaknesses at the same time. It's your combination sinners – your lecherous liars and your miserly drunkards – who dishonour the vices and bring them into bad repute.   THORNTON WILDER, *The Matchmaker*

Video

A Canadian psychologist is selling a video that teaches you to test your dog's IQ. Here's how it works: if you spend $12.99 for the video, your dog is smarter than you.   JAY LENO

This guy is selling a video of Jennifer Lopez having sex. Have you seen it? Frankly, I think it makes me look a little fat.   DAVID LETTERMAN

If you buy your husband or boyfriend a video camera, for the first few weeks he has it, lock the door when you go to the bathroom. Most of my husband's early films end with a scream and a flush.   RITA RUDNER

I was up on 96th Street today. There was a kid couldn't have been more than ten years old. He was asking a street vendor if he had any other bootlegs as good as *Death Blow*. That's who I care about. The little kid who needs bootlegs because his parent or guardian won't let him see the excessive violence and strong sexual content you and I take for granted.   JERRY SEINFELD

Violence

Have you heard about the woman who stabbed her husband thirty-seven times? I admire her restraint.   ROSEANNE BARR

Violence is the repartee of the illiterate.   ALAN BRIEN

The right to swing my fist ends where the other man's nose begins.

OLIVER WENDELL HOLMES

Beware of the man who does not return your blow: he neither forgives you nor allows you to forgive yourself.

GEORGE BERNARD SHAW, *Man and Superman*

This calls for a very special blend of psychology and extreme violence.

VYVYAN (ADRIAN EDMONDSON), *The Young Ones*

Virginity

I'm a virgin and I brought up all my children to be the same.   SHIRLEY BASSEY

They used to say that if you lost your virginity in Cork someone would be sure to find it before teatime and bring it back to your mother.   MAEVE BINCHY

A twenty-five-year-old virgin is like the man who was set upon by thieves – everyone passes by.   CHARLOTTE BINGHAM

Losing your real virginity is when you first come with someone, I believe. A bit like the Queen having two birthdays.   JULIE BURCHILL

He can remember the night he lost his innocence in the back seat of the family car. It would have been even more memorable if he hadn't been alone.

RED BUTTONS

I always thought of losing my virginity as a career move.   MADONNA

I remember the first time I had sex – I kept the receipt.   GROUCHO MARX

Men prefer to marry virgins because they can't stand criticism.

Virtue

Nothing is more unpleasant than a virtuous person with a mean mind.

WALTER BAGEHOT

The good die young because they can see it's no use living if you've got to be good.   JOHN BARRYMORE

He neither drank, smoked, nor rode a bicycle. Living frugally, saving his money, he died early, surrounded by greedy relatives. It was a great lesson to me.

JOHN BARRYMORE

Righteous people terrify me; virtue is its own punishment.   ANEURIN BEVAN

Good women always think it is their fault when someone else is being offensive. Bad women never take the blame for anything.

ANITA BROOKNER, *Hotel du Lac*

A lady is someone who never shows her underwear unintentionally.

LILLIAN DAY

Virtue may be its own reward, but most people are looking for a better deal.

SAM EWING

I do not know if she was virtuous, but she was ugly, and, with a woman, that is half the battle.   HEINRICH HEINE

Any of us can achieve virtue, if by virtue we merely mean the avoidance of the vices that do not attract us.   ROBERT LYND

When you can't have anything else, you can have virtue.   DON MARQUIS

(*on Carl Lewis*) I wouldn't be surprised if one day Carl's halo slipped and choked him.   ALLAN WELLS

Virtue has its own reward, but no sale at the box office.   MAE WEST

I used to be Snow White – but I drifted.   MAE WEST

Vulgarity

I've been accused of vulgarity. I say that's bullshit.   MEL BROOKS

Vulgarity is the garlic in the salad of life.   CYRIL CONNOLLY

Swearing is a compromise between running away and fighting.

FINLEY PETER DUNNE

When a driver gives you the finger, what does it mean? Am I supposed to feel bad? I mean, you could just give someone the toe really. I would feel worse if I got the toe than if I got the finger because it's not easy to give someone the toe. You've gotta get the shoe off, the sock off and drive . . .

JERRY SEINFELD

Waiters

Any man should be happy who is allowed the patience of his wife, the tolerance of his children and the affection of waiters. MICHAEL ARLEN

I went into a French restaurant and asked the waiter, 'Have you got frogs' legs?' He said, 'Yes', so I said, 'Well hop into the kitchen and get me a cheese sandwich.' TOMMY COOPER

Manuel will show you to your room – if you're lucky.
BASIL FAWLTY (JOHN CLEESE), *Fawlty Towers*

It's a good thing that life is not as serious as it seems to a waiter.
DON HEROLD

Waiter, there's no fly in my soup! KERMIT THE FROG, *The Muppet Show*

Wales and the Welsh

Never ask for directions in Wales, Baldrick, you'll be washing spit out of your hair for a fortnight.
EDMUND BLACKADDER (ROWAN ATKINSON), *Blackadder*

The Welsh are all actors. It's only the bad ones who become professionals.
RICHARD BURTON

Wales is the land of my fathers. And my fathers can have it.
DYLAN THOMAS

There are still parts of Wales where the only concession to gaiety is a striped shroud. GWYN THOMAS

We can trace almost all the disasters of English history to the influence of Wales. EVELYN WAUGH, *Decline and Fall*

Never get mixed up in a Welsh wrangle. It doesn't end in blows, like an Irish one, but goes on for ever. EVELYN WAUGH, *Decline and Fall*

Walking

I like long walks, especially when they are taken by people who annoy me.
FRED ALLEN

My grandmother started walking five miles a day when she was sixty. She's ninety-seven now, and we don't know where the hell she is.
ELLEN DEGENERES

People think I have an interesting walk. I'm just trying to hold my stomach in.
ROBERT MITCHUM

I went for a walk last night and my girlfriend asked me how long I was going to be gone. I said, 'The whole time.'
STEVEN WRIGHT

War

I have never understood this liking for war. It panders to instincts already catered for within the scope of any respectable domestic establishment.
ALAN BENNETT, *Forty Years On*

Memorial Day: we honour our war dead by getting in a car and driving until one of the kids throws up.
LEWIS BLACK

(*on the British war effort in World War One*) A war hasn't been fought this badly since Olaf the Hairy, chief of all the Vikings, accidentally ordered 8,000 battle helmets with the horns on the inside.
EDMUND BLACKADDER (ROWAN ATKINSON), *Blackadder Goes Forth*

George (Hugh Laurie): If we do happen to step on a mine, sir, what do we do?
Edmund Blackadder (Rowan Atkinson): Normal procedure, Lieutenant, is to jump 200 feet in the air and scatter oneself over a wide area.
Blackadder Goes Forth

We've been sitting here since Christmas 1914, during which millions of men have died, and we've advanced no further than an asthmatic ant with some heavy shopping.
EDMUND BLACKADDER (ROWAN ATKINSON), *Blackadder Goes Forth*

In war there is no second prize for the runner-up.
GENERAL OMAR BRADLEY

I'm sick of hearing about the wounded. What about all the thousands of wonderful guys who are fighting this war without any of the credit or the glory that always goes to those lucky few who just happen to get shot.

FRANK BURNS (LARRY LINVILLE), *M*A*S*H*

War is much too important a thing to be left to the generals.

GEORGES CLEMENCEAU

(*on the Six Day War*) If we lose this war, I'll start another in my wife's name.

MOSHE DAYAN

(*on Afghanistan*) They live in caves. So we came up with burrowing bombs. Doesn't that mean we're creating more caves? In some parts of the country it's got to be considered a re-development project.

WILL DURST

Men love war because it allows them to look serious. Because it is the one thing that stops women laughing at them.

JOHN FOWLES

The Gulf War was like teenage sex. We got in too soon and out too soon.

TOM HARKIN

We have smart bombs. They not only find the target, they knock on the front door and pretend to be the pizza delivery guy.

JAY LENO

I'll just have to sit this one out on the touchline with the half-time oranges and the fat wheezy boys with a note from matron, while you young bloods link arms for the glorious final scrum down.

GENERAL MELCHETT (STEPHEN FRY), *Blackadder Goes Forth*

The quickest way of ending a war is to lose it.

GEORGE ORWELL

The object of war is not to die for your country, but to make the other bastard die for his.

GEORGE S. PATTON

If it was the war to end all wars, why did they call it World War One?

COLIN QUINN

You can no more win a war than you can win an earthquake.

JEANNETTE RANKIN

Sometimes I think war is God's way of teaching us geography.

PAUL RODRIGUEZ

(*on nuclear warfare*) You may reasonably expect a man to walk a tightrope safely for ten minutes; it would be unreasonable to do so without accident for 200 years.   BERTRAND RUSSELL

War does not determine who is right – only who is left.   BERTRAND RUSSELL

All wars are popular for the first thirty days.   ARTHUR SCHLESINGER JR

Nuclear war would really set back cable.   TED TURNER

In a world without men, there would be no war, just intense negotiations every twenty-eight days.   ROBIN WILLIAMS

There will never be a nuclear war; there's too much real estate involved.
                                                          FRANK ZAPPA

In nuclear war, all men are cremated equal.

Washington

Washington is like a self-sealing tank on a military aircraft. When a bullet passes through, it closes up.   DEAN ACHESON

The Pentagon boasts more than seventeen miles of corridors; there are people wandering around still trying to deliver urgent memos pertaining to the Normandy Invasion.   DAVE BARRY

(*to Rudy Giuliani*) Frankly, Mr Mayor, I think your new hairstyle is the right way to go. After all, in Washington, the cover-up is always worse than the truth.
                                                HILLARY RODHAM CLINTON

I always like to go to Washington D.C. It gives me a chance to visit my money.
                                                          BOB HOPE

There was a scare in Washington when a man climbed over the White House wall and was arrested. This marks the first time a person has got into the White House unlawfully since . . . President Bush.   DAVID LETTERMAN

Washington is the one place where you can't take friendship personally.
                                                          TONY SNOW

Water

I never drink water – fish fuck in it.   W.C. FIELDS

It's not the taste of water I object to; it's the after-effects.   RONALD KNOX

Whenever someone asks me if I want water with my Scotch, I say I'm thirsty, not dirty.   JOE E. LEWIS

Patsy Stone (Joanna Lumley): Water? What's that?
Edina Monsoon (Jennifer Saunders): It's a mixer, darling. You mix it with scotch.   *Absolutely Fabulous*

Water, taken in moderation, cannot hurt anybody.   MARK TWAIN

I mixed this myself. Two parts H, one part O. I don't trust anybody!
                                                      STEVEN WRIGHT

Wealth

Fortune-hunter: a man without wealth whom a rich woman catches and marries within an inch of his life.
                       AMBROSE BIERCE, *The Enlarged Devil's Dictionary*

Bill Gates made a pact with the Devil. The Devil said, 'You can have $100 billion, but you have to go through life looking like a turtle.'   DANA CARVEY

A rich man is nothing but a poor man with money.   W.C. FIELDS

If you can actually count your money, then you are not really a rich man.
                                                      J. PAUL GETTY

I never wanted to be a millionaire; I just wanted to live like one.
                                                      WALTER HAGEN

If Bill Gates put all his $98 million under his mattress and fell out of bed, it would take him eighteen minutes to hit the floor.   RICH HALL

I don't care how rich he is – as long as he has a yacht, his own private rail-road car and his own toothpaste.
                       SUGAR KANE (MARILYN MONROE), *Some Like It Hot*

In this country you're guilty until proven wealthy.   BILL MAHER

I get so tired of listening to one million dollars here, one million dollars there. It's so petty.   IMELDA MARCOS

Wealth: any income that is at least one hundred dollars more a year than the income of one's wife's sister's husband.   H.L. MENCKEN

If you live in Beverly Hills they don't put blinkers in your car. They figure if you're that rich you don't have to tell people where you're going.   BETTE MIDLER

Every day I get up and look through the Forbes list of the richest people in America. If I'm not there, I go to work.   ROBERT ORBEN

Do not be fooled into believing that because a man is rich he is necessarily smart. There is ample proof to the contrary.   JULIUS ROSENWALD

Someday I want to be rich. Some people get so rich they lose all respect for humanity. That's how rich I want to be.   RITA RUDNER

Homer Simpson: Well, he's got all the money in the world, but there's one thing he can't buy.
Marge: What's that?
Homer: (thinks) A dinosaur!   *The Simpsons*

One can never be too thin or too rich.

                                    WALLIS SIMPSON (DUCHESS OF WINDSOR)

Weather

Thanks to modern science we now know that lightning is nothing more than huge chunks of electricity that can come out of the sky anytime, anywhere, and kill you.   DAVE BARRY

Barometer: an ingenious instrument that tells us what kind of weather we are having.   AMBROSE BIERCE, *The Devil's Dictionary*

Any man who is married can appreciate why we have named our hurricanes after women.

                    ART BUCHWALD, *I Never Danced in the White House*

(*to Lilith*) What brings you to Seattle, the constant rain?

                    FRASIER CRANE (KELSEY GRAMMER), *Frasier*

We shall never be content until each man makes his own weather and keeps it to himself.

JEROME K. JEROME, *Idle Thoughts of an Idle Fellow*

A study shows men are hit by lightning four times as often as women – usually after saying, 'I'll call you.'   JAY LENO

The British, he thought, must be gluttons for satire: even the weather forecast seemed to be some kind of spoof, predicting every possible combination of weather for the next twenty-four hours without actually committing itself to anything specific.   DAVID LODGE, *Changing Places*

It's so hot Republican Congressman are going into gay bars just for the cold stares.   BILL MAHER

On cable TV they have a weather channel – twenty-four hours of weather. We had something like that where I grew up. We called it a window.

DAN SPENCER

Everybody is talking about the weather but nobody does anything about it.

MARK TWAIN

If it's zero degrees outside today and it's supposed to be twice as cold tomorrow, how cold is it going to be?   STEVEN WRIGHT

Weddings

It's the wedding season again. You can tell because the average bridal magazine currently weighs more than the average bride.   DAVE BARRY

I had a fairytale wedding – Grimm.   MARTI CAINE

He noticed that the bride was pregnant. So at the wedding everyone threw puffed rice.   DICK CAVETT

Two TV aerials meet on a roof, fall in love, get married. The ceremony was rubbish but the reception was brilliant.   TOMMY COOPER

Music played at weddings always reminds me of the music played for soldiers before they go into battle.   HEINRICH HEINE

You can always spot the father of the bride – he's the one signing over his retirement fund to the caterer.   JOE HICKMAN

June is the traditional month for weddings. The other eleven are for divorce.
JOE HICKMAN

In a survey six per cent said a good place to have sex is a wedding reception. I remember when you just kissed the bride.
JAY LENO

A bride at her second wedding does not wear a veil. She wants to see what she is getting.
HELEN ROWLAND

The idea behind the tuxedo is the woman's point of view that men are all the same, so we might as well dress them that way. That's why a wedding is like the joining together of a beautiful, glowing bride and some guy. The tuxedo is a wedding safety device, created by women because they know that men are undependable. So in case the groom chickens out, everybody just takes one step over, and she marries the next guy.
JERRY SEINFELD

A wedding is a funeral where you smell your own flowers.
EDDIE WILSON (EDDIE CANTOR), *Kid Millions*

Weekends

Ah, Monday morning. Time to pay for your two days of debauchery, you hungover drones.
MONTGOMERY BURNS, *The Simpsons*

What is it with the weekends now? I swear to God every guy I've fucked since Memorial Day wants to know what I'm doing this weekend. They just don't get it. My weekends are for meeting new guys so I don't have to keep fucking the old ones.
SAMANTHA JONES (KIM CATTRALL), *Sex and the City*

Weight

Women should try to increase their size rather than decrease it, because I believe the bigger we are, the more space we'll take up, and the more we'll have to be reckoned with.
ROSEANNE BARR

I recently had my annual physical examination, which I get once every seven years, and when the nurse weighed me, I was shocked to discover how much stronger the Earth's gravitational pull has become since 1990.
DAVE BARRY

At least my mother could never tell me that my eyes were bigger than my belly.
ROY 'CHUBBY' BROWN

Why do people suck in their stomachs when they weigh themselves? So they can see the scale.
MARTA CHAVES

I found there was only one way to look thin – hang out with fat people.
RODNEY DANGERFIELD

Al Gore's so fat that the Liberty Bell is now the second biggest thing with a crack.
DAVID LETTERMAN

(*recalling his arrest*) The most horrific thing that happened was that I was photographed with my shirt off and I was fat. Can you imagine two worse things than being fat and gay?
GEORGE MICHAEL

There's more of your blood sitting in test-tubes around the world than presently circulating in your veins. You have tried every fad drug that has ever existed. More money has been poured into your quest for 'Twiggy-ness' than goes in aid to most third-world nations . . . and somehow you're two stone overweight!
SAFFRON MONSOON (JULIA SAWALHA), to Edina, *Absolutely Fabulous*

Sam Malone (Ted Danson): Whatta you up to, Norm?
Norm Peterson (George Wendt): My ideal weight, if I were eleven feet tall.
Cheers

Sure, you look heavier on TV, but Anna Nicole Smith is getting really huge. Her calves are so fat they moo.
JOAN RIVERS

The chief excitement in a woman's life is spotting women who are fatter than she is.
HELEN ROWLAND

Outside every thin girl is a fat man trying to get in.
KATHARINE WHITEHORN

I'm not overweight. I'm just nine inches too short.
SHELLEY WINTERS

Orson Welles

It's like meeting God without dying.
DOROTHY PARKER

The sad thing is that he has consistently put his very real talents to the task of glorifying his imaginary genius.
JOHN SIMON

Westerns

An adult Western is where the hero still kisses his horse at the end, only now he worries about it.
MILTON BERLE

I want you to round up every vicious criminal and gunslinger in the west. Take this down. I want rustlers, cutthroats, murderers, bounty hunters, desperados, mugs, pugs, thugs, nitwits, half-wits, dimwits, vipers, snipers, con men, Indian agents, Mexican bandits . . . muggers, buggerers, bushwhackers, hornswagglers, horse thieves, bull dykes, train robbers, bank robbers, ass kickers, shit kickers, and Methodists!

HEDLEY LAMARR (HARVEY KORMAN), *Blazing Saddles*

I started out playing the villain in Hopalong Cassidy Westerns. I got $100 a week and all the horseshit I could carry home.   ROBERT MITCHUM

I wouldn't say when you've seen one Western you've seen the lot; but when you've seen the lot you get the feeling you've seen one.

KATHARINE WHITEHORN

Widows

Rich widows are only second-hand goods that sell at first-class prices.

BENJAMIN FRANKLIN

The comfortable estate of widowhood is the only hope that keeps up a wife's spirits.   JOHN GAY, *The Beggar's Opera*

The only woman who knows where her husband is every night is a widow.

What do you call a man who has lost 95 per cent of his brainpower? A widower.

Oscar Wilde

The sovereign of insufferables. He had nothing to say and he said it.

AMBROSE BIERCE

If, with the literate, I am
Impelled to try an epigram.
I never seek to take the credit;
We all assume that Oscar said it.   DOROTHY PARKER, *Oscar Wilde*

Wills

Death is not the end. There remains the litigation over the estate.

AMBROSE BIERCE

Where there's a will there's a lawsuit.   OLIVER HERFORD

Harold Wilson

Double-talk is his mother tongue. He is a man whose vision is limited to tomorrow's headlines.   IAIN MACLEOD

(*on his supposedly humble background*) If Harold Wilson ever went to school without any boots, it was merely because he was too big for them.
HAROLD MACMILLAN

He is going around the country stirring up apathy.   WILLIAM WHITELAW

Wine

A meal without wine is like a day without sunshine, except that on a day without sunshine you can still get drunk.   LEE ENTREKIN

I was reading a periodical about wine, and they had an ad for the 'perfect breakfast wine'. Let me tell you something, if you're drinking wine for breakfast, you don't care if it's perfect.   JAY LENO

A bottle of wine contains more philosophy than all the books in the world.
LOUIS PASTEUR

A good general rule [with wine] is to state that the bouquet is better than the taste, and vice versa.   STEPHEN POTTER, *One-Upmanship*

You can tell German wine from vinegar by the label.   MARK TWAIN

We want the finest wines available to humanity, we want them here and we want them now.   WITHNAIL (RICHARD E. GRANT), *Withnail and I*

Michael Winner

To say that Michael Winner is his own worst enemy is to provoke a ragged chorus from odd corners of the film industry of 'Not while I'm alive!'
BARRY NORMAN

Michael Winner's films are atrocious, but they are not the worst thing about him.

Winning

Anybody can win – unless there happens to be a second entry.
GEORGE ADE

Winning is everything. The only ones who remember you when you come second are your wife and your dog.
DAMON HILL

Winning is not the most important thing; it's the only thing.
VINCE LOMBARDI

Winning is only important in war and surgery.
AL MCGUIRE

Victory goes to the player who makes the next-to-last mistake.
JACKIE MASON

When you win you eat better, sleep better and your beer tastes better. And your wife looks like Gina Lollobrigida.
JOHNNY PESKY

Men hate to lose. I once beat my husband at tennis. I said to him, 'Are we going to have sex again?' He said, 'Sure, but not with each other.'
RITA RUDNER

You can become a winner only if you are willing to walk over the edge.
DAMON RUNYON

Son, when you participate in sporting events, it's not whether you win or lose: it's how drunk you get.
HOMER SIMPSON, *The Simpsons*

The trouble with the rat race is that even if you win, you're still a rat.
LILY TOMLIN

Wisdom

The saddest aspect of life right now is that science gathers knowledge faster than society gathers wisdom.
ISAAC ASIMOV

Some folks are wise and some otherwise.
JOSH BILLINGS

Wise men never say what they think about women.
SAMUEL BUTLER

A man begins cutting his wisdom teeth the first time he bites off more than he can chew.
HERB CAEN

Knowledge speaks, but wisdom listens.
JIMI HENDRIX

The only true wisdom consists of knowing that you know nothing.
BILL S. PRESTON (ALEX WINTER), *Bill and Ted's Excellent Adventure*

He is a wise man who has his afterthoughts first.

Wives

In life, it's not who you know that's important, it's how your wife found out.
JOEY ADAMS

In my house I'm the boss, my wife is just the decision-maker.
WOODY ALLEN

I'm thinking of taking a fifth wife. Why not? Solomon had a thousand wives and he is a synonym for wisdom.
JOHN BARRYMORE

You know what the difference is between my wife and a terrorist? – You can negotiate with a terrorist.
FRANK CARSON

(*on his ideal wife*) I don't care if she doesn't know how to cook – so long as she doesn't know a good lawyer.
ERROL FLYNN

I've had so many wives, I can't remember all their names. To keep it simple, I just called them all 'Plaintiff'.
LEWIS GRIZZARD

I have learned that only two things are necessary to keep one's wife happy. First, let her think she's having her way. And second, let her have it.
LYNDON B. JOHNSON

It's not a good idea to put your wife into a novel; not your latest wife anyway.
NORMAN MAILER

I never mind my wife having the last word. In fact, I'm delighted when she gets to it.
WALTER MATTHAU

There's only one thing wrong with wife swapping. You get another wife.
SCOTT ROEBEN

A woman who takes her husband about with her everywhere is like a cat that goes on playing with a mouse long after she's killed it.
SAKI, *The Watched Pot*

A man who says his wife can't take a joke forgets that she took him.
OSCAR WILDE

Whenever you want to marry someone, go have lunch with his ex-wife.

SHELLEY WINTERS

This time of year makes me sad. It was ten years ago today that I lost my wife. I'll never forget that poker game.   HENNY YOUNGMAN

Women

(*on his ideal woman*) Sometimes it's Britney Spears and sometimes it's Carrie Fisher. I can't tell if I've got a Lolita complex or an Oedipus complex.

BEN AFFLECK

Until Eve arrived, this was a man's world.   RICHARD ARMOUR

Whatever you do, keep clear of thin women. They're trouble.

ALAN AYCKBOURN, *A Small Family Business*

Women were brought up to believe that men were the answer. They weren't. They weren't even one of the questions.   JULIAN BARNES

If a woman has to choose between catching a fly ball and saving an infant's life, she will choose to save the infant's life without even considering if there are men on base.   DAVE BARRY

Here's to woman. Would that we could fall into her arms without falling into her hands.   AMBROSE BIERCE

Girls have an unfair advantage over men; if they can't get what they want by being smart, they can get it by being dumb.   YUL BRYNNER

A woman who has the divine gift of lechery will always make a superlative partner.   ALEX COMFORT

How strange. I usually get some sign when Lilith is in town: dogs forming into packs, blood weeping from the walls.

NILES CRANE (DAVID HYDE PIERCE), *Frasier*

Women want men, careers, money, children, friends, luxury, comfort, independence, freedom, respect, love, and three dollar pantyhose that won't run.

PHYLLIS DILLER

There are only three things to be done with a woman. You can love her, suffer for her, or turn her into literature.   LAWRENCE DURRELL, *Justine*

My understanding of women only goes as far as the pleasures. When it comes to the pain, I'm like every other bloke. I don't want to know.

ALFIE ELKINS (MICHAEL CAINE), *Alfie*

Women are like elephants to me: nice to look at, but I wouldn't want to own one.

W.C. FIELDS

The great question that has never been answered, and which I have not yet been able to answer, despite my thirty years of research into the feminine soul, is 'What does a woman want?'

SIGMUND FREUD

There's really nothing wrong with a woman welcoming all men's advances, as long as they're in cash.

ZSA ZSA GABOR

Girls are always running through my mind. They don't dare walk.

ANDY GIBB

I love women. They're the best thing ever created. If they want to be like men and come down to our level, that's fine.

MEL GIBSON

Women are frightening. If you get to forty as a man, you're quite battle-scarred.

HUGH GRANT

There's a bit of a stripper in every woman.

MELANIE GRIFFITH

Women say they want a man who knows what a woman's worth. That's a pimp.

RICH HALL

A woman's mind is cleaner than a man's: she changes it more often.

OLIVER HERFORD

A woman needs to know but one man well to understand all men; whereas a man may know all women and not understand one of them.

HELEN ROWLAND

Man has his will – but woman has her way.

OLIVER WENDELL HOLMES, *The Autocrat of the Breakfast-Table*

Lady: most often used to describe someone you wouldn't want to talk to for five minutes.

FRAN LEBOWITZ

The female sex has no greater fan than I, and I have the bills to prove it.

ALAN JAY LERNER

Whatever women do, they do best after dark.   JOHN V. LINDSAY

Women, can't live with them . . . end of sentence.
                              JACK MCFARLAND (SEAN HAYES), *Will and Grace*

Felix Unger (Jack Lemmon): Funny, I haven't thought of a woman in weeks.
Oscar Madison (Walter Matthau): I fail to see the humour.
                                                        The Odd Couple

You don't know a woman till you've met her in court.   NORMAN MAILER

The females of all species are most dangerous when they appear to retreat.
                                                              DON MARQUIS

Any man who says he can see through a woman is missing a lot.
                                                             GROUCHO MARX

Do you know why the Lord withheld the sense of humour from women? So that
we may love you instead of laugh at you.   BEVERLY MICKENS

Things bounce off men, but ladies are different. They have softer flesh.
                                                             ROGER MOORE

Women would rather be right than reasonable.   OGDEN NASH

I prefer the company of women. I'm buzzed by the female mystique. I always
tell young men, there are three rules: they hate us, we hate them; they're stronger,
they're smarter, and most important, they don't play fair.
                                                          JACK NICHOLSON

There are two kinds of women: those who want power in the world, and those
who want power in bed.   JACQUELINE KENNEDY ONASSIS

Women: you can't live with them, and you can't get them to dress up in a skimpy
Nazi uniform and beat you with a warm squash.   EMO PHILIPS

A woman without a man is like a trailer without a car; it ain't going nowhere.
                              POLLY the PISTOL (KIM NOVAK), *Kiss Me, Stupid*

I'd much rather be a woman than a man. Women can cry, they can wear cute
clothes — and they're the first to be rescued off sinking ships.
                                                           GILDA RADNER

A woman is like a teabag. It's only when she's in hot water that you realise how strong she is. NANCY REAGAN

No woman is all sweetness; even the rose has thorns. JULIETTE RÉCAMIER

A smart girl is one who knows how to play tennis, piano and dumb. LYNN REDGRAVE

When a man says 'fine', he means everything's fine. When a woman says 'fine', she means, 'I'm really ticked off, and you have to find out why.' JOHN ROGERS

A wise woman puts a grain of sugar into everything she says to a man, and takes a grain of salt with everything he says to her. HELEN ROWLAND

Changeable women are more endurable than monotonous ones. They are sometimes murdered but seldom deserted. GEORGE BERNARD SHAW

Bart, a woman is like a beer. They look good, they smell good, and you'd step over your own mother just to get one! HOMER SIMPSON, *The Simpsons*

Women: you can't live with them, you can't live without them. That's probably why you can rent one for the evening. JIM STARK

I could never be a woman, 'cos I'd just stay home and play with my breasts all day. HARRIS TELEMACHER (STEVE MARTIN), *L.A. Story*

A woman's place is in the wrong. JAMES THURBER

Women can be icons of beauty, hourglasses of femininity, teetering along on high heels and everything. And they should play on their vulnerability and cry or whatever to get their own way. VIVIENNE WESTWOOD

We men are driven to find Miss Right – or at least Miss Right Now. ROBIN WILLIAMS

Women have served all these centuries as looking-glasses possessing the magic and delicious power of reflecting the figure of man at twice its natural size. VIRGINIA WOOLF, *A Room of One's Own*

Women and calendars are good only for a year. SPANISH PROVERB

Words

For women the best aphrodisiacs are words. The G-spot is in the ears. He who looks for it below there is wasting his time.   ISABEL ALLENDE

If there's one word that sums up everything that's gone wrong since the War, it's 'Workshop'.   KINGSLEY AMIS, *Jake's Thing*

A synonym is a word you use when you can't spell the word you first thought of.   BURT BACHARACH

The most beautiful words in the English language are not 'I love you', but 'it's benign'.   HARRY BLOCK (WOODY ALLEN), *Deconstructing Harry*

Everybody wants you to 'have a nice day'. That's the trouble with 'have a nice day' – it puts all the pressure on you. Now you've got to go out and somehow have a good time – all because of some loose-lipped cashier.
                              GEORGE CARLIN

Frasier Crane (Kelsey Grammer): Dad, you're twisting my words. I meant 'burden' in its most positive sense.
Martin Crane (John Mahoney): Oh, as in 'Gee, what a lovely burden'?
                              Frasier

The most beautiful words in the English language are 'not guilty'.
                              MAXIM GORKY

'Two-in-one' is a bullshit term, because one is not big enough to hold two. That's why two was created.   MITCH HEDBERG

I wonder about things, like, if they call an orange an 'orange', then why don't we call a banana a 'yellow', or an apple a 'red'? Blueberries, I understand. But will someone please explain gooseberries to me?
                              'REVEREND' JIM IGNATOWSKI (CHRISTOPHER LLOYD), *Taxi*

Always and never are two words you should always remember never to use.
                              WENDELL JOHNSON

Why not add a few more 'ers' to the word 'stutterer'?   CRAIG KILBORN

At the beginning there was the Word – at the end just the Cliché.
                              STANISLAW LEC

The two most beautiful words in the English language are 'cheque enclosed'.
DOROTHY PARKER

The trouble with words is that you never know whose mouths they've been in.
DENNIS POTTER

She used clichés like coasters – a place to rest her mind before picking it up and using it again.
JANET SCHWIND

Man does not live by words alone despite the fact that sometimes he has to eat them.
ADLAI STEVENSON

Words skittered out of his mouth like cartoon dogs on freshly-waxed linoleum, frantically going nowhere.
AMY TAN

Only presidents, editors and people with tapeworm have the right to use the editorial 'we'.
MARK TWAIN

Why are there five syllables in the word 'monosyllabic'?
STEVEN WRIGHT

Why is 'abbreviation' such a long word?
STEVEN WRIGHT

If a word in the dictionary were misspelled, how would we know?
STEVEN WRIGHT

Work

I do most of my work sitting down; that's where I shine.
ROBERT BENCHLEY

All I've ever wanted was an honest week's pay for an honest day's work.
MASTER SGT ERNEST G. BILKO (STEVE MARTIN), *Sgt Bilko*

Oh, you hate your job? Why didn't you say so? There's a support group for that. It's called EVERYBODY, and they meet at the bar.
DREW CAREY

Some people are much like blisters: they don't show up until the work is done.
SAM EWING

One of the saddest things is that the only thing a man can do for eight hours a day, day after day, is work. You can't eat for eight hours a day, nor drink for eight hours a day nor make love for eight hours.
WILLIAM FAULKNER

When I asked you to build me a wall, I was hoping rather than just dumping the bricks in a pile, I was wondering if you could find the time to cement them together, you know in the traditional fashion.

BASIL FAWLTY (JOHN CLEESE), *Fawlty Towers*

If you have a job without aggravations, you don't have a job.

MALCOLM FORBES

By working faithfully eight hours a day you may eventually get to be a boss and work twelve hours a day.

ROBERT FROST

Be nice to nerds. Chances are you'll end up working for one.

BILL GATES

When you go to work, if your name is on the building, you're rich. If your name is on your desk, you're middle class. If your name is on your shirt, you're poor.

RICH HALL

Work is the greatest thing in the world, so we should always save some of it for tomorrow.

DON HEROLD

I like work: it fascinates me. I can sit and look at it for hours.

JEROME K. JEROME, *Three Men in a Boat*

When your work speaks for itself, don't interrupt.

HENRY JOHN KAISER

Some people are so busy learning the tricks of the trade that they never learn the trade.

VERNON LAW

Saying we're in a slow recovery, not a recession, is like saying we don't have any unemployed, we just have a lot of people who are really, really late for work.

JAY LENO

At Microsoft a minority employee is one who has a girlfriend.

CONAN O'BRIEN

Work is the curse of the drinking classes.

MIKE ROMANOFF

I think Mr Smithers picked me for my motivational skills. Everyone always says they have to work twice as hard when I'm around.

HOMER SIMPSON, *The Simpsons*

I continue to work because the alternative is so awful – sitting in an armchair with a rug over my knees, waiting for the guy with an hourglass in his hand and a cowl over his head to tap on the window.   ERIC SYKES

Is sexual harassment at work a problem for the self-employed?
VICTORIA WOOD

World

I have recently been all round the world and have formed a very poor opinion of it.   THOMAS BEECHAM

It's a funny old world – a man's lucky if he gets out of it alive.
SAM BISBEE (W.C. FIELDS), *You're Telling Me*

The trouble with the world is that everybody in it is three drinks behind.
HUMPHREY BOGART

After one look at this planet any visitor from outer space would say, 'I want to see the manager.'   WILLIAM S. BURROUGHS

Did you ever get the feeling that the world is a tuxedo and you're a pair of brown shoes?   GEORGE GOBEL

I can picture in my mind a world without war, a world without hate. And I can picture us attacking that world because they would never expect it.
JACK HANDEY

Maybe this world is another planet's hell.   CHRISTOPHER MORLEY

All the world's a stage and most of us are desperately unrehearsed.
SEAN O'CASEY

If the world comes to an end, I want to be in Cincinnati. Everything comes there ten years later.   WILL ROGERS

It's a small world, but I wouldn't want to paint it.   STEVEN WRIGHT

Worry

Maddie Hayes (Cybill Shepherd): I wouldn't want you losing any more sleep over me.
David Addison (Bruce Willis): Believe me, if and when I find myself over you, the last thing I'll be thinking about is sleeping.   *Moonlighting*

Sometimes I lie awake at night and ask, why me? Then a voice answers, 'Nothing personal, your name just happened to come up.'   CHARLIE BROWN

Remember, today is the tomorrow you worried about yesterday.
DALE CARNEGIE

If you see ten troubles coming down the road, you can be sure that nine will run into the ditch before they reach you.   CALVIN COOLIDGE

As a cure for worrying, work is better than whisky.   THOMAS ALVA EDISON

The reason why worry kills more people than work is that more people worry than work.   ROBERT FROST

Tell your troubles to a bartender: who ever heard of a shrink giving you one on the house?   JACKIE GLEASON

Worry is interest paid on trouble before it falls due.   WILLIAM RALPH INGE

The Venus de Milo is a good example of what happens to somebody who won't stop biting her fingernails.   WILL ROGERS

Never worry for fear you have broken a man's heart; at the worst it is only sprained and a week's rest will put it in perfect working condition again.
HELEN ROWLAND, *Reflections of a Bachelor Girl*

I worry that the person who thought up Muzak may be thinking up something else.   LILY TOMLIN

I drive way too fast to worry about cholesterol.   STEVEN WRIGHT

Writers

A writer is a controlled schizophrenic.   EDWARD ALBEE

The freelance writer is a man who is paid per piece or per word or perhaps.
ROBERT BENCHLEY

(*to an author who had sent him an unsolicited manuscript*) Many thanks. I shall lose no time in reading it.   BENJAMIN DISRAELI

No author is a man of genius to his publisher.   HEINRICH HEINE

A good many young writers make the mistake of enclosing a stamped, self-addressed envelope, big enough for the manuscript to come back in. This is too much temptation to the editor.　　　　　　　RING LARDNER

There are no dull subjects. There are only dull writers.　　H.L. MENCKEN

The shelf life of the modern hardback writer is somewhere between the milk and the yoghurt.　　　　　　　JOHN MORTIMER

Two people getting together to write a book is like three people getting together to have a baby. One of them is superfluous.　　GEORGE BERNARD SHAW

Writers are a little below clowns and a little above trained seals.　　　　　　　JOHN STEINBECK

Writing

I love deadlines. I like the whooshing sound they make as they fly by.　　　　　　　DOUGLAS ADAMS

I love being a writer. What I can't stand is the paperwork.　　PETER DE VRIES

Writing is like driving a car at night. You can only see as far as the headlights, but you make the whole trip that way.　　E.L. DOCTOROW

The pen is mightier than the sword and considerably easier to write with.　　　　　　　MARTY FELDMAN

All good writing is swimming under water and holding your breath.　　　　　　　F. SCOTT FITZGERALD

All writing is creating or spinning dreams for other people so they won't have to bother doing it themselves.　　　　BETH HENLEY

Writing a novel is like making love, but it's also like having a tooth pulled. Pleasure and pain. Sometimes it's like making love while having a tooth pulled.　　　　　　　DEAN KOONTZ

I like to write when I feel spiteful; it's like having a good sneeze.　　　　　　　D.H. LAWRENCE

When once the itch of literature comes over a man, nothing can cure it but the scratching of a pen.　　　SAMUEL LOVER, *Handy Andy*

Writing books is the closest men ever come to child-bearing.

NORMAN MAILER

Multiple exclamation marks are a sure sign of a diseased mind.

TERRY PRATCHETT

Writing is the only profession where no one considers you ridiculous if you earn no money.
JULES RENARD

Wrong

The major difference between a thing that might go wrong and a thing that cannot possibly go wrong is that when a thing that cannot possibly go wrong goes wrong it usually turns out to be impossible to get at or repair.

DOUGLAS ADAMS, *Mostly Harmless*

Sometimes I lay awake at night and I ask, 'Where have I gone wrong?' Then a voice says to me, 'This is going to take more than one night.'

CHARLIE BROWN, *Peanuts*

I may have my faults, but being wrong isn't one of them.   JIMMY HOFFA

There's nothing wrong with hitting someone when his back is turned.

HOMER SIMPSON, *The Simpsons*

X

Xenophobia

I don't want to talk to you no more, you empty headed animal food trough wiper! I fart in your general direction! Your mother was a hamster and your father smelt of elderberries.

FRENCH SOLDIER (JOHN CLEESE), *Monty Python and the Holy Grail*

Switzerland, though lovely, is very full of the Swiss.

GEORGE MIKES, *How to be Poor*

Saudi Arabia says they compiled a list of all the known terrorists in Saudi Arabia. I think that's called the phone book.   JAY LENO

A gesticulation is any movement made by a foreigner.   J.B. MORTON

After shaking hands with a Greek, count your fingers.   ALBANIAN PROVERB

Do not trust a Hungarian unless he has a third eye in his forehead.
CZECH PROVERB

If a Russian tells you it's dry, put your collar up.   UKRAINIAN PROVERB

One German a beer; two Germans an organisation; three Germans a war.
POLISH PROVERB

Take from a Spaniard all his good qualities and there remains a Portuguese.
SPANISH PROVERB

Yawn

A yawn is a silent shout.   G.K. CHESTERTON

Imitation is the sincerest form of flattery, except when you yawn.
EVAN ESAR

Youth

(*to his doctor, late in life*) I haven't asked you to make me young again. All I want is to go on getting older.   KONRAD ADENAUER

Youth would be an ideal state if it came a little later in life.
HERBERT ASQUITH

If you want to recapture your youth, just cut off his allowance.
AL BERNSTEIN

I'm trying very hard to understand this generation. They have adjusted the timetable for childbearing so that menopause and teaching a 16-year-old to drive will occur in the same week.   ERMA BOMBECK

Boys do not grow up gradually. They move forward in spurts like the hands of clocks in railway stations.   CYRIL CONNOLLY, *Enemies of Promise*

Youth is a period of missed opportunities.   CYRIL CONNOLLY

The young always have the same problem — how to rebel and conform at the same time. They have now solved this by defying their parents and copying one another.   QUENTIN CRISP, *The Naked Civil Servant*

It is only rarely that one can see in a little boy the promise of a man, but one can almost always see in a little girl the threat of a woman.

ALEXANDRE DUMAS, FILS

Only the young die good.   OLIVER HERFORD

A boy becomes an adult three years before his parents think he does, and about two years after he thinks he does.   LEWIS B. HERSHEY

Youth has been a habit with some so long they cannot part with it.

RUDYARD KIPLING

If you had seen me in my teens you would have bolted for the door without picking up your coat.   JOANNA LUMLEY

I was a fourteen-year-old boy for thirty years.   MICKEY ROONEY

Youth is too important to be wasted on the young.

GEORGE BERNARD SHAW

When I was growing up, there were two things that were unpopular in my house. One was me, and the other was my guitar.

BRUCE SPRINGSTEEN

Z

Zips

(*on old age*) First you forget names, then you forget faces. Next you forget to pull your zipper up and finally, you forget to pull it down.

GEORGE BURNS

Men don't feel the urge to get married as quickly as women do because their clothes all button and zip in the front. Women's dresses usually button and zip in the back. We need men emotionally and sexually, but we also need men to help us get dressed.   RITA RUDNER

Nothing has done so much to bring husbands and wives together as the dress that zips up the back.

Zoos

A petting zoo is a great place if you want your kid's clothes to end up inside a goat's stomach.
BILL DWYER

A zoo is a place devised for animals to study the habits of human beings.
OLIVER HERFORD

INDEX OF CONTRIBUTORS